POWER, REALISM AND CONSTRUCTIVISM

Framed by a new and substantial introductory chapter, this book collects Stefano Guzzini's reference articles and some less well-known publications on power, realism and constructivism. By analysing theories and their assumptions, but also theorists following their intellectual paths, his analysis explores the diversity of different schools, and moves beyond simple definitions to explore their intrinsic tensions and fallacies. Guzzini's approach to the analysis of power – both within and outside International Relations – provides the common theme of the book through which the theoretical state of the art in IR is reassessed.

A novel analysis of power and the potential and limits of realism and constructivism in International Relations, *Power, Realism and Constructivism* will be of interest to students and scholars of international relations, international political economy, social and political theory, and the study of power.

Stefano Guzzini is Senior Researcher at the Danish Institute for International Studies, Denmark, and Professor of Government at Uppsala University, Sweden.

The New International Relations

Edited by Richard Little, *University of Bristol*, Iver B. Neumann, *Norwegian Institute of International Affairs (NUPI), Norway* and Jutta Weldes, *University of Bristol*.

The field of international relations has changed dramatically in recent years. This new series will cover the major issues that have emerged and reflect the latest academic thinking in this particular dynamic area.

International Law, Rights and Politics
Developments in Eastern Europe and the CIS
Rein Mullerson

The Logic of Internationalism
Coercion and accommodation
Kjell Goldmann

Russia and the Idea of Europe
A study in identity and international relations
Iver B. Neumann

The Future of International Relations
Masters in the making?
Edited by Iver B. Neumann and Ole Wæver

Constructing the World Polity
Essays on international institutionalization
John Gerard Ruggie

Realism in International Relations and International Political Economy
The continuing story of a death foretold
Stefano Guzzini

International Relations, Political Theory and the Problem of Order
Beyond international relations theory?
N.J. Rengger

War, Peace and World Orders in European History
Edited by Anja V. Hartmann and Beatrice Heuser

European Integration and National Identity
The challenge of the Nordic states
Edited by Lene Hansen and Ole Wæver

Shadow Globalization, Ethnic Conflicts and New Wars
A political economy of intra-state war
Dietrich Jung

Contemporary Security Analysis and Copenhagen Peace Research
Edited by Stefano Guzzini and Dietrich Jung

Observing International Relations
Niklas Luhmann and world politics
Edited by Mathias Albert and Lena Hilkermeier

Does China Matter? A Reassessment
Essays in memory of Gerald Segal
Edited by Barry Buzan and Rosemary Foot

European Approaches to International Relations Theory
A house with many mansions
Jörg Friedrichs

The Post-Cold War International System
Strategies, institutions and reflexivity
Ewan Harrison

States of Political Discourse
Words, regimes, seditions
Costas M. Constantinou

The Politics of Regional Identity
Meddling with the Mediterranean
Michelle Pace

The Power of International Theory
Reforging the link to foreign policy-making through scientific enquiry
Fred Chernoff

Africa and the North
Between globalization and marginalization
Edited by Ulf Engel and Gorm Rye Olsen

Communitarian International Relations
The epistemic foundations of international relations
Emanuel Adler

Human Rights and World Trade
Hunger in international society
Ana Gonzalez-Pelaez

Liberalism and War
The victors and the vanquished
Andrew Williams

Constructivism and International Relations
Alexander Wendt and his critics
Edited by Stefano Guzzini and Anna Leander

Security as Practice
Discourse analysis and the Bosnian War
Lene Hansen

The Politics of Insecurity
Fear, migration and asylum in the EU
Jef Huysmans

State Sovereignty and Intervention
A discourse analysis of interventionary and non-interventionary practices in Kosovo and Algeria
Helle Malmvig

Culture and Security
Symbolic power and the politics of international security
Michael Williams

Hegemony & History
Adam Watson

Territorial Conflicts in World Society
Modern systems theory, international relations and conflict studies
Edited by Stephan Stetter

Ontological Security in International Relations
Self-identity and the IR state
Brent J. Steele

The International Politics of Judicial Intervention
Creating a more *just* order
Andrea Birdsall

Pragmatism in International Relations
Edited by Harry Bauer and Elisabetta Brighi

Civilization and Empire
China and Japan's encounter with european international society
Shogo Suzuki

Transforming World Politics
From empire to multiple worlds
Anna M. Agathangelou and L.H.M. Ling

The Politics of Becoming European
A study of Polish and Baltic post-Cold War security imaginaries
Maria Mälksoo

Social Power in International Politics
Peter Van Ham

International Relations and Identity
A dialogical approach
Xavier Guillaume

The Puzzle of Politics
Inquiries into the genesis and transformation of international relations
Friedrich Kratochwil

The Conduct of Inquiry in International Relations
Philosophy of science and its implications for the study of world politics
Patrick Thaddeus Jackson

Arguing Global Governance
Agency, lifeworld and shared reasoning
Edited by Corneliu Bjola and Markus Kornprobst

Constructing Global Enemies
Hegemony and identity in international discourses on terrorism and drug prohibition
Eva Herschinger

Alker and IR
Global studies in an interconnected world
Edited by Renée Marlin-Bennett

Sovereignty between Politics and Law
Tanja Aalberts

International Relations and the First Great Debate
Edited by Brian Schmidt

China in the UN Security Council Decision-making on Iraq
Conflicting understandings, competing preferences 1990–2002
Suzanne Xiao Yang

NATO's Security Discourse after the Cold War
Representing the West
Andreas Behnke

The Scandinavian International Society
Primary institutions and binding forces, 1815–2010
Laust Schouenborg

Bourdieu in International Relations
Rethinking key concepts in IR
Edited by Rebecca Adler-Nissen

Making Sense, Making Worlds
Constructivism in social theory and international relations
Nicholas Greenwood Onuf

World of Our Making
Rules and rule in social theory and international relations
Nicholas Greenwood Onuf

Maritime Piracy and the Construction of Global Governance
Edited by Michael J. Struett, Jon D. Carlson and Mark T. Nance

European Integration and Postcolonial Sovereignty Games
The EU overseas countries and territories
Edited by Rebecca Adler-Nissen and Ulrik Pram Gad

Power, Realism and Constructivism
Stefano Guzzini

POWER, REALISM AND CONSTRUCTIVISM

Stefano Guzzini

LONDON AND NEW YORK

First published 2013
by Routledge
2 Park Square, Milton Park, Abingdon, Oxon, OX14 4RN

Simultaneously published in the USA and Canada
by Routledge
711 Third Avenue, New York, NY 10017

Routledge is an imprint of the Taylor & Francis Group, an informa business

© 2013 Stefano Guzzini

The right of Stefano Guzzini to be identified as author of this work has been asserted by him in accordance with sections 77 and 78 of the Copyright, Designs and Patents Act 1988.

All rights reserved. No part of this book may be reprinted or reproduced or utilised in any form or by any electronic, mechanical, or other means, now known or hereafter invented, including photocopying and recording, or in any information storage or retrieval system, without permission in writing from the publishers.

Trademark notice: Product or corporate names may be trademarks or registered trademarks, and are used only for identification and explanation without intent to infringe.

British Library Cataloguing in Publication Data
A catalogue record for this book is available from the British Library

Library of Congress Cataloging-in-Publication Data
Guzzini, Stefano.
 Power, realism, and constructivism / Stefano Guzzini.
  p. cm.—(New international relations)
 Includes bibliographical references and index.
 1. Power (Social sciences) 2. International relations. 3. Constructivism (Philosophy)
 4. Realism. I. Title.
 JC330.G89 2013
 320.01—dc23
                                                                    2012028418

ISBN: 978-0-415-64046-6 (hbk)
ISBN: 978-0-415-66304-5 (pbk)
ISBN: 978-0-203-07174-8 (ebk)

Typeset in Bembo
by RefineCatch Limited, Bungay, Suffolk

For Alva, Anna and Miro

CONTENTS

List of figures   *xiii*
Acknowledgements   *xiv*

Introduction: power and the study of politics   1

PART I
Power   **13**

1 Structural power: the limits of neorealist power analysis   15

2 The use and misuse of power analysis in international theory   47

3 From (alleged) unipolarity to the decline of multilateralism? A power-theoretical critique   61

4 Niklas Luhmann's conceptualization of power   77

5 Pierre Bourdieu's field analysis of relational capital, misrecognition and domination   93

PART II
Realism   **107**

6 The enduring dilemmas of realism in International Relations   109

7	The different worlds of realism in International Relations	136
8	Foreign policy without diplomacy: the Bush administration at a crossroads	146
9	Robert Gilpin: a realist quest for the dynamics of power	152
10	Susan Strange's oscillating realism: opposing the ideal – and the apparent	175

PART III
Constructivism 187

11	A reconstruction of constructivism in International Relations	189
12	The concept of power: a constructivist analysis	217
13	'The Cold War is what we make of it': when peace research meets constructivism in International Relations	237
14	Alexander Wendt's constructivism: a relentless quest for synthesis (with Anna Leander)	247
15	Imposing coherence: the central role of practice in Friedrich Kratochwil's theorising of politics, international relations and science	268

Epilogue: the significance and roles of teaching theory in International Relations — 286

Bibliography — *304*
Index — *332*

FIGURES

0.1	The domains and levels of power	10
1.1	An analytical model of David Baldwin's relational power analysis	26
1.2	Morriss's dispositional conceptualization of power	30
1.3	A dyadic conceptualization of power phenomena	41
2.1	Keohane's rational actor approach	53
11.1	A conceptual synopsis of Pierre Bourdieu's *le sens pratique*	208
14.1	Wendt's synthesis in *Social Theory of International Politics*	257

ACKNOWLEDGEMENTS

A research that spans over two decades needs institutional support. Mine started with the *Studienstiftung des Deutschen Volkes* (the German Scholarship Foundation) which provided me with a generous student grant for four and a half years. This grant, in turn, allowed me to study away from home with no financial consequences. It also provided me with a certain sense of self-confidence that I may have the abilities to aim for the better universities. I was also granted a PhD fellowship by the Italian government and from the European University Institute in Fiesole (Florence). Some of the research in the following chapters was done, and the opening chapter published, while I was a PhD student there. It is difficult to overestimate the importance of those years for me. My first job was at the Central European University in Budapest. The CEU has an incredibly stimulating student environment which had a strong influence on me: Chapter 11 is dedicated to my students there; the Epilogue reflects on my teaching experiences there. But during my six-year stay, the CEU also offered me two sabbatical semesters during which I could spend more time on research. At the Copenhagen Peace Research Institute, I spent two very productive years (almost one-third of the chapters here are connected to my time at COPRI), before the Danish government decided to close it for political reasons. It was joined together with other research institutes into a follow-up organisation, the Danish Institute for International Studies, which has provided me with a solid base for almost ten years. My thanks go to both DIIS and the Department of Government at Uppsala University for agreeing to a joint deal which allows me to combine the good teaching environment in Uppsala with the special research environment at DIIS. Last but not least, I wish to thank the *Hanse Wissenschaftskolleg* (Hanse Institute for Advanced Studies) in Delmenhorst which offered my wife, Anna Leander, and me fellowships and hosted us during the academic year 2007 to 2008. That year was wonderful in many regards and got me back on track with my research agenda. My gratitude goes to all these fellowship organisations and institutions which gave me support, inspiration and uninterrupted time spans for research (the most precious good). I hope this book can return part of the favour.

I have also incurred many personal debts during the past 20 years of research, most of which I hope to have acknowledged in the notes to each individual chapter. A list of names would be far too long: my teachers in different places, including the early studies in Saarbrücken that put me on the IR track; my fellow students and my PhD supervisors at the EUI; our small team and famous absentee landlord at COPRI who pushed us to good research; my colleagues and students in Budapest, Copenhagen, Uppsala, and in Madrid, Bremen, PUC-Rio during my guest professorships, as well as in the many PhD workshops I taught around Europe; many colleagues and friends elsewhere, as well as, and for the entire period, my wife. As we all know, even casual talk in a conference corridor, or with family, friends and students in a pub or at dinner at home, can sometimes give important hints or remove some intellectual blockage. It is not possible to be conscious of all those inspirations, but I am aware of their existence and significance. Careful readers will undoubtedly detect many other people's handwriting explicit or hidden in the following pages. They will miss many of my students' challenges and ideas which pushed me forward. I am not sure I can ever repay this.

Looking back over the past two decades, I mainly see our family quartet. It is customary to acknowledge the family, and it is quite usual to believe one's family to be in some sense special, at least to ourselves. I am no exception. Whenever we are together, I cannot help but see us as an improvising quartet, taking turns accompanying when others make a solo, phrasing melodies and counterpoints while we play our common tunes. This book has unfortunately little of that joy – or anger and melancholy, for that matter – of our time spent together. But it could only be dedicated to you.

Stefano Guzzini
Frederiksberg, June 2012

The authors and publishers would like to thank the following for granting permission to reproduce material in this work:

Stefano Guzzini, 'Structural Power: The Limits of Neorealist Power Analysis', *International Organization*, vol. 47, no. 3, pp. 443–78. © 1993 Cambridge University Press. Reprinted with permission.

Stefano Guzzini, 'From (Alleged) Unipolarity to the Decline of Multilateralism? A Power-theoretical Critique', in Edward Newman, Ramesh Thakur and John Tirman (eds), *Multilateralism Under Challenge? Power, International Order and Structural Change*. © 2006 United Nations University Press. Reprinted with permission.

Stefano Guzzini, 'The Enduring Dilemmas of Realism in International Relations', *European Journal of International Relations*, vol. 10, no. 4, pp. 533–68. © 2004 Sage. Reprinted with permission.

Stefano Guzzini, 'The Different Worlds of Realism in International Relations', *Millennium: Journal of International Studies*, vol. 30, no. 1, pp. 111–21. © 2001 Sage. Reprinted with permission.

Stefano Guzzini, 'Foreign Policy Without Diplomacy: The Bush Administration at a Crossroads', *International Relations*, vol. 16, no. 2, pp. 291–7. © 2002 Sage. Reprinted with permission.

Stefano Guzzini, 'Strange's Oscillating Realism: Opposing the Ideal – and the Apparent', in Thomas C. Lawton, James N. Rosenau and Amy C. Verdun (eds), *Strange Power*, 215–28. © 2000 Ashgate. Reprinted with permission.

Stefano Guzzini, 'A Reconstruction of Constructivism in International Relations', *European Journal of International Relations*, vol. 6, no. 2, pp. 147–82. © 2000 Sage. Reprinted with permission.

Stefano Guzzini, 'The Concept of Power: A Constructivist Analysis', *Millennium: Journal of International Studies*, vol. 33, no. 3, pp. 495–521. © 2005 Sage. Reprinted with permission.

Stefano Guzzini, 'Imposing Coherence: The Central Role of Practice in Friedrich Kratochwil's Theorising of Politics, International Relations and Science', *Journal of International Relations and Development*, vol. 13, no. 3, pp. 301–22. © 2010 Palgrave. Reprinted with permission.

Stefano Guzzini, 'The Significance and Roles of Teaching Theory in International Relations', *Journal of International Relations and Development*, vol. 4, no. 2, pp. 98–117. © 2001 Palgrave. Reprinted with permission.

Stefano Guzzini and Anna Leander, 'A Social Theory for International Relations: An Appraisal of Alexander Wendt's Disciplinary and Theoretical Synthesis', *Journal of International Relations and Development*, vol. 4, no. 4, pp. 316–38. © 2001 Palgrave.

Every effort has been made to contact copyright holders for their permission to reprint material in this book. The publishers would be grateful to hear from any copyright holder who is not here acknowledged and will undertake to rectify any errors or omissions in future editions of this book.

INTRODUCTION

Power and the study of politics

When I told Jean Lauxerois, a philosopher, translator of German and Greek philosophy, and then teacher at my former high school in Germany (Saarbrücken), that I was going to write a PhD thesis on power, he was not surprised: it seemed logical and coherent with my earlier interests. I was taken aback by that remark. After all, I had spent quite some time studying other things. Only a couple of months earlier, I had been admitted to a PhD programme with a proposal on the sociology of knowledge in IR. To me, researching on power did not seem to be my long-time scenario. In addition, being apparently quite obstinate in my interests did not strike me as a very good thing. But with hindsight, it is always easier to see the logic of certain developments, which does not mean that it could not have come otherwise.

By looking back upon this first research cycle which has spun now for almost 25 years, it does seem to me that Lauxerois was right. Power is probably the overarching theme of this research, but only, as I was to find out, because it covers a wide variety of problematics, far more than analyses and theories in international relations, and not only there, usually acknowledge. In fact, in the course of my research, the relationship between the phenomenon of power and analysing/theorising global politics began to change, indeed reverse. I started out busily working on the concept of power as *the* means to improve the theorising of global politics. By now, the conceptualisation of global politics has almost become the means to further the understanding of power. Both approaches – the research on each one being sufficient to fill libraries – are present and needed in the analysis of power, whose meaning is changing and multiple, but not arbitrarily so. It is quite a lot, though. When Steven Lukes told me that I should try to write a PhD on power in IR, since there had not been one before that time, I stretched my arms as wide as I could and asked whether there was not an easy reason for this absence. In typical manner, he shrugged off my remark as if it were almost irrelevant, and here I was, embarking on my new journey. As a result, my research is characterised by a series of coping strategies in an attempt not to get overwhelmed by the topic and its different problematics. I am not sure how many times, if at all, I succeeded.

1 Realism and power

As an undergraduate student in Germany, while many other students were attracted by Marx and the Frankfurt School, I took a seminar on Kissinger and his time in the US government. I was interested in international affairs for different reasons. Many of the reform discussions in 'domestic' politics came to a standstill during the Cold War because 'the international situation would not allow it'. German Ostpolitik was always also domestic politics. And so was the NATO dual-track decision and the gigantic mobilisation against the Euromissile deployment in Germany. Young men were asked to spend 12 months of their life, sometimes more, preparing for war.

Furthermore, being born five kilometres from the French border in the Saarland made 'external affairs' a daily and concrete reality 'at home'. Indeed, the very border and the connected wars had marked the history of almost all the local families. Saarbrücken had long been part of one of the duchies of the Holy Roman Empire, before it became French, then again German in the eighteenth century, then part of the *département de la Sarre* during the First French Empire, again German after the Napoleonic wars, and a battleground during the Franco-Prussian war (the battle of Spicher(e)n). After the First World War, the Saar became a mandate under the League of Nations in 1920 (governed by the UK and France, with direct French control of the industry), voting overwhelmingly to join Hitler's Reich in 1935, before it became a French protectorate after the Second World War, voting against pro-German parties, participating as an independent country in the Olympic Games in Helsinki of 1952, before refusing a European Statute in 1955 (an independent entity under the auspices of the now defunct Western European Union – which would have made it European territory and hence probably the core of the EU), and joining the *Bundesrepublik* in 1957 (on a constitutional provision ready to be used again for the German reunification in 1990), while still keeping the local franc for two years or so. At a border, politics is international, even if the border does not move for a while, or no war is fought on its behalf.

But why Kissinger? This was partly a coincidence. The University of Saarbrücken is a small and peripheral university, particularly in Political Science (the department has since been closed). This was the only IR course on offer in that semester. But that is not the whole story. I was surely attracted by the sense that, 'there', 'real' politics was taking place. No writers project such a picture of tragic heroism as realists do, Kissinger being surely no exception. If politics was by nature international, if ruling the world was tragic, the intricacies of 'power politics' were to be the core of my interest.

Having turned to realism for the sake of understanding politics through 'power', I was soon to be disappointed. As many chapters of this book testify, despite its central role of power, realism had put me on several wrong tracks for its analysis. To begin with, as many who were educated in IR can testify, power is often used as the killer argument, the ultimate put-down: something happened 'because of power' (or: the power position, superior power, the drive for power, etc.). But then, when checking out what was actually meant by 'power', arguments often turn quite messy. All realists are probably aware of the intrinsic circularity of power arguments of the sort that 'A won because it had more power'; and we know 'it had more power because it won'. Dealing with this potential circularity led to the many 'paradoxes of unrealised power', as David Baldwin (1979: 163) critically calls them, as when observers had to make sense of the US defeat in Vietnam. Either the USA was more powerful but lost, and hence the causal link from power to influence was gone. Or the causal link was there, but that meant the USA was (militarily) weaker than Vietnam, which was surely not what appeared in the balance-of-power sheets, although the latter were now busily redrawn to accommodate ex post the unexpected outcome.

Some realists tried to avoid that circularity. But when they cut through the direct causal link between power (usually understood as resources or 'capabilities') and influence or control of outcomes, that is, when they did not simply infer power from influence or control over outcomes, they ran into a dilemma. No longer able to automatically explain influence from power undercut the very reason why they were interested in power in the first place. Nobody wants to know resources just for their own sake. Hence, many returned to or simply upheld the idea of some causal link, then inevitably ending up with an analysis of conversion failures, in which otherwise superior power was lost in transition, a statement which had the advantage of being unfalsifiable, since ex post anything in that conversion can be analysed as a failure (for this critique, see Baldwin 1979). 'And how do we know it was a failure? Because . . . they lost.' There was no way out of the circle, if the concept of power or the causal status of the analysis was not itself revised.

A second dead-end in the realist (but also others') treatment of power is connected to this. Even if we went along and defined power through its base or resources, how do we aggregate resources – military, financial, cultural, moral, and others – into one single unit? This assumes a common measure into which the different units can be converted. Unfortunately, no such thing exists, at least not in an objective sense (for a constructivist reading of this conversion, see below). In other words, by assuming a single measure of power, balance-of-power theories applied what Robert Dahl had repeatedly called the 'lump of power' fallacy (Dahl 1976: 26). The underlying reason for this missing convertibility is that power cannot be conceptualised in close analogy to money, at least not for the purpose of building an explanatory (and causal) theory of action. As Raymond Aron, a classical realist, argued many years ago (and I insist on his overlooked argument several times in this book), whereas economists can reduce the variety of preferences (guns or butter) into a unified utility function through the concept of money, and whereas people can apply this in real existing monetarised economies in their everyday economic behaviour, there is no equivalent in politics. In real world politics, we have no existing measure to tell us how much a billion inhabitants weigh in power as compared with a nuclear weapon, or hundreds of them. And this qualitative difference undermines the attempt to model power in analogy to money. Put into power jargon: power is not just less 'fungible' (convertible across domains) than money, although it is this, too. What is important, however, is that by being so, power cannot fulfil the same functions in political exchanges as money does in economic ones: it does not provide a standardised measure of economic value (Baldwin 1993a: 21). A difference of degree becomes a difference in kind – and a difference overlooked by most realists, not least by Waltz (1986) and Mearsheimer (2001) who explicitly use the analogy of power and money.

A third problem in established power analysis has to do with the very character of power which makes it difficult to even conceive of it as capabilities alone. As Dahl and Baldwin insist, power is relational. The relational conceptualisation of power takes place in the context of post-Weberian definitions of power. Max Weber had defined power as any chance (and not 'probability', as it is often translated) 'within a social relation to impose one's will also against the resistance of others, regardless of what gives rise to this chance' (Weber 1980 [1921–2]: 28). For Dahl, 'A has power over B to the extent that he can get B to do something that B would not otherwise do' (Dahl 1957: 202–3). Hence, the main characteristic of a relational approach is that it locates power in a human relationship, thus distinguishing it from the sheer production of effects (power in nature). At the same time, 'relational' is not to be confused with 'relative' in that it means something different from the bottom of a balance sheet where power corresponds to one's net 'amount' when the power (or, worse, the resources) of others has been taken into account.

Such relational concepts of power take issue with a vision of power in terms of its resources or instruments: power exists in and through a relation; it is not the possession of any agent. In a famous example, Bachrach and Baratz (1970: 20–1) illustrate this with reference to a situation in which a sentry levels his gun at an unarmed intruder, whom he orders to halt or else he will shoot. If the intruder stops it seems the threat has worked: the sentry has exercised power. Not necessarily, they say. If the intruder was himself a soldier, he may obey because that is what a soldier does when receiving an order from a sentry. The alleged power resource was ineffectual here, since it was the intruder's value system that made him obey, not the gun. Inversely, if the intruder does not obey and gets himself killed, we may again not be seeing a power relationship. Since the intruder apparently valued entering the base more than his own life, the killing only shows the ultimate powerlessness of force (violence) in the face of a suicide attack. (In a more strictly Weberian reading, however, it would be fair to say that the sentry exercised power in imposing his will – not to allow anyone unauthorised to enter the base – against the resistance of the intruder.) But this example can be pushed to its extreme: the intruder may have wanted to commit suicide and gets the sentry to do it for him. In this case the intruder, by 'forcing' the sentry to shoot him, exercises power over the sentry.

The central point is that no analysis of power can be made without knowing the relative importance of conflicting values and preferences in the mind of the power recipient, if not also of the supposed power holder. The capacity to sanction and the resources on which the sanctions are based are a part of power analysis, but in themselves insufficient to attribute power, since what counts as a sanction in the specific power relation is itself dependent on the specific values and preferences in the minds of the people involved.

By now, not much is left of the put-down killer argument. If power is inferred from effects, the concept is circular; if it is not inferred because no direct causality exists, power is indeterminate, and hence is not centrally relevant. If power cannot be measured because it lacks fungibility, we do not know when it is 'balanced' nor when it has been 'maximised', both being statements that assume a possible general measure (and there goes realism as an explanatory theory). If power is not a resource or property, but a relational phenomenon dependent on the specific encounter of people with their values and preferences in their historical context, then the analysis of power moves fundamentally to the interpretivist camp. Far from being its ultimate trump card, power is realism's central weakness. Taking power seriously means leaving realism.

2 Power and constructivism

Constructivism is part of the interpretivist family of social theories. As such, it cannot conceive of power in terms of resources alone. People act towards objects on the basis of the meaning they give to them: objects themselves do not determine their meaning. Nuclear missiles may be mighty weapons; small Luxemburg does not fear its relatively huge French neighbour because of them. *A fortiori*, constructivism is not prone to repeat the lump-of-power fallacy, where all possible power resources would be mixed and added. Such an aggregate power (resource) assessment, independent of the actor's understandings and the contingent situational setting, would be not only wrong, but conceptually impossible.

This makes constructivism more receptive to a relational understanding of power. Yet, constructivist theorising would give a communicative twist to this, insisting on the role of open or tacit recognition which, in turn, relies on a wider social or cultural context. Such recognition is typically based on conventions, and it applies to both resources and status. As mentioned above, resources are given weight not by themselves, but by shared understandings in social relations. Before diplomats can count, they have first to agree on what counts. Similarly, the recognition of a general power status is social. The simple reference to resources is not enough when the definition of what is considered crucial for great power status shifts. The Russian government may at times be justified in thinking that other countries' concentration on matters other than material resources for defining rank and status – as, for instance, in the insistence on good governance, human rights, etc. – is a ploy to keep it out of Olympus. On the other hand, no criteria for rank are 'natural'; they all evolved historically. It is just as much a convention to determine it in terms of purely material or military resources. Hence, for a constructivist understanding of power, just as individual communications are part of and make sense within the context of a language at large, the relational aspect of power is conceived in this wider manner so as to allow social norms to become visible in their role for the constitution of power in its recognition.

As a corollary of the interpretivist and communicative setting, constructivists will not use power in terms of an efficient cause. Power is part of constitutive relations and effects. A master does not 'cause' a slave; instead, both, and their respective powers, are constituted through this master–slave relation. For the same reason, constructivism will view power in an often impersonal and hence also not necessarily intentional way. Invoking certain metaphors or historical analogies can be very influential, whether intended or not, since they mobilise a pre-given understanding. The particular way in which issues are framed empowers certain arguments and actors at the expense of others. If a situation is understood in terms of the 'lessons of Munich', pleading for negotiations becomes an indefensible act of 'appeasement'; an understanding in terms of the lessons of the First World War would make negotiations an act of prudence to pre-empt a further escalation which nobody wanted. This power of existing biases is 'impersonal' to the extent that it is done through a set of common understandings or discourses, rather than reducible to the interpretation of one person; it is intersubjective not subjective. But, as with language, to be effective it requires people to mobilise it.

Finally, constructivism is interested in the power aspects of performativity. If the categories with which we order the world are themselves part of, and can significantly affect, the order in the (social!) world, then they are a crucial element in understanding power in any society (see Chapter 11). So does, for instance, the category 'failed states' interact with some states in their self-understanding and subjectivity (and behaviour), and therefore not only describes but affects the social world. It also prompts and legitimates certain actions, which would not have been legitimated by other categorisations, such as international interventions which overrule the otherwise fundamental norm of sovereignty. An interest in the category and measure of power has given way to a concern with the power of categorisation and measurement.

Such a performative analysis may also be reflexively applied to power analysis itself by looking at the way in which the analysis of power affects power. Which way of defining power increases the status (and responsibility) of certain actors rather than others? As later chapters will show, definitions of power as 'structural power' or 'soft power' are not politically innocent, nor are they intended to be. They redefine authorised and legitimate action and the call for responsibility or liability. There is a 'power politics of power analysis'. In fact, and this may sound odd to some readers, constructivism places politics back into the centre of the analysis. For what could be more political than the issue of the *Definitionshoheit*;

that is, the struggle for the sovereign authority to name and define what makes an issue an issue in the first place? Bourdieu sees power in the (legitimate) monopoly of imposing the vision and division of the world.

However, while constructivism may be a good antidote against a property conceptualisation of power, against an (efficient) causal understanding of power, while it may be a good entry into the reflexive effects (and hence power) between knowledge and social reality, the way we use it in IR (myself included) leaves one of the cognitive interests we have in power largely unanswered: we want to know power to understand political rule in a comprehensive manner.

3 Structural power and international rule

David Baldwin, one of the external examiners, asked the opening question during my PhD defence. In fact, it was just a seemingly easy comment for me to react to. Although I do not recall the exact wording, the gist was that I had used power as explanans in my analysis, but that many saw it as explanandum. I do not recall how I got out of this, but I surely had no good answer. That little comment encapsulates a central tension and further complication of power analysis. Rather than a mere means for understanding outcomes or influence, power is often the aim of the analysis. In many power analyses, it is both.

It is not difficult to see why precisely in the study of international relations, power could appear as both the means and end of the analysis. With no world government, the international system seemed to miss not only an ordering authority, but a polity altogether. In a sense, therefore, it was possible to think of world politics as the simple aggregation, and balance, of agent capacities. Power then became a central variable in a double causal link. Power understood as resources or 'capabilities' was an indicator of the strength of actors, and consequently of the capacity to affect or control events. Likewise, a general capacity to control outcomes has been used as an indicator for the ruling of the international system: by knowing who can be expected to win conflicts, we would also know who or what governs international politics, which, given the absence of a world polity, was all there was to know about power as political order and government. Power was both the means and end of the analysis.

But once the causal link between capabilities and outcomes is broken, as we have seen in the first section above, the relationship between power and rule needs to be rethought as well. Agent power is no longer the sufficient means to understand international power or rule. It is probably not unexpected that scholars in International Political Economy, dealing with capitalist markets and their systemic effects, have been particularly interested in rescuing the understanding of international power or rule from the analysis of sheer capabilities. As I have argued in my earliest piece (Chapter 1), they kept the focus on three components usually overlooked in the established power analysis, namely power in terms of unintended effects, indirect institutional power affecting outcomes by changing the rules of the (institutional) games, and in terms of the impersonal power of structures which mobilise a bias constituting individual opportunities. The thrust of these analyses is to take the focus away from direct power-to-power relations towards power structures and the more institutionalised settings in which social relations occur. In doing this, they either kept an agency concept of power in which they added the indirect institutional or unintended effects of agency (agency power through 'structural effects'), or they moved to an understanding of power located at the structure ('the power of structures' to effect).

In other words, structural power analysis in the international political economy tries to overcome the difficulty of conceiving power along the resource–outcome–rule line by starting from the other end; but it is not always clear whether such approaches get us out of the two problems we have met before. On the one hand, they tend to overplay the causal strength of power in their analysis. Moving backwards from rule to outcome faces similar problems to those met when moving from resources to outcomes. 'The USA won because of its structural power' faces the same translation or conversion questions as does classical resource-based analysis. It often appears to offer an answer when in reality it begs the question: power cannot just be substituted for cause. And in order to keep its alleged causal efficacy, it ends up overburdening the concept of power by adding more and more items into it, something I have called the overload fallacy of power analysis. The second problem is that these analyses tend to substitute power for rule, or conflate the two, now only reversing the order.

In my own work (see Chapter 1), I have proposed to keep the concepts of power (as an agency concept) and governance or rule (as a structural concept) apart, while combining them in a power analysis. Although this resolves some problems, I did not eventually much address rule as such. Worse, although I did see that the analysis of power conflated micro and macro levels, and hence overburdened the concept of power, I did not see that the analysis, mine included, traded on, and often conflated, two different domains.

4 The domains of power analysis

When Dahl analysed power through the conflicts of interests and their management at the municipal level, he was not interested in the outcomes for their own sake, or even just in the patterns of rule. He was interested in the wider concerns of 'who governs?', namely the nature of US democracy as such. The significance of the study, and the furore it provoked with defenders and critics alike, derives from its methodological innovations for a behavioural power analysis, but also from the political message: the apparently 'elitist' USA could be seen as 'pluralist', its democracy not as unhealthy as is often portrayed. Had he come up with the opposite result – something entirely possible with his approach – much good conceptual discussion, informed by the attempts to prove him wrong, may never have seen the day.

In turn, Lukes was not mainly interested in domination, when he criticised Dahl and Bachrach and Baratz, by pointing to a third dimension of power. This dimension, often tacit and akin to Gramsci's concept of hegemony, looks at those social relations in which conflicts of interests do not even arise because people have come to acquiesce, and not necessarily in a conscious manner, to the existing asymmetric rule. Being a sociologist who had studied Durkheim, his analysis was certainly informed by this focus on domination, but his aim and target was not sociological in the strict sense. His concern was a democratic concern with personal autonomy or freedom which he saw curtailed or pre-empted by this more insidious form of power, and which the other power analyses would not even be able to see as power because of their assumptions.

Both Dahl and Lukes use one type of power concept to elucidate another, crossing the micro–macro divide. Dahl starts bottom–up from the level of interaction, comparing influences, and infers the state of US democratic government, at least at the municipal level. Lukes works top–down, by seeing how social rule prevents, indeed pre-empts citizens from developing their full autonomy and freedom.

But both also cross domains (see now also Haugaard 2010). Their analyses start from the empirical sciences and explanatory theories, yet tie their findings back to classical political science, with the central focus of how government and 'its' subjects relate to each other. One could call this classical political analysis also normative, since it relates to classical issues of political values. This denomination would only be correct, however, if it were not narrowed to 'ethical' issues alone, discussed in terms of moral philosophy as is often done today, and almost excluding its empirical content. For classical political analysis asks constitutive questions about the nature of the state, of power, of government, of sovereignty, etc., which it understands not only as normative, but at the same time also as empirical. For my purposes, therefore, rather than contrasting an allegedly normative or theoretical with an empirical domain, I will distinguish between two different ways of harnessing both together in our attempts to explain/understand different facets of the world. For lack of better words, let me call them respectively the domains of political theory and explanatory theory, or the domains of constitutive and applied knowledge.

Now, if one crosses the macro–micro divide of power analysis with the two domains of power analysis, then the matrix shown in Figure 0.1 would appear. The matrix can do entirely without naming power, but for all of the dark-shaded terms used, 'power' could be substituted. This field of power concepts or connected terms gives a sense of the vast variety of concerns we mobilise when we embark on power analysis. For one, the significance of concepts is driven by the concerns they address. The matrix suggests how wide they are. For even an indicative list of power-connected terms in the light-shaded boxes shows why power seems so ubiquitous: be it concerns of social theorising (e.g. understanding cause) or of philosophy (e.g. understanding freedom), they often rely on a detour of power analysis (and specifically dedicated power concepts) for making their points, whether consciously or not. In

	Political theory (domain of constitutive knowledge)	Explanatory theory (domain of applied knowledge)	
	Polity/Socio-political order	
Macro level	Common good	Government/governance Rule/domination/hegemony	Hierarchy Stratification
Micro level	Freedom Responsibility	Autonomy Independence	Ability/capacity Influence	Disposition Cause
	Subjectivity	Agency	

FIGURE 0.1 The domains and levels of power

Note: Dark shading refers to primary power concepts; light shading refers to centrally related terms.

fact, a good way to use the matrix is to specify the exact concerns one wishes to address with and through power analysis.

Furthermore, the matrix suggests that even if we explicitly relate only to one power term, it always reverberates with debates in the other ones. Hence, as useful as an analytically narrower usage of power may be, we should not forget that in our political discourse – which often influences what is socially relevant knowledge – that narrower usage is always connected to others. That mutual connection also explains why it is so suggestive to explain one power concept through another. Yet I believe that nothing is gained by conflating one with the other and that, indeed, the specific relations and links between these concepts need time and again to be problematised in our analyses.

The matrix finally invites us to be very careful about those alleged links between these power phenomena. It is not self-evident to me that all there is to social and political order is the effect of other power concepts, or the other way round. The matrix is not meant to imprison us in connecting only the boxes within. In fact, if anything, it should alert us to the inherent risk of such reductionism.

Before concluding, let me add two more points concerning power concepts and domains. One is about an apparent omission. One central, indeed crucial power concept is not mentioned: authority and the related issue of legitimacy. It is perhaps no coincidence that it is a fundamental concept for Max Weber, who straddled the two domains (in trying to emancipate a sociology of the state from legal approaches to it) and the two levels (in his defence of a interpretivist methodological individualism for understanding social ontologies like capitalism). Indeed, I would place it in the exact middle of the matrix, where domains and levels meet and potentially overlap.

As for the two domains, I had initially also envisaged three, including a practical one based on practical knowledge or historical experience, as in the classical political realist (Weberian) tradition (for a more thorough discussion, see Guzzini 2007). But today I think that the practical discourse, rather than constituting a third domain apart, is probably better understood as a historical attempt to keep the two domains united under a common label, an undertaking which would fit Weber's more general approach. That historical attempt did not succeed. Hence my distinction in those domains, albeit argued analytically, is historically contingent. One could argue, for instance, that Foucault's approach, although more in the constitutive domain, is another but contemporary attempt to bridge both sides or, rather, to encompass them into a wider approach.

In general, it seems to me that the analysis of power is returning to these Weberian days and connecting the domains again. In the aftermath of Weber, much of power analysis, and surely in IR, has focused on the explanatory domain, as do my own analyses in the following chapters. But it seems we understand that we can neither reduce the explanatory domain to the constitutive one, as we did more than a century ago, nor the other way round as we have done in more recent decades. The reception of Foucault, and his pairing with scholars like Bourdieu, and other post-Weberian (also rationalist) schools, testify to a return to visualising the two domains together without reducing them to each other. While doing so, power, substantially re-apprehended, recovers the central place it used to have in our understanding of politics – and vice versa. Yet, by now, I am far more wary about the exact role it can play.

This leads me back to where the research on power began. Although realism eventually turned out not to offer the expected solution on my research path, and indeed became an obstacle on its way, the quest for understanding politics which brought me there did profit from having being de-routed towards international relations. In the realm of global politics, observers must constantly problematise the understanding of its socio-political order – something too often taken for granted in methodologically national studies – including its relation to war and violence.

The following chapters engage power mainly within the explanatory domain. As such, they are necessarily embedded within different social theories. Conceptual analysis can never be done on neutral ground or a blank sheet. Concepts derive their exact meaning from the theories in which they are embedded. Hence, it is normal that all the following power discussions are intrinsically related to theories, within or outside IR. However, with some translation (and some mutual blind spots and misunderstandings), concepts also travel across theories. And so I use theories to assess their power concepts, and, in reverse, I sometimes use the translation of different power concepts to expose the limits of theories. Besides the check for coherence, conceptual analysis can hence be used for both internal and external assessments of theories, while those very theories are necessary to apprehend the different ways in which power can be conceived in the first place. We cannot do without -isms, although there is no need to turn them into religions (indeed, there is just as much a risk of them becoming religious by being not aware of them as by being obsessed by them). This book can hence be read as a way to use social theories to improve our understanding of power, just as much as using power analysis as a way to improve our theories of international relations.

5 A short chapter outline

The book is divided into three parts. Each part includes three chapters of a more theoretical nature – constitutive and/or applied – and another two on theorists. The latter, perhaps unusual feature has to do with my concern about cognitive interests. Just as concepts of power have to be read in their theoretical context, and power analyses in terms of their theoretical assumptions, the purpose and significance of these analyses is connected to certain cognitive interests. Although those interests are often widely shared, focusing on the research agendas of individual scholars is a good way to get at them. In a sense, the always precarious coherence of individual cognitive interests provides a second type of contextualisation for the analysis of power.

For this collection, I have followed one of the traditions by keeping the chapters intact, because that is the way they had been initially conceived and referred to. I could have followed another tradition and cut some overlaps (e.g. the section on Luhmann in Chapter 12 can be skipped because of the longer development in Chapter 4, some passages in Chapter 7 are similar to others in Chapter 10) while interrupting the flow of the individual chapters. I appeal to the generosity of the readers and their good sense to read quickly through those passages where my argument sounds already familiar. To some extent, however, these overlaps are important. Appearing in different argumentative contexts, they show how the three main topics of the book are interrelated, something which is not always so evident from the arguments at their first appearance. I hope that the positive side of some repetition will outweigh its drawbacks.

PART I
Power

1
STRUCTURAL POWER
The limits of neorealist power analysis

The origin of this conceptual analysis lies in a basic puzzle. How did power analysis increasingly turn from a defense to a critique of realism? I shall argue that the turn from realism to neorealism, with its consequent reliance on economic methodology, in fact diminished the substantial range of the original concept of power. This chapter will contend that taking power analysis seriously leads beyond neorealism.

Some recent studies by authors dissatisfied with neorealism have attempted to widen the power concept to include what has been called structural power. Their common claim is that the focus on strategic interaction or the bargaining level of analysis does not capture important power phenomena. I shall argue that these notions of structural power involve three distinct meanings, of which only one can be shown to be compatible with the interactionist choice-theoretical power concept that underlies the neorealist approach.

Finally, this chapter claims that none of the structural power concepts is able to provide both a comprehensive and a coherent power analysis, either because it still omits particular power phenomena or because it overloads the concept of power. Instead of pursuing the track of continuously widening the concept, this chapter will propose a pair or dyad of concepts. The word "power" will be reserved as an agent concept, and the term "governance" will represent effects not due to a particular agent, whether individual or collective. More generally, I shall use the term "power analysis" to encompass both concepts and to deal with the link between power and international governance.

For helpful comments and suggestions on drafts of this article as early as June 1990, I am indebted to James Coleman, Robert Cox, Stephen Gill, Pierre Hassner, Anna Leander, Steven Lukes, Reinhard Meyers, Heikki Patomäki, Susan Strange, Ole Wæver, and the editor and two anonymous referees of *International Organization*. I would also like to thank Peter Taylor and Holly Wyatt who helped me to improve the language.

By approaching power from the methodological level, this chapter presents a more systematic analysis than those that either take the form of reviews or enumerations of different approaches or else do not consider the literature beyond David Baldwin's work.[1]

A last preliminary remark concerns the underlying definition of neorealism in the argument pursued here. The contribution of neorealism has been the systematic use of an economic mode of explanation in international relations (IR). This implies both (1) the Waltzian use of market theory and (2) the rational-actor model used in the game-theoretical approach and most prominently by Robert Keohane and Joseph Nye, Jr.'s later research program. It is on this ground that insights from the traditional realist and liberal traditions recently have been integrated.[2] The thorny question of whether Waltzian (so-called structural) neorealism is indeed linked to a rational-choice (individualist) model has spurred a major debate.[3] The position followed here is in essence closer to that of Alexander Wendt and Richard Ashley. Martin Hollis and Steve Smith are right that neoclassical economic theory allows, indeed requires, a double causation at the individual and market levels. Ashley and Wendt are also right to argue that the structural explanation presupposes the existence and the constancy of the actor's preferences. Indeed, only by presupposing *homo economicus* (Kenneth Waltz's like-unit), a being who wants to survive in his environment (basic preference) and manages to do so by rationally calculating the costs and benefits of alternate actions, can market (anarchy) constraints be understood. Economic theory is very powerful because it conceals and inextricably links these two levels. At the market level, dynamics are the result of individual utilitarian value-maximizing behavior. At the individual level, the static market constraints are the permanent background against which the strategic behavior of individuals is articulated. To allow for the explanatory articulation of the two levels of neoclassical theory, both individual preferences (in the macroanalysis) and the so-called invisible working of the market (in the microanalysis) must be taken for granted theoretically and held constant in the analysis. Without them, marginal economics could not work. In other words, rational choice and a Waltzian analysis are merely the two different levels of the same economic (utilitarian and interactionist) approach.

---

1 See, respectively, Sklar (1983), and Caporaso and Haggard (1989). Baldwin (1980) is the last reference in Evans and Newnham (1990).
2 Keohane and Nye (1987), in particular, see p. 729, wherein Keohane and Nye explicitly subsume liberalism and realism under a rational-actor model but with different conceptions of the nature of environment and other actors' goals. See also Nye (1988), and, explicitly, Keohane (1989 [1988]). For the purpose of this argument, only the neoinstitutionalist and regime approaches that use an economic mode of explanation can be criticized accordingly.
3 See Ashley (1984), Wendt (1987, 1991), and Hollis and Smith (1991). See also the rejoinders: Wendt (1992b), and Hollis and Smith in the same issue (1992).

The argument will be pursued in three steps. A first part will introduce the methodology of this conceptual analysis and the power concept underlying neorealism. Next, I will analyze three meanings of structural power. Finally, I shall propose a more coherent power analysis characterized by a dyad of concepts.

A conceptual critique of power in neorealism

The particular analysis and criticisms of recent conceptualizations of power proposed here call for a short justification of why at this particular moment a new conceptual analysis of power is required. After some major methodological assumptions regarding conceptual analyses in general have been outlined, an appraisal of the previous power debates in IR will introduce the underlying concept of power in neorealism.

Aims and limits of a conceptual analysis

The present analysis is not concerned with the empirical assessment of power; rather, it proposes a conceptual analysis of power and does so in the particular situation of a discipline in crisis. Currently, the discipline of IR is recovering from a state of disarray exemplified by the creation of a new discipline – namely, international political economy (IPE) – and the establishment of new and legitimate research areas on the fringes of mainstream research, such as critical theory, feminist theory, and poststructuralist approaches. At times like this, reconceptualizations are unavoidable: they constitute the first stage in theory reconstruction. Conceptual analyses serve to clarify and systematize the meaning of the very tools that different theories can then use to formulate explanations. In this respect, it is essential to recall that concepts are the basis for explanations and are not explanations as such. There might be theories involving power that can be checked empirically, but there are no concepts that can be checked in this way. Theories explain, concepts do not. Thus, this conceptual analysis falls short of claiming to provide *the* theory of power. The aim of this conceptual analysis is to provide a *pre*theoretical check of the coherence with which the concept of power is used in explanations and extended in recent writings for and against neorealism. It represents a logical control of theories before they are applied to empirical material.[4]

The theory dependence of the concept of power entails that there is no single concept of power applicable to every type of explanation. This implies that a limited range of views about power can be held that are both reasonable and yet different, possibly even incompatible (Connolly 1974: ch. 1). At least three different reasons have been put forward to argue for the concept of power as being "essentially contested."

---

4 This is also a requisite of a strictly positivist approach that insists on the prior clarification of the central variables and their meaning. For a classic statement, see Hempel (1965).

First, power always implies an element of counterfactual reasoning; that is, the judgment of the significance of a given set of abilities (power) presupposes an implicit statement about the unaffected state of affairs. Power implies potential change, which in turn implies a counterfactual situation of potential continuity. Since counterfactual situations are difficult to assess empirically, so this argument runs, no decisive proof can be brought in favor of one approach.

Second, it has been argued that the concept of power (as related to personal autonomy or interests) cannot be disentangled from normative discourse (see esp. Lukes 1974). Derived from this idea is the view in IR that "incommensurable" paradigms or ideologies meet in an "interparadigm debate."[5] Thomas Kuhn's concepts provided a welcome explanation for the discipline's difficulties in accumulating knowledge at a time when realism had lost its hegemony. The interparadigm debate argued for the establishment and recognition of rival schools of thought that cannot be subsumed under any form of revised realism. Once accepted, however, Kuhn's concepts became a welcome protective shield used by realists (and others) against attacks from other schools. Now, the concept of incommensurability legitimizes business as usual at the price of a predefined pluralism.[6] A specific historical stage of the debate in IR has become reified into rigid categories. These categories are inherently heterogeneous and are becoming increasingly confused with the (Anglo-American) ideological triad of conservatism, liberalism, and radicalism without any theoretical discussion of why specific ideologies would require particular theories and methodologies.[7]

Therefore, I shall not develop a so-called realist as opposed to a so-called liberal/pluralist or so-called critical/Marxist concept of power, assuming such things exist. Given that concepts of power are widely used as central *explanatory* variables, I find the underlying metatheoretical differences that characterize modes of explanation to be a more fundamental level at which those concepts can be distinguished. This third reason for essential contestability is a constructivist approach that is arguably more Kuhnian than the interparadigm debate. By mode of explanation, I mean the particular cluster of ontologies (agent/structure) and epistemologies (naturalist/interpretivist) that underlie theories and their reconstruction of reality.[8] Alexander Wendt and Raymond Duvall have written: "Although social ontologies do not directly dictate the content of substantive theories, they do have conceptual and methodological consequences for how theorists approach those phenomena they seek to explain, and thus for the development of their theories" (Wendt and Duvall 1989: 55). Concepts are not self-sufficient. They derive their meaning more generally from their modes of

---

5 Banks (1985). For the term "ideology" in IPE, see Gilpin (1987b). For an impressive list of the widely proposed trilogies, see Rittberger and Hummel (1990: 23).
6 For this attitude, see esp. Holsti (1985).
7 For more details, see Guzzini (1988, 1992: esp. chs 10 and 16).
8 For the same metatheoretical division, see Carlsnaes (1992: 249).

explanation and particularly from the theories (e.g., realism) in which they are embedded.[9] As will be shown, power is significantly different if conceived in an interactionist, dispositional, or intersubjective/structuralist approach.[10] This insight, which informs the whole of the following conceptual analysis, could be called explanatory perspectivism. It implies that concepts can be checked on the basis of their coherence within their respective theoretical frameworks.[11] It furthermore entails that, for the purpose of this study, it makes no significant difference who is the particular reference for power, provided the theory using power is constructed in the same mode of explanation. For instance, interactionist rational-choice approaches and the power concept they include remain basically the same in the analysis of nuclear brinkmanship, organizational agenda-setting, or personal threats. They also remain alike across the different spheres to which they are applied, whether economic, social, financial, or others. Power is distinguished through its role in explanatory frameworks, not through the fields to which it is applied.

In this way, I make two major claims. First, I try to show that concepts of structural power rightly identify the basic paradox of recent developments in realism. The neorealist move to an economic model will be shown to reduce the explanatory value of the concept of power.

The second claim is a theoretical argument against what Michael Banks once called "realism-plus-grafted-on-components," that is, the tendency of common wisdom in IR to incorporate reasonable insights without keeping track of whether doing so leads to an internal inconsistency (Banks 1984: 18). By criticizing already developed power schemes in political theory, I attempt to show that the concept of power cannot be extended indefinitely without becoming inconsistent with the underlying framework of analysis. This applies, of course, to both neorealist concepts and their challengers alike.[12]

The twist of the argument presented here is to make a paradox work. Realists generally believe that whatever one can say about their story, it is a story on power writ large. My contention is that by turning neorealist, they are in fact restricting themselves to a limited view of power. Some realists will not care, and the paradox will not work. Some realists might, however, hesitate and become curious about the wisdom of sticking to or moving to a choice-theoretical mode of explanation and its assumptions in which their central concept is underrated. Taking power seriously might lead realists beyond neorealism.

---

9 This is now widely acknowledged across rather different conceptualizations. See e.g. Barnes (1988), Clegg (1989), Merritt and Zinnes (1989: 27).
10 I use the word "structuralist" in the traditional sense of social theory, where it refers to theories that rely on holistic explanations. Waltz's approach has been, unfortunately for the interdisciplinary debate, sometimes labeled structuralist. I will refer to Waltz as a neorealist.
11 For a similar approach, see Joseph (1988).
12 For a similar approach, see Kratochwil and Ruggie (1986).

The neorealist concept of power

Concepts of structural power are but the latest in a series of attacks on realism through conceptual critiques of power. The neorealist concept of power itself reflects this long-standing debate.

According to traditional realism, the workings of the international system can be explained through the underlying distribution of power. This type of analysis typically identifies the contenders, their diverging interests and intentions, the open or tacit clash of wills, and the prevailing outcome. It shows which of the means that have been employed have proved most efficient. This allows the power of actors to be assessed not only for the power confrontation in question but also for future ones. One can deduce the relative power positions of actors by measuring the share of the most effective means they have under their control and can then derive guidance for future policy. This mix of explanatory and policy-planning characteristics has made the national interest as expressed in power such a "parsimonious" and ubiquitous tool in traditional IR.

However, this conception of power has often been held to conceal an essentially circular argument both for the assessment of the outcome and for the amount of power. On the one hand, it claims that (the distribution of) power is the main criterion for the explanation of outcomes. On the other, in some cases the outcomes are the main criterion for the assessment of power(s). Among other critiques, this essential circularity spurred the first major criticisms of the concept (Haas 1953, Claude 1962). As a reaction to this criticism, researchers in IR have either carefully avoided the concept of power[13] or tried to state specific power links and measure the means more rigorously. It is in this context that we must see two prominent reconceptualizations of power in IR, which both use a choice-theoretical approach. This is done not by Waltz, who leaves the concept unchanged, but by Baldwin and by Keohane and Nye.[14] Baldwin attempts systematically to apply insights from the pluralist literature in political theory to IR.[15] Keohane and Nye explore the limits of traditional power analysis in the context of transnationalization. Even though Baldwin criticizes their use of the concept of interdependence, these two influential reworkings of the concept have many crucial points in common. Both approaches take a choice-theoretical model as their underlying methodological starting point. Both are aware of the above-mentioned tautology, which derives from defining power in terms of resources. Both stress the importance of apprehending power resources only after a careful contextual analysis that Keohane and Nye subsume under

---

13 James Rosenau (1980 [1976]), distinguishes between "capabilities" as a property concept and "control" as actual influence over outcomes.
14 Keohane and Nye (1977: 18). For Baldwin's more systematic account, see the next section in this chapter.
15 For examples of the "pluralist" approach, see Dahl (1968) and Polsby (1980).

"asymmetrical interdependency." Finally, both emphasize the need to specify the context, that is, the issue-areas (and possibly also regimes) from which "vulnerability," resources, and thus potential power derive. (For instance, military resources are not necessarily useful when employed in a financial context.) As a result, they propose a choice-theoretical power analysis that focuses on specific "bargains" and the translation process from agent resources, which derive from particular contexts (interdependence), via strategic interaction to influence over outcomes.

Again, this new version of a realist power analysis has been found wanting. In the following section, these critiques will be presented systematically and criticized in turn.

Beyond neorealism? Meanings of structural power

Some recent studies have attempted to widen the power concept to include what has been called "structural power." I shall argue that these new notions of structural power involve three different meanings, namely, *indirect institutional power, nonintentional power, and impersonal empowering* (see Table 1.1). Only one of them is yet compatible with the underlying framework of neorealism, and none is able to provide a framework for the analysis of power phenomena that is both encompassing and coherent.

The criticisms were largely inspired by the so-called power debate in political theory. All the stages of that debate were replayed in IR. James Caporaso's and Stephen Krasner's concepts of structural power within IPE draw on Peter Bachrach and Morton Baratz's "second face of power," which tried to integrate notions like nondecision making or agenda setting. Stephen Gill and David Law's use of structural power derives from Steven Lukes's "third dimension" of power, which proposes to focus on the very power-intensive situations in which conflicts

TABLE 1.1 Meanings of structural power and related concepts

	Power as the production of		
Author	Indirect institutional effects	Unintended/unconscious effects	Impersonally created effects
Krasner	Metapower	—	—
Strange	Structural power	Structural power	—
Caporaso; Caporaso and Haggard	Structural power	—	Structural power, locational power
Gill and Law	Structural power	—	Hegemony/structural power
Ashley	—	—	Hegemony in the realm of *doxa*

of interests are systematically ruled out before they can be voiced. Finally, Susan Strange and Richard Ashley extend power concepts beyond the "power debate."[16]

Power as a relational concept: Indirect institutional power as an update of neorealist power analysis

One meaning of structural power is "indirect institutional power." Krasner's concept of metapower has to be understood as control over outcomes not via direct confrontation but by changing the setting in which confrontation occurs. Even though this seems to depart from the usual neorealist power analysis, a comparison with Baldwin's framework will show that it is in fact compatible with the assumptions of the economic approach. This concept is unsatisfactory, however, because it is too restrictive even for an agent-based concept of power.

Krasner tries explicitly to extend his particular regime analysis to embrace a form of power analysis. He analyzes how the regime concept can be located within the same conversion process from resources via power to influence (over outcomes) that we have already met in Keohane and Nye. He thus follows the traditional realist assumption that regimes are, in the last resort, still a function of the distribution of power and the relations among states. However, there need not always be congruity among power distribution, regimes, and related behavior or outcomes. In other words, there is a time lag of adjustment that allows for a certain autonomy of the realm of norms, as well as an interactive process between (power) base and norms (Krasner 1982a: 499). Therefore, lags and feedbacks between power base and regime are the basic puzzles of Krasner's research program. Krasner makes two points about the interaction of power and regimes. First, he argues that changes of regimes alter the context in such a way as to render particular resources more important for power capability than others. The approach thereby recovers part of what one could call the historically contingent character of power resources.[17] Second, regimes can, after a time lag, be conceived of as independent sources of influence.

However, through a shift of the argument, power and regime are not only two different sources of influence but regime is in fact reduced to a source of power. Krasner has defined "power" as potential control over resources and conceived of "power resources" as those phenomena that can be used to exercise influence. It follows that normative structures and regimes can be envisaged as just another type of power source and their potential control as just another form of power. Then, one could argue, Krasner's two approaches to power and regime are fused into one. Krasner has taken this logical step by defining a second level of power relations:

---

16 See, respectively, Bachrach and Baratz (1970) and Lukes (1974).
17 For this argument, see Aron (1962: 64).

> The boundaries of this work can be more clearly delineated by distinguishing between two categories of political behavior. Relational power behavior refers to efforts to maximize values within a given set of institutional structures; meta-power behavior refers to efforts to change the institutions themselves. Relational power refers to the ability to change outcomes or affect the behavior of others within a given regime. Meta-power refers to the ability to change the rules of the game. Outcomes can be changed both by altering the resources available to individual actors and by changing the regimes that condition action.[18]
>
> (Krasner 1985a: 14)

Since regimes are a source of power, any intentional attempt to change regimes or to set new institutional frames for actors' capabilities must be integrated into power analysis. This is an indirect form of power and is often hidden or tacit. Krasner argues his case by referring to the Third World and its attempt to change the institutional settings in which North–South relations occur in order to upset the relational power advantage of the North.[19]

This wider concept of metapower is consistent with neorealism's economic foundations. One way to see this is to recognize the parallel between Krasner's metapower and the power approach as developed by Baldwin, who works explicity with an economic exchange model like that underlying neorealism.[20]

Baldwin defends a so-called relational approach to the analysis of power. In this approach, a power base or power resource cannot be assessed by sole reference to the power holder. Baldwin's preferred example is a coercive attempt in which a person threatens another with a gun and shouts "your money or your life." [S.G. 2012: This is a mistaken attribution. The example derives from Bachrach and Baratz (1970).] The sanction of killing and the visible means for realizing it generally provide a powerful threat. Yet, if the threatened person is preparing to commit suicide, or does not value life so highly, the coercive capacity of the threat is reduced accordingly. Awareness of this relational aspect can also be consciously used as a defense against threats. President Harry Truman tried to impress Joseph Stalin in Potsdam in 1945 by telling him that the United States had developed an

---

18 For a very similar approach, see Nye (1990b: 166–8). Above the traditional "command power," he conceives of a form of power, called "co-optive power" or "soft power," which (1) expressed in terms of resources, is derived from intangible resources like the rules in regimes and cultural and/or ideological attraction and (2) expressed in terms of power exercises, consists in structuring the situations in which power relations occur.
19 Krasner's argument was made in the context of the U.S. and the U.K. decisions to "react" against this attempt by quitting the United Nations Educational, Scientific, and Cultural Organization (UNESCO).
20 The best general presentation in political theory of the choice-theoretical approach to power remains Barry's 1975 essay reprinted in Barry (1989 [1975]). See also Baechler (1978) and Bartlett (1989). In addition, see Dowding (1991), whose distinction between "outcome power" and "social power" reflects exactly Krasner's twofold approach.

atomic bomb. Stalin, however, by feigning indifference, reduced the impact of this possible bargaining chip. Thus, any power instrument becomes a potential power resource only if its control is seen to be valued by other actors in the interaction. Power comes out of this relation, not from the power holder alone.[21]

Yet, the fundamental theoretical reason why Baldwin argues in favor of power as a relational concept, and not a possession, is to resist the money–power analogy. This approach, stemming from the social exchange literature, treats power as a resource to be exchanged in an interaction for influence. The rejection of this analogy marks the three major elements of Baldwin's power analysis: the concept of fungibility,[22] the multidimensional character of power, and the prior relational analysis of specific policy-contingency frameworks.[23]

The high fungibility of money rests on two main characteristics: first, its high liquidity as a medium of exchange based and dependent upon, second, its function as a standard of value.[24] Yet, for Baldwin

> the owner of a political power resource, such as the means to deter atomic attack, is likely to have difficulties converting this resource into another resource that would, for instance, allow his country to become the leader of the Third World. Whereas money facilitates the exchange of one economic resource for another, there is no standardized measure of value that serves as medium of exchange for political power resources.
>
> *(Baldwin 1979: 165–6)*

Because power is not fungible, it is multidimensional, i.e., its scope (the objectives of an attempt to gain influence; influence over which issue), its domain (the target of the influence attempt), its weight (the quantity of resources), and its cost

21 On this particular point, see Baldwin (1980: 500–1, 1985: 22).
22 The term "fungibility" refers to the idea of movable goods that can be freely placed and replaced by others of the same class. It connotes universal applicability or "convertibility" in contrast to context specificity. For Baldwin, money is defined by its fungibility. He obviously refers to an ideal type of money, i.e., the most liquid part of the various money aggregates, and the fact that the standard-of-value function is fulfilled mainly in developed national economies and only to a limited extent on the international level.
23 Keohane follows this approach when, by arguing for issue- or regime-specific analyses, he specifically criticizes Waltz for this fungibility assumption. See Keohane (1986: 184).
24 Baldwin (1971a: 393). For a similar argument, see Wolfers (1962: 106). Aron states that only the characteristics of money allow economists to reduce the multiplicity of individual choices to a single scale of preferences. Since neither power nor "national interest" can play this role, economics cannot be the model for international theory. By criticizing Kaplan, Aron thereby anticipates and rejects Waltz's research program. Waltz explicitly acknowledges Aron's argument. He counters by claiming that the missing standard-of-value characteristics of power is not a problem for theory building but a practical problem that arises during its application. He thereby overlooks Aron's argument that the reason why money is not analogous to power lies in the lack of a theoretical analogy between utility and national interest. For the two arguments, see Aron (1962: 98); and Waltz (1990), respectively.

(opportunity costs of forgoing a relation) must be made explicit. Without these qualifications, any statement about power is, for Baldwin, close to meaningless. Another consequence of low fungibility is that power can rest on various bases, and no single power base (military resources, for instance) can be held a priori to be the most decisive in any attempt to exert influence.

This multidimensional character leads to the last characteristic of any power approach in Baldwin's terms: the specification of the situation, that is, the policy-contingency framework (see Figure 1.1). A relational concept of power requires a prior contextual analysis (Baldwin 1979, 1985: 285). At this point, the inextricable link of the economic approach's two levels can be shown. For the agent, this policy-contingency framework corresponds to the structural level of an economic approach. Only by analyzing the particular market in which (economic) actors meet is a precise assessment of the interaction possible. In this respect, Baldwin's multidimensional context resembles Keohane and Nye's issue-areas or regimes rather than the general Waltzian structure. On the other hand, agents' behavior in the long run shapes the underlying structure that constrains future actions. It is exactly on this microeconomic dynamic of structural theories that Krasner's approach of indirect power can be located.

In order to draw the analogy between Baldwin's and Krasner's approaches, a last element is needed: the necessary inclusion of societal norms in the analysis. This results from the fact that exchange is possible not only in money economies but also in situations of barter. Indeed, in such contexts there also exists a medium of exchange, even though it is a very crude one. Therefore, the analogy of barter exchange and power relations is theoretically possible (Martin 1977: 29).

Baldwin writes:

> The exchange of approval for advice, of compliance for money, or of one favor for another does not require measurement in terms of commensurate units of value – at least not so long as we speak of it as direct exchange (barter). It is only when indirect exchange and the fairness of exchange are discussed that standardized measures of value begin to matter. One of the exchange theorists' most important insights concerns the way societal norms function as *primitive* measuring rods that make indirect social exchange possible.
> *(Baldwin 1978: 1240, italics in original)*

Thus, one not only needs a contextual analysis and a study of the historical background but one also must be familiar with the *societal* background of norms. This has the important consequence that any technological, political, cultural, or normative development that improves the efficacy of certain resources in affecting outcomes can, in turn, become a target for attempts to gain influence. Therefore, two strategies are possible to improve one's potential power in a given situation: to cause either a quantitative improvement of the relevant situational power resources or a change in the environment that defines the situationally relevant power resources. The latter is exactly what Krasner defines as

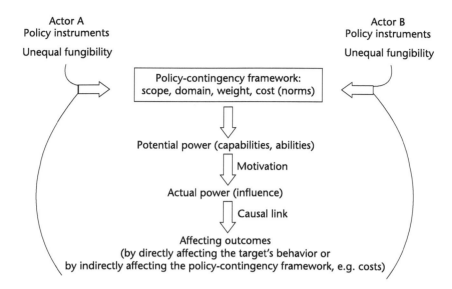

FIGURE 1.1 An analytical model of David Baldwin's relational power analysis

metapower. Thus, the intentional agenda setting that Krasner tried to integrate into realist power analysis can indeed be coherently accounted for within the methodology used by neorealists.

Baldwin's approach (as synthesized in Figure 1.1) will serve as the reference point for discussing the other two meanings of structural power.

Power as a dispositional concept: Nonintentional power and the limits of neorealist power analysis

The second distinct meaning of structural power is still conceived at the level of agents but refers to an action's unintended (and sometimes unconscious) effects. This meaning cannot be simply grafted onto a neorealist understanding of power, because the latter links power to intentionality. It can be linked to a dispositional concept of power. This section will show how the second meaning of structural power can successfully supplement Krasner's concept. In the final part of the chapter, dispositional approaches of this sort will be shown to be unsatisfactory because their concept of structure is too limited.

Strange's work illustrates this notion of structural power as "nonintentional power." She developed her concept in opposition to the literature of American hegemonic decline.[25] The expression of decline is chosen on purpose. One of the

---

25 The reference definition of hegemonic stability theory has been given by Robert Keohane (1980). Yet, it seems too much tailored for his regime approach, neglecting the collective-good argument. For a convincing argument, see Snidal (1985: 581).

theses of the hegemonic stability theory states that a declining hegemonic power presages a declining provision of the international public good. For Strange, the decline school is based on a fallacious inversion of this thesis, namely, that the declining provision of international public goods would indicate the declining power of the hegemon. She tries to show that the United States is not unable but just unwilling to provide, or help to provide, basic functions of a global political economy. Her concept of structural power is crucial to pointing to the global reach of a so-called transnational empire with the United States at its center.

She uses structural power to refer to the increasing diffusion of international power, in both its effects and its origins, due to the increasing transnationalization of nonterritorially linked networks. Structural power is, on the one hand, a concept similar to Krasner's intentional metapower: the ability to shape the security, financial, productive, and knowledge structures (Strange 1985: 15). Here, power is structural because it has an indirect diffusion via structures. On the other hand, Strange understands power as structural because it refers to the increasingly diffused sources and agents that contribute to the functioning of the global political economy.[26] Taken together, the provision of global functions appears as the result of an interplay of deliberate and *nonintentional influence* of decisions and nondecisions made by governments and other actors.[27] To Strange, then, the international system appears as if run by a "transnational empire," whose exact center is difficult to locate because it is not tied to a specific territory, but whose main base is in the United States (Strange 1989). In other words, even though actors in the United States might not always intend or be able to control the effects of their actions, the international structures are set up in a way that decisions in some countries are systematically tied to and affect actors in the same and other countries.

The September 1992 crisis of the European Monetary System shows that structural power also exists outside the United States. German reunification led to inflation that was controlled only partly through a reversal of prior fiscal policies. The German Bundesbank then exported the problem via higher interest rates. These higher rates helped to trigger a speculative attack on the British pound and the Italian lira. This, in turn, involved so much money moving across borders that central banks quickly judged interventions to be too costly for both the inflating DM and the deflating monetary reserves of the attacked currencies. Thus, one basic reason for these effects is a specific policy mix decided by the German government together with the strained social consensus in Germany. Germany's position and sheer "weight" within the European system gives it the privilege of avoiding some of the painful adjustments others are facing. It manages

---

26 For a concise presentation of recent power concepts with a similar analysis of Strange's approach, see Badie and Smouts (1992: 148–56).
27 See Strange (1984: 190–1) and Strange (1988), where this notion is developed most fully. For the empirical analysis of U.S. nondecisions, see Strange (1986: ch. 2).

a transnational currency as if it were a national one.[28] Yet, for particular actors, many of what appear to be purely domestic decisions in fact significantly affect other actors, whether intentionally or not. Actors in Germany have a great deal of nonintentional or nonconscious power to which all the other participants in the international game must nevertheless adapt their behavior (typically in worst-case scenarios). Or, to use an image of Pierre Hassner's for the description of a condominium: it does not make any difference to the trampled grass if the elephants above it make love or war. This structural power is underrated if one analyzes power only in cases of specific contests in which different intentions clash.

The remaining part of this section will analyze the two implicit claims of this form of structural power. First, it will show that economic approaches can include the study of nonintentional effects but cannot include them in the concept or analysis of power itself, instead referring to these effects as either random effects or simply good or bad luck. Second, nonintentional power can, however, be accounted for by a methodological individualist position. Strange's approach is based not on a relational but on a dispositional concept of power.

For the exclusion of nonintentional effects from the concept and analysis of power, we return to Baldwin's framework as the choice-theoretical reference point. Baldwin tries to elaborate a policy-oriented, manipulative, and thus agent-focused theory of power. Yet, his power concept has been pulled increasingly toward a type of reasoning that focuses on outcomes and not on a manipulative agent. In other words, Baldwin seems to be torn because of a conceptual dilemma that is also applicable to Krasner's concept: his conceptual approach to power expands to include all effects that influence outcomes, whereas his *actual* policy analysis argues for a power concept that is limited to the intentional agent. We could describe this in William Riker's terminology as a dilemma in which Baldwin's aim is the study of statecraft through a "recipe-like" concept of causality (and power), while his conceptual analysis pulls him toward a "necessary and sufficient" kind of causality.[29] Whereas the former focuses on manipulative techniques, the latter aims at a full explanation of what affects the outcome, whether overtly or covertly. According to Baldwin, "although Riker may be correct in asserting the superiority of the latter concept of causality for some types of science, the former concept is more useful in the policy sciences and will therefore be employed here" (1985: 26). Yet, as Riker says, "The more profound difficulty with recipe-causality, however, is that it takes as fixed all relevant variables, except the manipulative one.... If a non-manipulative variable in the

28 With regard to the management of the U.S. dollar, this critique has a longer tradition. For one example, see Aron (1984: 44). It is important to note that the power to avoid or to export adjustments can, in the long run, undermine the very base of "national" power. This argument is most thoroughly made in David P. Calleo's work; see e.g., Calleo (1982, 1987). See also Senghaas (1992: 55).
29 Riker (1969: 116). The recipe-like concept is defined as the production of effects through the manipulation of nature.

antecedent condition does have a relation to the effect, then it must be involved in the cause, even though recipe-causality does not admit it" (Riker 1964: 346). In his attempt to preserve power as an operationalizable causal concept, Baldwin incorporates more and more items to account for the exact contextual assessment of manipulative techniques; yet, he avoids providing the full account of the causality chain toward which this very extension pulls his analysis. To cite Riker again:

> The difference between the two kinds of causality is, like the difference among definitions of power, a difference in orientation toward outcomes. In recipe-like causality, the full explanation of the effect is not the problem. Rather the problem is to explain how the effect can be made to occur. *If no manipulative technique is available, cause may be non-existent.* By contrast, in the necessary and sufficient condition kind of causality, the center of attention is on the effect rather than on manipulative techniques. Here the full explanation of outcomes is at stake. Hence, cause cannot be non-existent, although it can be unidentified.
>
> *(Riker 1964: 347, emphasis added)*

The choice of a recipe concept of power deprives the analysis of those causal factors that cannot be linked or reduced to the agent's conscious manipulation of the resources at hand. Power as the production of unintended effects is not captured because it falls outside the causal link between A's intention and B's changed behavior. The only exception that the pluralist power literature accepts, the rule of anticipated reaction, is a case of imputed intentions, but intentions nevertheless. Therefore, by reducing the analysis of power to the establishment of a causal chain from A's intention to the outcome, a choice-theoretical approach cannot theoretically incorporate the idea of power as unintended effects *into the concept of power*.

This does not mean that these unintended effects are forgotten in a choice-theoretical analysis. Riker's important point consists of showing that by sticking to a specific mode of explanation, these unintended effects must be dealt with either as environmental constraints or as purely random phenomena. Since manipulative power entails the idea that one can change the course of affairs, those excluded items appear as a kind of fate against which even the most powerful actors remain powerless. The far-reaching consequence of this apparently innocent methodological move lies on the level of political action and responsibility. If we have to face fate, then there is nothing to do. Yet, Strange's insistence on unintended effects attempts to show that agents could make a difference if they wanted. Her widened concept of power aims at shedding light on the possibilities for change and on the (political) responsibility for non-manipulative effects that a limited concept of power must disregard.

Concepts of structural power suggest that this widening of the concept needs to integrate a structural element into the power concept. In fact, this is not true. One can leave intentionality out of an agent-based power concept, but it is then necessary to relax the empiricist assumptions, the interactionist approach, and the general causal analogy. Thus, the analytical chain starts not from an agent's intentions but from basic actions. That this conceptualization is not just a theoretical possibility can be shown by referring to a recent redefinition of power in exactly these terms.

Peter Morriss bases his analysis on a concept of power that he distinguishes from mere influence by pointing to the profound dispositional character of power: power, to him, refers to a capacity, ability, or dispositional property: "So power, as a dispositional concept, is neither a *thing* (a resource or vehicle) nor an *event* (an exercise of power): it is a *capacity*."[30] Since power is defined as an ability, every basic action, controlled by will, at the disposal of an actor can be considered as power. The capacity to influence by will is thus a criterion to distinguish power from a (dispositional) property.

Morriss goes on to distinguish, as shown in Figure 1.2, three categories of ability (Morriss 1987: 54). Since this conceptualization of power is based on "effecting," Morriss disposes also of a category for nonintentional power. "Nonepistemic" abilities are those that are effected in an uncontrolled way, such as when agents are unaware of their capacities and their consequences or they

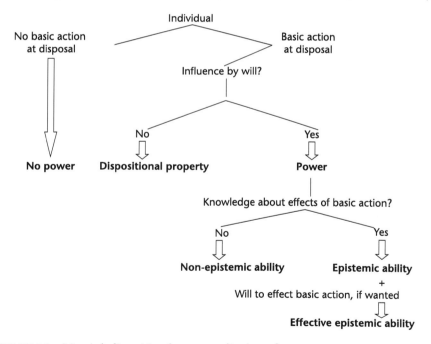

FIGURE 1.2 Morriss's dispositional conceptualization of power

30 Morriss (1987: 19; emphasis in original). On pages 15–18, Morriss criticizes the pluralists for their excessive empiricism in requiring the actual exercise of power as a condition for its existence. He calls this the "event-fallacy." For a discussion of both fallacies in IR and IPE, see Garst (1989: 20–2).

choose the wrong basic action for the intended outcome. This category is able to take account of Strange's idea of nonintentional power, which looks at power from the "receiving side." Morriss shows that whenever "we want to work out what people might do to us, it is non-epistemic power we are concerned with" (Morriss 1987: 54).

This stress on mere capacities and not their exercise seems at first hand close to the traditional power analyses in IR. The important difference is that those approaches posited a direct link between the *control* of outcomes and capacities, whether they are implemented or not. Strange's structural power looks at power from the point of view of the diffused power effects and stresses the uncontrolled consequences of power actions.[31]

The major difference of such a dispositional approach from an interactionist rational-choice approach is that these consequences are part of the power assessment and are not just random. This contradicts approaches like Klaus Knorr's, for instance, who explicitly and coherently refuses to accept such a form of nonintentional power. Knorr dismisses François Perroux's concept of dominance, which is close to Strange's structural power, as purely incidental and therefore irrelevant for power analysis (Knorr 1973: 77–8). This exclusion of nonintentionality privileges the manipulative actor's (or power holder's) view and leaves the analysis of power with a specific blind spot, namely, the tacit power of the strong. If neorealism goes on following this route, it is to be expected that criticisms of the kind implicit in different structural power concepts will continually reappear. Hence Baldwin acknowledges, without further discussion, that "concepts of power that allow for the possibility of unintended influence may be more useful to the student of dependency and autonomy than other power concepts" (Baldwin 1980: 499).

Power as a structural/intersubjective concept: impersonal power

The last of the three meanings of structural power and related concepts can be generically described as "impersonal power" because the origin of the produced effect is not located at the level of actors. Here, two different conceptualizations can be distinguished. The first could be described as a positional concept that focuses on the impersonal bias of international relations, which systematically gives an advantage to certain actors due to their specific positions or roles in the international system. The second stresses the link between knowledge and power, arguing that power requires prior intersubjective recognition. Both approaches explicitly attempt to abandon the underlying choice-theoretical

---

31 Coming to the second side of her power approach, the diffusion not of the effects but of the origins of power, Strange does, however, individualize a privileged actor, the "international business civilization." In other words, nonintentional power is very unevenly distributed throughout the international power structure. See Strange (1990).

mode of explanation. These concepts, too, are unsatisfactory because they tend to overload and thus render incoherent the single concept of power. This section will present the two approaches; the next section takes their insufficiencies as the basis for developing a different power analysis derived from a dyad of concepts.

The first more positional approach to power has been introduced by James Caporaso. He accepts the centrality of power, yet gives it a double twist in order to incorporate the link between the global political economy and less developed countries' economic and political development. The focus on "bargaining power in asymmetrical interdependence" is considered insufficient.[32] He acknowledges that dependence is, on the bargaining level, no criterion for a qualitative differentiation of less developed countries.[33] Yet, he integrates the "second face" of power, derived from Bachrach and Baratz, to save a concept of dependency. This is called structural power. Implicitly, he also repeats an ambiguity that can be found in the work of Bachrach and Baratz.[34] Their nondecision making can mean both the inherent bias of any organization that benefits some more than others (nondecisions as "structural bias") and the conscious manipulation of the bias to affect outcomes in an advantageous way (nondecisions as "antedecisions"). Caporaso refers to the latter in his definition of structural power as "the ability to manipulate the choices, capabilities, alliance opportunities, and payoffs that actors may utilize" (Caporaso 1978a: 4). This is in line with Krasner's concept of metapower. Yet, he also speaks of "the social structuring of agendas [that] might systematically favor certain parties," which is definitely an *impersonal* concept.[35]

In a similar vein, Gill and Law try to overcome the dominant behavioral power paradigm in IR and IPE by a concept of structural power that is said to capture better the indirect forms of power (see Gill and Law 1988, 1989). Explicitly following Lukes, they begin by distinguishing three dimensions of power: overt, covert, and structural.[36] Later, they introduce a direct/indirect distinction. Although they are not explicit, they seem to rely on individual action as the distinctive criterion. Thus, overt and covert power are linked to agents' decisions and nondecisions in pursuing their interests, whereas structural power

---

32 Caporaso (1978a: 4, 1978b: 28). The quotations allude, of course, to Keohane and Nye's *Power and Interdependence*.
33 Caporaso (1978a: 2, 1978b: 18). This point has been most elegantly made by Lall (1975).
34 This ambiguity has been largely neglected in the literature. For an exception, see Debnam (1984: 24).
35 Caporaso (1978b: 33). In more recent writings, Caporaso retreats slightly from this latter position. He retains the basic division between relational (agent-based) and structural power approaches. Yet, together with Stephen Haggard (1989), he now concludes that these forms of power are not necessarily competing categories: they both refer to (different kinds) of resources that affect outcomes understood as bargains. For a critique of this argument, see the third section of this chapter.
36 For a similar account, based on Steven Lukes's three dimensions, see Krause (1991).

refers to "material and normative aspects, such that patterns of incentives and constraints are systematically created" (Gill and Law 1988: 73).

Their "impersonal material setting" is nearly synonymous with the functioning of markets. Through markets, the structural power of capital is exercised.[37] The state–market nexus becomes the very center of the analysis.[38] Gill and Law focus on the relationship between the political organization of the global political economy into nation-states and the power of capital. On the one hand, international anarchy enhances capital's bargaining position, allowing it to play one country against another; on the other hand, national sovereignty can reduce capital's power through statist intervention, such as welfarism, mercantilism, and the public sector. The absence of a world government is as much a structural prerequisite for the power of capital as a limitation to the potentially global reach of market-economic activities. Hence, in the material part of their approach, the logic of the market overtakes the balance of power or regimes as the central and slightly mechanistic explanatory variable, which provides the basic causality and predictive virtue (Gill and Law 1989: 485).

However, Gill and Law also stress a second, normative aspect of structural power/hegemony. This is the basic link between structural power and Antonio Gramsci's analysis of hegemony, which, following the work of Robert Cox, they want to transfer to the international level. True, no realist would dispute the derivation of norms from power relations, the conservative bias of law in the hands of the ruling group, the importance of the normative setting for specific historic global political economies (regimes of accumulation), or, finally, the anticipated ruling of power where its overt demonstration is not needed.[39] However, the Gramscian approach derives the ruling ideology from a class analysis, that is, from the sphere of production.[40] It goes beyond crude materialism by pointing to the fact that the ruling elite can co-opt part of the ruled into a "historic bloc," which makes orthodox revolutionary politics impossible. The research program of this power approach consists of finding the new transnational historical bloc and the way its (neoliberal) discourse and practice suborn dependent classes and preempt their opposition.

---

37 For the definition of capital, see Gill and Law (1989: 480–1). Note that the terms "power of markets" and "structural power" are sometimes used interchangeably; see Gill and Law (1988: 97).
38 The state–market nexus "politicizes" (in an Eastonian way) international economic relations. The analysis is centered around the two competing authoritative allocation mechanisms (for values or resources) that exist: states and markets. See Czempiel (1981, 1989).
39 On the first point, see Morgenthau (1948: 342ff.); and on the second, see Waltz (1969 [1967]: 309). Note in this context Antonio Gramsci's interest in the Italian Realist tradition (Niccolò Machiavelli, Gaetano Mosca, Vilfredo Pareto) in Gramsci (1981).
40 Cox insists on the rooting of hegemony in social forces, to avoid repeating Machiavelli; see Cox (1983: 164).

This latter point, in particular the consensual aspect of power, has been developed by Ashley in the second impersonal conceptualization of power as power/knowledge. The consensual aspect is traditionally handled through the concept of legitimacy that, in the usual reading of Max Weber, distinguishes between power (*Macht*) and authority/rule (*Herrschaft*). *Herrschaft* requires legitimacy, that is, a form of internal acceptance by the power addressees (Bobbio 1981: 226). The poststructuralist twist can be seen in the metatheoretical location of phenomena of power. This means that consensus is conceptualized not only in an agent's recognition but also as produced and reproduced outcomes of rituals and discourses that are not intentionally effected by particular actors. Legitimacy understood as the result of a social contract is an insufficient concept to account comprehensively for consensus and governance (Foucault 1977: 188). In this formulation, the consensual aspect of power entails, but means certainly something more than, a shift of focus to a kind of Weberian approach wrapped in a Gramscian blanket.[41] This approach has, then, its specificity not only in the actual meaning given to power but also in the realm to which it is applied. It does not analyze power *in* IR and IPE as reflected in its discourse but the power *of* precisely this discourse. The poststructuralist critique aims at that level at which such power practices are concealed, that is, the metatheoretical level which underlies realist analysis and consequently its deliberate policies.[42] The realist discourse is attacked as a power practice itself.

Ashley expands what one could call a "communicative" approach (Little 1989, Kratochwil 1988: 272) to a Foucauldian genealogical power conceptualization. His genealogical attitude can be summarized as an attempt to reveal the power practices that bind, conquer, and administer social space and time, that is, the emergence of "disciplines" (Ashley 1987: 418).

Crucial for this understanding of power is a specific concept of practices that includes not only interactive influence attempts but also rites, routines, and discourses. Thereby one disposes of an intersubjective level of analysis different from an objectified or even determinist structure as well as from an intentional agent. Rites and routines are not just a constraint or a resource for agents; they also empower agents. In this approach it makes sense to speak of the power of rites. According to David Kertzer, "The power of the rite is based in good part on the potency of its symbols and its social context.... People's emotional involvement in political rites is certainly a key source of their power" (Kertzer 1988: 179, 180).

There are two ways in which rites can be linked to power. First, they can obviously be used as a means or source of an intentional influence attempt. A

---

41 For the stress on *Herrschaft*, see Albrecht (1986). For the Gramscian wording, see Klein (1988: 134).
42 The most radical power critique at the metatheoretical level is the poststructuralist branch of feminism. See Runyan and Peterson (1991: 75–6 and 97–8).

recent example is the Western propaganda that modeled Saddam Hussein as a modern Adolf Hitler. The "powerful" analogy constituted a means to stimulate widespread approval of U.S. foreign policy in those European circles that usually are rather critical of it. Second, rites can also empower agents. In this case, the power of rites is impersonal, because it does not originate in an actor. But at the same time, it is not objective or natural – like the power of hurricanes, for instance – because rites are not powerful independent of agents. The symbol of Munich can be intentionally invoked by actors, but it keeps a particular hold on Western political discourse and thus also on policymaking since 1938. Its power is constantly renewed or shaken by more recent applications. The rallying power of a national flag can be used by politicians, but the symbol escapes their control; it "governs" independently of particular intentions, albeit not independently of the practices and the meaning given to it by the group of actors involved.

Ashley derives such a form of impersonal power from the work of Pierre Bourdieu. Fundamental here is Ashley's introduction of Bourdieu's concept of "*doxa*." Bourdieu distinguished *doxa* both from orthodoxy (a kind of established truth or common wisdom) and from heterodoxy (orthodoxy's official contender). The two latter concepts refer to the universe of open discourse and argument and depend on each other. *Doxa*, on the other hand, refers to the self-evident background of the established order on which the contest between orthodoxy and heterodoxy is articulated. Even though the realm of *doxa* is necessary to set the stage, its contingency is not acknowledged: "Every established order tends to produce the naturalization of its own arbitrariness." Writes Bourdieu:

> In the extreme case, that is to say, when there is a quasi-perfect correspondence between the objective order and the subjective principles of organization (as in ancient societies) the natural and social world appears as self-evident. This experience we shall call *doxa*. . . . The instruments of knowledge of the world are in this case (objectively) political instruments which contribute to the reproduction of the social world by producing immediate adherence to the world, seen as self-evident and undisputed, of which they are the product and of which they reproduce the structures in a transformed form. . . . The theory of knowledge is a dimension of political theory because the specific symbolic power to impose the principles of the construction of reality – in particular, social reality, is a major dimension of political power.
>
> (Bourdieu 1977: 164, 165)

The domain of *doxa* represents a system of normalized recognition through continuous practice that ceases to work (and incidentally also to exist) exactly at the moment when conscious legitimation is needed. Thus, Ashley locates impersonal empower*ing* explicitly at an intersubjective level, where knowledge is constituted and acting and thinking space defined. There roles and practices are constructed, and they then operate systematically and nonintentionally, that is "naturally," not only to exclude issues from the agenda but also to prevent the very definition of such issues and their possible solutions. Ashley writes that "the political power of hegemony ... is neither a 'power over' other actors nor a 'power to' obtain some consciously deliberated future end among ends. The power of hegemony resides precisely in the capacity to inhabit a domain of *doxa* and to competently perform the rituals of power naturalized therein" (Ashley 1989: 269).

We can use a critique of neorealism as an illustration of Ashley's "dissident" power analysis. The latter would attempt to counter the closing-off procedures that the move toward neorealism "effected" in the face of the increasing dissolution of the discipline's boundaries in the 1970s. The qualitative difference between international and domestic politics, that is, anarchy and sovereignty, already had been attacked by the older behavioral claim that methodologically the study of internal and external policies is alike, by the rising importance of transnational actors that undermine the concept of sovereignty, and by bureaucratic politics that question the notion of a unified or rational actor. Waltz's reformulation of realism restored the categorical dichotomy and thus provided the discipline with a defining boundary. Waltz's defense comprised the off-loading of transnational and infranational phenomena into the area of foreign policy analysis (hence political science), thus preserving a systemic realism. Its effect, or its power, derived from its ability to rescue IR as a respectable and legitimate discipline – respectable through its commitment to economic methodology and legitimate because it could not be "reduced" to any other field in the social sciences' division of labor. Waltz's neorealism was so "powerful" not because its parsimonious balance-of-power theory could uncover more things about the real world than we knew before but because it mobilized the scientific community's longing for a paradigmatic core. By preempting specific heterodox views, Waltz's discourse prepared the ground on which the legitimate debate of the discipline between neorealism and neoinstitutionalism could take place. In other words, it did not provide a convincing answer to the anomalies of the discipline, but it was successful in mobilizing established conceptions of the legitimate way to approach them.[43]

Consequently, this strong metatheoretical outlook of poststructuralism is at once the historical symptom of a discipline in crisis and the necessary outlook of an explanatory framework that seeks to disclose knowledge trapped in the positivist rational-choice discourse of neorealism.

Since the authors of this third meaning of structural power have themselves departed explicitly from the choice-theoretical basis of neorealism, what is at issue here is not whether these structural approaches of power can be integrated into neorealism; rather it is whether they are internally coherent and whether their insights are necessarily linked to a power analysis.

---

43 See Kenneth Waltz (1979 and 1986). In the latter work, Waltz does not respond to the move to the metatheoretical level on which Ashley's critique is pitched.

A power analysis with a dyad of concepts

This final section deals with the fallacies inherent in possible overextensions of the concept of power and proposes a solution that distinguishes between two *concepts*, power and governance, that must be put together in a comprehensive power *analysis*.

Overload fallacies of structural power

The three following fallacies illustrate the impossibility of limiting power phenomena to a single concept at either the agent or the structural level. The first fallacy is trying to extend an agent concept to cover all power phenomena. This problem is linked to the concept of human agency itself. Following Dennis Wrong, the fallacy consists of not distinguishing between intentional and nonintentional action. By failing to make this distinction (and by not reserving the exercise of power for intentional and responsible action), one inevitably makes the effect of power coincide with human action. For this reason Wrong limits the concept of power to the capacity to produce intended effects including unintended, but foreseen side effects (Wrong 1988 [1979]: 3–5). Unforeseen effects are considered important for any analysis in social science and part of a more general concept of influence but are not generally considered relevant to the concept of power as such. Yet, foresight does not seem to be a good criterion for the distinction of power relations from general agency because it would result in giving too much emphasis to the viewpoint of those who exercise power as opposed to those who have to bear its consequences (Barbalet 1987: 6). Morriss's argument remains valid at this point; if one conceives of power as a way of "effecting," as Wrong also does, then unintended effects must be included.[44]

Thus, the initial problem remains: how to avoid collapsing all power phenomena into agency? Lukes, aware of this difficulty and the shortcomings of intentionalist approaches, starts by saying that the "effecting" must be considered significant for a particular reason (and is therefore contestable). His distinctive criterion is not intention and its link to responsibility but "interest furthering."

Yet, this approach points to the second possible fallacy of structural power as impersonal empowering: pluralists refuse it because it would entail the "power-as-benefit fallacy." Deducing power from positive effects produces the anomaly

---

44 One of the reasons for the reluctance to incorporate nonintentional power is the relationship between the concepts of power and responsibility in agent-oriented theories. It seems, however, to be going too far to conclude that since it is difficult to assess responsibility in cases where unintended effects have been produced, such effects must necessarily be excluded from power analyses. The extent of responsibility must be judged case by case. For both the intended and unintended consequences of action, the capacity to effect an outcome (i.e., power) is a necessary but not sufficient condition for an actor's responsibility.

of the free rider, whose interests are furthered by the system but who remains nevertheless at its mercy. It seems odd to describe the free rider as necessarily powerful (Polsby 1980: 208).

Even more carefully developed individualist approaches suffer from this shortcoming. Morriss, for instance, explicitly attempts to include such impersonally produced effects. For this purpose, he introduces the notion of passive power to account for the cases where we "don't want to differentiate between people who *do* get something and people who *can* get it, but we want to distinguish these people from those who *cannot* get it." Morriss then defines passive power as being "passive in both senses: no choice is involved because you *could not* intervene to prevent the outcome occurring; it would come about *in spite of* anything you might do" (Morriss 1987: 100, 1989 [1987]: emphases in original). This illustrates the "benefit fallacy": deduce power from rewards (Barry: 315). Morriss accepts the charge, yet considers it beside the point:

> There is no need to claim that because someone benefits she must cause her good fortune, nor that she can control it. All one need do is note that a status quo that systematically benefits certain people (as Polsby agrees it does) is relevant in itself.... Yet if the social system performs in such a way as systematically to advantage some individuals or groups, it certainly seems odd not to take account of this.
>
> *(Morriss 1987: 105–6)*

I agree that it would be a great mistake in an empirical analysis of a specific outcome to neglect how the structural bias on the normative, institutional, or economic level affects the very way power relations are built up, conceived, understood, and decided. But why must we take account of it by integrating it into the concept of power as such, especially if we refuse, as Morriss does, the argument of power as a subcategory of cause? Impersonal effect or structural bias may be part of any power *analysis*, but it cannot be part of the *concept* of power if the latter is actor-based, as in the case of the pluralists' relational conception or Morriss's dispositional one.

The third fallacy represents a mirror image of the first one, namely, a form of structural reductionism. All the approaches considered so far take into account the policy-contingency framework, or whatever the authors prefer to call the contextual part of their analyses. The notion of impersonal power seems to require a founding outside the agent, not within the person's intention (in the narrow behavioral approach) or action (in the wider individualist approach). This has provoked major critiques. By not sufficiently stressing the fundamental agent reference of power, the criticism runs, the concept of power becomes either synonymous with structural constraint, thus rendering structural power a contradiction in terms (Lukes 1977: 9), or else it becomes a rather amorphous all-encompassing concept like social control (Wrong 1988 [1979]: 252).

This critique stems from writers whose concept of power rests on a rather strong concept of agency, as, for instance, in the agency assumptions of rational-choice theories (desires, beliefs, preferences, rationality, choices) or, in a different vein, as in the case of Lukes, for whom power becomes attached to personal autonomy and the moral discourse of freedom and justice. Both approaches retain, on the other hand, a very thin concept of structure. Obviously, if structures are just seen as constraints, then structural power is a contradiction in terms. But this is due not to a supposedly inherent agency reference for power phenomena but to an insufficient conceptualization of structures.

The solution must include an idea of structures as not constraining, but enabling or facilitating. In one attempt to rescue a concept of structural power that is not a contradiction in terms, Hugh Ward distinguishes between power derived from two different kinds of resources (Ward 1987). Some resources are personal in the sense that they activate individual-specific relations. Other resources, however, are due to a general setting that makes no distinction among agents from within the same category. These structural resources enable actors or facilitate their actions. They thus differ from personal resources, and control over them can be called, as Ward suggests, structural power.

This reconceptualization of structure is still unsatisfactory. Ward uses the perfect market as his model. The market model can account for the enabling feature of structures only through the provision of resources that agents can use to alter their abilities. The assumption of perfect competition never calls into question the origin and maintenance, that is, the reproduction of market positions. The strength of economic analysis is its understanding of the market dynamics of the established actors. It is still not convincing for the explanation of growth, economic development, or the dynamics of creating competitive advantages. Yet, once one accepts that structures are inherently biased for this reason and tend to reproduce such biases, it becomes clear that one must conceive structures more dynamically. One must in fact expand the small structuralist account of a logic of the market not reducible to agency to one of markets as institutions that work with and through a specific set of intersubjective rules and practices. These structures constitute power practices that are continually allocating and reallocating agents to categories that are differently affected by the working of the bias. After all, not everyone is, say, an employer, and not everyone can or is empowered to be one. Whereas agent concepts are compelled simply to treat this as fate, structural constraint, or (poor) luck, it seems more reasonable to set up a power analysis in which empirical scrutiny determines whether it is in fact a question of luck or power.

Thus, whereas Morriss's solution, passive power, was questionable due to its attempt to integrate bias into the *concept* of power, Ward's proposal is insufficient because it leaves the systematic furthering of specific interests out of the entire power *analysis* by reducing impersonal empowering to the control of preexisting structural resources.

Power analysis including agent power and impersonal governance

There is a seemingly easy theoretical solution to this problem. Not one, but two concepts are necessary to account for the range of power phenomena, namely, (agent) power and governance. This solution avoids concealing the agent–structure tension within the concept, as Morriss does, or reducing empowering to an objective and general constraint/opportunity, as happens with Ward. This implies a shift away from an economic to an intersubjective and constructivist approach, but the substantial problem of the agent-structure divide remains.

The choice of using "power" as the agent referent of power phenomena and "governance" as the intersubjective referent is conventional. One could have chosen either to use another set of words or to follow Michel Foucault and reserve the concept of power for the impersonal part of power phenomena.[45] My decision is to follow more common (English-language) usage and reserve the concept of power for the agent level. In such cases, power concepts have often been accompanied by more impersonal concepts taken from the family of authority (see esp. Lukes 1979).

This dyad of concepts needs a particular theory of agency and structure. With regard to agent power, it requires a dispositional conceptualization of power as a capacity for effecting, that is, transforming resources, which affects social relationships.[46] Using power as a dispositional concept can account for the first two meanings of structural power.

Governance can then be defined as the capacity of intersubjective practices to effect. This includes both the social construction of options that is at the heart of the Gramscian analysis and the routine mobilizing of bias that affects social relationships, more present in poststructuralist writings. For all their differences, they both conceive cooperation as more than a phenomenon of an instrumentalist relation, where one looks for the best way to "cooperate under anarchy" or where the regimes, as an outcome of this instrumentalist cooperation, influence the brute clash of forces beyond the resulting invisible hand of the balance of power. Order is conceived of not only as the result of individual forces of will but also as the prior constitution of these forces. The structured international realm is also always a form of society/order/system in which agents are constituted – and not just the other way around. This could be exemplified by the way international discourse on development and its agencies have constructed the particular problematique of development and the so-called Third Worlder who needs to be developed (DuBois 1991). It is then under this recognized identity that these agents are either empowered or disempowered to take part in international relations.

---

45 The French language distinguishes between *puissance* (Latin *potentia*) and *pouvoir* (Latin *potestas*), where the first term refers to a potential or ability and the second, to an act. Moreover, a third term, *Pouvoir*, is used to denote centralized power or government. Foucault's insistence on the diffusion of power is explicable as a countermove to a traditional conception of sovereign (i.e., centralized) power.
46 For a recent and similar definition of power, see Patomäki (1991: 234).

Structural power

Poststructuralists would insist that governance for this reason is not necessarily something material to be attached to some persons and not to others, but a diffused process passing through agents.[47] It is reproduced and realized via practices, habits, dispositions, and sometimes even through the construction of the agent's identity (see Figure 1.3). Therefore, one must resist the attempt to invariably "individualize" the origins of power, the genesis of the produced effects. This individualization necessary for blaming agents begins to appear deceptive when one analyzes governance. There the discourse of individual blame is simply misplaced.[48]

Allowing for a wide approach to power phenomena does not, however, entail acceptance of all the power approaches presented above. The proposed solution explicitly excludes power analyses that argue for a restriction to an agent-based power concept, for they are compelled to avoid the power-as-benefit fallacy by introducing not a second concept of the power family but a random concept: luck. Keith Dowding's rational-choice approach to power has gone so far as to acknowledge the systematic interest furthering that pushed Morriss to conceive of passive power. Quite consistently, he must then treat it as "systematic luck." This concept refers to the privileges and advantages that stem from the social positions of specific actors, but for which they apparently did nothing (Dowding 1991: 137). By reducing systematic bias to a question of luck, this approach leaves out of the picture the daily practices of agents that help to reproduce the very system and positions from which the advantages of the lucky are derived. This means that social reproduction can be understood as a ritual of power that not only rests on those who benefit from the system but also needs all those who, via their conscious or unconscious practices, help to sustain it. There is no prime mover. Power lies both in the relational interaction of agents and in the

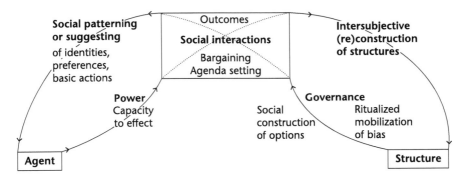

FIGURE 1.3 A dyadic conceptualization of power phenomena

---

47 This applies for both of Foucault's later periods. For the 1970s, see Foucault (1975: 31–34); and for the 1980s, Bernauer and Rasmussen (1988: 18–20).
48 For a critique of this unwelcome "interference of conspiracy theory," see Wæver (1989b: 23).

systematic rule that results from the consequences of their actions. To quote Foucault, "People know what they do; they frequently know why they do what they do; but what they don't know is what what they do does" (quoted in Dreyfus and Rabinow 1983: 187). Routine actions can constitute rituals of power that suggest the realm of the possible. They construct (and deconstruct) the horizon of the thinkable and feasible that continuously enframes agency and preempts or co-opts alternative discourses and practices.

Power analysis, as the comprehensive account of power phenomena, must call into question the relationship between the different forms of power and of governance. By focusing on power, one needs, for instance, to integrate an analysis of governance via the social patterning of structures. Social interactions mobilize rules for agenda setting that privilege specific agents, that is, the agent's actual power in a bargain is fostered by the system's governance. This is done neither through direct bargaining nor via indirect institutional agenda setting. Only in this way can the power of the German Bundesbank in the above-mentioned example be fully understood. Thus, with a dyad of concepts one can account for Strange's concept of structural power, which she sees as more than the "power to set the agenda of discussion or to design (in American phraseology) the international 'regime' of rules and customs" (Strange 1987: 565).

On the other hand, by focusing on governance, one needs to conceptualize power via the way the identities of agents are constantly redefined. This Foucauldian theme about the intersubjective constitution of agency might appear farfetched in times of stability. Yet, in periods of apparent transition and of an elusive agent and power, Foucault's ideas might be particularly interesting. Just as in Foucault's research program about the constitution of the modern self, so, in international theory, there is a research program about contemporary agency. Moreover, it seems that (1) the constitution of firms, individuals, and nations (not states), for example, as international agents, (2) their definition, and (3) their recognition are resisted by the (realist) international community. Neorealism's inherent conservative bias can at times be healthy but is more and more resented as a disciplinary ritual whose effect consists of marginalizing alternative thought and politics. In other words, in times of an "international" apparently in transition, the theory most resistant to the analysis of change predicts as most probable an eternal return of anarchy. It thereby counters the constitution of recognized international agency and, thus, the latter's power. An analysis of this *doxic* power of neorealism can identify this discourse and its bearers (academics and statesmen) and can bring them under a general power analysis.

Consequences for the study of power phenomena in contemporary IR and IPE

This reconceptualization of power and governance substantiates already existing critiques of neorealism. Via a conceptual analysis of power that integrates power and governance, neorealism's lack of historicity and its consequent legitimation of status quo power relations can be exposed.

To illustrate the first point, let us again take Krasner's concept of metapower. Krasner conceptualizes regimes as an influence on outcomes, that is, as something linked to the power base, but with a lag. In this way, he used regimes and normative structures as possible resources of power and their potential control as a form of power, namely, metapower. In this context the normative structure becomes an object, similar to material sources, on which to dwell.[49] This reduction of regimes to objects makes it possible to analyze the structural environment as a set of given constraints and opportunities and not as something that is being continually reshaped by the historically constituted and intersubjectively reproduced societal biases.

In a similar vein, Waltz's formulation practically rules out change at the structural level. By limiting structural change to the first level (anarchy versus hierarchy) and by defining anarchy as the lack of international government, the model constructs a thinking space for change in only one direction. There is change if and only if power becomes concentrated in the hands of one actor and if and only if this hegemony produces a unique sovereignty. This leaves untouched the constitution of the realm we take for granted as international and its significant changes.[50] However, as the preceding discussion has shown, to account for governance requires a focus on the social construction of such relations and, indeed, of the identity of the relevant actors (Wendt 1992c: 397). Thus, a dyadic power analysis will inevitably problematize the basic anarchy/sovereignty on which neorealism is built.[51] In response to Waltz's poor account of change, recent works have tried to integrate change at the second tier of Waltz's neorealism (Buzan, Jones and Little 1993). Yet, as long as they leave the historicity of the formal dichotomy of anarchy and sovereignty untouched, circularly defined, and reified, such projects cannot remove the basic shortcoming. For many abovementioned authors who conceptualized structural power, a dyadic power analysis points to a nonformalistic understanding of an international system of rule beyond the "anarchy problematique."

The static concept of structure in economic approaches also explains why Krasner and Caporaso, although referring to the same literature, develop two different concepts of structural power that derive from the ambiguity in Bachrach and Baratz's approach, Krasner, starting from an intentional choice-theoretical approach, sees current regimes as given and conceives of power relations only where intentional attempts to change an existing regime

---

49 In other words, the reduction of regimes to *objects* clashes with an implicit shift to an intersubjective ontology; see Kratochwil and Ruggie (1986: 764–5).
50 For a criticism of Waltz's neorealism as unable to account for the change from the medieval to the modern system, see Ruggie (1986 [1983], 1993).
51 For a thorough appraisal of the concept of sovereignty, see the writings of R.B.J. Walker (e.g., 1991).

can be detected: the Third World against the international liberal regime (assuming such a thing exists). Yet, regimes are not only a means (as for Krasner) for power relations but are, as Caporaso shows, in fact effecting exactly such power relations. Had Krasner from the beginning of his analysis included a problematization and historization of the impersonally empowered status quo, that is, used a dyad of concepts, this mistake would not have been made.[52] As a result, Krasner's analysis and neorealist power analysis in general itself tend to normalize specific power relations, namely, the unvoiced power of the status quo.

Thus, and this is the second important point, these very practices of power analysis and power politics are part of an ongoing reshaping and reproduction of legitimate discourses and politics. This implies that the whole power analysis must be conceived of as an intersubjective one. Individual power, understood as ability, is couched in an environment that is not just any objective regime or a position in the market/balance of power but an intersubjective realm where rituals of power continually set the stage.

It seems reasonable to expect that this impersonal empowering should be part of any power analysis. It could not in fact coherently be part of a choice-theoretical version of realism, of an individualist dispositional power approach, or of any approach that objectivizes regimes, balances of power, and/or markets.

Therefore, this power analysis, characterized by a dyad of concepts, can claim not only to avoid some traditional logical fallacies of power concepts but also to retain the major insights present in concepts of structural power. Its task is not to argue that either power or governance or both are always the most significant criteria for the explanation of an event. This is to be judged empirically case by case. But, it makes the claim that conceptualizations that do not unnecessarily exclude power phenomena from the construction of research hypotheses should be preferred, because they place fewer constraints on the answers to be found in empirical analysis.

Epilogue: beyond the unquestioned plausibility of power

As I have argued, recent concepts of power have endeavored to widen the scope of power analysis to include the three features we have met in the conceptualization of structural power: power as indirect institutional, unintended, or impersonally created effects. These attempts to use "power" to account for an international system of governance or hierarchy or authority highlight the insufficiencies of the concept of anarchy as it is used in traditional IR and IPE theory. "Governance" points to the systematic understatement of effective rule, of authority relations at the international level where the concept of sovereignty in a system of self-help might not meaningfully matter anymore. This has profound

---

52 For a convincing account of the dynamics of power positions that accounts for Caporaso's and Krasner's frameworks as different stages of power institutionalization and struggles, see Gaventa (1980: 21).

consequences for the articulation of neorealist theory. In a system of self-help, the ruling of the international system is simply the result of the clashing of national powers. The international order is made out of the hierarchy of state forces. Therefore, in realist theory, national power(s) become(s) the central variable in explanations. Leaving the system of self-help to whatever a structured or functionally differentiated system entails, however, means that power alone is no longer able to explain the "logic" of the international system. This is the central insight of regime theory. Yet, all the neorealist extensions of the concept of power that are aimed at preserving its central explanatory role have been unsuccessful in integrating important features of a comprehensive power analysis, as shown with respect to the three meanings of structural power. Instead of increasingly widening the concept of power, I propose a dyad of concepts, keeping power as an actor-based concept and not subsuming governance under it. Power analysis is about that link between agent capacities and systematic ruling and cannot be reduced to any of them.

This kind of power analysis prepares the ground for a better understanding of the dynamics of the international system, the political responsibilities therein, and the possible places for change. Even governance that is impersonal is realized via human action. The basic reason to preserve a widened power analysis is hence an obvious emancipatory purpose that this chapter shares with most structural power analyses. Although the relation between power and governance is far from explaining every single outcome, this approach does not exclude power phenomena a priori. Rather, it leaves the assessment of possible short-term and long-term political action to the empirical case. The governance of the system and its identification of powers are not taken for granted, but its pattern of change is examined via the long-term strategies that were or were not used to influence it. This power analysis does not deny a realm of necessity but allows for a wider conception of political action. Particularly for realists, who tend to believe that politics is the art of the possible, this power analysis points to a wider realm of the possible.

This brings me to a final remark. An inherent risk haunts power analyses: very often, power arguments are so "powerful" as to close debates. They are immediately plausible code words; that is, the use of a power argument is sometimes not an explanation any longer but a substitute for one. Instead of opening the analysis, the power argument becomes its final stroke. From being a possible help, it becomes a hindrance to understanding. Yet, this chapter seeks to show that the concept of power is neither self-evident nor unusable if reworked systematically.

Perhaps this unquestioned plausibility of power is linked to the fact that power politics represented a kind of general international theory. Since the international order, rule, or system was difficult to grasp at first sight, the distribution of power would give us the basic indication of who was responsible for controlling that international system. Power was a shortcut. Yet, once the realist link between agent power and international rule ceases to be clear, power explanations do not carry the same weight as before. The dyad of concepts makes it clear that power alone is not what we were looking for. Power becomes just a specific "momentum" in a wider analysis of power phenomena. In other words, power loses its function as a main theoretical indicator.

Accordingly, the concept of power must accept a more humble place. A concept can do no more than the theory in which it is embedded. By itself, it does not provide such a theory. It is even less of a solution to the missing paradigm in IR and IPE, that is, the satisfactory conceptualization of "the international." Anarchy, system, regime, society, system of rule, and governance are all vague descriptions that hide a central vacuum in IR and IPE theory reminiscent of the concept of the state in domestic political theory. A conceptual analysis of power may be a way to show possible spaces for political action and to lay bare the theoretical vacuum, but it cannot fill it.

2

THE USE AND MISUSE OF POWER ANALYSIS IN INTERNATIONAL THEORY

Power is ubiquitous. No theory and hardly any explanation in International Relations (IR) or International Political Economy (IPE) can do without it. At the same time, power is one of the most under-researched concepts in the discipline. In IR, conceptual pieces on power barely make it more than every four years or so into our scholarly publications.

This state of affairs is paradoxical. For power is certainly no self-evident or secondary concept. Dictionaries usually cite more than twenty meanings. And also in IR, it has been used in innumerable and increasingly polyvalent ways. For reasons of clarity, one scholar (Rosenau 1980), went as far as to drop it from his vocabulary and to replace it either by capabilities as a property concept, or by control as actual influence over outcomes.

Moreover, power is a central concept in IR theory, in particular in its long-time dominant school of thought, realism. For Morgenthau (1948), power was the consequence of the drive for domination, the immediate aim of all political action, and the essence of international politics. Yet, whereas he still felt compelled to discuss the origins of the essence of politics as power – origins he found in human nature – this effort has remained unrivalled, and also strangely unattempted (for this critique, see Krippendorff 1977: 36), even in the realist camp.

More generally, power has been of central importance in IR, because it seemed essential for the understanding of two central issues: who (one or more) can be expected to win a conflict? And, related to this, who (one or more) governs international politics? Power, traditionally understood as resources or capabilities has been used as an indicator for the strength of actors, and

For helpful comments on an earlier draft, I am grateful to David Baldwin, Anna Leander, Michael Merlingen and Ronen Palan.

consequently of the capacity to affect or control events. Likewise, a general capacity to control outcomes has been used as an indicator for the ruling of the international system. In other words, IR assumed a double causal link between these two facets in a way comparable to Robert Dahl's (1961) famous power analysis in *Who governs?* (the city of New Haven). There Dahl assessed power empirically by checking who prevailed in crucial decision-making. In the case of a consistent pattern across issue-areas, he would have deduced a hierarchical power structure. In its absence, i.e. when many different actors prevailed in different crucial municipal decisions, he judged the local government as pluralistic.

This chapter argues that the resurgence of some power analysis in the last twenty years, mainly in IPE and contructivist IR, challenges these tacitly assumed links between resources and control over outcomes, as well as between control over crucial outcomes and general rule. More precisely, the chapter makes two arguments. First, with regard to the link between resources and outcomes, the discussion will show that power cannot play the central role it assumes in both neorealism and neoinstitutionalism. Second, with regard to the understanding of 'rule' and 'governance', different 'structural power' approaches have shown the need to make more encompassing power concepts in order to capture important facets of international rule. These approaches, derived mainly within IPE, run the risk, however, of overplaying the causal strength of their analysis, and of understating the non-materialist aspects of rule or governance.

The argument will be laid out in three steps. To begin with, the realist-dominated power discussion prior to the neoinstitutionalist reformulation of the 1970s–80s will be presented. Here it can be shown that power is meaningless, if used as a 'lump' concept as required by balance of power theories. In the second section, I then show that neoinstitutionalist attempts to rescue at least the facet of power concerned with the link between resources and outcomes are caught in a dilemma: either they keep a more generalisable analytical framework, by sacrificing the significance of power, or they keep a causal explanatory role for power at the expense of a parsimonious and generalisable analysis. The third section finally demonstrates the utility of concepts of power derived from structuralist IPE approaches for understanding international rule, but indicates, with the hindsight of constructivist approaches, their overly materialist bias.

The theoretical uselessness of realist and neorealist lump concepts of power

In his turn to a more scientific theory of realism, Waltz touched neither upon the underlying concept of power, nor on the central place of balance of power theory in classical realist writings. Waltz uses micro-economic theory for an approach which focuses on the systemic level of analysis. Analogous to markets, the balance of power sets the range of options available to actors. In turn, markets and hence the balance of power system, are 'made by actions and interactions of its units, and the theory is based on assumptions about their behavior' (Waltz 1979: 117).

Relying on economic theory, Waltz assumes an analogy between the role of power in IR and the function of money in neoclassical economics (for the following, see also Guzzini 1998: 136–7). The striving for utility maximisation which can be expressed and measured in terms of money, parallels the national interest (i.e. security) expressed in terms of (relative) power.[1]

In an astonishingly overlooked argument, Raymond Aron (1962) opposed this very transfer of economic theory to IR theory. First, for Aron, it made little sense to liken the maximisation of security as expressed in power to the maximisation of utility as expressed in terms of money. Aron (1962: 28–9) argued that there are three classical foreign policy goals (puissance, security, glory/ideals) that cannot be reduced one into the other. Having no single aim, no optimal rational choice could happen. In the language of rational choice, foreign policy is indeterminate since alternative ends are incommensurable. If this were correct, then rational choice theorists (e.g. Elster 1989: 31–3) accept that their approach cannot be applied for explanatory purposes (see also Guzzini 1994: 83–6).

Aron's claim is based on the different degree of fungibility of money and power resources. The commensurability of means and aims presupposes a high degree of fungibility of power. The term fungibility refers to the idea of a moveable good that can be freely substituted by another of the same class. Fungible goods are those universally applicable or convertible in contrast to those who retain value only in a specific context. Yet whereas fungibility seems a plausible assumption in monetarised economies, in international relations, even apparently ultimate power resources like weapons of mass destruction might not necessarily be of great help for getting another state to change its monetary policies (see, in particular, Baldwin 1989: 25, 34, 209).

Aron did, of course, recognise that economic theory can be used to model behaviour on the basis of a variety of also conflicting preferences. But for him, with the advent of money as a general standard of value within which these competing preferences can be put on the same scale, compared, and traded-off, economists were able to reduce the variety of preferences to one utility function. In world politics, for reasons of its lacking real-world fungibility, power cannot play a corresponding role as standard of value. With no power–money analogy, there is also no analogy between the integrated value of utility and the national

---

1 The relationship between power and security is not clear in Waltz (see also Grieco 1997: 186–91). He explicitly stresses that states maximise security, not power. At the same time, neorealists assume states to be rank maximisers or relative gain seekers, hence my formulation. Important for my argument, and consistent with realism, is that such gain be measured on a common scale (the final rank), which is established with reference to power.

interest (security) (Guzzini 1993: 453). Consequently, (realist) theoreticians in IR cannot use economic theory as a model (Aron 1962: 102).

In a later, indeed very late, response to Aron, Waltz (1990) said that the analogy between power and money is not vitiated by a qualitative difference. Rather, the problem is simply one of measurement. Power, Waltz argued, does none the less function as a medium of exchange. Yet, although diplomats might agree on some approximations for their dealings, Waltz's argument misses the central point: for making the theoretical model work, power needs to be an (objectivised) standardised measure of value, as well (for this punctual reminder, see Baldwin 1993a: 21–2).

The critique of the fungibility assumption of power is most damaging for balance of power theories. If power is segmented, if capacities are issue-specific, then the positioning of power in a general balance is guess-work. Therefore, balance of power theorists literally need a lump concept of power which assumes that all elements of power can be combined into one general indicator. Given this central, albeit weak dimension of their theory, even sophisticated theoreticians have resorted to rhetoric instead of arguments to defend their position. Hedley Bull, for instance, after assessing the difficulties to arrive at an over-all concept of power, at some point candidly writes that 'the relative position of states in overall power nevertheless makes itself apparent in bargaining among states, and the conception of overall power is one we cannot do without' (Bull 1977: 114). His first argument, deriving power *ex post* from its effects, comes close to the usual power tautologies. The second argument, well, is no argument at all (on the level of observation). And yet Waltz (1979: 131) finds it convincing enough, when he asserts that the 'economic, military and other capabilities of nations cannot be sectored and separately weighted'.

It is here, where regime theorists and neoinstitutionalists part company with neorealists. Relying heavily on Baldwin's work, Robert Keohane and Joseph Nye (1977) had already argued for issue-specific power structures. Later, Keohane (1986: 184) explicitly criticised Waltz's fungibility assumption and argues that power concepts are only useful within circumscribed issue areas where fungibility can be assumed. Waltz remained unimpressed and answered:

> Obviously, power is not as fungible as money. Not much is. But power is much more fungible than Keohane allows. As ever, the distinction between strong and weak states is important. The stronger the state, the greater the variety of its capabilities. Power may be only slightly fungible for weak states, but it is highly so for strong ones.
>
> *(Waltz 1986: 333)*

Waltz's defence, however, is inconsistent. If power resources were so highly fungible that they could be used in different domains, then one does not need to argue with their variety: economic capabilities can be used for producing political, social or cultural outcomes. If one assumes a great variety of capabilities, one implicitly assumes that a strong state is strong not because it has a lot of overall power, but because it possesses a high level of capabilities in distinct domains. This is still no case for the fungibility of power as desperately as balance of power theories would need it.

As Baldwin a long time ago already showed, a single international power structure relies either on the assumption of a single dominant issue area or on a high fungibility of power resources. Since both are of little avail, it 'is time to recognise that the notion of a single overall international power structure unrelated to any particular issue area is based on a concept of power that is virtually meaningless' (Baldwin 1979: 193).

Power in IPE:
The neoinstitutionalist link between resources and outcomes

The rebirth of power analysis in IR/IPE has to do with what Baldwin called the 'paradox of unrealised power'. In a regional conflict, the major power of the world was apparently unable to lay down the rules and had to accept a humiliating military and political defeat against the Vietcong. Some scholars, in the academic equivalent of the stab-in-the-back theories fashionable among some US military, tried to explain away this paradox by identifying the lack of 'will' on the side of the US to use these resources, i.e. so-called conversion failures. An explanation based on alleged conversion failures implies that the war did not show the relative weakness of the US (in spite of its tremendous capabilities), simply its unrealised strength. Consequently, any event could be explained *ex post* so as to suit any assumption about the distribution of power. In other words, such an explanation had the scholarly implication that power cannot be empirically assessed at all. As so often, the trouble with this type of power analysis was not that it was wrong, but that there was no way it could go wrong.

Neoinstitutionalist analysis has, however, opted for a more sophisticated approach. If power is not a lump concept, but must be understood within specific issue areas, then two different theoretical tracks can be pursued. On the one hand, one could accept the apparent lesson of the Vietnam War and argue that control over resources, even issue-area-specific ones, does not necessarily translate into control over outcomes. Power no longer functions as a determining cause. On the other hand, one could try to stick to a strong causal role for power, one in which the link between valued resources and outcomes is not loosened. This can be done by further specifying the situational context that defines which policy instruments can count as actual power resources in this particular issue area.

As I will argue, these two very valuable attempts have problems of their own. They express a dilemma. They can stick to a generalisable explanation in which, however, power plays no longer a central role, or propose a causal, but situation-specific concept of power which is inconsistent with generalisable explanations.

Non-causal power and prediction

Regime analysis maintains the basic causal approach of realism in which the distribution of power is the main independent variable for explaining international events. It supplements it, however, by including an intervening or, at times, autonomous variable (Krasner 1982a, 1982b), be it called regimes or simply institutions: 'power measured in terms of resources may look different from *power measured in terms of influence over outcomes*. We must look at the "translation" in the political bargaining process' (Keohane and Nye 1977: 18, original emphasis).

This approach, which was meant to supplement realism, paradoxically risks stripping power analysis of its predictive character. Indeed, in *Power and Interdependence*, Keohane and Nye showed that realist explanations were of little use in the context of complex interdependence, whereas they were useful in the context of power politics. But they had no theory that anticipated when which context applied (not that this would be easy, or perhaps even feasible). They offered a typology of explanations, in place of a theory which could explain *ex ante* why in a certain situation one should use one model rather than the other. In that sense, their approach repeated earlier approaches which distinguished different types of actors or different contexts in international anarchy – and their predicament, so masterfully captured by Arnold Wolfers (1962: 86): 'One consequence of distinctions like these is worth mentioning. They rob theory of the determinate and predictive character that seemed to give the pure power politics hypothesis its peculiar value.'

Indeed, Robert Keohane increasingly came to have doubts about the causal role of power. While discussing hegemonic stability theory, he shows empirical anomalies of the 'crude' version, which derives the existence of regimes solely from shifts in the distribution of power. A more sophisticated version needs to rely on an aspect of the unit-level, namely leadership.

> Rather than being a component of a scientific generalization – that power is a necessary or sufficient condition for cooperation – the concept of hegemony, defined in terms of willingness and an ability to lead, helps us to think about the incentives facing the potential hegemon.
>
> (Keohane 1984: 39)

In his model, the determination in the explanation shifts from interests defined in terms of the distribution of power, to rational choice made on the basis of given interests defined in terms of 'power, expectations, values, and conventions' (Keohane 1984: 75). See Figure 2.1 for a simplified model of Keohane's rational actor approach.

But in this model, only predictions of a very limited kind are possible – with a secondary role for power. Power is assumed to be one of the two primary motivations for rational action. Similarly, the distribution of power is part of the actor's definition of interests of an actor. Yet, we are still far away from predicting

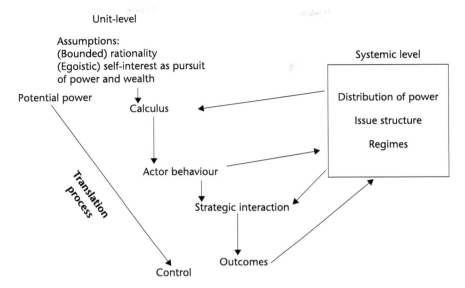

FIGURE 2.1 Keohane's rational actor approach
Source: Based on Keohane (1984).

possible outcomes. In this model, prediction is no longer based on power resources, but on rational choice. But similarly, the rational calculus helps us to predict behaviour in strategic interaction, not its outcome.[2]

Causal power and educated guesses

Decreasing the causal explanatory value of power as the central link in the translation from resources to outcomes, Robert Keohane emphasises instead the role of rationality and regimes on strategic interaction. David Baldwin, on the other hand, wants to keep a strong causal link between power as control over relationally valued resources and as control over outcomes. The price for this, however, is that power analysis must potentially become very narrowly circumscribed to particular instances, where no prediction is possible. Whereas the first institutionalist move kept, however limited, predictive capacity of a theory, based on rational choice and not on power, this second move saves a central causal role for power at the price of predictability in IR/IPE.

2 Rational choice can predict behaviour under the condition that we do firmly assume egoism as underpinning the maximisation of utility. True, the rationality assumption is perfectly compatible with altruism (Keohane 1984: 74). Leaving this assumption open, however, implies that the very same approach is compatible with any outcome to be explained: only *ex post* it can describe why an actor decided this way – or the other. Consequently, removing the assumption of egoism turns the rational choice approach into a mere taxonomy and robs it of its predictive power (see also Schmalz-Bruns 1995: 354).

Baldwin defines power as the capacity to get somebody else to do what he or she would not have done otherwise. This effect is not limited to empirical changes in behaviour, but applies also to attitudes, beliefs or the propensity to act (Baldwin 1989: 7). He circumscribes the use of power for three reasons: the already mentioned problem of fungibility, the relational character of power, and the inevitably counterfactual character of power analysis.

Baldwin's conception is shaped by his relational understanding of power. In Keohane and Nye, this relational aspect is present to the extent that power derives from relations of vulnerability interdependence defined by the high cost to be paid for substituting these resources. Baldwin, on the other hand, begins with individual, not collective actors, with relations, not resources. Baldwin's preferred example for the relational character of power might serve as illustration. If a suicide candidate is threatened with a gun to choose between his money and death, he might not feel threatened at all. The gun-bearer has no power over the suicide candidate in this relation. [S.G. 2012: This is a mistaken attribution. The example derives from Bachrach and Baratz (1970).]

In other words, power comes not (only) out of the utility attached to resources, but exists through the actual value systems of human beings in their relations with each other. The major difference is that personal value systems cannot be simply assumed in the empirical power analysis, as they can in utilitarian action theories. Instead, the researcher has first to analyse the value systems of the interacting parties in order to establish whether there are power resources in the first place.

For this reason, Baldwin (1979: 165, 1985: 285) insists that one can only study power, if understood as a causal variable, in well circumscribed 'policy-contingency frameworks' (for the following, see Guzzini 1993: 451–6). The context then specifies the scope and domain of power, as well as the norms and values within which interaction takes place. Once circumscribed, power can be defined as a causal antecedent to an outcome. Baldwin follows Lasswell and Kaplan to the extent that a power base 'refers to the causal conditions that gives influence its effectiveness. Thus, by definition, ineffective influence attempts cannot employ "influence bases"' (Baldwin 1985: 23). Keohane, by keeping contextual analysis to a fairly general level, can make probabilistic predictions on behavioural outputs, but not outcomes, leaving power as a secondary variable. Baldwin's attempt to keep power a central causal determinant forces him to include all the necessary information into a contextual analysis, thereby making predictions on the basis of power impossible.

Besides the relational concept of power, the lack of fungibility, and the potential need to have a very elaborate contextual analysis prior to the assessment of power, it is the unavoidably counterfactual character of power which makes Baldwin's approach to power both causal and yet little generalisable. Counterfactuals are no easy matter in empirical sciences. Since power relations involve getting somebody else to do what he or she would not have done otherwise, one can assess power *ex ante* on the basis of what this foregone action would have been. With that move, power analysis stops being a central element of building middle-range theories, but instead appends itself to an action theory to be meaningful (this applies also to Keohane). A good example can be found in Baldwin's (1985: 154) discussion of economic sanctions in the Peloponnesian War. The sanctions failed to deter war. To assess the importance of economic sanctions, one needs, however, to know what would have happened in the case economic sanctions had not been applied. More precisely, one needs to know whether war was inevitable or not. For realists, war would have been inevitable because the rise of Athenian power had been provoked by the necessity of Sparta's balancing behaviour. Economic sanctions could not have worked. The scholarly assessment of the role of economic sanctions is then dependent on a more general action theory which defines the (*ex ante*) counterfactual expectations against which influence attempts can be judged.

Consequently, Baldwin's approach with its much greater sensitivity to personal and historical idiosyncrasies has little generalising capacity, despite its clear causal character. Indeed, as Keohane warily noted about Baldwin's approach, if 'we defined each issue as existing within a unique "policy-contingency framework", no generalisations would be possible' (Keohane 1986: 187).[3] Baldwin himself faces this problem of prediction in his analysis, when he writes that counterfactual 'discussion may amount to little more than "educated guesses", but this is preferable to ignoring the problem' (Baldwin 1985: 22). What is left is no longer an economistic, but a historical institutionalist approach (see also Leander 2000a).

Rule in IPE: structural power and governance

With the link between resources and control weakened, the second link between the distribution of control over outcome as indicators of international rule might not be worthwhile studying at all. And yet, this is where IPE has made its most important contribution to power analysis. In fact, concepts of structural power redefine the context within which strategic interaction takes place, the resources considered important for assessing capabilities in the first place, and the outcomes that should be included in power analysis. Their common claim is that the sole reference to the first link, as done by neoinstitutionalists, is insufficient, if not biased, for understanding rule in the international system.

But opening up power analysis to political economy comes at a price. Some approaches indulge in some vain hope that by simply retuning the concept of power in a more structuralist way, one could safeguard its central causal explanatory power. And all of them tend to neglect the less materialist part of rule, that part which is now the focus of much constructivist/post-structuralist literature.

---

3 Baldwin (1979: 167–8) responds to this charge by arguing that this is not necessarily so. But neither is it to be excluded: the extent of necessary situational analysis is itself an empirical question.

Structural power as indirect institutional power

Shortly after the publication of *Power and Interdependence*, James Caporaso (1978b) tried to clarify the difference between a behavioural and structural understanding of power. His critique parallels Bachrach and Baratz's (1970) famous critique of Dahl's power analysis. Caporaso (1978a: 4) criticises behavioural approaches of power, on the ground that they neglect 'the ability to manipulate the choices, capabilities, alliance opportunities and pay-offs that actors may utilise'. Here, structural power refers to the conscious manipulation of the institutional setting within which bargaining relations take place. Many important issues are decided before they reach the bargaining stage, indeed, often because they never reach it – hence, Bachrach and Baratz's reference to non-decision-making.

Clearly, intentional agenda setting is an important facet of power analysis. Despite opposite claims, however, it is compatible with behaviouralist approaches. It is still intentional action aimed at changing the context within which strategic interaction takes place. Therefore, it is probably better to express the difference in terms of structural versus relational power, as two facets of the same action theory. In the same year as *Power and Interdependence*, Cheryl Christensen (1977) had already proposed a structural power concept which would take into account the (power) effects of the situational setting within which interaction occurs. Similarly, Susan Strange (1985: 15) distinguishes between relational and structural power, and Joseph Nye (1990b: 166–8) between 'command' power and 'soft' or 'co-optive' power.

Consequently, regime theory can coherently integrate this facet of power. Stephen Krasner (1985a: 14) distinguishes between relational power and meta-power. The first refers to the 'ability to change outcomes or affect the behaviour of others within a given regime. Meta-power refers to the ability to change the rules of the game.' In fact, what this does is to stress the importance of the feedback effect that action can have on regimes which define the background for rational calculus, a link already present in Keohane's approach (see Figure 2.1).

Structural power as non-intentional power

A more original contribution of structural power concepts in IPE has been the stress on non-intentional power. The late Susan Strange (1988) suggested that we should think of power backwards from its effects, and not in terms of intended outcomes. Her concept of structural power stresses both the diffusion of the origins of power (and the variety of power resources), and the diffusion of its effects (for a more thorough analysis of Strange's approach, see Guzzini 1998: 176–83). For her, power no longer lies mainly with states or with military capabilities, but with the international control of credit and knowledge, for instance. Similarly, there is no reason to exclude all those crucial effects that might not have been intended from power analysis. Whether interest rate policies of the German Bundesbank were intended to destabilise the European Monetary System is less significant than the fact that only a few players could have effected such an outcome. As an old Chinese saying has it, it makes little difference to the trampled grass beneath whether the elephants above it make love or war.

This analytical shift from intentions to effects diminishes the importance of the neoinstitutionalist approach for understanding power, based on resources, interests and rationality. It focuses on systematic, not on chosen features of power. As I have shown elsewhere (Guzzini 1993: 456–61), such an approach is compatible with an individualist approach, yet not with a behaviouralist one. Economic approaches can include unintended consequences (Elster 1989), but they cannot include them into their concept of power. Should they? This depends on whether the implications of keeping non-intentional power out of power analysis are considered significant. At stake is that such unintended effects are then considered purely incidental and hence irrelevant for the assessment of power (Knorr 1973: 77–8).

We have reached here the heart of a political debate. Power is a concept which has a variety of purposes (Morriss 1987: 37–42). To mention two: power is used in practical contexts in which we are interested in what we can do to others and what others can do to us. It is also important in moral/legal contexts where it functions as an indicator of effective responsibility: if actors could not have done an act (if they had not the capacity to do so), they cannot be found guilty for it. The first indicates the realm of action, power becoming an indicator of politics as the art of the possible. The second assesses possible blame. By limiting the practical context to only those actions with which we intend to affect others, we rule out any moral judgments on those actions that affect others, whether intended or not. Leaving out non-intentional power mobilises a status quo research bias and blinds us for the tacit power of the strong. Hence, it seems that those scholars interested in international rule were right to stress power as the production of unintended effects. As Baldwin (1980: 499) noted, without much developing it himself, 'concepts of power that allow for the possibility of unintended influence may be more useful for the student of dependency and autonomy than other power concepts'.

Structural power as systematic bias

Caporaso's concept of structural power repeats the ambiguities of Bachrach and Baratz's non-decision-making approach, an ambiguity which has largely passed unnoticed (for an exception, see Debnam 1984: 24). On the one hand, Bachrach and Baratz talked about (intentional) agenda control. On the other hand, Caporaso (1978b: 33) referred to the impersonal 'mobilisation of bias' when he mentioned the 'social structuring of agendas that might systematically favour certain parties'. Such an understanding of power was common currency in dependency writings, both Marxist and non-Marxist (for the latter, see, in particular, Galtung 1971). They are still used in IPE in the Gramscian School

(Gill and Law 1988, 1989) whose concept of structural power refers 'to material and normative aspects, such that patterns of incentives and constraints are systematically created' (Gill and Law 1988: 73).

Such a conceptualisation can be criticised on two accounts. First, it conflates power with benefits. Here, I would argue that although it is important that systematic bias be part of any *power analysis*, thus contradicting behaviouralist approaches, it should not be collapsed into the *concept of power*. Second, I will argue that a Gramscian theoretical underpinning is too limited to account for forms of impersonal and consensual power.

Structural power as systematic bias has been criticised for deducing power from rewards, the so-called benefit fallacy of power (Barry 1989 [1987]: 315). Nelson Polsby (1980: 208) explicitly mentioned the case of the free-rider who certainly profits from a certain systemic arrangement, but who basically remains at its mercy. One would not necessarily ascribe power to free-riders.

But the benefit fallacy exists only within a causal framework itself. To say that a system benefits certain people does not mean that they caused that benefit or that they control it.

> All one need do is note that a status quo that systematically benefits certain people (as Polsby agrees it does) is relevant in itself . . . Yet if the social system performs in such a way as systematically to advantage some individuals or groups, it certainly seems odd not to take account of this.
> *(Morriss 1987: 106, 105)*

In other words, in terms of the second link between rule and outcome, systematic benefits are relevant.

And here it is very important, within which framework of analysis such systematic interest-furthering is conceived. Rational choice approaches can, of course, account for the privileges and advantages that stem from the social position of actors, but for which they did nothing. They can do so, but then only as 'systematic luck' (Dowding 1991: 137). As a consequence, we have no choice but to live with this fateful polity. Power, understood as an indicator of the art of the possible, is ruled out. By reducing a systematic bias to a question of luck, this approach leaves out of the picture the daily practices of agents that help to reproduce the very system and positions from which these advantages were derived. For this reason perhaps, Dowding (1996: 94 and ff.) rephrases his approach and now explicitly includes systematic luck into power analysis which he very correctly then links to normative debates.

If, on the other hand, we grant that such systematic benefits should be part of a power analysis, it is preferable not to include them in the very concept of power. Instead, I referred to it within the context of the concept of rule (or governance), not power. Elsewhere, I have argued that doing otherwise produces an overload of the concept of power (Guzzini 1993: 468–74), as if adding the word power to structure would suffice to have a structural causal determinacy.

The second ground on which this concept of structural power shows weaknesses, is the theoretical underpinning of consensual rule in Gramsci's concept of hegemony. By presenting their approach, Gill and Law explicitly refer to Steven Lukes' (1974) critique of Dahl. In distinguishing three dimensions of power, Lukes had criticised the overly empiricist approach in Dahl which rules out from power analysis many, although not all, situations in which the behaviour of an actor was influenced without any visible bargaining or conflict. The one exception which can be included into behaviouralist analysis is the 'law of anticipated reactions' in which actors, anticipating reward or punishment, adapt their action accordingly. It thus includes consent in the sense of an obliged behaviour against the original intention of one actor. This exception is still permissible in this framework of analysis because it keeps the causal link between intentions, here imputed, and influenced behaviour. Lukes' third dimension of power, however, stresses those situations in which consent results not from any obligation or threat, but from the internalisation of values and ideas. Whereas in the law of anticipated reactions, consent follows an adaptation process, here nothing of that sort is necessary.

Lukes mentions Gramsci as one inspiration for the third dimension. Gramsci's concept of hegemony refers indeed to the role of ideology in pre-empting collective action against existing rule. This ideology is considered self-evident and hence is naturalised for the collectivity. Yet, the basis of this ideology is to be found in the realm of production. And here it seems increasingly difficult to define a strict relationship between the sphere of production, particular social classes, and ideologies (for the best application of this approach, see Rupert 1995). Similarly, the reproduction of structures is not as mechanistic as presupposed in neo-Marxist writings, but can be conceptualised as rituals of power. In other words, although one does not need to leave a materialist context entirely, the more hermeneutical scholars might rely on neo-Weberian approaches such as Bourdieu's field theory (1980, 1982). This theory employs a less materialist background for the establishment (and analytical definition) of social groups whose power is derived from forms of economic, social, and cultural capital (for applications of Bourdieu's power approach to IR, see Ashley 1989 and Guzzini 1994, 2000a).

A final reason to reassess the materialist bias of structural power approaches in IPE is their tendency to objectify or naturalise structures. In this regard they face a similar criticism as levelled against the macro-level of regime analysis. By presupposing intersubjective units of analysis (rules, norms, symbols), these approaches need also an intersubjective ontology (Kratochwil and Ruggie 1986). Whereas neorealism is eventually too individualist for this, structuralist approaches tend to objectify structure. Theories assuming intersubjective units then open up for a social constructivist understanding of power.

Such a constructivist understanding is already implicit in Bull and explicit in Baldwin. When Bull defended the lump concept of power, he said that it is one we cannot do without. In classical diplomacy, with its balancing and band-wagoning, its arbitrations and compensations, diplomats must find a common understanding of overall power. In other words, diplomats must first agree on what counts before they can start counting. Similarly, Baldwin writes that barter exchange is a better approximation for power relations than money. This points to the essential role of trust and, in particular, of social conventions in translating the value between different goods. In this regard, money is not basically different from power: its fungibility is an effect of social conventions, not of some inherent or objective criteria (Baldwin 1971a: 595–6, Guzzini 1994: 54–6, Kratochwil 1996: 212, Hall 1997: 593, Guzzini 1998: 231–4).[4]

Conclusion

This chapter has argued that recent approaches in IPE have challenged the presumed double link in power analysis, that is, between control over resources and control over outcomes, and between control over outcomes and rule/governance. It has argued that the power concept that undergirds balance of power theories is analytically useless. Moreover, it has shown that institutionalist attempts to remedy this problem run into a dilemma: they either maintain a probabilistic predictive framework, but reduce the importance of power therein, or they maintain a strong causal role for power, yet at the price of stripping power analysis of its predictive capacities. Finally, concepts of structural power, mainly developed within IPE, have shown a different understanding of the second link between outcomes and international rule, stressing non-intentional power and the systematic bias of the international system. As such, both links have been thoroughly rethought within IR and IPE.

Unfortunately, this does not mean that the use of power in international analysis has become more precise. Power is still a short cut for understanding international affairs, its undiscussed ubiquity an indicator of intellectual laziness. In other words, power has been a short-circuit for leaving things unexplained despite opposite appearance (Guzzini 1993: 478). Taking the recent power debate seriously could avoid power arguments still being used as apparently sensible answers whose only certainty is to kill theoretical reflection and sensible empirical research.

---

4 This does not mean that fungibility equally applies in economics and IR. The original argument, now correctly phrased in sociological terms, still holds: in real world politics, the social conventions of power translations are much more politically contested than the naturalised use of money in functioning market economies. Fungibility is hence still different in these two spheres and Aron's critique still applies.

3

FROM (ALLEGED) UNIPOLARITY TO THE DECLINE OF MULTILATERALISM?

A power-theoretical critique

This chapter deals with the claim that the decline of the institution of multilateralism[1] is but a logical outcome of the present distribution of international power (Krauthammer 1991). This claim is inspired by power materialist approaches which assume both a significant impact of international structural change on state behaviour, and that institutions are ultimately just a reflection of the distribution of state power.[2] In case of a large power preponderance, the leading state can be logically expected to pursue a policy of primacy which maximizes its foreign policy autonomy (Huntington 1993b). It will guard itself from international institutions that acquire an autonomous dynamic antithetical to its power position. In such a circumstance, it would unilaterally bypass or retreat from

---

A very rudimentary version of this chapter was presented at the author workshop of the research project 'Multilateralism under challenge? Power, institutional order and structural change', supported by the SSRC and UNU (Washington DC, 29–30 November 2004). An earlier draft of this version was presented during a guest lecture at the Institut d'Études Politiques de Bordeaux and a research seminar at the Danish Institute for International Studies. For comments and suggestions there and in correspondence, I am indebted to Jens Bartelson, Dario Battistella, Barry Buzan, Aida Hozic, Peter Viggo Jacobsen, Elizabeth Kier, Richard Ned Lebow, Jonathan Mercer, Edward Newman, Kuniyuki Nishimura, Gorm Rye Olsen, John Gerard Ruggie, Beth Simmons, Ramesh Thakur, John Tirman and Jason Weidner. All the usual disclaimers apply.

1 In the following, multilateralism is understood as a primary or fundamental institution of international society, as distinguished both from secondary institutions like organizations and regimes, as well as from simple acts of multi*national* coordination. See Buzan (2004a) and Reus-Smit (1997). Such an understanding is compatible with Ruggie's more qualitative definition of multilateralism, as an institution which coordinates relations among states on the basis of generalized principles of conduct. See Ruggie (1992).
2 For one classical statement, see Krasner (1982b).

them in order to reassert its primacy.[3] Since multilateralism is an institution based on *generalized* principles and diffuse reciprocity – hence diluting exceptionalist prerogatives simply based on power – it almost by definition clashes with a strategy of primacy. For, although (defensive) realists can envisage the increased use of multilateralism in order to reassure other states (Mastanduno 1997), the institution of multilateralism requires the leading power to curtail its autonomy and capabilities. It will have to forgo part of its power, if not its preponderance, in the name of its own security and world order (Hoffmann 1978, Jervis 1993). This being unlikely, or so the argument goes for power-oriented realists, common principles will yield to power when primacy faces multilateralism.

In this chapter, I will analyse what amounts to a double causal claim, namely that the distribution of international power (unipolarity) determines the nature of US foreign policy (primacy-plus-unilateralism) and that such policy is antithetical to international multilateralism. My analysis will not question the existence of a unilateralist turn in US foreign policy (accelerating recently, but dating back earlier) which challenges several areas of the existing multilateral order.[4] But on the basis of recent conceptual analyses of power, I argue that the general thesis of a causal relationship between unipolarity and a decline of multilateralism does not hold. Such systemic explanations misconceive the role power can play in social science explanations. I will make this point in three steps.

First, I illustrate the indeterminacy of systemic power analysis for assessing the general causal claim by comparing the present debate with the hegemonic decline debate of the 1980s. This comparison shows that systemic power analyses have explained the same outcome by opposite power dynamics, once a decline and once a rise in US power. It also shows that US unilateralism is not necessarily antithetical to all components of multilateralism. Hence, the causal chain does not work in its two main links.

Second, I show that this contradiction is not fortuitous but intrinsic to the properties of the concept of power in International Relations. For the very assessment of this unipolarity is contingent on a series of often implicit definitional moves which have been discarded in political theory. They end up privileging a view of power as a property concept and not a dispositional and relational concept, and as being unidimensional (mainly military or material) and not multidimensional. Once these assumptions are questioned, two implications follow: it undermines the possibility of an overall concept of power necessary for polarity analysis, as well as the overall assessment of US power which turns out to be much more ambivalent. Linking this finding up with the first section, I conclude that, since power is not measurable, claims to a specific unipolarity cannot be independently checked to save the causal links of a systemic power analysis going from unipolarity to the decline of multilateralism.

---

3 For this argument, see Krasner (1982a) and (1985a), written in the context of the Reagan administration's withdrawal from UNESCO.
4 For the unilateralist turn, see for example, the essays collected in Malone and Khong (2003).

In a third step, I will use a constructivist twist to the conceptual analysis of power in order to assess whether a particular conception of power, if shared, has an actual effect on world order. Precisely because the distribution of power resources does not determine outcomes, but is often understood to do so, the capacity to shape the definitions of power is not mere semantics, but has political effect. This move reverses the relationship between the two central concepts. Rather than seeing unprecedented preponderance as the cause of unilateralism, it shows how a successful (neoconservative) policy of US unilateralism could foster a certain understanding of power which, if it becomes shared by the international society, will have real power effects akin to the alleged effects of unipolarity.

The indeterminacy of polarity explanations: Unipolarity, unilateralism and the logic of Hegemonic Stability Theory in reverse

The implicit hypothesis of most observers is that the present preponderance of the US in world affairs explains its increased use of unilateral and bilateral policies. Such a hypothesis trades on a theoretical assumption that power differentials significantly shape the definition of state interests and behaviour, whether directly and somewhat naturally or via the decision-making elite's perception of them.[5] This theoretical assumption is flawed, and systemic power approaches with it, as a comparison with Hegemonic Stability Theory (HST) shows.

The causal link between the distribution of power and the nature of the international system (or its regimes) is purely systemic. Its basic causal relationship is not new. It has been played out in the 1980s during the debates about the alleged US decline. But then, its logic ran in reverse. Whereas today it is allegedly obvious that unilateralism is the result of unipolarity, during the heyday of HST, US decline was held responsible for the decline of multilateralism. I will use this curious reversal to illustrate the indeterminacy, if not arbitrariness, of general systemic power arguments in International Relations.

HST had its heyday after the US had started to dismantle the system of Bretton Woods, a system it had significantly helped to inaugurate and manage. The theory drew on a historical analogy with the inter-war period. The inter-war breakdown of the international liberal order was interpreted as the direct result of missing leadership.[6] Then, the UK, seen as the declining hegemon, was no longer able, whereas the US was perhaps able, but not yet willing to support the international liberal order. When the Nixon administration unilaterally declared

---

5 In other words, the present chapter does not follow Kenneth Waltz in his claim that structural realist approaches can function and yet be indeterminate for state behaviour, a claim hardly shared by any realist and often not followed by himself. For realist rejoinders to Waltz, see, for example, Mastanduno (1997: 52–3), and Elman (1996).
6 For this analogy, see in particular Gilpin (1971, 1981) and Kindleberger (1986 [1973]).

the fixed Gold–Dollar link suspended, commentators saw the US repeat the British experience.

HST is an extension of a classical realist thesis, that high power differentials are conducive to stability. In the words of Kenneth Waltz (1969 [1967]: 312), "Extreme equality is associated with extreme instability". It derives its specificity by linking this idea to a rationalist theory of public goods (Snidal 1985). Such public goods can be understood in the classic realist way as the provision of international order (Gilpin 1981, Webb and Krasner 1989), as an international economic order for mercantilists (Kindleberger 1986, Gilpin 1987b), or as international regimes for neo-institutionalists (Keohane 1984). Multilateral institutions are usually connected to the last two. And indeed, that hegemons have been at the origins of multilateral institutions is at the core of standard approaches to multilateralism (Ruggie 1992).

Flowing from its collective good formulation, HST makes three central propositions.[7] First, the emergence of a hegemon is necessary for the provision of an international public good (hegemony thesis). Second, the necessary existence of free riders (and thus the unequal distribution of costs for the provision) and/or a loss of legitimacy will undermine the relative power position of the hegemon (Entropy thesis).[8] Third, a declining hegemonic power presages a declining provision of the international public good (Decline thesis).[9]

Showing with some detail the causal propositions of HST illustrates an obvious puzzle for the causal link between the present unipolarity and the alleged decline of multilateralism in both its causal links. For the US of the immediate post-1945 period had a similar unipolar/hegemonic position and yet did not pursue a policy which was antithetical to multilateralism.

The logically most satisfying solution to the puzzle would consist in devising a hypothesis in which the optimal provision of an international public good would be connected to a certain equilibrium of power, not more and not less. In one case, the weakened hegemon would be no longer able to go multilateral; in another the emboldened hegemon would, by objective forces propelled, be no longer willing. However, this solution trades on the existence of a general measure of power, which, as the next section shows, is missing.

A special "unipolarity"?
The pitfalls of power as aggregate resource analysis

It is a curious feature that the ubiquity of power analysis in IR has largely remained unshaken by the multiple warnings that the concept of power cannot

---

7 For a more thorough presentation from which this is taken, see Guzzini (1998: ch. 10).
8 For an explicit use of "entropy", see Kindleberger (1976: 18, 24).
9 Robert Keohane does not belong to those who subscribe to this aspect of HST, arguing that multilateral regimes, once created, can be perfectly sustained without a hegemon.

shoulder the explanatory weight assigned to it. This section shows that the "unipolarity breeds the decline of multilateralism" thesis systematically misconceives of the dispositional, relational and multidimensional character of power in the understanding of social interactions and their outcomes. Through the detour of conceptual power analysis, it questions the very possibility of a general polarity analysis and hence of the starting point of the causal link under scrutiny: unipolarity. For this reason, I argue that assigning to the present unipolarity a special quality is eventually arbitrary.

Power: dispositional, relational and multidimensional

The very idea of unipolarity assumes an overall concept of power in which different resources can be consistently aggregated. It moreover assumes that resources as such are sufficient to predict or understand outcomes (such as unilateralism). The critiques of such assumptions are legion and I will only briefly rehearse them here.[10]

The difficult relationship between power understood as resources and power as control over outcomes has been an evergreen in IR power debates.[11] On the one hand, power analysis is most interested in the control of outcomes, not resources as such. Yet, defining power in terms of control over outcomes produces an obvious risk of circularity.[12] Hence, mainstream power analysis goes back to resources and basically stipulates its link to control over outcomes in probabilistic terms. The underlying idea of causality with regard to the outcome is kept.

This is either at odds with the dispositional character of power, or needs to be very heavily qualified for the relational character of power. Peter Morriss has shown that in its most general understanding, power is neither a thing (or property, or resource), nor an event (which shows itself only if realized in an outcome), but an ability: a capacity to effect a certain action (Morriss 2002 [1987]: 19). Dispositions translate into effects only under specific conditions. In a social context, such a disposition is understood in a relational way. In its Weberian understanding, power refers to the capacity to get others to do something they would not have otherwise done. For understanding the latter, one needs to know the preferences and value systems of the actors at hand.[13] To use an extreme example: killing a person who wants to commit suicide at all costs is usually not understood as an instance of power. Power does not reside in a resource but stems from the particular relation in which abilities are actualized. Hence, in order to

---

10 For more extensive treatment in IR, see in particular Baldwin (1989, 2002) as well as Guzzini (1993, 2000c).
11 An early and still valid statement can be found in Keohane and Nye (1977) and its revised editions.
12 Realists are perfectly aware of this. See most recently Mearsheimer (2001).
13 As is well known, Steven Lukes would also include a third dimension of power in which this very value system is affected so that no visible conflict arises. See now the revised edition: Lukes (2004).

find out whether a certain action (*not* just the possession of the resource) indeed realizes an instance of (social) power, the distribution of resources says quite little independently of the specific conditions which apply to the social relations at hand. Power is situation-specific.

Moreover, power is a multidimensional phenomenon. This is linked to the fact that power in political relations cannot be thought in an analogy to money in economic exchange, both in practice and theory. Whereas different preferences and different markets can be gauged through the fungibility of money, which allows also the observer to reduce this multiplicity on a single aggregate scale, no such scale exists for power in real world politics.[14] While (in monetarized economies), money is the real world measure of wealth, there is no equivalent currency to measure power. This is not merely a theoretical problem that would be resolvable with some conceptual work;[15] it derives from the different status in practice. As a result, there is no overarching issue structure, as suggested by polarity analysis. And abilities in one area might not affect from one issue area to another (or the effect cannot be controlled for). The multidimensional character of power goes hand in hand with an issue-specific vision of world politics. It also means that attempts to construct a more general theory of linkage are doomed from the start: such a theory of linkage would assume that we had indeed a measure which would allow us to move from one issue area to another, a measure whose very absence is however the reason why we have different issue areas to start with.

There have been different reactions towards these findings. Although realists are usually committed to neglect or downplay these difficulties (Waltz 1986), some have contributed to the debate by rethinking the role of power even if it cannot be measured,[16] by accepting that issue-specificity applies to world politics (Buzan, Jones and Little 1993), or arguing that the problem of fungibility is not as big as assumed,[17] yet without really answering Aron's and Baldwin's critiques (Guzzini 2004c).

Unipolarity, influence and legitimacy

These characteristics of power have significant implications for the "unipolarity breeds the decline of multilateralism" thesis by questioning the taken-for-granted assessment of unipolarity. On the one hand, it qualifies (and simultaneously widens) the assessment of significant resources. Here, US preponderance appears less clear cut. More importantly, it moves from resources to the analysis of actual

---

14 The central place of the missing money–power analogy for the use of an economic approach to political science/IR has been discussed in Aron (1962: ch. 3).
15 As attempted by Waltz (1990).
16 See in particular the thoughts by Wohlforth (1993, 2003).
17 Art (1996). See also the ensuing debate: Baldwin (1999) and Art (1999).

influence and then to authority showing that legitimacy is not just a function of resources, even soft ones.

Wohlforth's reference study does acknowledge the difficulty of having a single issue area, and hence bases the assessment on the "decisive preponderance in *all* the underlying components of power: economic, military, technological and geopolitical" (Wohlforth 1999; emphasis in original). Yet, there are several difficulties with this assessment.

First, as in this case, unipolarity analysis tends to concentrate on mere material resources (see below for "soft power") for assessing power. This misses two qualifications. First, the nature of international society affects the respective value of abilities, their resources and the relevant issue areas.[18] This is an old idea, running from Wolfers (1962) through Keohane/Nye (1977) and the English School (Buzan 2004a) to constructivism - inspired approaches (Wendt 1999). It simply means that, in a context of international relations which can no longer be satisfactorily described as Hobbesian in most parts, but has aspects both of a society of states and a transnational world of societies (Czempiel 2002), power is to be thought of in quite different ways at the same time. It is not obvious that US (or any other) military resources are usable against friends in the same way as against enemies. The important implication is that they then no longer qualify as unconditional sources of "power" in those relations *in the first place*.

A second qualification derives from the reductionist understanding of influence through resources alone, where the distribution of resources is a shorthand for international order or governance. Such an approach assumes that by aggregating instances of influence in particular social interactions, one can get a comprehensive picture of authority relations in the international system.[19] Going this road, however, conflates the aggregation of instances of influence with authority. Authority is linked to legitimate rule which can obviously not be reduced to material matter alone. Indeed, in one school of thought, power is the opposite to violence (Arendt 1969): the most powerful police is the one which does not need to shoot. In such an Arendtian understanding, it is connected to the capacity to create things in common (Arendt 1986 [1970]).

Taking these two arguments together, one can conclude that the link from resource to control over outcomes is only applicable to a situation-specific analysis, and that the link from mere material resources, via influence to general authority is even weaker.

As a result, a more comprehensive understanding of power is needed. This applies both to the bases of power (abilities) and to the more social understanding of power applicable to present international affairs. Stressing the multidimensional character of power, Nye (2004: 4) rejects the label of unipolarity for the

---

18 This is the way Barry Buzan modifies classical unipolarity analysis in Buzan (2004b).
19 De facto, this applies Robert Dahl's strategy for assessing "Who governs?" to the international level. See Dahl (1961).

present world. Sticking to his power approach derived from Weberian sociology, Michael Mann (1986) includes economic power in which the US does not have clear lead,[20] as well as political and ideological power on which he finds the present US fundamentally wanting (Mann 2003). Focusing directly on the concept of power, Christian Reus-Smit (2004: ch. 2) argues that to understand power correctly today, it needs to be conceived as relational not possessive, primarily ideational not material, intersubjective and social, not subjective and non-social. And again, he finds the US wanting in most. In both cases, only the superiority of its military seems to be unquestioned.

Joseph Nye's concept of "soft power" seems to belong to the same category insofar as it does not understand power simply in terms of resources but as actual influence, and includes non-material sources. And yet Nye's use is more ambivalent and at times differs in an important way.

Nye's concept of soft power is akin to attraction and consensus, and used for pointing to the legitimacy component of power. Just as Susan Strange's (1988) reconceptualization of power as "structural power", which included a knowledge structure comprising technology and culture, Nye (1990a, 1990b) formulated "soft power" as a reaction against the US decline debate of the 1980s. But even in his most recent statement of it, there is a tendency to analyse soft power in terms of objective resources ("objective measure of potential soft power"), based on the relative number of US movies, patents, high-level universities, and so forth (Nye 2004: 34). Now, stressing the difference between resources and influence, he does note that some (popular) cultural items, even if diffused, do not imply a political stance in favour of the US. Also, he gives three different sources of soft power in culture, national values and foreign policy. But, or so the argument can be read, since the US has strong resources in culture, and is allegedly leading the West in terms of values, better public diplomacy becomes the only crucial variable for actual US attractiveness – and anti-Americanism the default residual variable, should it fail. The real value of the other resources is more or less taken for granted. That means that the focus of the power analysis does not really engage with the social and intersubjective component of legitimacy, but slides into a classical *conversion failures* study so much criticized earlier by Baldwin in the wake of the Vietnam war. When allegedly overriding power seemed not

---

20 The assessment of the economic sector is widely debated. For some, the US economic and technological lead is obvious from (recent) growth rates, the health of high technology sectors, and so forth. Those scholars, like Mann, who argue that there exist roughly three poles, tend to focus on other items. First, they stress that in the economic sector, EU member states can no longer be counted individually: to the outside, there is one market of a comparable size to the US; in trade terms, and also to a lesser extent with regard to monetary policies, there is one single representation and one central bank. And then one can add that Japan leads in patents, Germany has just overtaken the US as the world leading manufactory exporter (despite the very high euro), and so on. Since there is no common measure of economic power, one cannot really adjudicate between these positions.

to translate into influence, that was not because the US lacked sufficient power, but because of conversion failures (lacking political will, that liberal press backstabbing, etc.). Hence, we have again the curious finding that the same outcome can be explained by opposite causes (power or powerlessness). The problem here is not just indeterminacy. It is what Baldwin called the "paradox of unrealized power" which makes power analysis unfalsifiable and arbitrary. The value of resources is ultimately objectified and all misfits in terms of influence are explained away via incompetent agency: power resources never fail, only politicians do.

Soft power can be read to apply this logic to the issue of legitimacy: soft power resources never fail, only public diplomacy does. It then falls short of taking the social and intersubjective component of legitimacy into account, as Reus-Smit rightly notes (2004: 64–5). Reminding the US administration that a clever lion knows when to be a fox could miss the point. If one takes power seriously, then one would have to look at the problem not just in terms of the packaging (public diplomacy) (Edelstein and Krebs 2005), but more fundamentally of the content, i.e. the legitimacy of the US specific American vision and project of the international order (not to be confounded with the wider Western, let alone the liberal or the democratic, project).

From the missing measure of power to power perception?

In view of the difficult measurement of power, some power analysis has moved from the actual distribution of aggregate power resources to their perception. Applied to our argument here, the causal link would then start from a perceived unipolarity to the decline of multilateralism. Moreover, such an explanation could perhaps answer the contradiction with which this chapter started: the perceived unipolarity in post-1945 is of a different kind to the one today. Although William Wohlforth developed this argument for another context, it could be reapplied for the present one. When discussing US primacy, Wohlforth does see similarities in the preponderance of Britain between 1860–70, post-1945 US and post-1989 US. Yet, according to him, what sets the present situation apart is the perception of power.[21] Whereas the rational expectation in the past was that the respective leadership position would be passing, now it is not. From this, one could derive the argument that the present situation has no historical comparison.

---

21 Wohlforth (1999: 18–22). Wohlforth also argues that the comprehensive power resources of the US are superior. That argument hinges however on an assumption that power is measurable, on which he himself is critical. Moreover, he uses a definition of power which is only material, and allows the know-how of private firms to be simply capitalized for states. Although this is justified so as to make historical comparisons with earlier periods more coherent, the very understanding of how power is historically contingent, is a point Wohlforth does not deal with.

Unfortunately such an attempt seems to beg the question. If the material component of power has no causal force alone – if it does not "impress" itself unambiguously – then the significant part of the causal explanation moves towards perceptions. But why does the expectation of a leadership in decline ask for multilateralism in 1945, but for unilateral retrenchment in the 1970s and 1980s? In other words, a recourse to perceptions opens up an explanatory regress and risks being adjusted ad hoc to save a realist type of power analysis.

What all this shows is that the general argument, although presented in a forward causal link from unipolarity, is in fact running backwards. Changes in US foreign policy outlook and international multilateralism are read back into an assumed and ultimately unquestioned power link, which is then adjusted to serve the explanatory needs of the day.[22] The classical risk of circular power statements resurfaces.

Unilateralism as a strategy to redefine power

The fact that there is no measure of power has posed perhaps more problems to the (realist) observer than to the (realist) diplomat. Whereas the former still look out for a measure that would help to fix systemic analysis,[23] the latter meet those observers who do not deduce power in any objective way, but understand it from the way practitioners understand it. Since we miss a measure of power, practitioners have to rely on secondary indicators and read power from events. Yet events do not determine a certain vision of power, as the above mentioned indeterminacy and hence circularity of such argument shows. Still, since power as a measurable fact is still crucial in the language and bargaining of international politics, measures of power are agreed to and constructed as social fact: diplomats try and need to agree first on what counts before they can start counting (Guzzini 1998: 231).

This moves the analysis of power away from the illusion of an objective measure to the political battle about defining the criteria of power, which, in turn, has political effects. Concepts of power are not merely external tools to understand international politics, but intervene into it. This moves the analysis on to constructivist ground since it is interested in how knowledge reflexively interacts with the social world.[24]

Based on such an analysis, I discuss a possible reversal in the relationship between unipolarity and unilateralism: whereas the earlier sections have shown that unipolarity does not cause the decline of US multilateralism, nor international

---

22 For earlier statements of this line, see Strange (1987).
23 See the ongoing quest from Frei (1969) to Mearsheimer (2001).
24 For the most recent definitional statement on constructivism, see Adler (2002). Constructivists have also a wider understanding of power in international affairs, which goes beyond the Weberian one, but given the focus of the present chapter, this is not further elaborated. See Guzzini (1993), and now Barnett and Duvall (2005a).

multilateralism (although US power in certain issue areas can be used to such effect, if US administrations chose to do so), this section argues that US unilateralism can become a strategy to attain the diplomatic (social) equivalent of the alleged effect of unipolarity.

Performative and reflexive aspects of the concept of power

Some concepts, such as power, play a special role in our political discourse. They interact with the world they are supposed simply to describe. This means that besides understanding what they mean, their analysis has to assess what they do.[25] Two issues stand out for our present discussion. Power is firstly connected in our political discourse to the assignment of responsibility. "For to acknowledge power over others is to implicate oneself in responsibility for certain events and to put oneself in a position where *justification* for the limits placed on others is expected" (Connolly 1974: 97, original emphasis). Moreover, there exists a reflexive "looping effect" (Hacking 1999) of power definitions with the shared understandings and hence working of power in international affairs.

This link to responsibility makes out of power a concept which is closely connected to the definition of political agency, or politics *tout court*. The traditional definition of power as getting someone else to do something he or she would not have otherwise done implies an idea of counterfactuals. The act of attributing power redefines the borders of what can be done. In the usual way we conceive of the term, this links power inextricably to "politics" in the sense of the "art of the possible/feasible". Lukes (1974) rightly noticed that Bachrach's and Baratz's (1970) conceptualization of power sought to redefine what counts as a political issue. To be "political" means to be potentially changeable; that is, not something natural, objectively given, but something which has the potential to be influenced by political action. In a similar vein, Daniel Frei (1969: 647) argues that the concept of power is fundamentally identical to the concept of the "political"; i.e. to include something as a factor of power in one's calculus, means to "politicize" it. In other words, attributing power to an issue imports it into the public realm where action (or non-action) is required to justify itself. In return, "depoliticization" happens when by common acceptance no power was involved. In such instances, political action is exempted from further justification and scrutiny.

Such a performative analysis of concepts is not new in IR, in particular with regard to the concept of security. Barry Buzan and Ole Wæver have proposed a framework of security analysis around the concept of "securitization". According to them, security is to be understood through the effects of it being voiced. It is part of a discourse (for example, "vital national interests") which, when successfully mobilized, enables issues to be given a priority for which the

---

25 For the following and for a more detailed account of this turn in conceptual analysis as applied to power, see Guzzini (2005).

use of extraordinary means is justified. In its logical conclusion, "securitization" ultimately tends to move decisions out of "politics" altogether (Wæver 1995; Buzan, Wæver and de Wilde 1998; see also Huysmans 1998).

US power and special responsibility: justifying exemptionalism

Connolly's original analysis relates to situations where power holders see none of their power involved. No power means no responsibility, thus discharging actors from justifying their actions. Critiques of their actions almost inevitably end up in challenging the understanding of power: there is supposedly no power only because the narrow definition of power precludes seeing it. Hence, a change in the definition of power, if shared, will affect political discourse and action. A classical example of this usage in IR can be found in Susan Strange's concept of structural power which she developed in the mid-1980s against the backdrop of alleged US hegemonic decline. She showed how "non-decisions", as well as unintended consequences of actions are part of any power analysis.[26] Indeed, making the US aware of such non-intentional effects is consequential: the next time, such effects need to be included into one's justification of action.

But the present debate turns this relationship between power and responsibility onto its head: the power holder no longer downplays its power for keeping aloof of criticism, it heavily insists in its power-thus-responsibility so as to justify a worldwide interventionism. If it were true that the US enjoys a very large power and superiority, then it is only natural that it assumes a large responsibility for international affairs. Insisting on the special power of the US triggers and justifies a disposition for action. Here, the insistence on the special nature of unipolarity gives the responsibility – power link a special twist, not dissimilar to the classical realist view that international politics cannot be apprehended with the same norms as domestic politics.[27]

There are two steps in this argument which can combine responsibility with a justification always already given. A first and direct one is the traditional defence of interventionism. With such preponderance of power, there is no safe way to retreat to one's own shores. A second step is more tenuous, but actually derives from Hegemonic Stability Theory: US unipolarity introduces a hierarchical element into world order. US primacy means that it has different functions and duties (responsibilities) than other states. From there, the final step to a right or even duty to unilateralism is not far. Its role as world policeman is no longer a choice, but actually a requirement of the system (see e.g. Kagan 1998). Being compelled to play the world leader means, in turn, that the rules which apply to

---

26 On the effect of "non-decisions", see Strange (1986); on the need to integrate ideas from dependency scholars into a concept of "structural power", see Strange (1984: 191). For the full statement, see Strange (1988: ch. 2).
27 For a classical (and moderate) defence of this position, see Kennan (1985–6).

all the others cannot always apply to the US. The US becomes an actor of a different sort: its special duties exempt it from the general norms. This is the basis of its tendency to exemptionalism, something which is difficult to accommodate within a multilateral framework.[28]

The political implications are clear. The more observers stress the unprecedented power of the US, the more they mobilize the political discourse of agency and responsibility tying it to the US and the US alone, and the more they can exempt US action from criticism, since it responds to the "objective" (power) circumstances of our time (e.g. Krauthammer 2002–3). This does not necessarily mean that unilateralism is to follow; but it makes that argument much easier to swallow. Inversely, the more observers see this "special responsibility" or exceptionalism as part of the problem, not of the solution to US security concerns (and international order at large), the more they might be inclined to double-check the alleged unipolarity (e.g. Kupchan 2002).

The power of unilateralism

Through the link of power to politics in our tradition of political discourse, definitions of power have a reflexive relationship with the world they are said simply to describe. The definition of power, if shared, has power effects in itself. As discussed above, it defines the realm of political justification and legitimacy. But it also provides practitioners with a socially constructed shorthand for their ranking and hence their leverage in any bargaining. The struggle for the right definition of power is not academic; by its potential effects, it is inherently political. Reaching and keeping definitional power over "power" is more widely consequential. For "the theory of knowledge is a dimension of political theory because the specifically symbolic power to impose the principles of the construction of reality ... is a major dimension of political power"(Bourdieu 1977: 165).

This leads to the last step in the analysis of the relationship between unipolarity and unilateralism, one in which the poles are reversed. Rather than seeing in the "logic" of unipolarity the cause for unilateralist US action (and the decline of multilateralism), US unilateralism, justified through non-relational and one-sidedly material definitions of power, can be part of a self-fulfilling prophecy leading to the alleged "logic" of unipolarity.

As the discussion of the first two sections tried to show, there is no logic of unipolarity, no inherent necessity in moving from the argument of unprecedented preponderance to the outspoken unilateralism in US foreign policy. Indeed, exactly because the US enjoys such preponderance, it could afford to be much more self-restrained (Walt 2002b). Yet, if power is defined in mainly military terms, not only the US acquires a very special place, but it also means that

---

28 For a more general argument about US exemptionalism, see Ruggie (2005).

the very functioning of the international system is understood as one which is "ultimately" one of military security.

In such a remilitarized environment, questions of legitimacy are redefined. For the sake of this argument, we can follow Fritz Scharpf's understanding that legitimacy derives usually from both responsiveness (input) and efficiency (output). In an international order defined fundamentally by military competition, with no international society worth its name, legitimacy is provided, or so it seems, mainly from the output side. On Mars, force is the only source of a necessarily shallow legitimacy. The contract is purely Hobbesian: authority through security. Joseph Nye (2004: 63) is aware and wary of this kind of argument, since it allows (the illusion of) an ex post legitimization of an otherwise illegitimate unilateralism.

The crux of this somewhat paternalist legitimation through some future order is that it can push the verification of the claim indefinitely. Having an interpretation of power that raised the US to the pinnacle as the only country able to do anything, even should it fail, it did the right thing responding to its special duty. There is no way to disconfirm this logic. If order has not yet been found, given the unprecedented (read: military) power position of the US, the only way forward is to do more of the same and let the US try to fix it again, being the only authority there is. The logic is a kind of Microsoft theory of security: the problem is not that there is too much Windows, the problem is that there is still not enough.

At some point in time, repeated US unilateralism would have contributed to reduce the international society to military order, and security to military strategy, and so eventually produce the very vision of unipolarity from which all is supposed to derive. The chain of the self-fulfilling prophecy is this: (1) a presumed but wrong causal link between power (unipolarity) and behaviour (primacy-plus-unilateralism) based on a wrong reduction of power to resources and moreover to material ones, allows (2) a justification for a special responsibility which exempts the sole superpower from the usual rules, hence (3) a remilitarized unilateralism which requires a retreat from the multilateral demilitarizing regime network and (4) by these very actions, increasingly enforces a definition of power in purely military terms, which (5) becomes the accepted and intersubjectively shared meaning and understanding of power in international society, that (6) finally *leads to* a world of Mars in which legitimacy is reduced to efficient coercion. This chain is the effect of a neoconservative understanding of the world which actively changes the world, not just responds to it. And the socially constructed character of the concept of power is crucial in every link of this chain.

Most of the critics of unipolarity mentioned so far are concerned and aware of this reflexivity, that is the very significant real world effect an erroneous definition of power ultimately can have. As Buzan (2004b: 171) puts it, "The salient point is . . . which interpretation of unipolarity gets accepted within the US – and indeed the other great powers – as the prevailing social fact. It is the accepted social fact that shapes securitization." And continuous securitization ("hyper-securitization", as Buzan calls it) would indeed change the nature of international society.[29]

It is hard not to be reminded of the by now (in)famous quote made by a senior adviser to President George W. Bush, reported by Ron Suskind. The adviser insisted that people like Suskind were part of the "reality-based community" which thinks about solutions in terms of the existing reality. "That is not the way the world works any more . . . We're an empire now, and when we act, we create our own reality" (Suskind 2004). That sentence acquires an even more fundamental significance when put into the context of a reflexive analysis of power.

As mentioned by Buzan, such self-fulfilling effects are of course contingent on the acceptance of certain understandings. Power discourse in its link to responsibility is open to both its classical use as a critique of power holders, as to its new twist where it exempts the especially powerful from norms applicable to others.

Conclusion

This chapter has applied the recent conceptual analysis of power to the thesis that unipolarity predisposes for a US foreign policy of primacy and unilateralism and hence for a decline of multilateralism as an institution. It found this thesis wanting in both links. More specifically, it made three claims.

First, as a discussion of Hegemonic Stability Theory showed, the decline of multilateralism can as well be connected to an alleged decline in hegemony as to its opposite. This illustrated that there is no determinate link between the distribution of power, the foreign policy of the leading power and its effect.

Second, I argued that this indeterminacy of systemic power analysis is not fortuitous, but results from the very characteristics of the concept of power. Usually the analysis assumes a concept of power which is based on resources not relations, and on the one dimension of the military (including material factors supportive of it, such as economy and technology) not on its multidimensionality. Yet, once these conceptually untenable assumptions are loosened, power analysis becomes relation and situation dependent. This widens the assessment of significant resources which, in turn, makes US preponderance appear less clear cut, and, indeed, any analysis in terms of a general unipolarity difficult to defend.

Third, precisely because we have no objective measure of power, it is crucial to analyse the relationship between knowledge about power and politics itself. Like the national interest, balance of power arguments are part of the common language of the international society.[30] It is important not just because theories are built upon it, but because practitioners understand and base actions on it. This shifts the analysis of polarity arguments further, from what they could mean and

---

29 For a more detailed argument on these lines, see also Guzzini (2002a).
30 For this analysis of the national interest, see Weldes (1999).

explain to what their use, if shared, *does* not just to the common understanding, but also to politics and the social fact of power itself. In this context, this chapter shows the special role power has in our political discourse by linking it to the definition of the political realm, to responsibility and hence the need to public justification. Here, the stress on unipolarity, far from requiring the US to justify its deeds as it had in the past, has been twisted to condone, if not require a US policy of primacy that undermines multilateralism. Moreover, the use of one-dimensional power concepts to support a claim to a special unipolarity mobilizes a discourse which remilitarizes the understanding of international politics. Repeated unilateralism which is informed by this militarized understanding, has the potential to affect the shared understandings of power which actually decide what power means and does. This might indeed end up creating the social fact of "unipolarity" which appears objective and no longer questionable to international actors.

4
NIKLAS LUHMANN'S CONCEPTUALIZATION OF POWER

Prologue

Given the recent sociological turn in International Relations (IR) theory, usually labelled "constructivism," it is hardly surprising that more seemingly remote theories are also joining the stage, such as Niklas Luhmann's systems theory. For there are good reasons for IR theoreticians to have a closer look. First, Luhmann's theorizing of self-reference and "reflexivity" – crucial for constructivists (cf. Guzzini 2000a), and others too – cuts across all his theory in an extent perhaps unparalleled by another social theory. His theory is based on operationally closed, self-referring, and yet cognitively open social systems. Second, and related, Luhmann insists on a distinct yet parallel treatment of psychic and social systems, and of different social systems, such as politics, economics, law and science, to the effect that his theory necessarily includes a parallel treatment of "action," knowledge and of knowledge production. As a result, his theory allows us to observe in parallel, i.e. it runs an epistemology which is necessarily a sociology of knowledge, besides analyzing how science has become, and functions as, a social system.

Earlier drafts of this chapter have been presented at the ECPR Joint Session of Workshops, Copenhagen (April 2000), which included a whole section on reflexivity, and at the 42nd Annual convention of the *International Studies Association* in Chicago (21–5 February 2001). I am particularly grateful to the participants of the ECPR workshop for their comments on earlier versions and the many suggestions provided by their own papers (see many of them collected in Albert and Hilkermeier 2004), and again to Mathias Albert for discussing the paper at the ISA. I also gratefully acknowledge comments and criticisms by Fiona Adamson, Bernt Berger, André Brodosz, Barry Buzan, Lene Hansen, Friedrich Kratochwil, Anna Leander, Michael Merlingen, Gunther Teubner, Ole Wæver, and in particular Oliver Kessler. Perhaps in a way more than usual, the usual disclaimers apply.

His theory therefore shares the main characteristics of constructivism, at least in my reconstruction (cf. Guzzini 2000a; see also Adler 2002), namely

1 being particularly sensitive to the distinction between the level of action (proper), the level of observation and the relationship between the two;
2 having an epistemological position which stresses the social construction of meaning (and hence knowledge);
3 having an ontological position which stresses the construction of social reality.

Power is crucial for constructivist theorizing, since it handles the relationship between the social construction of meaning and the construction of social reality. For constructivists, the categories we use, as they are shared, have an effect on the social world. To some extent, statistical categories "produce" what counts as significant facts, and function as the "authoritative" way of understanding the world. Moreover, human beings – but not natural phenomena – can become reflexively aware of attributions and influence their action in interaction with them. This "looping effect" (cf. Hacking 1999: 34) is one of the reasons for the importance of "identity" in constructivist writings. And as a final point linking the social construction of knowledge and the construction of social reality, constructivists stress the importance of self-fulfilling prophecies. If money is money and not just paper, because people identify it as such, then it ceases to be so the moment this shared attribution goes missing. When people stop trusting money, money will *through this very action* become untrustworthy. *Realpolitik* becomes political reality not because of the alleged iron laws of world politics, but because of the combined (and sticky) effect of actors believing in its truth (cf. Guzzini 2004a).

The initial puzzle for this chapter is, however, that Luhmann's constructivism-inspired social theory reserves a much more limited place for power. Given this tension, the following analysis has the general purpose of introducing Luhmann's concept of power as a way to illustrate the different possible strategies to turn a constructivist meta-theoretical commitment into a social theory. This chapter shows that, in comparison with other social theories of the recent sociological turn, which tended to broaden the concept, Luhmann aims at defining power in a narrower way.

This, in turn, relates to a further claim, namely that the role of "media of communication" in Luhmann's social theory derives from two theoretical inspirations which might produce an internal tension. On the one hand, Luhmann proposes a theory of media of communication. His vision of history, although not teleological, displays a certain logic insofar as social organization is becoming both more complex and also more complex in its dealing with that complexity. As we will see, media of communication are said to have originated historically exactly to handle this complexity. Power is such a medium. Politics, in turn, happens whenever observation takes place with this medium. On the other hand,

Luhmann's theory of social systems has a synchronic element which becomes increasingly important in his latest writings. Here, he takes the differentiation of society into different subsystems for granted and is mainly interested in mapping out their different internal logic of reproduction. In this undertaking, the media of communication, although having a general reference point in society, become intrinsically connected to one particular system, in this case tying (political) power to the political system.

Hence, to put my claim in a different way: whereas a focus on communication and the role media play therein tends to see power in a more diffused way typical for constructivism in IR, the definition of the medium with regard to one particular subsystem provides a narrowing and opens a series of definitional moves which are unusual in recent power analysis, such as the tying of power to negative sanctions only. In a nutshell: power and politics are intrinsically connected, yet in one case, the medium power is the driving force, defining where politics lies in the social system; in the other, the political system encapsulates politics and hence narrows the scope of the medium "power."

In the next section, I analyze Luhmann's concept of power as a medium of communication and provide illustrations from IR to show its usefulness for constructivist analysis. The following section discusses power in Luhmann's theory of social systems. It highlights the definitional strictures arising from tying power to the analysis of one system in particular, strictures which are less useful for constructivist analysis, as illustrated by a very short comparison with Bourdieu's field theory.

Power as a medium of communication

In his 1975 book on power, reprinted without any change in 1988, Luhmann (1988 [1975]) bases his understanding of power mainly on the social exchange (cf. Blau 1964) and community power literature (cf. Dahl 1958, 1961; Polsby 1980), which was prominent in the USA at the time. This starting point is unusual for more recent, usually more sociological approaches on power (see the survey in Clegg 1989), which have been criticized for being rather too structuralist (cf. Lukes 1977; Wrong 1988 [1979]). Moreover, this type of literature has an individualist understanding of social interaction and is therefore meta-theoretically incompatible with Luhmann's functionalist approach. Yet, this background offers one good way to apprehend Luhmann's concept of power by following the steps of how he "systemizes" the community power literature. He tries to retain the particular Weberian inspiration and re-conceptualizes it into a systemic social theory.

Power: causal, relational, multidimensional

The basic inspiration of the community power literature is Max Weber's definition of power as getting somebody else to do something against his or her will.

As a result, this literature defines power as a *causal* concept, but not of the earlier mechanic version (e.g. Russell 1960 [1938]). Luhmann explicitly follows Dahl (1968) in taking "will" or preferences seriously. Hence this conceptualization of power needs to refer to both individual and interactive preference rankings and foregone alternatives, i.e. sanctions and cost analysis. Moreover, power is also a *multidimensional* concept insofar as resources in one domain might be of little use in another (a claim with which Luhmann will have some difficulties, see below). Moreover, Dahl would insist that power is a *relational*, not to be confused with a *relative*, concept. In other words, power does not reside in capabilities or resources, but in the effect they can have in the relationship between actors. We can talk about power only if intention has been affected – in the extreme case, will has been broken – in a relationship. As such, power is, finally, a *counterfactual* concept, since it means that action has been affected which would have been different otherwise.

Dahl's concept has been fundamental for the so-called community power literature which is in many ways at odds with Luhmann's social theory. This literature had been written as an open attack against elitist approaches, insisting on the empirical verifiability of power claims (cf. Dahl 1958), a move too positivist and empiricist for Luhmann's meta-theory. Also, this literature is self-consciously methodologically individualist, again something systems theory wants to break with.

The system-theoretical and communicative twist

Luhmann must give a non-empiricist and non-individualist twist to these conceptualizations of power. Inspired here by Parsons, he defines power as a medium of communication (cf. Luhmann 1988 [1975], 2000: 18ff.). Media of communication, like power or money, are seen to have developed as a response to the rising complexity of modern societies. As throughout his theorizing, Luhmann is interested in the ways in which systems have been able to cope with (and, in turn, generate) increasing complexity. With the development of written communication and its accrued distance between information, understanding and acceptance/refusal, symbolically generated media of communication become necessary, because of their function of reducing complexity and disposing in favor of acceptance. They create motivations for the acceptance of communication, in order to avoid that this distance is perceived as making communication too complicated, or even impossible (although he later parts company with Parsons' general theory, this view is constant throughout, see Luhmann 1990: 179).

In a later elaboration, Luhmann argues that media of communication originate in particular when the risk arises that communication is not accepted, even though such acceptance would be useful for solving important (for power, political) problems. Luhmann argues that the invention of writing increases the storage capacity of social memory. This heightens the risk of seeing communication refused, since previous refusals are stored and can be mobilized in an impersonal way and without the social control in direct interaction (cf. Luhmann 2000: 37–8).

Such media function hence as a supplementary institution of language. They represent a "code of generalized symbols" that steer communication and, through this, the transmission of "selection impulses." So does power affect *alter's* selection of alternatives through the implicit or explicit threat of negative sanctions. For communication exists only if *ego* or *alter* are affected in their respective "selections" – what an individualist approach would call "choices" or "decisions." Other media of communication, such as money, truth and love, also affect selections, but on the basis of something else.

In a neo-Weberian vein, power is a symbolically generated medium of communication which presupposes that *both* partners see alternatives whose realization they want to avoid. This Weberian formulation is, however, recast into the framework of his systems theory. The realization of power (*Machtausübung*) arises, when the relation of the communication partners to their alternatives to be avoided (*Vermeidungsalternativen*) is such that *ego* wants to avoid them relatively more than *alter*. Power as a medium links up one combination of alternatives to be avoided with another, yet preferred one. It ensures that this is visible to the communication partners. For Luhmann (1988 [1975]: 22) the code of power *communicates* an asymmetrical relation, a causal relationship, and motivates the transmission of selections of action from the more powerful to the less powerful one. It is based on the control of access to negative sanctions (cf. Luhmann 1990 [1981]: 157).

There is an important communicative twist in Luhmann's theory, which is quite unique and useful for constructivist theorizing. The twist occurs through a small, but heuristically very consequential move which is perhaps more explicit in later writings: power does not (only) ensure asymmetrical coordination of action, but (also) regulates the communicatively generated *attribution* of causality. "Thus power is present only when the participants define their behavior in correspondence to a corresponding medium of communication" (Luhmann 1990 [1981]: 157). Power is not only permitting a certain type of communication, but is itself in fact socially constructed through communication.[1] Still more constructivist, Luhmann (1990 [1981]: 163) argues that the process of the causal attribution of power, in turn, has an effect on the actual relationships of power. In other words, despite the apparently technical functionalism, Luhmann's interest in communicative theory leads him to develop a strong vision of the social construction of reality, at least for a while. Only the "social" referent here is not an individualist mind, but intersubjective communication systems and media.

---

1 This has been an important theme in the move to more structural/impersonal power concepts in IR. See, for instance, Friedrich Kratochwil (1988: in particular 272) and Richard Little (1989). For a discussion, see Guzzini (1993).

This communicative component allows a constructivist re-reading of IR theorizing, as the next section will illustrate with the discussion of power substitutes.

The substitution of power: illustrations from IR

Power is simply an attribution of causality in the communication. The exact weighing of alternatives in a relational concept of power is, however, hardly possible for the problem of double contingency. To make such communication possible, it needs therefore to develop substitutes for the medium which would fulfill the same function of stabilizing expectations. Those substitutes, in turn, become a symbolically generated code of power.

Hence substitutes similarly fulfill the task of complexity reduction. For Luhmann, substitutes to power include *hierarchies* (already presupposing a ranking); *history* (attributing power through past events), and related to this, *prestige/status* and *the example of previous significant events*; and finally, *rules deriving from contracts*. In all these cases the direct communicative recourse to power is replaced by a reference to symbols, that normatively oblige all parties and take account of the presupposed power ranking (cf. Luhmann 1988 [1975]: 10).

In IR, this idea of substitutes for power has been the daily bread of much theorizing. Hedley Bull (1977) referred to the "great powers" (that is to hierarchy) as an *institution* for ordering the anarchical society. Vertzberger (1986) has done much work on the role of history in decision-making including its substitute for actual power realizations. More constructivist inclined scholars refer to the discursive or symbolic construction of power as legitimacy through the mobilization of collective memory (cf. Campbell 1992, 1993; Khong 1992; Weldes 1999). The Cold War obsession of domino theories and "keeping commitments" so visible in the difficult US disengagement in Vietnam only makes sense when we consider the concern about power substitutes, like reputation, which actually cannot be divorced from power as such.

In the very classical understanding of the role of diplomacy, realpolitik diplomats, i.e. those who orient their action according to the balance of power, need substitutes that account for power, so as to avoid that its measurement be each time found out, and fought out, on the battlefield. Many of the classical realists have been concerned about the very absence of such a consensus on the practical level. Kissinger, for instance, deplores the fact that with the advent of nuclear weapons the relationship between power and politics has been loosened, and that power has become both more awesome and more "abstract, intangible, elusive" (Kissinger 1969: 61). In his eyes, it was crucial that diplomats came to a shared understanding of power, independent of its actual use. To make the traditional balance-of-power politics and diplomacy work, the central coordinates, references and symbols, such as national interest or power, must have a translatable meaning. For compensations cannot be used to ease tensions if their value is deeply contested; nor can balancing diplomacy have its effect of moderating conflict, if there is no common understanding on the point of equilibrium (for a longer discussion, see Guzzini 1998: ch. 7 and 231ff.).

Therefore, during the Cold War, some IR scholars have understood their responsibility in contributing to find commonly acceptable substitutes for power. Daniel Frei (1969) urged his peers in his inaugural lecture to help politicians to come up with a generally (i.e. socially or communicatively) accepted measure of power. Such a measure, which implicitly acknowledges a constructed nature of power, would help to stabilize diplomacy in the Cold War.

Spinning the argument further, Luhmann (1988 [1975]: 10–11) claims that, should science ever become able not only to propose substitutes but actually to measure power, this would destroy these substitutes and hence affect reality itself. He feels confident, however, that whatever scientists might come up with, it would be just another set of substitutes and not a real measure of power – and that politics would blissfully ignore it anyway.

Power and the political system

As we have seen in the previous section, power defined as a medium of communication has the potential to be basically everywhere, at least wherever a causal attribution in action or a certain selection in communication is needed. So, Luhmann seems at first sight to go down the road of defining power in a fairly ubiquitous manner. Yet, it is exactly against such approaches, which he finds represented by Bourdieu's symbolic power, for instance, that Luhmann (2000: 13–14) wants to narrow down the concept. His theory of social systems provides the way for this move.

Power and the autopoiesis of the political system

In 1975, Luhmann started with a very wide concept of power which, like all symbolically generated media of communication, is omnipresent in society. Since this is far less the case in his later writings, it may warrant a central (and lengthy) quote. Opening a chapter on the "social relevance of power," Luhmann writes:

> Like language, symbolically generated media of communication have one necessary systemic reference: society. They pertain to problems of the whole society, and regulate constellations, which are possible at any time and anywhere in society. They cannot be restrained and isolated into subsystems, in the sense, for instance, that truth would play a role only in science, or power only in politics. There are constellations in connection with doubly contingent selectivity, which cannot be eliminated out of the "horizon of possibilities" (*Möglichkeitshorizont*) of human interaction. Wherever humans communicate with each other, there exists the probability of a transfer of selection patterns in one form or another. (A different

assumption would be a good sociological definition of entropy.) Wherever humans communicate with each other, there is the probability that they orientate themselves by taking the possibility of a mutual harming into account, thereby having influence on each other. Power is a life-world based universal of social existence.

(Luhmann 1988 [1975]: 90, my translation)

Although strictly speaking this society-wide reference of power is not given up in his later writings, this section will claim that his focus on *autopoiesis* and the different logics of societal subsystems such as politics or law increasingly ends up entangling certain media with certain systems, here power with politics.

But what exactly is autopoiesis? Luhmann's social theory distinguishes organic, psychic and social systems. Systems have an internal side and an environment, made up mainly by other systems. Between some social systems there can be special relationships, which Luhmann's theory calls "structural coupling," such as that, for example, between the systems of politics and of law. For all their differences, psychic and social systems are conceptualized in an isomorphic way. Functional autopoietic systems come to exist when (1) they reproduce themselves, by (2) following an internal logic driven by a system-specific binary code. For instance, the social system of "science" which has become autonomous in well-differentiated societies, functions (i.e. observes) according to the code "true/untrue." The system builds up certain expectations about its environment which it then sees confirmed or not, in a binary way.

This quite ingenious conceptualization allows Luhmann to have his cake and eat it, too. On the one hand, it permits an inner logic through an operational closure, since there is one binary code which steers "understanding" from inside the system. On the other hand, the system is cognitively open and not deterministic, since the feedback from the environment, deciphered in the binary way of the code, influences its reproduction.[2]

The move to Luhmann's theory of social systems has, however, rather profound consequences for the conceptualization of media of communication. These are consequences which seem at odds with much constructivist theorizing, also in International Relations.

---

2 It is perhaps important to add that Luhmann proposes a rather unique and very radical constructivist epistemology here which still allows a minimal realist ontology. The environment is not a neutral ground upon which different visions are tested. It is an amorphous thing of which we only "know" its "reaction" in terms of what the system in its reproduction expects from it. The feedback cannot be likened to a correspondence theory of truth, but corresponds simply as an external check which tells the system (here, science) whether its expectations were confirmed or not. Hence, Luhmann claims to have a constructivist position which differs both from a realist version of a correspondence theory of truth and from an idealist position whose epistemology gives up any reference to reality (see respectively Luhmann 1990: 260ff. and 92f.).

First, and less consequential, it implies for Luhmann, that every reference to humans needs to be replaced by organic, psychic or social systems. That move, which is perfectly coherent within his theory, breaks with the classical conception of how to link up different fields of society. (Human) agents cannot link up, only systems can. Whereas more classical approaches allow for power, money and other phenomena to be used at the same time in an interaction by (human) agents, Luhmann's systems theory must ascribe all this to observation done by different systems. The linkage is done through the simultaneity of observations by different systems. Corruption, for instance, can be observed at the same time as the codes of the legal and political system.[3] As mentioned earlier, if such inter-systemic links are of a certain stability, Luhmann talks of "structural coupling." Yet, structural couplings are again, and must be, a system-internal representation of a certain part of the environment. This reinforces the "inner logic" of the code. All agency is constructed within system via social attributes to persons (understood as artifacts).

Relatedly, this vision of reducing language to communication seems to strip language of the hermeneutic thickness typical of at least some types of constructivism. Let me give as an example his argument with regard to pluralism in his chapter on world society (cf. Luhmann 1997). He argues that different culturally defined systems in the world cannot be understood by observers who accept this pluralism. Since the observer cannot have a view from somewhere, no Archimedian point, independent of any of these cultures, pluralism must accept an "in-the-world" observation which is at the same time "out-of-the world" and hence becomes self-contradictory. But this argument only follows when understanding is conceived in a non-hermeneutic manner. In this, the argument recalls the classical rebuttal by Bernstein (1983) that Kuhn's (1970 [1962]) incommensurability thesis (and its related holistic theory of meaning) is not, or is less of, a problem for those who conceive of the observer as translator (see also Kuhn 1970). Similarly, in order to conceptualize the observer, Pizzorno (1994 [1993]) has used Simmel's (1908: 509–12) idea of a "stranger," as opposed to a foreigner, defined by being at the same time in and outside of the community. There is no *a priori* reason to believe that the paradox is better resolved through time (observation of observation . . .), as Luhmann repeatedly proposes.

But there is a second theoretical move which accomplishes the increasing linkage of power to the political system and less to society as such. Luhmann makes the consequential move to bind specific binary codes which steer the autopoietic reproduction of systems to specific media of communication (cf. Luhmann 1990 [1981]: 196). Indeed, media are "coded" in and for the emergence of autonomous social subsystems. Hence, for instance, the medium of communication "truth" is linked to the binary code true/untrue in the autopoiesis of the social system of science, and the medium power is similarly linked to

---

3 For this point and example, I am indebted to Oliver Kessler.

the binary code of power superiority (*Machtüberlegenheit*) and power inferiority (*Machtunterlegenheit*) (cf. Luhmann 2000: 88f.).

Consequently, this seems to do exactly what Luhmann admonishes in this early quote: it ties specific media closer to "their" subsystems. The theory of symbolically generated media of communication and his theory of social systems pull in different directions. In the first, power is tied to a general reference to society which makes it potentially ubiquitous. In the second, it is tied to a binary code of one social subsystem, the political.

The relationship between power and politics: The case of negative sanctions

The underlying reason for tying power further to one system has more to do with the logic of Luhmann's theory of social systems, and less to do with the theory of symbolically generated media of communication. It is this same logic, rather than Luhmann's theory of media of communication, which leads to a further narrowing of the concept of power: political power is based solely on negative sanctions which, in turn, relate mainly to physical violence.

For Luhmann, power is indeed inextricably connected to negative sanctions, that is, the threat of a punishment, but not to positive sanction or the offer of a reward (cf. Luhmann 1988 [1975]: 23, 2000: 45ff.). Positive sanctions are not part of power although they can be turned into such, when they change the preferences of another actor such that he/she perceives the foregoing of the reward as a threat. Power exists only if an action which would have detrimental effects is avoided.

In this context, Luhmann explicitly refers to Baldwin's analysis (Baldwin 1971b) which has been consequential in International Relations. He shares the assessment about the difference between positive and negative sanctions: positive sanctions must be realized to work, negative sanctions have been a failure when they are applied. Yet, he disagrees with Baldwin's idea of keeping both under a common heading, namely power (cf. Luhmann 1988 [1975]: 120, n. 50). Luhmann distinguishes between influence and power: influence can be based on "uncertainty absorption," "positive and negative sanctions," but only the last is defined as power (cf. Luhmann 2000: 43ff.).

This is a very consequential move, since it undermines the very Weberian base of the concept of power. The reason why Baldwin makes so much headway on positive sanctions is exactly that classical political science has been too concerned with threats of inducing change in behavior and thereby underplayed the role of other-than-military instruments for conducting foreign policy (cf. Baldwin 1985). If power has to do with getting someone else to do what he or she did not intend to do, then what matters is to change the intention and/or action of the other, not the way this is done. For Luhmann, however, only those means count which threaten a situation one wants to *avoid* and hence it harks back into a very classical, if not realist, political theory. Why?

In his earlier writings, Luhmann thinks that the inclusion of positive sanctions into the concept of power would make it impossible to distinguish between power and other forms of influence enabled by other media of communication like money – or even love (cf. Luhmann 1988 [1975]: 120, n. 50). In his late book on the political system, he develops this thought. He argues that positive sanctions are by-and-large conducted through and with the medium money and have therefore more the form of an exchange (although debatable, this is not pursued here). The economic system is hence the locus which develops the main opportunities for the use of positive sanctions. Although this can be used by the political system, it is nothing specific to it. Indeed, the difference between these sanctions and the main medium attached to them is crucial for understanding the differentiation between the economic and the political system in the first place (cf. Luhmann 2000: 45–6). For setting something specifically political aside, the "specifically political medium of power" (*ibid.*) is more narrowly defined as related to only negative sanctions.

At this point, Luhmann makes clear that the special role of negative sanctions has to do with the special role of physical violence for understanding politics. For him, violence is both the negation, and yet also the fundamental base, of power. From early on, he follows Parsons' view that power and constraint (*Zwang*), which in the last resort means physical violence, are antithetic. Let's mention again that a medium of communication has the role to ensure that *alter* and *ego* are not asked every single time to negotiate their relation, to play out all the alternatives they might have. Hence, communication media ensure that some alternatives do not arise, as it were, in order to stabilize expectations about the relationship. Communication must ensure an effect on *alter*'s action without *ego* acting itself. By substituting *ego*'s action for the communicated threat of it, physical violence *replaces* communication itself. Therefore, it cannot be power as such.

Yet, according to Luhmann, the monopolization of physical violence has allowed the political system to emerge in the first place. Moreover, it represents at the same time the extreme case of a power-constitutive alternative that actors would prefer to avoid (cf. Luhmann 1988 [1975]: 64). Hence, physical violence becomes a "symbiotic mechanism" which founds power (and no other medium of communication but power), because of its nearly universal applicability and latency (cf. Luhmann 1988 [1975]: 62, 2000: 62).

Luhmann's link between physical violence and power revisited in IR

This chapter started by stressing Luhmann's Weberian concern with power. Part of the post-Weberian literature on power went down the direction of the social exchange literature, as does Luhmann's earlier more Parsonian systems theory. Here, power is increasingly analyzed in other areas, where even some exchanges can be seen as part of the phenomenon of power, and also through other means, such as consensus built on authority, legitimacy, norms, but also sheer habit. But by now, we have reached another Weberian lineage, important for the lawyer

Luhmann: the political realism of German public lawyers in the wake of Weber, Schmitt and Morgenthau (cf. Koskenniemi 2000), where power is likened to constraint and obedience (cf. Luhmann 2000: 48) and the fascination with physical violence as the ultimate, but systemically independent, backing of the rule of law is shared.

In this field, IR scholars seem quite at home, since IR has usually been more concerned with the role of violence than much political science. And yet, exactly for this reason, IR offers a series of arguments which seem to undermine Luhmann's "realist" component in his understanding of power.

As mentioned above, Luhmann argues that violence is the ultimate power constituting action alternative, although not power itself. This assumes that violence is always that action which power-inferior actors (or systems) would most prefer to avoid. In other words, Luhmann assumes that the organized form of physical violence is necessarily the most threatening action across domains. But, as wary Soviet governments have shown with regard to détente politics, they felt more threatened if competition was played out in economic terms rather than military ones. One could reply that the role of factors other than physical violence was parasitic on the existence of mutually assured destruction (MAD). But this simply reinforces the argument. If MAD indeed had the effect of ruling the ultimate use of force out, then physical violence is only an ultimate threat under certain conditions, namely a primarily military communication. It is not all that difficult to imagine several power relations in which the ultimate threat of physical violence would simply be inefficient: nuclear warheads might not be the right means to influence interest rates of other countries, let alone the ones of allies.

This example points to a series of theoretical reductions in the link between politics, power, negative sanctions, and physical violence, as proposed by Luhmann. The first has to do with what the power literature calls the lacking fungibility of power.[4] Whereas money functions as both standard of value and as measuring rod in the economic system, power cannot do the same for politics (cf. Guzzini 2000c). There are so many substitutes for power exactly because there is no equivalent to money: I might know how to translate butter into guns (via money), but how do I translate population numbers, convertible currencies, universal language and military equipment into each other? The political world is sectored, and power multidimensional. Since Luhmann uses the analogy of power and money, he is forced to overstress the homogeneity of negative sanctions in which, at least in principle, physical violence can substitute any other form.

This represents, however, a second reduction: the confusion of negative sanctions with physical violence. Negative sanctions are strictly speaking only those

---

4 The classical statement on the power–money analogy in IR can be found in Arnold Wolfers (1962). For a critique of the fungibility assumption, see Raymond Aron (1962: 97–102), and then in particular David Baldwin (1985, 1989).

things one would like to avoid. As the above-mentioned example shows, this is not necessarily military punishment, not even "in the last resort." IR theorists have struggled with the impact of "amity/enmity" for understanding international relations (cf. Wolfers 1962; Buzan 1991). Based on this, one could formulate a paradox: in enmity relations, usually characterized by a high military or violent component, "de-securitization" – i.e. the moving out of the military agenda – can be a bigger threat for the actor weaker in other spheres (cf. Wæver 1995). In amity relations, however, non-physical threats are bound to be more efficient. Following the realist creed and taking the ultimate value of physical violence for granted has repeatedly led superpowers to mishandle their relations with their allies (cf. Guzzini 1998: 104–5).

Hence it seems to be the assumptions of Luhmann's political realism in the analysis of power which ask for the equivalence of negative sanctions and physical violence, not his theory of communication media, let alone the development of international relations which is not or no longer a purely Hobbesian international society. But the implications of this critique are wide-ranging. If there are significant political situations, where threats are more efficient if they are not backed by physical violence, but by other means, then, even if we limit power to negative sanctions, the specificity of the political cannot be found there. The theoretical aim of defining power narrowly in order to apprehend the specificity of the political system (and of politics!) sacrifices insights of the power literature for an aim not reached. Trying to define the "political" through power becomes a hindrance for the understanding of power – indeed for the very Luhmannian constructivist insights generated by his theory of media of communication.

Was it necessary? Constructivism and power beyond Luhmann

Whereas Luhmann's theory of media of communication attaches power to a societal reference, his theory of social systems ties it to the political system. In order to show the specificity of that system, power is moreover reduced to negative sanctions, understood as being based ultimately on physical violence. By distinguishing between positive and negative sanctions, Luhmann tries to carve out a concept of power which is not equivalent to influence and which allows us to define the specificity of the political in modern societies.

He certainly succeeds in narrowing the concept, avoiding the tendency to produce ubiquitous concepts of power. His insistence on physical violence can also serve as a good reminder for constructivist theorizing – not because it would contradict constructivism, but because the very construction of a Hobbesian society, the self-fulfilling prophecies of agents whose identity is intrinsically connected to a definition of politics in terms of violence is less researched than questions of norm diffusion, for instance.

But the theme of this section is whether his aim at defining politics through power enforces a stricture too narrow for power. A short comparison with another social theory compatible with constructivism can illustrate a way of handling power more in line with Luhmann's own communicative approach.

For the present argument, Bourdieu is a good comparison, since his theory is similarly reflexive (cf. Bourdieu 1990) and comes in many regards close to Luhmann's. This applies in particular to his theory of fields which have a similar role as social systems have for Luhmann. A field stands both for a patterned set of practices which suggests competent action in conformity with rules and roles, and for the playing (or battle) field in which agents, endowed with certain field-relevant or irrelevant capital, try to advance their position (cf. Bourdieu 1980).

This social subsystem is, however, not mainly defined by its functionality as compared to the entire system, but relies intrinsically on a historically derived system of shared meanings which define agency and make action intelligible. Its boundaries are an empirical question. Being historical, fields are open and change over time. But their inertia, their *habitus* (field-specific shared disposition), their internal (open) logic, what Bourdieu calls the *sens* (referring both to "meaning" and "direction"), produces an inward-looking reproduction which can take over many of the features of Luhmann's autopoiesis.[5]

Whereas the theory of fields is not dissimilar to Luhmann's vision of *social* systems, this is less the case for Bourdieu's theory of stratification based on his theory of capital. Here is perhaps the biggest difference with Luhmann's theory of social systems, because these forms of capital both link up different fields, and set them apart, since their role and efficacy are different from one another. In other words, they play a similar role to the societal reference of Luhmann's media of communication. Bourdieu distinguishes between economic, social, and cultural capital (symbolic capital being a fourth but slightly different notion). Agents are endowed with different amounts of these capitals. Conversely, their capital has not always the same efficacy depending on the context in which it is used. Having lots of economic capital might not be of much use in being well positioned as an artist, although it certainly influences the way the artistic field is structured. Indeed, to some extent the very identity of these fields/subsystems is closely connected to the particular mix of the capital relevant there.

The concept of power which results is therefore varied and multidimensional, and centrally focuses on the component so important for constructivists: the link between the social construction of knowledge and the construction of social reality. "The theory of knowledge is a dimension of political theory because the specific symbolic power to impose the principles of the construction of reality – in particular social reality, is a major dimension of political power" (Bourdieu 1977: 165; see also Bourdieu 2001).

Such a theoretical framework has several advantages for constructivists. First, the not-strictly-materialist definition of capital allows for field-specific analysis and

---

5 For a more detailed discussion in IR, see Guzzini (2000a), and in International Political Economy (IPE), see Leander (2000a).

for linking up fields. For this, however, Bourdieu still keeps a concept of an agent, even if individualists might find it over-socialized. Moreover, it also allows for an understanding of hierarchy within and across fields which can coexist with a diffusion of centers of power, similar to Luhmann's understanding that functional differentiation has turned the world "acentrical" and "heterarchic" (Luhmann 1997: 157). Related to this, Bourdieu's theory allows us to see power relations in every single field, without, however, reducing all relations to them. Finally, this field theory allows us to have a more contingent theory of fields/subsystems which is not deduced from a teleology of complexity as in Luhmann's theory.

In other words, Bourdieu's analysis divorces the understanding of power from the understanding of the political system. It is curious to see that Luhmann (2000: 13–14) overlooks this point. He explicitly rejects Bourdieu's conceptualization of symbolic power, because power so defined is to be found in all parts of society and hence conflates the political system with society at large. But this only occurs if politics is inextricably linked to the political system which, in turn, is linked to (the medium and code) power – a link which Luhmann makes, but Bourdieu does not.

As a result, Bourdieu also has little trouble countering Luhmann's other critique, namely that such conflation inhibits the study of what has been historically institutionalized under the concept of politics, namely "the politics referring to the state and its decision-making practice." Bourdieu is Weberian enough to assess the specificity of the bureaucratic field and of the state (cf. Bourdieu 1989) without, however, necessarily reducing politics to the political system and the state.

Epilogue

Luhmann's theory of media of communication presents a unique and elaborate constructivist understanding of power. Based on an internal critique and a comparison with Bourdieu's field theory and concept of symbolic power, this chapter has argued that his theory of social systems, however, unduly restricts these insights by connecting the medium of power to the political system. Whereas in the communicative theory, politics is when observation happens with the medium of power, and has thus a general societal reference, in Luhmann's theory of social systems, power becomes intrinsically connected to negative sanctions and physical violence and to what the state does. The very aim of defining the specificity of the political system through power seems to be Luhmann's guiding cognitive interest, an interest perhaps detrimental for his own constructivist understanding of power.

This epilogue spells out the constructivist idea that political theories are part of the political reality they try to understand and that no definitional choices are therefore innocent. There are some peculiarities about the concept of power which need to be taken into account when making such theoretical choices (for a more detailed account on the nature of conceptual analysis, see Guzzini 2002b).

Hence this epilogue is no longer about what power *means*, but what it *does* when it is used in political discourse. As Peter Morriss has argued, power is used in (three) particular contexts to specify "the art of the possible" and to assign blame or responsibility (cf. Morriss 1987: 37–42). Similarly, William Connolly (1974) had earlier argued that there is an irremediable connection between power and responsibility and that calling something an issue of power means "politicizing" it: it implies that things could have been otherwise; it asks for political justification.

This link does not escape Luhmann. He himself notices a relationship between one form of influence, based on "uncertainty absorption" and responsibility (cf. Luhmann 2000: 43). Moreover, when discussing the reasons for tying the concept of power to the political system and "the politics referring to the state and its decision-making practice," Luhmann claims that a wider concept of symbolic power could apparently make people err in the belief "that such things could be influenced by criticism or through reforms of state politics" (Luhmann 2000: 14). Yet, although the state and politics as social practices and institutions are sticky, they are not immutable. Even if Luhmann's definition of power, by defending politics from justifications apparently unwarranted in his theory, effects a construction of reality that consciously reproduces the prevalent self-definition of the political system.

5

PIERRE BOURDIEU'S FIELD ANALYSIS OF RELATIONAL CAPITAL, MISRECOGNITION AND DOMINATION

The study of power is taking place within two domains with distinct research logics, namely political (ontological) theory and social (explanatory) theory. At the same time, it includes analyses at the micro-level, often expressed as 'power-to' and at the macro-level, often coined in terms of 'power-over'. To capture these different components of the analysis of power, a family of power concepts has developed.

Informed by political theory, power has often been connected to the 'nature' of politics. At the macro-level, it relates to questions about order, indeed the state or governance in general. At the micro-level, power is considered to be the condition for the possibility of autonomy or freedom (and hence responsibility). But power has been a major inspiration in a part of social theory, too, where it is the object not of philosophical deliberation and constitutional design, but explanation. And here we meet the analysis of domination (or social stratification), as well as concepts of power which are tied to ideas of agency and influence, i.e. the study of how resources and latent capacities (or 'potentials') help us understand which agents prevail in the outcomes of their interaction. Such social theories of action tend to look at power in terms of influence, understood, at times, as a subcategory of 'cause' (Dahl 1968). In between the two levels and two domains, or across them, is the analysis of authority.

Government (order), autonomy (freedom), domination (rule), influence (cause) – that a single concept should stretch all the way from the nature of politics

---

This is a considerably shortened and revised version of a paper presented at the annual convention of the ISA in Chicago (22–5 March 2006). I apologise for not having been able to update and rethink it as much as I would have liked to, but am grateful to those who anyway encouraged me to go for a revision, as Vincent Pouliot already did a long time ago. For comments on the paper, I am grateful to Rebecca Adler-Nissen, Dan Nexon, and in particular Anna Leander.

to the study of individual outcomes might look strange to a contemporary scholar, educated in cutting concepts to their operational minimum. To make some headway through this problem, we need to understand that researchers use power in different ways. 'Power' stands both for the totality of *analyses* which refer to any of these concepts, and, confusingly, also for the individual *concepts*, like government or influence, with which it is often used interchangeably. To make things worse, *theories* of power (or domination, etc.) usually stipulate relationships between several of those concepts within a systematic whole, like Dahl when he wants to understand (macro-political) government through (micro-social) influence (Dahl 1961). The different nature of its usages, usually unacknowledged, has produced much confusion.

My chapter on Bourdieu's power analysis for IR must be understood in this context. I will organise it as a response to two unsatisfactory ways to deal with this confusion. The first way consists in widening the *concept* of power to take all different facets of an *analysis* of power into account, a move I dubbed the 'overload-fallacy' of power (Guzzini 1993: 468ff.). The overload-fallacy arises when scholars try to have all the facets of power analysis brought together within a widened concept of power, which then fails to clearly state the relationship of the different power concepts to each other within a wider theory. Such a tendency exists among structural power concepts. In response, I had proposed to keep the different components apart, and think of a power analysis which includes a series of central concepts within the family of power concepts. The result was a four-tier dispositional power analysis around a twofold agent power concept (which included non-intentional and indirect institutional power) and two intersubjective governance or impersonal power concepts (social construction of options and ritualised mobilisation of bias which affect the identities of agents) tied together in a dynamic model (Guzzini 1993). This was a first step providing a coherent meta-theoretical setting able to combine Lukes and Foucault, so to speak. But, although inspired by Bourdieu (see also Guzzini 1994), this analysis left off with an under-determined social theory.

The other unsatisfactory way consists in keeping the concepts apart, but not developing how they can relate to each other (for a recent example of this in IR, see Barnett and Duvall 2005a). Suggesting a solution, this response ends up providing merely a non-explanatory taxonomy. Whatever the intention, making mere classifications of power concepts invites analysts to just pick and choose, and possibly combine, with not much concern for the theoretical terms upon which such combination may or may not be possible. And the caveat that these power concepts are possibly incommensurable (hence also possibly commensurable) leaves us after the taxonomy where we were before. Such taxonomies do not move our knowledge of power further, but simply survey the field and remind us of its diversity. If the overload strategy limited theoretical development by subsuming all under a single concept, the taxonomic solution, or indeed the 'taxonomic illusion', does so by de facto neglecting it.

A closer look at Bourdieu's analysis of power can avoid both problems. This chapter will claim that Bourdieu can provide some guidance for combining these different facets within a coherent social theory of power and domination. At the same time, in my reading at least, the recent interest in Bourdieu can be seen at the crossroads of this sociological theorising, and the revival of political theory, as exemplified by the reception of Foucault. I think that Bourdieu's approach can provide a starting point for tying these strings together.

Whether or not his theory provides the answer to all puzzles of power analysis (which I would not expect), it forces the analyst to think about the relationship between different concepts within a wider power analysis. And it shows that this is possible without repeating the overload-fallacy or resorting to a taxonomic (illusionary) solution. Indeed, even the problems of actually applying Bourdieu's framework to IR, when it was derived from domestic social theory, can provide fruitful research tracks for IR scholars.

The chapter proceeds by spelling out his theory in the context of the sociological and linguistic turn before analysing some of the ways and problems in applying it to the sphere of IR.

Analysing power and domination in a relational field theory

The analysis of power will start with the component in Bourdieu's field theory which is called 'power'. He defines it as a form of (relational) capital. But that is obviously not the end of the story. Fundamentally, power is only a means in the wider analysis of domination. Hence, the present section will also develop the other elements of his analysis of domination, namely symbolic violence and the role of language in domination, social stratification, and finally the field of power and its relations to the state.

Power as (relational) capital

For Bourdieu, power is tied to the control of resources which correspond to (and reproduce) the organising principles of fields. In fact, to some extent fields and forms of capital are co-constitutive: because certain spheres of society have acquired a self-sustaining autonomy, they can be seen as 'fields' which, in turn, are ruled by the specific competences accrued to agents in view of the distribution of specific capitals. The economic field empowers agents endowed with economic capital, the field of art those with artistic capital, and so on. And having much economic capital does not make a respected painter (although some transfer can happen).

This analysis of capital avoids a series of typical reductionisms. For one, such a conceptualisation rejects the attempt to read any single capital as the most 'fundamental' or generally applicable. But it also avoids a second reductionism. Power is not in the resource as such, but is defined through its role within the field. Only what affects a field's logic and hierarchy counts as capital. To some, this may appear close to the classical circularity of power explanations which tie resources to actual control, and where hence power can be always re-defined through its effects. But Bourdieu does not see it as a causal analysis, where the possession of an (independent) resource is meant to affect a (dependent) outcome. He wants to understand what makes a resource a power resource in the first place. And so, in his analysis, it makes no sense to define capital independently from the particular logic of the field. Instead, making the very definition of capital dependent on the field allows for a context-specific and *relational analysis of power*. It also opens up the difficult, but in terms of power analysis crucial, question of *fungibility*, i.e. to what extent capital valuable and valued in one field may be so also in another field, or, indeed, more widely, how different capitals are made (or not) measurable in each other's terms, made convertible (see below on the field of power).

A similar stress on a relational, not a property, concept of power, the necessarily issue- or field-specific analysis of power, and the central issue of fungibility have been the core conceptual battles of David Baldwin in his analysis of power (Baldwin 1985, 1989). There is still a difference, though. Baldwin tends to define the relational aspect in an interactionist mode, where the effect of a resource is dependent on the values and preferences of the parties involved in the contest. Bourdieu's theorising problematises and systematises the origins of these values and preferences within the logic of the fields and, in particular, in the *habitus*. It enables a context/field-specific assessment of power, and yet, as in all more structuralist accounts, also a more 'typified' assessment.

To further stress the relational component of his analysis, Bourdieu ties all analysis of capital to his notion of 'symbolic capital'. Capital is never only in the material or ideational resource itself, but in the cognition and recognition it encounters in agents. A relational analysis of power always insists on the complicity, or, as Bourdieu sometimes prefers calling it, the connivance that exists between the dominating and the dominated. Hence, for Bourdieu, symbolic capital can be attached to all forms of capital. More specifically, symbolic capital is the form which any capital will take, if it is recognised, i.e. perceived through those very conceptual categories which are, however, themselves the effect of the distribution of capitals in the field (Bourdieu 1994: 117, 161).

Symbolic violence, misrecognition, and 'doxic subordination'

From this relational approach to capital, Bourdieu renews Weber's analysis of *Herrschaft*, succinctly understood as the chance that a command stands to be obeyed, or more precisely, as the fact that

> an expressed will ('order/command') of the dominating actors intends to influence the action of the subordinates and actually influences in a way such, that the latter act[,] as if they had turned the content of the command, for its own sake, into a maxim of their action ('obedience').
> *(Weber 1980 [1921–2]: 544, my translation)*

Doing so, Weber connected the idea of *Herrschaft* with actual rule (since it implies obedience), and tied it intrinsically to the idea of legitimacy, i.e. to a systematic acceptance by the subordinated. He famously saw the origins for this legitimation of rule in (legal) rationality, tradition, or charisma, thus characterising his three types of *Herrschaft* (for a more detailed account, see Guzzini 2007). Bourdieu further sociologises the origins of such obedience by lifting it out of Weber's individualist approach. This is where he introduces his concepts of symbolic violence, mis(re)cognition, and '*doxic* subordination' (*soumission doxique*).

In his understanding of symbolic capital, Bourdieu redefines 'recognition' away from a conscious consent or cognition towards a phenomenon where acts mobilise pre-existing schemes of cognition and behavioural dispositions, which agents have internalised in and through their practices with which they became a 'competent' practitioner within the field. In what I have elsewhere called Bourdieu's rule of 'non-reactive anticipation' (Guzzini 1994: 273ff.),[1] this results in a type of self-censorship which is the often unconscious practice by which agents conform to the expectations of their position in the field, 'the concession to a social universe which one makes by having accepted making oneself acceptable' (Bourdieu 2001: 114, my translation).

And it is in this unreflected mobilisation that Bourdieu sees the almost 'magical' origin of obedience, an obedience which works all the better if agents are not aware of it (Bourdieu 1994: 188), just as in Lukes' third dimension (Lukes 1974). Therefore, he speaks also of symbolic 'violence'. His is a redefinition of legitimacy as a pre-reflexive disposition to obey by conforming to expectations acceptable to, and made acceptable by, the *doxa* of the field, its paradigmatic truths. Just as with Foucault – but Bourdieu quotes Hume – the puzzle is not to find out how to achieve political order in liberal mass societies, but to understand why it is often achieved so easily, when it 'goes without saying' (Bourdieu 1994: 127–8).

'*Doxic* subordination' is hence the effect of this symbolic violence, a subordination which is neither the result of coercion, nor of conscious consent, let alone a social contract. Instead, the domination is based, as he writes, on a mis(re)cognition (*méconnaissance*) of that symbolic violence which works by not being recognised as such. It is based on the unconscious adjustment of subjective structures (categories of perception) to objective structures. And so, according to Bourdieu, the analysis of '*doxic* acceptance' is the 'true fundament of a realist theory of domination and politics' (Bourdieu and Wacquant 1992: 143, my translation).

Language and authority

One of the impersonal power components which I had detected in the IR power debate of the 1980s, the 'ritualised mobilisation of bias', was directly

---

1 This is obviously a reference to Carl Friedrich's 'rule of anticipated reaction' which is the only exception a Dahlian approach allows to non-intentional power, since it is the imputed intention of A (hence intention nevertheless) which affects the behaviour of B. Bourdieu takes the analysis out of this individualist and intentional framework.

derived from Bourdieu. It refers to the power which lies in the social construction of knowledge that suggests a certain 'order of things' (see e.g. Bourdieu 1980: ch. 8).

To make this version of impersonal power work, Bourdieu considers language very seriously. For only through the working of language and its capacity to fix concepts and schemes can he build a link from the social construction of knowledge to the construction of social reality. And he does this within an explicitly reflexive theory of power where categories and schemes to apprehend the social world interact with that world (see also my Bourdieu-inspired analysis in Guzzini 2000a).

This gives a twist to the usual understanding of authority and legitimacy again. Bourdieu's understanding of authority is not necessarily connected to an office or any other already officialised 'position'. It goes one step further, asking for the conditions under which that position became authoritative in the first place. Authority is placed within a wider analysis of dis/empowering which includes also the tacit legitimacy conferred by the logic of the field to certain dispositions to see and understand social reality. In this way, Bourdieu takes 'authority' away from a legal or personal context à la Weber, relying instead on a social and relational ontology of intellectual dispositions and linguistic categories.

In contrast to classical speech act theory, however, Bourdieu insists heavily on the social conditions which make such an act potentially successful. Not everyone is either in the position or, as mentioned above, more generally 'empowered' to command an open or tacit acceptance of his or her 'power of naming': not everyone is empowered or entitled to call things into being. And, given symbolic violence, not everyone will even try, but they could be pre-empted from doing so (from even thinking so) by the internalised dispositions and expectations within the field. And so Bourdieu does not mince his words when criticising Austin (and then Habermas) for neglecting the social conditions for the possibility of a speech act (see e.g. Bourdieu 2001: 149–74). This said, this may not be a very generous reading, since the speech act tradition after Austin, in particular Searle, includes also a socially thicker understanding of institutions for understanding the force of speech acts (as he acknowledges in Bourdieu and Wacquant 1992: 123).

But then, in an equally ungenerous reversal, Bourdieu was also criticised for overstating his point, thus leading his theory to assume an almost objectivist social positioning which empowers performatives. At least Bourdieu's critique of speech act theory would therefore tend to neglect the extent to which performatives are themselves contributing to the social positioning (for this critique, see Butler 1999). Again, the critique is correct in showing a tension in extricating the discursive and non-discursive. But the solution is most probably in the very abandonment of that distinction. Just as much as discursive analysis makes sense within a specific social space, Bourdieu seems committed to think the power of performatives (the 'social magic') as generated by the *habitus* and sense practice in a field mediated by language and indeed discourses.

Social stratification and elites

Social space is indeed another concept in Bourdieu's theorising. The focus here moves from the field-specific understandings of action, power and authority, to the overall picture within a theory of domination, i.e. from the (more) micro-level, albeit relationally understood, to the macro-level of power analysis. As we have seen, Bourdieu conceives of social groups in terms of their capital, in a rather classical way. But, again placing himself more in the succession of Weber than Marx, that capital had been defined in relational terms as emanating from (symbolic) recognition, hence coming closer to the idea of status groups. Can we map all these fields and capitals into a single social space?

Bourdieu has famously provided graphical representations of such a social space, defined by the distribution of what he found to be the two most important forms of capital (in France), economic and cultural, tied to allegedly meritocratic 'titles' (Bourdieu 1979: 40–1). The elite is located where the amount of capitals is high, but its different composition makes for competing elites, pitting the classical *Bildungsbürgertum* (cultural bourgeoisie) against the *Wirtschaftsbürgertum* (economic bourgeoisie). Moreover, again insisting on the parallel reading between subjective and objective structures, he relates life-style with social position, showing thereby how our categories for distinguishing people in the social space overlap with certain status symbols and (acquired) tastes.

Yet such groups are not automatically classes, understood as real existing political forces. Assuming otherwise is to commit the 'scholastic fallacy' of assuming that the scholarly categories and constructions used to understand the social world are shared by that world (Bourdieu 2000b: 156). Since groups do not necessarily develop a collective consciousness, whether false or not, 'social classes do not exist' (Bourdieu 1994: 28), in the sense that they cannot be read off the social map. A representation of the social space can show similarities or differences in the way groups experience their life. But the borders are open and groups are not 'out there', they have to be politically formed and constituted. In an ironic twist on Marx, Bourdieu criticises him for having taken his categories of analysis for the actual object – and yet, by the success of those categories to have contributed to making them become actual collective agents.

The field of politics, the state, and the field of power

After accounting for power and a theory of domination typical for the sociologist, Bourdieu also ventures into the classical macro-question of power for the political theorist: the question of 'government', here understood more widely as the question of political order and not just the study of the political system or its executive branch. And although the theory has a link, and needs one, that link is not so self-evident.

Bourdieu has to deal with the problem almost all sociologists face when they analyse the development of social subsystems and elites. In principle, there is nothing which makes any subsystem or field superior to another, no self-evident hierarchy. At the same time, there is a political hierarchy which has made political theorists start their theories from government or, indeed, the state. How, then, does one treat politics: as a political system, one among others? Or is it permeating everything? Or on top of everything?

Bourdieu's solution is not unusual, but it is worth developing. He does define the field of politics as one among others, also to be distinguished from the field of bureaucracy, for instance, which is more narrowly defined and attached to the actual state institutions. The field of politics is defined by a different stake. In a redefinition of Weber, he sees at stake the 'monopoly of the legitimate principle of vision and division of the social world' (Bourdieu 2000a: 64, my translation. Sometimes he also includes the physical world, see Bourdieu 1994: 91). As such, the stake is intellectual, since it is about the way the world is made sense of, how it is classified. As he says, the class struggle is importantly a classification struggle, since the categories with which we view and divide up the world can constitute social facts which, in turn, can be politically mobilised (Bourdieu 2000a: 67). This 'intellectual' twist explains the closeness of the political field to, and the inclusion of, social actors who handle ideas and who also give them authority, like scientists. Bourdieu insists that the political field comprises not only the professionals of politics, but also (court) journalists and academics, making it possible for ideas to 'circulate in a circle' (*circulent circulairement*, Bourdieu 2000a: 37), that is, within the field, thus increasing the latter's autonomy. Yet, ideas alone are not enough. They need to become '*idées-forces*', i.e. leading ideas, which means that agents who are part of the game of affecting the social world by changing its vision and divisions have to engage in the field and its political struggles.

And so politics is defined through a field which is horizontal or parallel to the others, although its stake is part of a wider system of domination. But at the same time, he introduces a wider encompassing field, what he calls the field of power (*champ de pouvoir*). This concept draws on the ambiguity of the French *pouvoir* which means both power and government (*potestas*). In its latter sense, it is always used for the entirety of the state, its territory, and people. A political theory of domination is hence not only about the field of politics, but about the field of power and its relation to the state.

The field of power is perhaps the least concrete of Bourdieu's fields. To be thought horizontally, not in a hierarchical position, this field amalgamates and overlaps with the fields of the economy, the bureaucracy, politics, and (elite) education, constituting and being constituted by the *Noblesse d'État* (Bourdieu 1989). It corresponds to the space in which the *rapports de force* between different types of capital are fought out. This struggle pits agents, not autonomous subjects, against others who are sufficiently endowed with specific capitals to dominate their respective fields and who defend the value of their capital against competing ones (the most important capitals here being cultural, economic, and political). In other words, the stake is the 'exchange rate' between capitals (Bourdieu 1994: 56). Precisely because power is not to be found in 'objective' resource but in relations of recognition – not just for the analyst but also the agent – an overall system of domination is the result of an ever ongoing fight to establish the rates of convertibility and hence hierarchy of capitals and social groups. It is the struggle for the dominating principle of domination (Bourdieu 1994: 34).

This field of power is not synonymous with, but closely related to, Bourdieu's understanding of the state which he defines as having the legitimate monopoly of both physical and symbolic violence (meant here as an ideal definition, just as in Weber). In its actual definition, the concept then overlaps with the idea of the field of power, since Bourdieu sees the state as endowed with a kind of 'meta-capital' which dominates the other types of capital by setting their rate and dis/empowering agents endowed with it (Bourdieu 1994: 109). That puts the state above the rest. And if the field of power may still be thought on the same level and overlapping with other fields, its stake, the control of the state, makes for a hierarchical setting, an ambiguity which commentators have been well aware of (see, for instance, Bigo 2011: 246–9).

A first conclusion

As I have earlier argued (Guzzini 1993), taking into account all the different facets of power IR scholars have detected requires a social ontology in which power is not understood as a cause, but as a disposition (capacity), in which its character is constituted through social relations, and which is attentive to the effects of legitimate domination that cannot be understood in terms of consent or contract. Just as in Lukes and Foucault, Bourdieu's power analysis includes that part of power which works by not being acknowledged, that part which makes agents conform not through external control mechanisms, but through some sort of internalised acceptance. He contributes to both the sociological and the linguistic turn. And his theory avoids not only the taxonomic illusion (which is alien to him), but also the overload-fallacy by clearly distinguishing different moments of power in his analysis without reducing all to a meta-concept.

Finally, the relational character also meets Foucault's concerns about power and the subject. The issue of subjectivity and identity can be accommodated within Bourdieu through the concept of the *habitus*, which functions like a depository of the collective memory in the field, going through and constituting agents in their social behaviour. Since agents are part of and positioned in different fields, their multiple *habitus* allow for a wider understanding of this identity or subjectivity, as shown by his discussion on the quite Foucauldian theme of how classificatory schemes interact with the identity and indeed the body (Bourdieu 1980: 117–34).

Bourdieu and the analysis of power in IR

With this understanding in mind, I will briefly sketch *some* inspirations which Bourdieu has provided and may provide for the study of power and domination in IR. The first part will develop his relational theory for a better understanding of what happens to power at the micro-level, developing the idea of reflexivity and performativity, and the second part will try to see how his understanding of social and political domination may shed light on world politics.

'The measure of power and the power of measure' (Guzzini 2009)

Bourdieu's approach to power is particularly important for guiding research towards the struggles and conventions which establish the value of different types of capitals. In fact, the very definition of power is a highly political issue since it influences the respective value of different power resources (or capitals). Indeed, on the international level this aspect of a struggle for imposing a certain weighting of capitals is perhaps more visible. The relational aspects of recognition and status are still far more open in international affairs. Hence, whether or not there is an overall measure of power (and there is none in any objective sense), due to the special role great power status plays in international affairs, diplomats need to 'make up' indicators for overall power. Given the need to trade gains and losses so as (not) to upset the ranking of power (also achieved through politics of compensation), diplomats have to come to agree on what counts before they can start counting (Guzzini 1998: 231).

These understandings of power are highly contentious precisely because of their political consequences. And so, to use just one example from the Cold War, the Soviet Union resisted those definitions of power whose stress on non-military factors would imply a decline in its status. Similarly, in the recent controversy about soft and hard (coercive) power, deciding what power really means has obvious political implications. Focusing more on the military side and hence stressing an unprecedented preponderance on the US military made it possible to ask the US to push its advantages further (since it is 'possible'), and at times even stress the duty of the US to intervene given its capacities (which relates back to the performative argument above). Or, stressing US soft power and its potential decline, analysts could advocate a much more prudent and varied foreign policy strategy sensitive to claims of legitimacy and cultural attraction (whether or not the legitimacy crisis is simply an effect of poor public diplomacy or of a more fundamental origin). Or, finally, insisting on the unipolarity of the present international system, such a power statement mobilises a justification for leadership and responsibility which, in turn, can justify the 'inescapable', and hence excusable, nature of unilateralism – and a consensus on multipolarity does the opposite (for a detailed discussion, see Guzzini 2006).

This ties in also to a more 'performative' analysis. There is a logical link from the 'symbolic violence' inherent in what I have called the ritualised mobilisation of bias to a more performative analysis of power, akin to, but not the same as in, the pragmatic linguistic tradition. Bourdieu calls the 'act of social magic' – which he himself calls a performative act – the attempt to make things become reality by giving them a name ('nominating' them) and succeeding in the imposition of this new vision and division of social reality (see e.g. Bourdieu 2001: 286ff.).

In IR, one could cite as an example of such a Bourdieusian analysis the way categories of vision and division within the military field have been altered empowering commercial actors, endowing them with *epistemic power* (Leander 2005b) – Bourdieu calls it *épistémocratique* (Bourdieu 2000b: 100) – and locking it (temporarily) into a new *doxa* (Leander 2011b). This *doxa* authorising arguments and capital of commercial agents, in turn, 'categorically' pre-empts ways to press for the accountability of commercial security forces (Leander 2010).

Now, in a curious reflexive link, the enunciation of 'power' itself can become part of a 'social magic' with significant consequences for social power. Naming something 'power' has performative power. This stems from its place in our political discourse where it is associated with the boundaries of the political and the attribution of responsibility (Connolly 1974; for a more detailed account in IR, see Guzzini 2005).

'Power' implies an idea of counterfactuals; i.e. it could also have been otherwise. The act of attributing power redefines the borders of what can be done. In the usual way we conceive of the term, this links power inextricably to 'politics' in the sense of the 'art of the possible'. Lukes rightly noticed that Bachrach and Baratz's (1970) conceptualisation of power – which included agenda-setting, non-decision making, and the mobilisation of bias – sought to redefine what counts as a political issue. To be 'political' means to be potentially changeable; i.e. not something natural, God-given, but something which has the potential to be influenced by agency. In a similar vein, Daniel Frei (1969: 647) notes that the concept of power is fundamentally identical to the concept of the 'political'; i.e. to include something as a factor of power in one's calculus means to 'politicise' it. In other words, attributing a function of power to an issue imports it into the public realm where action (or non-action) is asked to justify itself. In return, 'depoliticisation' happens when by common acceptance no power was involved. In the conceptual analysis of power, this depoliticisation has been taking place through the concept of 'luck'.

A field of power in world society?

When Richard Ashley tried to understand the specificity of international governance, he referred to Bourdieu both as an inspiration for an anthropological take on the international community, identified in the microcosm of realists (Ashley 1984, 1987), and later for studying the nature of international governance, understood, in Bourdieu's words, as an orchestra functioning without a conductor (Ashley 1989). This approach played on a beautiful paradox which Bourdieu would appreciate (and one would be able to appreciate through his theory, too). Ashley argued that, despite realist claims to the contrary, there is an international community under anarchy – and that it exists in the very realists who deny its existence. Indeed, this community is all the more powerful in the international system as its self-description, if not its theory, conceals its very existence; a theory which has, in many aspects, the status of common sense in particular among practitioners. By making the field and its practitioners think world politics in binary divisions of realism–idealism (its *doxa*), it establishes a hierarchy of signification, legitimating an orthodoxy of the world as it really is against a heterodoxy (heresy) of utopia and wishful thinking. With Ashley, realism is no longer a theory to study IR, it becomes itself a unit of analysis; realists are no longer subjects but objects of observation, not chroniclers of a world inevitably tragic, but inadvertent accomplices of its tragedy. Only, how representative is this picture for the present world elite or the field of power? When applying Bourdieu to the 'international', one of the major difficulties derives from this very sociological grounding needed for establishing the contours of 'international society/community' and where Ashley's choice of an ultimate highest elite might no longer persuade.

Still, Bourdieu's analysis may provide pointers for a sociology of international power that seems to evade us. It would first direct us towards the study of whether transnational/international fields exist and then whether some form of unified field or several fields exist, where the elites of such transnational fields meet to struggle over the rate of exchange of major types of capital.

The first research avenue would derive from the rather classical setup of Bourdieu's analysis. In a relatively customary way, the development towards modern societies unfolds through the increasing autonomisation of different social spheres. They come into existence as fields once they have achieved a certain autonomy of their reproductive logic. Hence, to stay within this tradition, the observer would need first to establish whether, on the international or transnational level, such autonomous fields have come into being.

Interestingly, there is not really a consensus as to how best to use Bourdieu in this context. For some, such fields are a privileged vantage point for understanding transnational interactions involving a range of heterogeneous actors that have acquired a certain autonomy from national fields (e.g. Madsen 2006; Bigo *et al.* 2007; Leander 2011a). For others, there are no such fields, as international and transnational interactions are too loosely held together and continue to mirror primarily nationally situated struggles (e.g. Dezalay and Barth 2002; Vauchez 2011).

But even if we take as settled that there are such transnational (although not global) fields, is this sufficient to arrive at some sort of unifying system of domination, an international field of power? Is there a *noblesse du monde* in the making? International society is seeing the emergence of multiple global elites as education, economy, political fields, and bureaucracy have become more interrelated.

And if there were a summit of the world elite, it is not the G7/8 or 20, but the yearly meeting in Davos (and the social forum meeting in Porto Allegre then for the counter-elite), in which a selected jet-set of the economy, finance, media, politics, and academia/think tanks meets (for a critical assessment of its power, see Graz 2003). But even if Davos stands for the attempt to mimic national fields of power on a global level, missing the particular connection to the state and the absence of such a unifying component would make it of a different kind. While

Bourdieu recommends comparisons, we need to take into account the different contexts within which the relational theory is applied.

Conclusion

Bourdieu's framework of power analysis is a systematic engagement with the sociological and linguistic turn in the social sciences. It offers the opportunity to provide a more coherent social theoretical setting for many power phenomena and concepts, including performative ones, that have surfaced over the last three decades in IR. This chapter has tried to show why Bourdieu's theory displays at least the potential to overcome a series of fallacies that power concepts in IR have experienced earlier. Yet, at the same time, the transfer of his mainly state-confined approach to an international field analysis, including the fields of politics and power, cannot be done in a one-to-one manner, but needs to look out for equivalences that do justice to the different types of relations. Finally, Bourdieu's approach is only one way to make the two lineages of power analysis meet in a comprehensive way; the political theory lineage which stresses questions of governance, order and the 'political', and the social theory tradition which is interested in the role of power for understanding particular outcomes and modes of 'domination'. And hence, Bourdieu's theory is just a starting point, a set of inter-related concepts of the family of power that allows significant questions and research about power (and domination); it is not a religion.

PART II
Realism

6

THE ENDURING DILEMMAS OF REALISM IN INTERNATIONAL RELATIONS

After the end of the Cold War, realism has been again on the defensive.[1] A first debate was triggered by a piece John Vasquez (1997) published in the *American*

The idea for this chapter started with a small piece entitled 'Has Anybody Ever Been a Realist?' which was submitted as a rejoinder to Legro and Moravcsik's (1999) article in International Security. I am indebted to Andrew Moravcsik and to Alexander Astrov for comments on this short piece. Earlier versions of this chapter, not always with the same title, were presented at the 41st Annual Convention of the International Studies Association in Los Angeles (14–18 March 2000), the annual convention of the Società Italiana di Scienza Politica in Naples (28–30 September 2000), at a workshop on realism in Copenhagen, and in various guest lectures at the University of Aalborg, the University of Wales at Aberystwyth, the Free University Amsterdam, the University of Copenhagen, the Norwegian Institute for International Affairs (NUPI), the Institute of International Relations (Prague), the Institute for Liberal Studies (Bucharest), and the University of Warwick. It was also exposed to characteristically undiplomatic critique in two workshop seminars at the late Copenhagen Peace Research Institute. My gratitude for comments, criticisms, and suggestions goes to these audiences and readers, in particular to Pami Aalto, Paul Dragos Aligica, Alexander Astrov, Pavel Barša, Andreas Behnke, Henrik Breitenbauch, Barry Buzan, Walter Carlsnaes, Alessandro Colombo, Petr Drulák, Lene Hansen, Gunther Hellmann, Patrick James, Pertti Joenniemi, Peter Katzenstein, Jan Karlas, Hans Keman, Robert Keohane, Petr Kratochvil, Anna Leander, Halvard Leira, Richard Little, Ian Manners, Michael Merlingen, Mammo Muchie, Iver B. Neumann, Henk Overbeek, Heikki Patomäki, Karen Lund Petersen, Fabio Petito, Liliana Pop, Ben Rosamond, Sten Rynning, Katalin Sárváry, Brian Schmidt, Jiří Sedivý, Ole Jacob Sending, Bastiaan van Apeldoorn, Colin Wight, Jaap de Wilde, Michael Williams, Anders Wivel, Ole Wæver, Maja Zehfuß, and several referees. An earlier version with the same title was published as COPRI Working Paper 43/2001. I finally want to thank Alexander Maxwell for copy-editing the final manuscript. The usual disclaimers apply.

1 In most, but not all, of this chapter, I follow Walt's (2002a: 199) proposal to focus on theories themselves, rather than on individual scholars who might embrace or combine different theories. Therefore, I refer generally to 'realism' (which can sound odd in English), supporting my argument by punctual documentation from the writings of scholars who are considered realists.

Political Science Review. In this blunt attack, Vasquez argued that realists reject the systematic use of scientific criteria for assessing theoretical knowledge. Vasquez charged (neo)realism either for producing blatantly banal statements or for being non-falsifiable, i.e. ideological. A second debate followed an article by Jeffrey Legro and Andrew Moravcsik (1999) in *International Security*. Realists were asked to accept that their recent work was good only because they have incorporated ideas and causal variables from other approaches. Here, realism is not denied scientific status. But by being allotted a small and usually insufficient terrain on the academic turf, realism becomes structurally dependent on a division of theoretical labour defined elsewhere.

Whereas these debates tended to focus on realism's recent developments, this chapter argues that they are but the latest manifestations of two intrinsic and enduring dilemmas of realism in International Relations (IR). I will call them the 'identity dilemma' and the 'conservative dilemma'.

As I will expose in more detail, realism's identity or determinacy/distinctiveness dilemma results from the fact that classical realists, when making more determinate empirical claims, usually relied on explanatory elements which were not genuinely realist. Much of the 'richness of the realist tradition' stems from these wider sources. As this chapter will show, the reason is to be found in the indeterminacy of its central concept of power, which can simply not bear the theoretical weight assigned to it. As long as realism needed no exact delimitation (its vocabulary being often confused with the discipline of IR at large), this was of little theoretical consequence. But in times of open theoretical debate, this necessary eclecticism leads to a dilemma: contemporary realism may be distinct from other approaches at the price of being theoretically indeterminate. It may also produce more determinate hypotheses which are then indistinguishable from (or worse, subsumable by) some other approaches in IR. In other words, while Legro and Moravcsik are right in their critique, they stop short of drawing the full consequences. They ultimately persist in the belief that realism, properly defined, can serve as an adequate explanatory theory. I claim that realist ambiguities are not accidents of recent realist research, but necessary consequences of an enduring theoretical dilemma.

Following Kissinger's (1957: ch. XI) analysis of Metternich, I propose to call the second enduring dilemma of realism the 'conservative' or justification/tradition dilemma. Faced with criticism of realism's scientific character or its findings, I will argue that realists have been repeatedly tempted to lean towards less stringent understandings of their own theory's status. Realism then refers to a philosophical tradition or more generally to 'an attitude regarding the human condition' (Gilpin, 1986 [1984]: 304). Yet, when realists want to retreat to a more 'traditionalist' position, they are caught by a dilemma which has existed since its beginnings in IR. Despite Morgenthau's (1946) early insistence on the intuitions of statesmen and the 'art' of politics, realism derived much of its appeal from its claim to understand reality 'as it is' rather than as it should be (Carr, 1946). But ever since the foreign policy maxims of *realpolitik* have ceased to be commonly shared knowledge or understood as legitimate politics, realism cannot refer to the world as it is and rely on its intuitive understanding by a responsible elite. Instead, it needs to justify the value of traditional practical knowledge and diplomacy. To be persuasive, such a justification comes today in the form of controllable knowledge. Moreover, since realism self-consciously refers to the world 'as it is, not as we would like it to be' (Mearsheimer 2001: 4), it necessarily requires a kind of objective status. In other words, by avoiding justification, realism loses its persuasiveness in times of a rational debate it decides not to address. Alternatively, by consistently justifying a world-view that should be natural and taken for granted, realist defences testify to realism's very demise. Today, there is no way back to a time when realism needed little justification.

In a last section, I draw some implications from these two dilemmas. I will argue that IR realism is fated to return to these dilemmas if it does not give up its own identity of the so-called first debate between realism and idealism. It is this relentlessly reproduced opposition which has generally impoverished IR realism as a branch of political realism – political realism is defined not only by its counter-position to a (utopian) 'ideal', whether or not this has really existed in IR, but also to an 'apparent' masking of existing power relations. It is a two-fold negation, both anti-idealist and anti-conservative. By concentrating on its practical knowledge, not its explanatory theory, and getting out of the 'first debate', IR realism would be free to join in a series of meta-theoretical and theoretical research avenues, which it has heretofore left to other schools. The need to defend IR 'realism' as such seems, therefore, too costly on strictly intellectual grounds – for realists, but also for IR at large.

The identity dilemma: The choice between determinacy and distinctiveness

Which realism?

In a general move to get realism out of the Waltzian straightjacket, it has become a commonplace to point to the diversity of realist writings, old and new (e.g. see Brooks 1997; Guzzini 1998), and this for good reasons. Realists are often at pains to recognize themselves in the portrayal of their detractors. Showing the 'richness of the tradition' can justifiably undermine some of the criticism.

But having nearly as many realisms as realist protagonists also produces a severe problem for realists themselves. At some point, the 'richness' argument begs the question of whether realism is a coherent tradition in the first place. It is paradoxical that IR (and indeed realists themselves) seem unable to agree on a definition of realism when this very school, we are told, has held sway over the discipline for so long. The most recent textbook on realism compares a series of often quite incompatible definitions and ends up with little more than a family resemblance or a certain 'style', concluding that 'we may not be able to define [realism], but we know it when we see it' (Donnelly 2000: 9).

One of the reasons for this difficult definition stems from the original confusion of realism and the early subject matter of IR. Many of the underlying assumptions believed to be unique to realism were not. This includes, most prominently, the micro-assumption of self-interest (and hence, disclaimers notwithstanding, instrumental rationality[2]) and the macro-assumption of anarchy, both widely shared among non-realists who did not dispute the absence of a world government setting international affairs apart from domestic politics, but only its necessity (e.g. see Claude 1962, Czempiel 1981, Deutsch 1968, Senghaas 1987). If defined just in terms of self-help under anarchy, definitions of realism are too encompassing, collapsing realism with the early self-definition of IR. In the recent exchange, for instance, Vasquez (1998: 37) defined the realist paradigm through three tenets, namely, the

---

2 The claim that realism implies a rationality assumption, shared both by realism's detractors (e.g. Keohane 1986: 164–5) and defenders (e.g. Grieco 1988, Glaser 2003), has produced an unnecessary debate. Some realists dispute the need for this assumption (e.g. Waltz 1986: 330–1, Schweller 2003: 324–5). Yet their rejoinder trades on any one of three mistaken arguments – a confusion between the level of action and the level of observation, the indefensible claim that Waltz has provided a purely systemic theory of IR, or the belief that the assumption of rationality has anything to do with the 'power of reason' to achieve progress, as even Kahler (1998) seems to suggest. First, the rationality assumption does not imply that actors always act rationally – they might misperceive, miscalculate, or erroneously think that no trade-off is implied. It simply means that theories which assume self-interest also assume that actors try to further or improve that interest in ways they believe most fit. As a shorthand, observers assume that this happens as if they assessed means for making ends meet in a world of scarcity. Again on the level of observation, this implies that instrumental rationality is a measuring rod with which to assess individual behaviour, whether or not that behaviour is then called rational. Quite logically, classical (e.g. Morgenthau 1962: Part 1, 1965, Wolfers 1962) and modern realists (e.g. Mearsheimer and Walt 2003, Mearsheimer 2001) have spent innumerable pages defending the 'correct' assessment of how to meet the national interest (US security) by improving the means–ends relation in US foreign policies. It is hard to see how Weber, the grandfather of this approach, and his followers in IR (e.g. Aron 1967, Morgenthau 1948) could do otherwise. Second, Waltz claims that his theory is a purely systemic theory in which final behaviour is the effect of socialization – a claim repeated by Schweller. Waltz's internal contradiction of relying both on micro-economics as theoretical inspiration (which, of course, assumes rationality) and some functionalist argument has been exposed in the past – Waltz's theory is in the last resort micro-driven (Ashley 1984, Wendt 1987) and needs a theory of action to function in the first place (Powell 1994, Guzzini 1998: ch. 9). As Wendt (1999) has later shown in more detail, Waltz's approach to 'socialization' falls short of overcoming this. Third, it is true that realists have scorned the possibility of profoundly changing the world through reason. But not believing in the ultimate 'power of reason' has nothing to do with a rational theory of action – individually rational behaviour might be constrained in such a way that its effects make collective or historical progress impossible. Indeed, even in the outspoken critique of liberal rationalism in his early book, Morgenthau defends realism as the correct way to be 'successful and truly "rational" in social action' (1946: 219). Inversely, a (primarily) non-rationalist theory of action can coexist with a progressive theory of history (see Wendt 2003). For a good discussion, see also Brooks (1997: 454).

assumptions of anarchy, of statism, and of politics as the struggle for power and peace. In such a case, it would be more correct, however, to follow Holsti (1985), who calls this wider category the 'classical tradition', which correctly includes non-realists.

A more distinctive definition is therefore warranted. If solely understood as a political theory, I assume that realism is characterized by a particular understanding of the two above-mentioned assumptions (a different way of defining realism will be introduced later). Realism's theory of action is based on a self-interest which is defined in a predominantly materialist way in order to distinguish itself from idealism. Moreover, the macro-assumption does not concern anarchy as such, but a theory of history which is cyclical, that is, pessimistic about progress.[3] It is this vision of history which, in the view of realists, sets realism apart not only from liberalism, but also from other materialist theories, such as Marxism (Gilpin 1987b: 43). The materialist theory of action and the cyclical theory of history together entail that international relations are necessarily a realm of power politics – materialist self-interest must look at the position of individual power and security first.

Looking for distinct definitions of the fundamental assumptions of realism comes with a risk – in the huge realist tradition, there will almost always be an exception. Likewise, some realists may find a description such as mine too narrow, if not consciously skewed in favour of realism's critiques (see e.g. the contributions in Feaver *et al.* 2000, Jervis 2003: 279, fn. 3). Yet, a more restrictive definition has become necessary over past decades, because we are now comparing quite different theories with each other. Realism has become just one box in the typologies of the Inter-Paradigm Debate. These boxes require a logical consistency if one school is to be demarcated from another. It is not fortuitous that in this period realists themselves, such as Waltz in his *Theory of International Politics* (1979), provided such a narrow definition. Hence, although a more narrow definition might look skewed in favour of realism's critiques, it is part of a game realism cannot avoid engaging in – it must find a distinct and logically consistent definition of itself (for this point, see also James 2002: 52).

This produces a tension. Realism is caught between the need to define a more restricted field for realism and the often justified sense that this very narrowness impoverishes 'realism' as compared with some of the work of its classical protagonists. Consequently, there has been a consistent drive to reappropriate more classical (and eclectic) insights – incurring the risk of also including non-specifically realist items once again.

This tension lies at the heart of the identity dilemma of realism in IR: formulations of realism can be either distinct or determinate, but not both.[4] I will argue

---

3 For an explicit statement about the centrality of this assumption in political realism, see Bobbio (1981). It is easily visible in IR realism (e.g. Morgenthau 1946, 1970 [1964], Wight 1966, Gilpin 1981).
4 This critique builds on Guzzini (1998), especially ch. 3.

that the fundamental reason for the realist identity dilemma lies in a concept of power which cannot offer what realism needs from it – an analogous role to money in utilitarian theories.

Power indeterminacy and the micro–macro link in realist theorizing

The concept of power has a demanding task in realist theories.[5] It is essential for a realist theory of action: whether for international anarchy or for reasons of human nature, international actors are bound to look for power, indeed to maximize their power position (or security, regarding which more will be said later). Moreover, 'power', traditionally understood as resources or 'capabilities', has been used as an indicator for the strength of actors, and consequently, of the capacity to affect or even control outcomes. Thus, power provides the micro–macro link of the theory: a general capacity to control outcomes can be used as an indicator for ranking international actors and for the ruling of the international system.[6]

Such a demanding task has, in turn, demanding implications for the very concept of power – it must be measurable (see e.g. Frei 1969, Walt 2002a: 222–3). For those realist scholars who concentrate on the micro-side of realist theory, power must be measurable, since they assume that international actors try to increase (relative) power or influence, something shared by both classical realists (e.g. Morgenthau 1948) and contemporary realists (e.g. Mearsheimer 2001, Zakaria 1998). The very idea of an increase needs a measure in order not to be void or arbitrary. The best increase (or maximization) of power or security is the observer's measuring rod for an efficient foreign policy. Those realists specializing in the macro-level need a measure of power to make sense of the idea of systemic power shifts or the very 'balance' of power. All must have an empirical equivalent of what 'more' power or 'equal' power means. They must have a measure.

Yet, Dahl had already insisted on one conceptual complication which vitiates the easy use of power in utilitarian theories – power is a relational and not a property concept (e.g. Dahl, 1968). Dahl's relational power is fundamentally connected to a Weberian understanding of social action, which also underlies Morgenthau's

---

5 It should be noted that part of this section draws on Guzzini (1993, 2000c).
6 In other words, much of realist IR assumed a double causal link between these two facets, comparable to Dahl's (1961) famous power analysis in *Who Governs?* In a laudable attempt to eliminate tautological power explanations, Mearsheimer (2001: 56) claims that power can only be defined as capabilities, not as control over outcomes. But that will not do. The maximization of power is a means for maximizing security – as Mearsheimer says himself. Maximizing security, however, implies a statement about outcomes, not just resources. If power is a means to an end, such as hegemony or dominance, then it includes an idea of control; if it does not, then realists would make the claim that amassing (military) resources is the end in itself – an (untenable) claim that virtually all contemporary realists shy away from.

theory. Weber understood power as the capacity to influence the other against his or her will. This requires a more interpretivist approach since observers have to assess the will and, hence, the respective value systems of the actors. Consequently, knowing resources does not necessarily say much about actual power, which resides in the specific human interaction or relation. Indeed, it implies that what counts as a power resource in the first place cannot be assessed *ex ante* independently from general norms, the actors' particular value systems, and the specific historical context of the interaction. In this tradition, power is not and cannot be a property concept. Morgenthau (1948: 14 ff.) understood that well when he distinguished between military power as a physical relation and political power, which is fundamentally a psychological relation influencing the other's mind. This parallels the Weberian distinction between violence or force and power. Morgenthau makes clear that military power alone is not enough to understand power relations in IR. But the implication is perhaps wider than Morgenthau himself thought. If resources cannot be independently defined from the interaction or relation, such an analysis is incompatible with the deductive balance of power theory on which narrow realism is based, but also with any attempt to have an *ex ante* theory of behaviour which could claim to be primarily materialist.

But even if we abstract from the relational character of power, even if we grant that all actors want to avoid being possibly threatened by material resources (mainly force), this still begs the question – how much, as compared to other options? Economists can express this in terms of a monetary value. Can political scientists do this with an analogous material value? The received wisdom in political theory would say that they cannot.

A first step in this argument must specify the terms of the analogy. To produce a power-materialist theory of action, one would need to assume an analogy between the role of power in IR and the function of money in neoclassical economics.[7] As Mearsheimer (2001: 12) put it – 'Power is the currency of great-power politics, and states compete for it among themselves. What money is to economics, power is to international relations.' In this analogy, utility (wealth) maximization, which can be expressed and measured in terms of money, parallels the pursuit of the national interest (i.e. security) expressed in terms of (relative) power.

This characterization addresses the debate concerning whether realism implies the maximization of power or security. In a move which allegedly sets neo-realism apart from classical realism, Waltz's theory assumes that actors maximize security, not power. Waltz wants to account for those situations where a further increase in power (then understood as mere capabilities) does not imply an increase in security.

The difference between maximizing power and security is, however, not as clear as it seems, neither in Waltz (for this critique, see also Grieco 1997: 186–91) nor in general. If it just means that power cannot be the final aim, but security,

---

7 For the following, see also Guzzini (1998: 136–7).

then Morgenthau would certainly agree – 'Whatever the ultimate aims of international politics, power is always the immediate aim' (1948: 13). So would Mearsheimer, who states that 'there is no question that great powers maximise security ... by maximising their share of power' (2001: 410 n. 46). No realist would sign a statement that in the pursuit of their national interest, states are expected to, or indeed rationally *should*, increase power even if it harmed their security. That a permanent worst-case assumption in the pursuit of power can produce a self-defeating strategy (if not a self-fulfilling prophecy) which a prudent statesman tries to avoid is old hat for classical realists (it is one of the central themes in Wolfers 1962), only to be rediscovered by defensive realists (Glaser 2003).

If, however, this distinction implies that, for a realist, security can be thought of totally independent from the pursuit of power, then it seems to contradict realism. Security might not be entirely reducible to relative gains for all realists, but it is never independent of it (see also James 2002: 52), just as in classical realism. In other words, (neo)realists assume states to have an aim of security which includes as means (or as an immediate aim) being rank maximizers, i.e. relative gain seekers. Important for my argument, and consistent with realism, is that such gains be measured on a common scale (the final rank), which realists commonly establish with reference to power.

After having established the terms of the analogy, we can now, in a second step, assess its validity. Here also, looking back into the literature is enough. In an astonishingly overlooked argument, Raymond Aron opposed this very transfer of economic theory to IR theory some 40 years ago. First, for Aron, it made empirically little sense to liken the maximization of security as expressed in power to the maximization of utility as expressed in terms of money. Based on historical evidence, Aron (1962: 28–9) argued that there are three classical foreign policy goals (*puissance*, security, and glory or ideals – here following Hobbes!) that cannot be reduced one into the other. Without a single aim, no optimal rational choice could occur. In the language of rational choice, foreign policy is indeterminate since alternative ends are incommensurable. If this were correct, then rational choice theorists (e.g. Elster 1989: 31–3) would accept that their approach cannot be applied for explanatory purposes (see also Guzzini 1994: 83–6).

Aron's claim is based on what the literature calls the different degree of 'fungibility' of money and power resources which undergirds the necessary multidimensionality of power. The term 'fungibility' refers to the idea of a moveable good that can be freely substituted by another of the same class. Fungible goods are those that are universally applicable or convertible, in contrast to those that retain value only in a specific context. Fungibility seems a plausible assumption in monetarized economies. In international politics, however, even apparently ultimate power resources, such as weapons of mass destruction, might not necessarily be of great help for getting another state to change its monetary policies.[8]

---

8 For the argument on fungibility, see in particular Baldwin (1980: 502).

Aron did, of course, recognize that economic theory can be used to model behaviour on the basis of a variety of preferences that also conflict. But for him, with the advent of money as a general standard of value within which these competing preferences could be put on the same scale, compared, and traded off, economists were able to reduce the variety of preferences to one utility function. In world politics, power lacks real-world fungibility, and thus cannot play a corresponding role as a standard of value. Without the power–money analogy, there is also no analogy between the integrated value of utility and the 'national interest' (security) (Guzzini 1993: 453). Consequently, in a chapter section appropriately entitled 'The Indeterminacy of Diplomatic-Strategic Behaviour', Aron (1962: 102) concludes that (realist) theoreticians in IR cannot use economic theory as a model.

Responding to Aron, Waltz (1990) acknowledged the centrality of Aron's argument, but said that the analogy between power and money was not vitiated by a qualitative difference. Rather, the problem was simply one of more complicated measurement. Power, Waltz argued, does nonetheless function as a medium of exchange. Similarly, when taken to issue by Keohane (1986: 184) on the fungibility assumption, Waltz remained unimpressed, answering:

> Obviously, power is not as fungible as money. Not much is. But power is much more fungible than Keohane allows. As ever, the distinction between strong and weak states is important. The stronger the state, the greater the variety of its capabilities. Power may be only slightly fungible for weak states, but it is highly so for strong ones.
>
> *(Waltz 1986: 333)*

Waltz's defence, however, is inconsistent. If power resources were so highly fungible that they could be used in different domains, then one does not need to argue with their variety: military or economic capabilities could be used for producing political, social, or cultural outcomes. If, however, one assumes a great variety of capabilities, one implicitly assumes that a strong actor is strong not because it has a lot of overall power, but because it possesses a high level of capabilities in distinct domains.

This is still no case for the fungibility of power. As a result, it is simply guesswork regarding how to aggregate power resources – there is no case for a 'lump' concept of power, as balance of power theories would require.[9] For if power resources cannot be necessarily aggregated, we have lost the indicator for predicting control over outcomes. Without this, we have no link to the final aim of security. What in the wake of the Vietnam War was called the 'paradox of unrealised power' (Baldwin 1979: 169) can always be rearranged by saying that another resource would have been more significant or (the *deus ex machina* of

---

9 Hence, by simply requoting Waltz, and then going on with business as usual, Zakaria (1998: 19, fn. 24) does not prove anything.

ex post fixing) that actors lacked the will to use their existing resources. Resources never fail, politicians and analysts do.

In view of these intrinsic theoretical problems, early institutionalist writers have criticized balance of power theories for assuming a single international power structure (Keohane and Nye 1977). They argued that if power is segmented, that is, if capacities are issue specific, then the positioning of power in a general balance is guesswork. As Baldwin has shown some time ago, a single international power structure relies either on the assumption of a single dominant issue area or on a high fungibility of power resources. Since both are of little avail, it 'is time to recognize that the notion of a single overall international power structure unrelated to any particular issue area is based on a concept of power that is virtually meaningless' (Baldwin 1979: 193).[10]

Given this central, albeit weak dimension of their theory, even sophisticated realist theoreticians have resorted to rhetoric instead of arguments for defending their position. Hedley Bull, for instance, after assessing the difficulties in constructing an 'over-all' concept of power, candidly writes that the 'relative position of states in over-all power nevertheless makes itself apparent in bargaining among states, and the conception of over-all power is one we cannot do without' (1977: 114). His first argument, deriving power *ex post* from its effects, comes close to the usual power tautologies. The second argument confuses the theoretical and practical levels.

It is precisely this confusion between the theoretical level and the level of actual politics on which Robert Art's and David Baldwin's most recent exchange on fungibility trades (Art 1996, 1999, Baldwin 1999). Art responds to Baldwin's by now classical, if neglected, theoretical charge by moving to the level of state actors' perception and action (Art 1999: 184–6). By this move, Baldwin's critique is reinterpreted to imply that policy-makers have no way to devise overall power measures. And then, Art has little difficulty in showing that they at least try to do so all the time.

But Art's argument is based on the initial move, which is a category mistake and hence does not add up to a rebuttal to Baldwin. Of course, Art is right that policy-makers can and often do come up with an idea of overall power and ranking. But what does that mean for realist *theory*? It means that rankings could differ according to historical circumstances, and various positions and assumptions policy-makers may have about the composition of material capabilities and the fungibility of such elements. This is, hence, a contentious issue for deliberation and potentially subjective assessment. Gorbachev apparently thought that military might was not all that important at the end of the day and changed course. Any measure, if politically shared and hence dominant, will do.

10 Indeed, some realists agree and draw the far-reaching conclusion that 'trying to think in terms of aggregate power has led, *inter alia*, to the overambitious and inconclusive debate about polarity and war' (Buzan, Little and Jones 1993: 61).

Indeed, if power assessments were not in principle malleable, it would make little sense to see so many writers, including Art (but also Joseph Nye (1990b) in 'Soft Power'), try to make our understandings of power converge on which resources 'really' count. But that is not what happens with money. With €10 we can generally expect to get goods which have no more expensive a price tag than €10, independent of whether we have a subjective feeling we should. Hence, having no real-life equivalent of money does not make a measure as such impossible, but it is not standardized. Moreover, this standard is necessary for making realist theorizing about 'increase or maximization' useful for a rationalist theory.[11] As Baldwin has reminded us before, to make the power–money analogy work, power needs to be an (objectivized) standardized measure of value, as well. Apparently, it is not (Baldwin 1993a: 21–2). For this reason, the repeated attempts to base realist theorizing on a power and influence improving or maximizing aim cannot be theoretically defended.

This discussion leads, therefore, away from realism to two constructivist points. First, although Bull and Art can easily show that diplomats might agree on some approximations for their dealings, this is not because they have an objectivized measure, but because they have come to agree on one. Far from being a materialist necessity, it is a social (and often politically bargained) construct. In classical diplomacy, with its arbitrations and compensations, diplomats must find a common understanding of overall power. Diplomats must first agree on what counts before they can start counting.[12]

This leads to a second and related constructivist point. Debates about the fungibility of power are part and parcel of the measure of power. Defining power is not an innocent analytical act – it is part of politics. Since it is not standardized, definitions influence the value of resources in power relations, the way power is assessed, and hence the way politics as the art of the possible is understood and conducted (for constructivism and conceptual analysis, see Guzzini 2002b). 'Defining the national interest' is in itself an act of power which affects what is politically thinkable and legitimate.

This leads to the conclusion that overall power is no objectively deductible variable. An interest in security, expressed as the maximization of rank through power, is indeterminate since, whether or not such a single aim exists, it cannot be expressed on one standardized yardstick. Consequently, the national interest expressed in terms of rank and 'power' is a hollow shell which has been, and indeed can only be, filled by auxiliary hypotheses on preference formation, be they liberal, institutionalist, or sociological, if inspired by a constructivist meta-theory (for the latter, see e.g. Weldes 1996).

11 Hence, it is not enough to footnote this exchange as a proof for the fungibility case in favour of realism, as in Deudney (2000: 10, fn. 22).
12 In this specific sense, measures of wealth and measures of power are similar, since they are institutional facts which only exist because people believe in them (see the classical money example in Searle 1995). Yet, as argued earlier, they differ in the amount of institutionalization and, hence, objectification they have in the real world.

As a result, realism needs to add something. Invariably realists have been relaxing their materialist assumptions. On the micro-level, for instance, Kissinger (1969) insisted upon diplomatic skills and types of foreign policy personalities and Morgenthau (1970 [1967]: 245) claimed that power cannot be equated with military might and is basically unmeasurable outside qualitative judgement (typically left unspecified). Once this micro–macro link had been forgone (not being able to deduce 'who governs' from resources) realists qualified the macro-level of anarchy. They defined different types of international systems that cannot be reduced to simple power polarity or polarization. Wolfers (1962: ch. 6) theorized amity and enmity along a continuum from the pole of power to the pole of indifference. Kissinger (1957: 1–3) distinguished revolutionary from legitimate international systems, while Aron (1962: 108–13) contrasted homogeneous with heterogeneous systems.

Among contemporary neoclassical realists, William Wohlforth explicitly relaxes materialist assumptions and joins adjacent terrain not because he downplays the concept of power, but because he thoughtfully engages with it. He faces the fact that power is not part of the solution to realist explanatory problems, but part of the problem (Guzzini 1993) – for all its centrality in the theory, 'power cannot be tested' (Wohlforth 1993: 306). Working from the indeterminacy of any realist power theory and the impossibility of measuring power, Wohlforth looks for a very situation-specific and interpretivist analysis of International Relations, giving special place to non-material capabilities and perceptions in an anarchical environment which is not primarily material, but social (for the last point, see Wohlforth 2003: 265 fn. 1).

Probably all classical realists have travelled on institutionalist or constructivism-inspired terrain. Blurring realist distinctiveness purchased better explanations, but the cost incurred has risen. When, in the wake of the Inter-Paradigm Debate, realism became just one theory among others, the present identity dilemma emerged – either realists keep a distinct and single micro–macro link through concepts of power and influence which, given the nature of the concept, provides indeterminate explanations or they improve their explanations, but must do so by relaxing their assumptions, hence losing distinctiveness.

Realism as indistinguishable science: 'Has anybody ever been a realist?'

The somewhat ironic implication of this argument is that if one defines realism as a coherent, distinct and determinate theory, there has indeed never been such a thing as a realist theory – the question is not 'Is anybody still a realist?', but 'Has anybody ever been a realist?'

It is only natural that, in response to its critiques, realists would refer to some classical thinkers to get out of the Waltzian straightjacket (Feaver et al. 2000). Although this argument contains some truth, realists draw the wrong implications, for a simple enlargement will only put realism back into the same dilemma. As the preceding section has argued, the assumptions and basic concepts of realist theorizing inevitably call for borrowing from elsewhere. In this, the present realist amendments to Waltz simply pursue a necessity already encountered by earlier realists. Indeed, the present critique is but a reiteration of Michael Banks's description of the 'hoover-effect' of realism, that is, its tendency to swallow everything valuable stemming from other paradigms. He called this strategy 'realism-plus-grafted-on-components' (Banks 1984: 18). The repeated realist endeavour to widen, and the repeated resistance of others to let this be *in the name of realism*, exemplify this basic dilemma of realism, once it is no longer the taken-for-granted language of IR and needs to be differentiated and justify itself. This problem lies within realist theorizing itself, not with its use by its detractors.

The 'conservative dilemma': The choice between tradition and justification

Legro and Moravcsik put the stakes very high – what should be the normal science of IR? They ask for a multi-paradigmatic synthesis on the basis of a causal theory of action which takes into account a variety of factors that can be linked to the four schools of thought they mention.[13] Indeed, they ask that any analysis start from such a multi-paradigmatic setting, and not from any version of realism. Realist explanations become one type among others, almost never sufficient alone and often, depending on the initial conditions, not even applicable.

Despite its similar outlook, such a move undermines the realist defence that all is about the specification of scope conditions (Schweller 1997). The difference lies in the understanding of indeterminacy and hence the sequence of the argument. Realists put scope conditions second. The analysis starts with a very parsimonious, realist structural account (e.g. Waltz) and is only subsequently qualified (the same strategy applies for the inclusion of other levels of analysis, see Sterling-Folker 1997). I think detractors are right to suggest that this stacks the deck too much in favour of realism. If indeterminacy derived just from the parsimony of materialist structural theorizing, then a later scope condition might work. Once it is understood that power is not strong enough to provide realism with a theory of action, the necessary micro–macro link, the very materialist

---

13 Such a synthesis with its exclusive emphasis on behaviour must leave out theories which at least partly focus their explanations on the reproduction of structures. This applies to purely holistic theories, but also all theories with a dual ontology (agency and structure), such as post-Gramscian approaches interested in the reproduction of the structures of power, or constructivist explanations interested in the reproduction of intersubjective life-worlds of meaning, or 'cultures', as in Wendt (1999). Indeed, Wendt is consciously trying to provide an even more encompassing theory in which the conditions for these individualist action theories are spelled out.

structural theorizing itself is at stake. As a result, scholars have to deal with the underlying reason for indeterminacy from the start.[14] As a result, a primarily materialist explanation in terms of the pursuit of power or security becomes just one possible starting point for which certain conditions need first to be united. Choosing realism would have to wait.

This implies that realism would become a sub-theory subsumed under a wider and, therefore, more encompassing theory. It is only in this particular, but very important sense that the realist rejoinders had a point when they saw in Legro and Moravcsik's writings an attempted hostile takeover. Realism would be reduced to the place where it is already for all non-realists – a special case in need of justification. For instance, the simple argument that materialism matters (see Feaver *et al.* 2000), in turn, no longer matters, since all other theories have always been able to integrate that component. What made the 'neo–neo debate' (Wæver 1996) so futile from the start is that Keohane *et al.* were not arguing that realists were always wrong – they simply tried to define the conditions under which they were. Neorealist defences, therefore, often missed the point, at least for the non-realist (see the debate in Baldwin 1993b).

But more than any other theory, realism cannot be comfortable with being subsumed under a theoretical roof which, by necessity, is not realist, for realism has always claimed an inherent superiority for its supposed closeness to reality. That reality *is* and it cannot only *sometimes be,* for then Pandora's box is open again regarding the limits of realism and 'its' reality.

Consequently, realism has to find a different line of defence. It is not allowed to cover the universe of IR either by expanding such as to include assumptions and causal variables from competitors or by defining purely theory-internal scope conditions. In this situation, one could construct a last logical defence by simply ditching the very need to justify realism and returning to business as usual – the problem lies with an erroneous conception of science, not with realism. Indeed, such a defence of IR realism has been proposed by Kenneth Waltz, whose recent anti-positivism can, however, no longer be considered at all representative of mainstream, contemporary IR realism. Yet, it does include a recurrent theme typical of realism as understood in this chapter – the reality check for a theory ultimately refers to the world of practice, not knowledge. I will use Waltz's last turn as a foil to exemplify the inherent logic of the second dilemma, i.e. the 'conservative dilemma of realism'.

The conservative dilemma of the realist tradition in IR

If realism is to be understood within the discipline of IR, this article applies a different type of definition. As in my earlier study (Guzzini 1998: ix–x), I define

---

14 This is supported by Waltz (1997), who consistently rejects the adding of variables such as perception and so on as extensions of his theory; for him, they do not fix, but abandon his theory.

realism in IR as a scholarly tradition characterized by the repeated, and for its basic indeterminacy repeatedly failed, attempt to translate the practical rules or maxims of European diplomacy into the scientific laws of a US social science. Realist IR scholars have always faced the same basic dilemma: either they update the practical knowledge of a shared diplomatic culture, but then lose scientific credibility, or reaching for logical persuasiveness, they cast their maxims in a scientific mould, but end up distorting their practical knowledge.

In 'Metternich and the Conservative Dilemma', one of the most evocative chapters ever written by a realist on realism, Kissinger (1957) depicts several facets of the politics of conservatism in a revolutionary era, a politics necessarily tragic. Conservatives must openly defend what should be tacitly taken for granted; they must strive for socialized values in a time in which values have become self-conscious. Put in the limelight of contestation and conflict, the conservative has three answers:

> fighting as anonymously as possible, has been the classic conservative reply ... To fight for conservatism in the name of historical forces, to reject the validity of the revolutionary question because of its denial of the temporal aspect of society and the social contract – this was the answer of Burke. To fight the revolutionary in the name of reason, to deny the validity of the question on epistemological grounds, as contrary to the structure of the universe – this was the answer of Metternich.
>
> *(Kissinger 1957: 193)*

But Metternich's answer confronted the same dilemma:

> While Metternich desperately attempted to protect 'reality' against its enemies, the issue increasingly became a debate about its nature and the nature of 'truth'. Had 'reality' still proved unambiguous, he would not have needed to affirm it. By the increasing insistence of his affirmation, he testified to its disintegration.
>
> *(Kissinger 1957: 202)*

Morgenthau stays paradigmatic with regard to this birth defect of realism in international relations in his attempt to preserve the rules of a conservative diplomacy of the 18th century in a 20th century in which nationalism, and to some extent democracy, had destroyed the very basis for its rule. Like Metternich, he does not concede the 'truly rational' (see Note 2) ground to adversaries, but confronts them on the question of 'the world as it really is'. Like Metternich, he eventually has to confront an audience which, by his very insistence on his realism, starts to question whether it is all that self-evident and natural.

Morgenthau follows a realist ritual in opposing what he perceives as dangerous idealist pipedreams. Interestingly enough, his opponents were initially the 'scientific men' of the enlightenment (Morgenthau 1946). Here, Morgenthau is still the (German) romantic, conservative critic of rationalism. Successive editions of his famous *Politics Among Nations* show his conversion to a rationalist conservatism.

Morgenthau's conversion to a 'scientific' self-image is best understood as an adaptation to his new environment. In crossing the Atlantic, the maxims of *realpolitik* became exposed to a political culture and foreign policy tradition defined in opposition to European foreign policy culture. He perceived it as much less accepting of the categorical distinction between the internal and the external aspects of politics, let alone the *Primat der Außenpolitik*.

Morgenthau tried his best to convince his adopted country(wo)men that such a world-view was useless before the disaster that had shattered the world in the midst of the last century. For him, such naivety had been responsible for the calamity. His approach combined the outlook of aristocratic European diplomacy with the new challenges that arose as societies became more tightly integrated and mobilized, and as legitimacy and domestic sovereignty became increasingly bound to broad popular consent (Morgenthau 1948: 74).

IR would be the academic support for the diffusion of the practical knowledge shared by the former Concert of Europe. Though diplomatic culture could no longer be reproduced by a transnational and often aristocratic elite, science was there to help the new elites to come to grips with the nature of international politics as conceived by realists. It is at this point that the evolution of realism, the perception of world politics from a US foreign policy perspective, and of the discipline of IR became inextricably linked. To enable the pre-eminent international power to fulfil its responsibilities, Morgenthau packaged the practical realist maxims of scepticism and policy prescriptions into a rational and 'scientific' approach.

But then Morgenthau faced the conservative dilemma. If realism is practical knowledge, then it can be said to exist in the cumulative lessons of history shared by a diplomatic community; it does not need explicit justification. Yet, if the same realist maxims are no longer or not necessarily self-evident and need justification in our democratic times, this foundation cannot simply rely on tradition; instead, it must argue with evidence which can be intersubjectively shared. To defend realism, Morgenthau was forced to take the second road, although he might have believed in the first.

For this reason, it is against the very tradition of realism to try to diminish its scientific status – a return to pure tradition would merely return it to the conservative dilemma. It would undermine the traditional appeal of realism, i.e. its claim to be analytical, unlike normative idealism. Realism brought positivity to IR. As Chris Brown (1992: 90) has very rightly pointed out, this pressure to be 'scientific' is, to some extent, preordained by the realist world-view itself. Realism claims to refer to an unproblematic reality, a claim that must invite objectivist methods. Retreating from this claim might save a classical version of realism – one which, however, is then hardly distinguishable from the wider classical tradition. Here, the second dilemma meets the first.

A critique of science as a defence of realism

It is curious to note that when realism is criticized from the more scientific branches of the discipline, some of its defenders easily embrace anti-scientific, if not anti-positivist ideas. Earlier, in the second debate, realists simply brushed aside any empirically controlled critiques of realist analyses, be they quantitative or not, as Morgenthau (1970 [1964], 1970 [1967]) and Bull (1966) famously did. Later, more explicit meta-theoretical and post-positivist arguments were used. When Bruce Bueno de Mesquita (1985) attacked IR for lacking scientificity, Stephen Krasner (1985b) retorted by (correctly) showing that even Lakatos is 'debating in an arena which has been defined by Kuhn, an arena in which the traditional view of science has been severely undermined'. In particular, Krasner argued that meaning and topic incommensurability, as well as competing normative prescriptions and 'the complex but often intimate relations with external communities', make claims about progressive shifts *across* paradigms extremely difficult. Basically, the discipline can only debate *within* given paradigms. After Krasner, Waltz (1997) and Wohlforth (2003) responding to Vasquez as well as Hellmann (Feaver *et al.* 2000: 169–74) responding to Legro and Morvacsik have also argued that if the science of IR encounters troubles with realism, this is not because realism is wrong, but because IR should not be a (positivist?) 'science'. Is no further justification needed?

I will concentrate on the most radical anti-positivist version, since it would provide the ideal solution to the conservative dilemma – it opposes the terms in which the dilemma is posed. In my reading, it comes in a version of scientific pragmatism, implicitly exposed in Waltz's answer to Vasquez. There, Waltz argues that science is actually not really possible, hence justification not conclusive, and therefore his theory is as good as one can get.[15] Hence, realism should be allowed to continue according to the pragmatist attitude that if it is not broken, do not fix it.

Waltz's (1997) rejoinder to Vasquez's critique seems to indicate the final destination of a journey he started with his *Theory of International Politics*. Increasingly, the underlying ambiguity of his concept of 'theory' is apparent. Waltz wanted scientific status for his theory. He appealed to some scientific respectability by using a neoclassical economic analogy and distinguished his theory from mere realist 'thought' (Waltz 1990). Yet even then, he was already careful to point out that positivist standards cannot really apply. Still, whereas his book talked about 'testing' theories against empirical evidence (Waltz 1979: 16, 123), the caveats about science have become much more prominent.

This curious use of 'theory' to evade the need for theoretical justification is probably based on a radicalized pragmatic understanding of science. This only

---

15 In a later rejoinder prefacing a book on the use of Lakatos for IR, Waltz openly endorses a post-positivist reading of Lakatos – 'Lakatos's assaults crush the crassly positivist ideas about how to evaluate theories that are accepted by most political scientists. He demolishes the notion that one can test theories by pitting them against facts' (2003: xii).

probable interpretation is based on the fact that Waltz has already used a Friedman-inspired pragmatic (yet then positivist) position for his book. Waltz retained three main features. First, in good non-empiricist manner, 'data does not speak for itself' – what counts as a fact is theory dependent. Second, assumptions and central concepts have to be as parsimonious as possible, but not realistic as long as they show empirical fit. Lastly, and contrary to the falsificationist ideal, this empirical fit is defined in a much weaker, 'pragmatic' way, since he admits that the distribution of power is actually difficult to assess and hence not really usable for disconfirming balance of power hypotheses (Waltz 1979: 124).

Now, Waltz even more explicitly restricts this position by claiming that 'success in explaining, not in predicting, is the ultimate criterion of good theory' (Waltz 1997: 916). Leaving aside the ambivalence of the term 'ultimate', this statement sits very uncomfortably with Friedman's positivist pragmatism. Here, being lax at the start by defining unrealistic assumptions is only possible because it is coupled with stringent tests at the end. This testing is done on explanation and prediction, since positivists do not see any qualitative difference between the two – the law of gravity explains past events in the same way as it predicts future events under similar conditions. Indeed, the stress on prediction is important for positivists since it allows the only really independent check of the empirical fit of a theory. Gary Becker (1986 [1976]), for instance, was always unhappy about economic explanations in terms of 'revealed preferences', since they could rearrange anything *ex post facto*.

With these moves, Waltz has systematically ruled out theoretical checks via (realistic) assumptions, (possible) predictions, and empirical testing. Here, the radical pragmatic argument comes in – the real world strikes back on those states who do not pursue policies that fall within the range of structural imperatives (Waltz 1997: 915). But *knowing* about this check then miraculously escapes the theory dependence of facts which he used to undermine stringent tests of his theory. Indeed, this question never actually arises, for this check occurs on another level altogether. Waltz does not care much about the 'artificial' world of researchers who devise tests for the explanation they put forward. He thinks about the more powerful vengeance of the material, 'real' world when its 'laws' are not observed. The check appears neither in the theoretical nor the controlled empirical world, but in the world of practice. In a curious way, Waltz's response divorces the world of knowledge entirely from the historical (and material) world, to be linked up through foreign policy practice. Put differently, Waltz argues for a theory dependence of facts when it serves to show that theories cannot be falsified (world of knowledge). There is, however, also a structural dependence of *policies* (world of practice) which can be used to check his theory (the link between the two). He does not answer, however, how we would actually *know* what this link is. How does Waltz know *what* actually struck back or that there was a strike to start with? Hence, this pragmatic position produces a huge justification deficit not only for defending its claims (which it admits), but for the initial choice of this theory as compared to any other.

Not having a justification for his theory choice is moreover important, since as with all realist theories in the past, Waltz's theory is easily criticizable for its potentially self-fulfilling effects. Contrary to constructivism, and consonant with positivism, Waltz seems to hold that the social and natural world are similar, at least in so far as, in materialist fashion, they are independent of the way we think about them. Positivists hold that basically there is no difference between the natural and the social sciences *and* that the subject (observer) to object relationship is unproblematic for the basic independence of the world from our thoughts. Constructivists hold that the *social* world is dependent on the way we think about it.[16] Now, how does Waltz know that actors inspired by his understanding (which cannot be empirically checked) are not reproducing the very things he sees in the world? Wendt, and decades of peace research, have argued quite conclusively that if everybody believed that they lived in a jungle, the world would look alike.[17]

In short, Waltz asks us to accept a theory (1) whose premises might be unrealistic, (2) which cannot be assessed in comparison with other theories, and (3) which informs explanations which cannot be assessed empirically, but (4) which should influence our thinking about the real world and hence our actions in foreign affairs (as if our thinking and actions are independent of that very real world) lest we be punished by the laws of the international structure for whose existence we have no proof. Consequently, this position has a permanent justification deficit and eventually does not escape the conservative dilemma of realism.

No pragmatist way out of the realist dilemma

I myself would defend realist reactions to empiricism or Lakatosian falsificationism (e.g. Walt 1997, Wohlforth 2003). But again, as with the first dilemma, realists draw the wrong implications. For even if we assume that Lakatos's sophisticated falsificationism is not tenable for the social sciences, this still does not make a case for returning to meta-theoretical business as usual on the grounds that realism's meta-theoretical value will be eventually decided by history or, as James (2002: 72) put it, by 'naturally occurring processes in society as a whole'. This defence simply begs the question and asks for even more meta-theory, not less (Elman and Elman 2002). It just reaffirms the conservative dilemma, for the classical tradition, including realism, would have no reason to be believed more than any other. Hence, when pragmatist arguments are taken seriously, they do not defend realism – as shown by the (fallen) realist Hellmann (2000), who eventually argued for retaining the common language of the entire classical tradition, be it realist or idealist.

---

16 For a discussion of constructivist tenets, see Guzzini (2000a).
17 For a discussion of the link between peace research and constructivism, see Guzzini (2004a).

Such a justification does not need to come in the form of formal modelling, as feared by many and expressed by Stephen Walt (1999). There are interpretivist versions of rationalism. But, surely, to have some wider appeal, it must come in a defence of the conceptual coherence of the theory, which this chapter seeks to question, and in some further assessment of how the empirical and theory interact and can be assessed between contending approaches (such as the 'trial' analogy advanced by Kratochwil 2000a). Perhaps it would make the life of qualitative research in IR easier if its defenders would refrain from simultaneously attempting to salvage realism's identity in IR, an endeavour which this chapter sees as basically impossible. It is here, again, where the two dilemmas meet.

Learning the lessons of the dilemmas: The trap of the perpetual first debate

Until now, this chapter has tried to show that realist debates are bound to reappear for two reasons intrinsic to the realist tradition. I have used present and previous debates to show that there is a systematic theoretical problem with the way realist theorizing has developed within IR which consists in not facing what I have dubbed the identity and the conservative dilemmas of realism in IR. If the dilemmas are left untouched, they provoke a continuing return to such debates, a necessary turning in circles, despite the increasing effect of overkill to which this chapter obviously contributes. For avoiding such a stale return, I want to argue, at last, that realism should try to get out of the vicious circle of critique and anti-critique into which it has trapped itself by perpetuating the often virtual 'realism–idealism' debate.

Realism as a twofold negation and the trap of the realism–idealism debate

In what follows, I argue that one of the underlying reasons why many realists do not face the implications of the identity (distinctiveness/determinacy) and the conservative (justification/tradition) dilemmas comes from the terms of the first debate, in which many realists feel compelled to justify realism. According to this self-understanding, realists are there to remind us about the fearful, cruel side of world politics. This distinct face of international politics inevitably appears when the diplomatic masquerade is over and world history picks up its circular course. By trying to occupy a vantage point of (superior) historical experience, science came as an offer that IR realism could not refuse.

IR realism has repeatedly been thought to have no other choice but to justify this pessimism by distancing itself from other positions, to be non-subsumable. It needed to show that whatever else might temporarily be true, there is an unflinching reality which cannot be avoided. Realism needed to point to a reality which cannot be eventually overcome by politics, to an attitude which would similarly rebuff the embrace of any other intellectual tradition. The 'first debate' is usually presented as the place in which this 'negative' attitude has been played out, indeed mythically enshrined. It is to this metaphorical foundation to which many self-identified realists return.

Yet, I think that the 'first debate' is a place where the thoughts not only of so-called idealist scholars, but also of self-styled realists are unduly impoverished exactly because they are couched in terms of an opposition. When scholars more carefully study this type of opposition, however, they quickly find out that many so-called realist scholars have been critical not only of utopian thought and social engineering, but also of *realpolitik*. In other words, political realism is not simply an attitude of negation, but of a twofold negation – in the words of R.N. Berki, realism must oppose both the conservative idealism of nostalgia and the revolutionist idealism of imagination (1981: 268–9, Griffiths 1992: 159).

Norberto Bobbio (1996: xiv–xvii) has developed this twofold negation in his usual lucid style as both a (conservative) realism which opposes the 'ideal' and a (critical) realism which opposes the 'apparent', a difference too few realists have been able to disentangle. For this double heritage of political realism is full of tensions. Realism as anti-idealism is status quo oriented. It relies on the entire panoply of arguments so beautifully summarized by Alfred Hirschman (1991). According to the *futility* thesis, any attempt at change is condemned to be without any real effect. The *perversity* thesis would argue that far from changing things for the better, such policies only add new problems to the already existing ones. In addition, the central *jeopardy* thesis says that purposeful attempts at social change will only undermine the already achieved. The best is the enemy of the good, and so on. Anti-apparent realism, however, is an attitude more akin to the political theories of suspicion. It looks at what is hidden behind the smokescreen of current ideologies, putting the allegedly self-evident into the limelight of criticism. With the other form of realism it shares a reluctance to accept beautiful ideas as what they claim to be. But it is much more sensitive to the ideological use of such ideas, revolutionary as well as conservative. Whereas anti-ideal realism defends the status quo, anti-apparent realism questions it. It wants to unmask existing power relations.

Some realists, such as E.H. Carr and Susan Strange, have oscillated between these two versions of realism.[18] Both have been strong critics of the status quo, not because it was wrongly led into a kind of utopianism, but because the ideological clothing used by the great powers of the day (the UK and France, and the USA, respectively), whether brandishing an apparent 'harmony of interests' or suggesting that 'there is no alternative', masked their power and responsibility. For Carr, this oscillation was necessary, since 'The impossibility of being a consistent and thorough-going realist is one of the most certain and most curious lessons of political science' (1946: 89).

---

18 For a more thorough discussion, see respectively Guzzini (2000b, 2001b). For the inclusion of Strange in the realist tradition, see also Guzzini (1998: 176–83).

Consequently, a privileged way for realists to learn from their endemic dilemmas would be to acknowledge the 'first debate' for the ritual it is (Thies 2002). On a purely disciplinary level, Brian Schmidt (1998, 2002) has already convincingly shown that the interwar period experienced no debate reducible to two camps coherently labelled 'idealists' and 'realists'. Similarly, many recent scholars on the realist tradition have emphasized the hybrid character of many of its more prominent protagonists, making them indistinguishable from some 'idealists'. Griffiths (1992) shows how Hedley Bull, often not included in the realist canon, comes much closer to a genuine realist position than Morgenthau and Waltz, both judged to be nostalgic or complacent idealists. In the most recent textbook on realism, Jack Donnelly comes to the conclusion that the (better) realist tradition, as exemplified by Herz and Carr, is the one which kept '"realist" insights in dialectical tension with wider human aspirations and possibilities' – a sense of balance 'sorely lacking in leading figures such as Morgenthau, Waltz, and Mearsheimer' (Donnelly 2000: 193, 195).

Realists should not recoil from the logical implication Donnelly's argument entails. If it is true that scholars such as Carr and Herz best express the 'nature' of the realist tradition, then the scholars most faithful to the realist tradition are paradoxically the most 'hedged', i.e. the least faithful to its assumptions and defining characteristics in the realist–idealist debate. It is only in this context that the unusually candid sentence on Donnelly's (2000) back cover makes sense – 'Donnelly argues that common realist propositions . . . are rejected by many leading realists as well.' This shows that the idealism of the continuing first debate is first and foremost the continuously reinvented 'other' logically required to make realist rhetoric and thought work in the first place (Guzzini 1998: 16), but rarely one which would be opposed in its entirety by leading realists, in particular the classical (and perhaps also the neoclassical) ones (Thies 2002).

In other words, I think it is counter-productive to defend IR realism's integrity at any price. In my understanding, it would be more coherent to accept that realism is a practical tradition which has not succeeded in translating its maxims into an explanatory theory. As a consequence, some of the 'realist' writings are good precisely because they are at variance with any realism narrowly and distinctively defined.

Instead of hunting after an elusive scientific theory of power politics, this is a non-realist's plea to concentrate on realism's practical knowledge, prudence, and sense of contingency. As should be expected, it is nothing new, but just another round in this continuing story of the realism debates. It joins, among others, Ashley's (1981) re-reading of Herz, Walker's (1989) plea to move realism beyond the determinism in Hobbes, and Kratochwil's (1993) focus on Kennan and realist practice.

Limits and opportunities of accepting the dilemmas

Some self-identifying realists (as much as some of their opponents) might not be ready to give up these wonderful identity-providing oppositions. For realism, moreover, this choice would be perceived as costly, since it implies the paradox that realist thought might be best served by abandoning the brand-name of IR realism and exploring the possibilities and limits of realism as a twofold negation. But, of course, no theoretical family feels immediately comfortable when having to embrace new bedfellows, let alone sleeping in new beds. Worse, thinking of realism as a twofold negation, while a more coherent way to account for a realist tradition, is no theoretical nirvana either. Rob Walker (1987: 85–6) has long argued that it is not clear why we should start from these dichotomies in the first place. Lastly, the feedback from the language of practitioners, in which the opposition between idealism and realism often prevails as the foundational dichotomy, makes such attempts difficult indeed, and seems to undermine one of the alleged strengths of realism as classically conceived – the resemblance of academics' and practitioners' language.

But perhaps realists are increasingly aware of the advantages gained from the acceptance of the dilemmas and the consequent choice to leave a distinct IR realism. Not all are happy with the strategy which consists in picking and choosing within the tradition to defend a version most congenial to a particular scholar. This is simply not rigorous enough truly to delegitimize opposite attempts to box realism in the simple-mindedly portrayed *realpolitik* which might do justice to some realist scholars at some time, but not to the intellectual tradition at large.

The second advantage of giving up the brand-name is that realists would be freer to concentrate on actual contributions in the debate. First, they could join the rationalist debate in IR in a different manner. Indeed, realists could more openly contribute to the recent reassessment of the concept of rationality which is largely being waged within the Weberian tradition in the social sciences (arguably also a political realist heritage) such as the Habermas-inspired rationalist critique of utilitarian rationalism (Müller 1994, 1995, Risse-Kappen 1995, Risse 2000). Rationalism does not equal rational choice.

A second avenue would be an opening up to more philosophical debates in IR in which some of the tenets of political realism might have been taken more seriously by others than by IR realists themselves. Many so-called post-structuralists (another of these slippery categories for enemy-image use) have shown no particular fear of discussing the fathers of political realism, from Max Weber to Carl Schmitt, as well as their Nietzschean lineage.[19] Foucault is inspired by, although not reducible to, such political realism.[20] Indeed, the conceptual discussion of power has been pursued largely outside of IR realism (Guzzini 1993). It is not quite clear why realists should leave that field eternally to others, even if this risks asking some hard questions for realism.

---

19 The literature here is growing rapidly. For its start, see the excellent early piece by Wæver (1989a), and also Campbell and Dillon (1993). For the recent engagement with Carl Schmitt in IR, see e.g. Behnke (2000), Colombo (1999), and Huysmans (1999).
20 For recent Foucaultian analysis, see e.g. Prozorov (2004) and Huysmans (2004).

Moreover, admitting that realism is best thought of as a twofold negation would lift realist self-understanding on to a more reflexive level where it would be able to answer the charge that realism is simply a special case of a wider approach proposed by neo-institutionalists, constructivists such as Wendt, and even the very classical IR realist tradition itself. The distinctions made by Wolfers, Kissinger and Aron mentioned above in the discussion on anarchy, all make place for *realpolitik* as a special case of world politics. It is therefore perfectly legitimate to claim that Keohane and Nye (via the Aron disciple Stanley Hoffmann) are the heirs of *that* richer realist tradition, rather than Waltz or Mearsheimer.[21]

In particular, realism could engage on the right footing with the present challenge by Alexander Wendt's (1999) version of constructivism. Wendt carefully addresses realists in building a more comprehensive synthesis in which both realism and institutionalism are now seen as a special case of a wider constructivist theory.[22] Again, Wendt does not say that world politics will never look like realists think it does. But since the materialist and individualist meta-theory on which realism is usually built does not hold, one has to find another, a philosophical idealist grounding for IR theory. As a result, there is no logic, but cultures of anarchy. If power politics exists, it is based on a self-fulfilling prophecy difficult to dispense with. All these would be claims that 'hedged' realists such as Aron could have engaged with. Whether or not one agrees with him, Wendt provides a meta-theoretical founding for such a view, something realists have not so far been able to offer. In addition, he offers a wider and more systematically argued theory than any 'hedged' realist has done in the past. In short, Wendt's constructivism is not just another idealism of the continuing 'first debate' – he defines both the meta-theoretical and theoretical scope conditions of realism's existence, something realists (beyond Copeland 2000 and Sterling-Folker 2002) should be reflecting upon.

This leaves us with the cost in terms of communicability, or shared experience, with regard to the world of practice. The misleading idealism–realism divide is very prominent in daily politics, and not only in the USA. Giving it up would put further strains on the already difficult communication between the world of the observers and the world of practitioners. Yet, I would claim that the issue is wrongly put and, if redefined, would no longer have these negative implications.

The negative implications of seeing realism on the level of observation defined differently than on the level of practice, double and not only simple negation, stem from the curious assumption that the language of observation has to imitate the language of practice (e.g. Wallace 1996). This assumption does not follow.

---

21 Note also that Keohane (1984: 8 fn. 1) finds it difficult fundamentally to disentangle his account from a 'non-representative' type of realism such as Stanley Hoffmann's.
22 For an analysis of Wendt's aim of a disciplinary and theoretical synthesis, see Guzzini and Leander (2001).

It is perfectly possible to be proficient in more than one language. Future scholars could, indeed should, be well versed in both the life-worlds of world politics, be it the language of diplomacy, the military, international business, or transnational civil society as well as in the life-world of academia, where truth claims have to be justified in a coherent manner (Guzzini 2001c). Being multilingual in this sense makes people aware of the reflexive relationship between the two worlds, a point perhaps more important for constructivism, but hardly superfluous for realism.

This leads directly to another negative implication which stems from the tacit, but unwarranted assumption that the world of observation is divorced from the world of practice. But there is already some reflexivity which has crept into political discourse and understanding. It is simply not true that the world of politics lacks self-observation. Indeed, *Ostpolitik* cannot be understood without the conscious attempt to alter the reference points within which Cold War diplomacy has been conducted (Wæver 1995). Reflexivity is hence not only a characteristic at the level of theory, but simply pushes the twofold negation one reflexive step further to a point where self-observation becomes part and parcel of world politics and has wider effects. Indeed, this reflexivity has been an important factor in shaping the end of the Cold War in Europe.[23] Refusing to admit this reifies a language about world politics which no longer necessarily holds. If consciously done, it is not a historical statement, but a status quo (political) argument about how world politics *should* be thought of. It transforms realism into precisely what Carr said it would be – a theory lacking any vision. There is no reason why realists should be compelled to take only this backward-looking position, nor do all (former) realists feel this need anyway.

Conclusion: after a '20 years' detour'?

Using two recent and earlier debates around realism as a foil, this chapter has tried to unravel two underlying and enduring dilemmas of the realist tradition. The main thesis of this chapter is that recurrence of such debates is not spurious nor a kind of generational rediscovery of realism and its critics. It is systematic as long as the two underlying dilemmas of the realist tradition in IR are not faced.

The identity or distinctiveness/determinacy dilemma resurfaced in the debate spurred by Legro and Moravcsik (1999) in *International Security*. Either realism tries to keep its theoretical distinctiveness and becomes indeterminate in its

---

23 This is a finding of the original book on the end of the Cold War debate which has not been undermined by later critiques. See Wendt (1992a), Lebow and Risse-Kappen (1995), and the debate which followed, which includes most prominently William Wohlforth (1998) and now also Brooks and Wohlforth (2000–1). See also the exchange between Kramer and Wohlforth in the *Review of International Studies* (Kramer 1999, 2001, Wohlforth 2000) and Petrova (2003).

explanation of the very indeterminacy of its central explanatory concepts, such as power or it strives for determinacy, but must then necessarily rely on auxiliary hypothesis and causal factors which are not uniquely realist. Therefore, the double implication of Legro and Moravcsik's critique, so acutely sensed by the realist rejoinders, is correct. Realism is basically no more than a special case in need of justification, a theory which can be subsumed under wider theorizing. Moreover, the embracing theories are intrinsically superior to genuinely realist theories in that they are used to problematize the scope conditions under which different sub-theories apply, i.e. they have integrated an element of theoretical reflexivity which has, in the past, been alien to much of realism.

The 'conservative dilemma' haunts realism when it gets caught in between science and tradition, as shown in the Vasquez-spurred debate, for realism cannot avoid a stance on science which goes beyond a simple evocation of 'tradition', however satisfactory it might seem to some of the realist rejoinders. There can be no return to a 'common-sense realism', as already argued by Spegele (1996). The moment realism is no longer the taken-for-granted background of 'good' political practice, it is itself in need of a justification. This justification cannot be provided by an appeal to its intrinsic superiority in grasping reality 'as it is'; its appeal needs to be backed by scholarly justification. But as long as this appeal to justification is either ignored or answered by some version of a scientific theory of power, it undermines the political and diplomatic insights of its practical tradition. Realism has been the repeated, and repeatedly failed, attempt to turn the practically shared rules of European diplomacy into laws of a US social science.

In other words, the debate around realism shows that the past 20 years have been a gigantic detour for realism. But realists cannot start anew as if nothing happened outside of realism and other approaches in IR. Cognizant of the enduring dilemmas of IR realism, I would hope that IR realists would not want to defend realism's integrity at any price. If there is no power–money analogy, there is no single aim for expressing state motivation. Hence, Grieco's (1988) acceptance that state motivations vary in principle and not only due to changing circumstances is more consistent with Aron- or Wolfers-inspired realism.[24] This would call for a theory of rational action much wider than mere distinct materialist utilitarianism, a theory which could also engage more fruitfully with constructivism-inspired approaches.

---

24 This contradicts Walt's (1999: 26 fn. 56) statement to the opposite. In other words, realism as a coherent theory might go the way of assuming an irreducible variety of state motivations (but then needs to answer how we derive them), instead of becoming a series of competing schools which can be used to play off contradicting evidence. In this case, however, it will no longer look distinctive from a wider rational action theory. The identity dilemma still applies.

Thus, IR realism should perhaps reconsider its tradition in a way that no longer mounts a defence of realism as a clearly distinguishable school of thought. If this is the best way to save some realist insights and to engage in arguments in the different meta-theoretical and theoretical debates in IR, so be it.

7
THE DIFFERENT WORLDS OF REALISM IN INTERNATIONAL RELATIONS

Whether or not there has been really as much renewal in the discipline of International Relations (IR), as the end of the Cold War seemed to call for, realists, for sure, have found themselves under closer scrutiny again. This came at a time when Realism might have lost its predominant *theoretical* status and yet still stood at the centre of much IR debate. For Realism provided the core to be criticised, as attested by the earlier poststructuralist critique via the neo–neo 'debate' to the recent constructivist turn.

The two books under review show, in their own ways, that if Realism is to define this core, it remains very elusive. Jack Donnelly's introductory textbook *Realism and International Relations* tries sympathetically and critically to re-compose a tradition of Realism as a philosophical orientation. This broad conception is the only one Donnelly is willing to defend. It is the result of a dilemma he continually encounters (and makes the reader feel, too). On the one hand, as stated on the back-cover, 'common Realism propositions . . . fail to stand up to scrutiny' (Donnelly 2000). This certainly runs counter to the very exercise of writing a textbook about a school of thought. On the other hand, Donnelly is genuinely interested in keeping the reference to some classical thinkers usually referred to as realists, in particular Thucydides, and also Niccolò Machiavelli. The retreat to Realism as a rather loose *Weltanschauung* is the attempt to square the circle, a possible solution that has its price, as this review will show.

The collection of essays in Michael Cox's (2000b) edited *E.H. Carr: A Critical Appraisal* seems far away from such a textbook enterprise. In many respects, it is. So, unavoidably, this essay will, by its focus on Realism, do less justice to its richness of themes and views. Yet this book can also be read as a way to cope

I am indebted to Chris Brown, Barry Buzan, Jaap de Wilde, Anna Leander, Richard Little, Sam Makinda and Katalin Sárváry for comments and suggestions on an earlier draft of this chapter.

with the elusiveness of the discipline's core. It is perhaps not accidental that the discipline has known a renewed interest in its classics, and more generally its great thinkers (Neumann and Wæver 1997). For in our times of contested knowledge, when world-views no longer command an encompassing understanding of the world, the great thinker provides an apparent coherence by bundling the discussion and debates in one *œuvre*, in one biography. And clearly, as the volume shows, Carr's own intellectual and personal life is uniquely rich to provide such a focal point. It does not, however, save Realism as a plausible and coherent research tradition.

Realism as a philosophical orientation

One can imagine what daunting task Donnelly faced. He was commissioned to write a readable, yet theoretically rigorous textbook on a school of thought for which he shares only some sympathies. By his own convictions, the book aims to steer the reader through the many failures of Realism, old and new, without however becoming the logbook of a gigantic theoretical detour. For Donnelly's own understanding of theory and theorising, Realism was to appear as a long-standing tradition, where the normative and the empirical were intertwined and not unduly divided, or the normative simply discarded. The book should show Realism in its internal tensions and not in its often caricatured one-sidedness. As a textbook, every chapter had to include a series of (excellent) questions for in-class discussions and an annotated bibliography. And yes, I forgot, 'please, do this in just about 200 pages'. Judging from the final product, I think Cambridge University Press was certainly well advised to choose him. Donnelly himself, however, might have sometimes wondered whether that chalice should not have passed him.

In the following I will not dwell on the many important, succinct yet subtle insights of the book as it unfolds. I strongly recommend anybody interested in Realism to read it. Instead, I will only concentrate on those aspects, where the dilemmas posed by the daunting task catch up with Donnelly. For this tells a much broader story; it reflects the inherent problems of understanding Realism in IR today, which has become ever more elusive, defensive, and in one important sense, marginal.

Problems start with what has to be the first chapter, the one defining 'Realism'. Gone are the times where this was either implicit and taken-for-granted or apparently obvious. But few would have guessed that after a first overview of competing definitions, Donnelly is left with little more than a family resemblance or a certain 'style', such that 'we may not be able to define [Realism], but we know it when we see it' (Donnelly 2000: 9). However honest an insight, it is hardly a good starter for this type of book.

Hence, despite there being nearly as many Realisms as there are Realists, Donnelly must find some characteristics which carve out his very subject-matter. He finds them in one macro assumption (anarchy, i.e. the lack of world government) and one micro-assumption (evil or egoistic human nature), which give rise to a theory of action that stresses power and conflict, as well as a sceptical normative agenda. He then goes on to classify realists along two lines, namely whether or not they derive their theory more from anarchy or human nature (structural vs. biological realists), and whether or not they are committed to an exclusively Realist approach (radical, strong and hedged realists, where the first is *de facto* an empty category). From there, one could have expected a matrix of Realism thinkers. But Donnelly then presents six paradigmatic models, Realism exemplars as it were, which are Thomas Hobbes, Thucydides' Athenian envoys [sic], Machiavelli, Hans Morgenthau, Kenneth Waltz, and the Prisoners' Dilemma. The structure of the book then elaborates on the basic characteristics of Realism. Each assumption gets one chapter. Two chapters deal with Realism-inspired theories (and contemporary US debates about them) and the last chapter is on Realism and morality.

In all chapters, Donnelly tries to show that Realism is fundamentally indeterminate. Despite Realist neglect or arguments to the contrary, it must include a substantial theory of state motivation, of hierarchy and order, of institutions, as well as a normative theory. For Donnelly, to make sense at all, Realism is necessarily 'hedged'. It is best understood as a 'philosophical orientation'.[1]

The chapter on human nature already provides the theoretical basis for this general claim. In this chapter, Donnelly convincingly, at least to this reviewer, shows that Realism-inspired explanations must refer to motivation. The 'structural dodge', as he calls the attempt to circumvent a substantial account of state motivation through an appeal to anarchy simply cannot work (Donnelly 2000: 51). Moreover, such a substantial theory cannot be reduced to a simple version of materialism. 'There is an inescapable variability and multiplicity in the motives of states' (Donnelly 2000: 65).

The implications of this double claim are far-reaching and inform the entire book. First, Realist theories have always oscillated between different types of motivations and resulting behaviour without ever being able to discriminate which will occur when (Donnelly 2000: 64). Second, the indeterminacy of (neo)realism is not a result of the systemic nature of the theory, but of its multiple and inconsistent assumptions (Donnelly 2000: 62). Consequently, the Realist tradition is unlikely ever to develop a useful general theory of international politics (Donnelly 2000: 65). This echoes nearly word for word Raymond Aron's classical dictum of the 'indeterminacy of the diplomatic-strategic conduct' for reasons of the irreducible multiplicity of state motivation:

> [I]f diplomatic conduct is not determined by mere power (*force*) relations, if power (*puissance*) is not the purpose of diplomacy as utility is for

---

1 He also refers to Realism as a 'research programme', which, for Donnelly, means less than a general theory. I neglect this Lakatosian term since it has much more stringent connotations than he would like to see applied to Realism. Yet, it is important insofar as Donnelly spends two long chapters discussing mainly neorealist research, besides his more philosophical chapters. For a recent (sympathetic) philosophical analysis of political Realism, see Portinaro (1999).

economics, then the conclusion is legitimate that *there is no general theory of international relations comparable to the general theory of economics.*

(Aron 1962: 102, original emphasis, my translation)

This is not all. For Donnelly, Realism is not only unable to provide a general theory; it is basically inconsistent, too. The same event explained by one Realist theory can also be explained by at least one other no less authentic Realist theory, yet inconsistent with the first one (Donnelly). Realism becomes 'a more or less loosely connected *set* of often inconsistent theoretical models rooted in shared pre-theoretical assumptions' (Donnelly 2000: 73, emphasis in original). The consequence of this argument is summed up at the end of the book when he writes that the (better) Realist tradition, as exemplified by Herz and Carr, for instance, kept '"realist" insights in dialectical tension with wider human aspirations and possibilities' (Donnelly 2000: 193), a sense of balance 'sorely lacking in leading figures such as Morgenthau, Waltz, and Mearsheimer'.[2]

Yet, here, Donnelly recoils from the logical implication of his own argument. If it is true that scholars like Carr and Herz most express the 'nature' of the Realist tradition, then the argument runs into a paradox. For, then, the scholars most faithful to the Realist tradition are paradoxically the most 'hedged', i.e. the least faithful to its assumptions and defining characteristics. It is only in this context that yet another candid sentence of the back-cover makes sense: 'Donnelly argues that common Realism propositions . . . are rejected by many leading realists as well'. (Which other tradition would be allowed to continue after such an indictment?)

This paradox is exacerbated, and not resolved, by Donnelly's claim to think of Realism as a style or a philosophical orientation with a long and important 'pedigree'. This all-accepting approach runs into the problem of Realism's distinctiveness.[3] It shows up in the necessary quotation marks around Realism (see above), if we start to talk about the nature of a Realist tradition, on a general level, within which then genuinely 'realist' insights are but one and insufficient pole in a dialectical argument. In other words, if Realism is understood as a philosophical orientation, then for it to be distinct, it becomes pretty much the one-sided radical neorealist version of Waltz and Mearsheimer, that Donnelly has shown to be basically mistaken. A distinct Realism would hence be similar to the caricature of Realism, which Donnelly wants to save it from. It would merely resemble a symbol, as rather harshly put by Inis Claude, another classical 'hedger':

[t]hese cases illustrate the widespread tendency to make the balance of power a symbol of Realism, and hence of respectability, for the scholar or

---

2 Donnelly (2000: 195). This is the basic argument underlying Berki (1981) who is mentioned once, and Griffiths (1992) who is not.
3 The determinacy–distinctiveness dilemma is one of the basic themes of Guzzini (1998). See also Legro and Moravcsik (1999).

statesman. In this usage, it has no substantive content as a concept. It is a test of intellectual virility, of he-manliness in the field of international relations. The man who 'accepts' the balance of power and who dots his writing with approving references to it, thereby asserts his claim to being a hard-headed Realist who can look at the grim reality of power without flinching. The man who rejects the balance of power convicts himself of softness, of cowardly incapacity to look power in the eye and acknowledge its role in the affairs of states.

(Claude 1962: 39)

In such a reading, it is this 'style', which makes us 'know Realism, when we see it', although we cannot define it. But Donnelly, very correctly I think, feels that this would be unfair to the majority of scholars, albeit mainly the elder ones, who used to refer to themselves as realists. 'Strong realists' are a marginal crowd, theoretically speaking, of course.

Therefore, Donnelly prefers to broaden Realism to this wider tradition playing out the tension between the two poles. But he cannot escape the paradox he put himself into. If Realism is the tradition, which systematically hedges the 'Realism' pole, then it would be more precise to call this the *classical* tradition in IR, and no longer Realism *tout court*, as actually done by K.J. Holsti in the *Dividing Discipline* (1985). For all his repeated references to the Realist contribution, the emphasis on egoism and anarchy is hardly enough to distinguish it from many non-Realist theories. Moreover, allowing Realism to take all the ground of the classical debates, would buy into the canonised but wrong Realist self-description of the first 'debate' in which allegedly only so-called idealists were stupid enough not to hedge (or, when they did, were said no longer to be idealists).[4]

To sum it up: either Realism is distinct but one-sided and wrong, or it is the rich tradition which Donnelly wants to save from neorealism, but then it is no longer distinctively Realism. When all is said and done, this latest textbook on Realism consequently and significantly ends by admitting that Realism would be best rejected (Donnelly 2000: 200).

After Donnelly's own discussion, it testifies to the academic power of neorealism in the US, and not to its theoretical strength, that he feels compelled to spend so much time discussing the recent works of Waltz and Mearsheimer, those indeed who have most tried to reduce the tradition of Realism to one single pole. Instead, he could have, as his argument implies, neglected them since their one-sidedness has pushed them out of the genuine 'nature' of the Realist tradition altogether.

When all was done, I wondered whether Donnelly would not have preferred to analyse and develop that part of the tradition he clearly appreciates. He could have looked at the different ways classical thinkers have been able to live with the

---

4 For a reassessment of the 'first debate', see Schmidt (1998).

dialectics between Realism and idealism/utopia or whatever they chose to call it. Also, he could have engaged with other scholars who have explored the richness as well as the internal tensions of Realism by taking some of its concepts more seriously, such as power (Richard Ashley) or security (Barry Buzan and Ole Wæver, R.B.J. Walker), all relatively unaddressed in the book. So one feels a sense of self-justification for Donnelly's weak defence of Realism, but also of a missed opportunity in the discipline, when the very last sentence of *Realism in IR* looks for support in Carr, a time-honoured Realist who 'is certainly right that sound theory and sound practice require a proper appreciation of both the strengths and the limitations of Realism' (Donnelly 2000: 202).

E.H. Carr: internal contradictions of a not-so-realist

According to Donnelly, Carr is not the canonical debunker of utopianism, but a dialectical thinker who expressed the self-contradictions of Realism. If there was still any need for such an argument, Cox's edited collection on Carr dispels any remaining doubts. Cox has assembled a variety of scholars to allow for a comprehensive assessment of Carr's intellectual biography. For Carr has not only experienced the *three* worlds of IR (diplomacy, journalism, and academia); he was, in his academic self, an international analyst and theorist, a consummate Soviet historian, and a historiographer. This variety makes the book a fascinating read in our days of specialised existence.

Apart from the good choice of contributors, Cox has made two further editorial decisions that paid out handsomely. First, he put a short and hitherto unpublished autobiographical note from 1980 at the very beginning of the book. Then, he did not unduly constrain his reflexes as a historian when sequencing the chapters; these allow for a very rich contextualisation of Carr's work. After the short autobiographical note, Cox provides us with a very good first introduction which sketches the themes to come. The book is then divided into four parts, *Life and Times*, *The Russian Question*, *International Relations* and *What is History?* This is not a chronological sequence in which Carr's work on the USSR would have come last. In fact, the Russian section is not really a historian's exegesis of Carr's interpretations; rather, it situates his general stance on Russia/USSR within the (British) intellectual debates of the Cold War whose end Carr was not given the chance to experience. As such it is the logical follower of *Life and Times*, which deals mainly with his professorship in Aberystwyth and his assistant editorship at *The Times*, i.e. until 1947 and 1946 respectively. For the very character of this review, I hope I will be forgiven, if I discuss mainly the last two parts.

Let me not concentrate on individual chapters, but on some overall impressions of Carr. It should be obvious that the following picture will be but a small, and necessarily much too coherent and continuous view on the multi-layered personal and intellectual profiles, as they emerge out of this volume. Still, the one profile, which emerges from the chapters and on which I will draw most, could be called 'the call of public responsibility in an elitist torn between reason and romance'.

Basically all contributors agree that Carr was an elitist at heart (see in particular Haslam 2000). The end of the First World War and the seesaw that followed it, struck this twenty-six year old Cambridge top graduate in Greek and Roman History, now at the Foreign Office, unprepared, as he himself writes. By reading the chapters, one is tempted to infer that Carr sometimes longed for, but nearly always resented, the *ambiance* of the British Empire of his youth for having been unable to foresee the changes that were to come, but also for having lulled young bright people like himself, its new elite, into complacency and self-indulgence.

In his understanding, responsibility fell upon elites, international powers and national leaders, to grasp and manage inevitable changes. In the dawn of the short twentieth century, neither his country nor himself had yet risen to their task. The effects of the war, but more of the Bolshevik Revolution, were an awakening for Carr. Given that he devoted thirty-five years and fourteen volumes to understanding the implications and consequences of this revolution (not its causes, as Fred Halliday (2000) notes), it is perhaps difficult to overstate its importance for him.

Carr's view of the inevitable changes refers to a position, noted by many contributors, that one could, parallel to 'legal positivism', call a kind of historical 'positivism' (Cox 2000a: 5). He did not fancy much discussions about counter-factuals in the past; one had to deal with the present as it was. On the one hand, Carr debunks the great teleologies of the future. On the other, he scorns the a-theoretical event chronicler. Indeed, *What is History?* is, as Anders Stephanson shows, mainly an attempt to cure his British fellow historians of their excessive empiricism (Stephanson 2000).

At the same time, however, Carr urged the historian, the observer and the politician not to miss their appointment with History as it unfolds. So, after having attacked all classical vantage points for understanding the course of History, he must come up with one of his own. He did so 'by distilling projections into the future from some relentlessly instrumentalised and continuous past experience'.[5] It is here where revolutions, as such, become important since they are held to herald epochal changes from which new patterns arise. The Bolshevik Revolution was clearly connected to Carr's vision of a Western decline as he experienced it. With it, historians were given the chance to catch a past incidence, which could help them to understand, and as responsible leaders, be prepared for and perhaps help to channel incoming historical tides. Despite all odds, reason has its place in History (Dunne 2000).

This curious, and fundamentally contestable, conception of History and historiography not only testifies to a sometimes heroic, albeit certainly romantic, elitism, but also to a creed in progress, hardly to be expected from such a canonical Realism.[6] In a chapter which beautifully bundles many argumentative strings

---

5 As critically noted by Stephanson (2000: 295).
6 See in particular the contributions by Fred Halliday and Anders Stephanson above, and Jenkins (2000).

in the book, Halliday coins this as a tension between 'reason and romance' in Carr (Halliday 2000). Halliday shows that the rationalist Carr did not share the typical Realist assumption of a cyclical theory of history (see also Bobbio 1981). The romantic Carr was attracted by nineteenth century Russian intellectuals and revolutionaries. During his posting at the British Legation in Riga between 1925 and 1929, Carr learnt Russian and started to write biographies like the ones on Dostoevski and on Alexander Herzen and his circles in exile, a strange choice of genre for somebody who believed in the great impersonal forces of History.[7] This makes it perhaps easier to put that Carr into context, who never relinquished to some inner optimism, some version of what he would call 'utopianism'. At the end of his life, he again openly prefers this attitude to cynicism (Carr 2000).

The tensions and contradictions of his vision of history help to understand Carr's peculiarly 'Realist' approach to international relations. To the extent that Realism is a mainly negative approach, opposing an 'other', Carr certainly qualifies, in what he calls his *esprit de contradiction* (Carr 2000: xv). Yet, as all the chapters of the second part show, it appears to me that Carr never sorted out two basically contradictory facets of the political Realism tradition. For political realists oppose 'reality' to two different things, to the ideal and to the apparent, a difference Carr did not disentangle.[8] This double heritage of political Realism is full of tensions, though.[9] Realism as anti-idealism is status quo oriented. It relies on the entire panoply of arguments so beautifully summarised by Alfred Hirschman (1991). According to the *futility* thesis, any attempt at change is condemned to be without any real effect. The *perversity* thesis would argue that far from changing for the better, such policies only add new problems to the already existing ones. And the central *jeopardy* thesis says that purposeful attempts at social change will only undermine the already achieved. The best is the enemy of the good, and so on. Anti-apparent Realism, however, is an attitude more akin to the political theories of suspicion. It looks at what is hidden behind the smokescreen of current ideologies, putting the allegedly self-evident into the limelight of criticism. With the other form of Realism, it shares a reluctance to treat beautiful ideas as what they claim to be. But it is much more sensible to their ideological use, revolutionary as well as conservative. Whereas the anti-ideal defends the status quo, the anti-apparent questions it. It wants to unmask existing power relations.

Carr's famous critique of the 'harmony of interests' is of this anti-apparent kind, but is easily misunderstood as anti-ideal Realism. Yet far from defending the real against a utopia that will never come, it unmasks a utopia dressed up as

---

7 Several contributors note the remarkable parallel to George F. Kennan, also posted at Riga, similarly shifting sides from the early need to contain illusionary hopes in the after-war period to the critique of the excessive militarisation of politics during the Cold War.
8 For this distinction, see Bobbio (1996 [1969]).
9 In this respect, there is a parallel with Susan Strange. See Guzzini (2000b).

real. For historical circumstances only, as he perceived them, the unmasking strikes at 'utopianism'. But any other ideology could do, as Carr clearly writes in *The Twenty Years' Crisis*. Being aware of the historical character of any ideology, Carr relies on Karl Mannheim's sociology of knowledge.[10] If Carr is seen in the anti-apparent Realism tradition, it comes as no surprise, that many radical writers see themselves in the tradition of the Realism Carr, such as, for instance Robert Cox and, in the volume itself, Randall Germain (Cox 1986 [1981], Germain 2000).

Since Carr does not deal with this tension, it is similarly not surprising that his basic categories in *The Twenty Years' Crisis* are fundamentally muddled and overblown, as early critics, better perhaps than much that followed in IR, already showed (see the discussion in Wilson 2000). Moreover, Carr shares all the pitfalls of such an approach. Its dialectics between the real and the utopian are never resolved, but relentlessly readjusted to meet the target of the day. For this is the only solution to the dialectical tension he offers. The anti-apparent Realism does not oscillate between the two poles at any single point in time, but *over* time, taking the truth of the day, whether reactionary or revolutionary, head on.[11]

Consequently, Carr's Realism of the war-years regresses into a mere rhetorical strategy, with which he tried to force political actors into a continuous dress rehearsal on the stage of History, so they can be prepared for when the curtain lifts. Paul Rich describes *The Twenty Years' Crisis* as a 'simple polemic concerned with securing in the medium to longer term a new political dialogue between the idealist Left, whom Carr saw as the major source of new ideas, and official policy-making' (Rich 2000: 205). And Tim Dunne insists that the Realism the book prescribes is not a theoretical construct, but an epistemic 'tool' or 'weapon' (Dunne 2000: 224). And indeed, what a Realism theory that would be, which does not recoil from optimism and which does not share a cyclical theory of history?

Conclusion: an invitation to history and theory

Realism seems not in safe waters yet. Donnelly's textbook on Realism, published by an authoritative publisher, ends up rejecting it. And Cox's collection of essays on one of the founding fathers of Realism in IR might invite readers to look up Carr again, but then shows in all his richness also his inconsistencies. Worse for realists, Carr was in fact not one of them, if the label retains any distinct meaning.

But this particular reading of both books conveys also a more positive message. Although the US market does not allow Donnelly to include classical thinkers without a somewhat apologetic justification (2000: 198), he does it nevertheless.

---

10 Mannheim (1936). For the influence on Carr, see Rich (2000: 201–3). For a more general assessment of its part in the intellectual origins and internal inconsistencies of Carr, see Jones (1998).
11 See his critique of Cold War containment in Carr (1961: 177).

Through Donnelly's example, the book could hopefully help to show that the theorisation of schools of thought cannot overlook a careful history of ideas, as well as a meticulous reading of texts. The book should certainly open up the readers' eyes for those classical thinkers, old and new, Donnelly respects. The world of contemporary Realism seems certainly too narrow for him.

If Donnelly's book revives another wider world, heir of a classical tradition, Cox's edited volume fills it with a content which, in turn, needs to be put into a historical context. For it is probably best not to read Carr any longer as more or less close to the one or the other pole in the sacrosanct 'first debate', a disease which anyway has befallen only IR. The persistence of this debate betrays both an obsessive Manichaeism, rather typical of the Cold War, and an internal logical need for Realism theorising. Instead, Carr is perhaps best seen as belonging to this generation of classical scholars who, after the shock of the First and the Second World Wars, became historically conscious of, and theoretically active with regard to the problems before them, like Max Weber, Raymond Aron, Karl Polanyi and István Bibó (Sárváry 1998). [S.G. 2012: see now: Sárváry (2008).] The evolution to mass societies, the industrial revolution, the rise of nationalism and self-determination, to name a few, redefined politics and concomitantly diplomacy and international affairs (Linklater 2000). It is not necessarily their answers, which are of course more or less time-bound, but their readiness not to divorce politics from economics or ethics, and to think both theoretically and historically, which constitutes the legacy put before us and which Realism in IR is perhaps less than ever able to address. What a different world, indeed.

8

FOREIGN POLICY WITHOUT DIPLOMACY

The Bush administration at a crossroads

The terrorist attacks on the financial and political–military centre of world power have become a defining moment for the foreign policy of the Bush administration. This moment provides 'an opportunity', as President Bush immediately declared in a TV interview, to wage international war against terrorism and, more generally, to redirect US thinking in international affairs.

The administration has made it clear that it wants to change strategy. President Bush has declared that international terrorism is a new type of war, the first 'war of the 21st century'. Since it is not an enemy with a face and territory, the strategy cannot just retaliate, but needs a long time frame to succeed. President Bush declared it an 'act of war' and spoke of US government action as 'patient', 'focused', 'steadfast in [its] determination'.

I will argue that the more fundamental reason for a need for change in US foreign policy, in particular of the Bush administration, has little to do with the attacks, but with its limited understanding of, and importance given to, the role of diplomacy in its security policy. It has pursued a strategy that is combining unilateralism (the idea that US international politics is something that can be decided alone at home) with a reliance on military assets. If it does not reconsider, US foreign policy runs the risk of repeating mistakes from the cold

---

This is a slightly edited and shortened version of a paper written in the week after 11 September and presented at the public Copenhagen Peace Research Institute (COPRI) roundtable on 'Terrorism and New Threats in the 21st Century', on 26 September 2001 in Copenhagen. I want to thank the unusually large audience for its feedback, and those who have taken time to read and comment on the article, namely Kateřina Borutová, Chris Browning, Barry Buzan, Tarja Cronberg, Stanley Hoffmann, Ulla Holm, Dietrich Jung, Morten Kelstrup, Ákos Kopper, Ekaterina Kristesashvili, Anna Leander, Zlatko Šabic̆, Davide Sparti, and Ole Wæver. A Danish version was published in *COPRI Nyhedsbrev* No. 11 (December 2001).

war. I consciously base my critique mainly on realist writers, simply to show that the present US foreign policy is debatable even in realist terms.

The war is not new

The US has been vulnerable for a very long time. During the cold war, security was based on a systematic vulnerability, which came under the name of 'Mutually Assured Destruction'. Deterrence was made to work all the better because both sides kept their mutual vulnerability: this made it least rational to start a war.

Nor would a military attack on countries harbouring threats to US security be something new. The US government has not recoiled from intervening unilaterally in countries that it considered to be threatening US security. The Monroe Doctrine allowed the American continent to be protected from outside interference, but then also helped subsequent US administrations to intervene militarily when they deemed it necessary. Some of these threats were non-territorial, like communism, and some were fighting a non-traditional guerrilla war. Cuba was the rogue state of the day, helping guerrillas around the world, from Angola to Bolivia – and experienced a half-hearted US invasion. The cold war against communism was not just defensive posture; it also meant military interventions elsewhere in the world.

And, certainly, this is not the first time the 'war on terrorism' has been declared; the elder President Bush declared it earlier. Many national liberation movements used to be called terrorists in their inception. And, ever since the Iranian Revolution and the western support of the Afghan Mojahedin against the Soviet invasion, subsequent US administrations have faced religious-nationalist attacks against US, indeed western, troops and civilians, like the attack on the discotheque 'La Belle' in Berlin which hosted many US soldiers, or the bomb explosion on a plane which came down over Lockerbie. Already then, US presidents retorted by attacking countries that were supposed to sponsor or host terrorism, like Reagan's attack on Ghaddafi and Clinton's Cruise Missiles against Sudan and Afghanistan.

The shortcomings of George W. Bush's foreign policy

This attack showed the shortcomings of the Bush administration's understanding of security, which is primarily military and unilateral. The National Missile Defense (NMD) Plan is symptomatic of this strategy, which seems to believe that military means are enough to achieve the highest possible invulnerability and that therefore diplomacy can be downgraded. It was pursued through a 'take-it-or-leave-it' diplomacy, which has succeeded in record time in antagonizing many sectors of the international community, including some of America's allies. Apparently, there was no need for outside moderation or indeed of any pre-emptive and creative diplomacy. US diplomacy was reduced to an instrument of stimulating support in favour of a self-reliance strategy already decided anyway.

The NMD is the logical corollary of a foreign policy that looks at questions of security as if they were questions of domestic safety. The territory of the US is like the sheltered wealthy suburbs where superior private and public security forces ensure that no violence can spill over from other more violent, and basically uncontrollable, neighbourhoods. The 'gated community' becomes the paradigm of US security thinking.

However, this strategy of military 'self-reliance' produces an important internal contradiction for US security when this order is challenged. Whereas, on a domestic basis, a legitimate police force can be regularly called in to mediate between the sheltered rich and exposed poor, there is no such thing on an international level. Hence, the US often felt called in as 'world policeman', a role with a rather delicate legitimacy. This administration acknowledged that more 'humility' with regard to unilateral military action was needed – yet without allowing multilateral action, such as the UN, to take its place.

Consequently, by having no multilateral or pre-emptive diplomatic component, yet feeling the sudden need to police, the tendency of a remilitarization of US foreign policy is but a logical, albeit paradoxical, corollary of the Bush administration's security policy. It leads to a paradox insofar as it seems to imply that the US lacks one thing in particular, namely military power, when it outshines everybody else to a degree it never did in its history. Moreover, it easily tends to get into an escalatory spiral, since it implies that defeat can only happen because 'we did not use all our power', an idea played out by the German military after the defeat of World War I and the US military after the Vietnam war. The problem with this argument is that it can never be wrong. For as long as not absolutely all means were used – a total war, as it were – one can always argue that 'we would have won, if only we had . . .'. A military logic is allowed to overtake a political one. In short, the US tends to reverse Clausewitz's dictum, where politics now becomes the prolongation of war with other means, and not vice versa, a US tendency already deplored by Raymond Aron during the cold war (Aron 1976).

The National Security strategy, as exemplified by the NMD, did not mean the isolationist retreat of the US from world politics, since it ensured that no 'power above' the US could arise, a world politics issue of no mean proportions. Rather, it meant the retreat of the US from any type of engaging and conflict-preventive diplomacy in which the US would embed itself in a wider system of international governance.

Two scenarios

If the attack has opened a window of opportunity for US diplomacy – not because the US faces a 'new' vulnerability, but because the underlying ideas of its security strategy have flaws – then there are broadly two scenarios. In one, the Bush administration will police the world to make it fit its own ideas about it; in the other, it could use the brutal awakening from the illusion of 'Fortress America' to rethink the bases of its own security strategy.

The first scenario results in further militarizing US foreign policy. The US would simply pursue its tendency to propose 'take-it-or-leave-it' policies. In this version, US diplomacy will attempt to gather support where possible (intentionally then misnamed as 'multilateralism'), and do it alone when this is not forthcoming.

Such a scenario would repeat a series of mistakes that earlier observers of US foreign policy had already brandished during the cold war. George F. Kennan thought that the Truman administration misunderstood his containment policy as an end, rather than as a means (Kennan 1967). He thought that the western vulnerability was psychological and political. Therefore not NATO (which he opposed), but the Marshall Plan was the appropriate answer to it. Kennan insisted that the strength of democracy would finally prevail in the competition between the systems and he invited his fellow citizens to reform and improve their own society as the best way to win the cold war (Kennan 1958). This statement also clearly refers to the risk of using international affairs to win domestic 'wars', something which the US had experienced during the McCarthy hearings. President Bush's declaration, 'who is not for us, is against us', might stand for this line. Colin Powell's early (pre-anthrax attacks) statement that the US would not change its way of life might fit into a line of thinking closer to Kennan.

The second major shortcoming of this (cold war) strategy is that it keeps the realm of diplomacy very limited. Yet, diplomacy will be needed. As the attack clearly showed, a military posture will hardly suffice to avoid future ones. The US is and will stay vulnerable. For the 'war against terrorism' or the 'attack on democracy' stands for something different. It stands for the acknowledgement that the principles according to which this form of international terror makes politics are not compatible with international society; the principles of terrorism, not a religion or civilization. This, besides human mourning, is the ground upon which so many countries felt solidarity with the US.

Yet, the US administration's search for complete independence of its will in international affairs undermines the very possibility of a diplomacy worth its name. While Kennan chastised the military emphasis of US foreign policy towards the communist threat and urged that the cold war be won by improving the health of democratic societies, Henry Kissinger insisted that any unilateral quest for invulnerability – any search for 'absolute security', as it were – was destined to provoke absolute insecurity for others and hence to undermine the very possibility of a functioning international Concert, a legitimate system of international diplomacy (Kissinger 1957: 2). Not accepting its own limits within the world order, the US would become the main actor to actually undermine it.

This implies that such a US diplomacy be part of the international community, that is, that it sees other international actors as subjects and not only objects of its policy. The US has to take more seriously the possibility that it itself needs to play to the rules of this international game. If this was an attack against democracy, then the attacked West must more than ever think about a world order that could be more legitimate. Military might without a vision for which it should be used might ensure short-term gains, it would not be efficient in combating terrorism.

Defining national security in such a way as to make any international governance that includes control over parts of US policy impossible has not and cannot produce security. Not paying into the UN is only one issue, here. Such an attitude has produced and will produce reactions against a perceived arrogance of power. Classical diplomacy teaches moderation and awareness of the negative effects of hubris. True, this arrogance is not something for which this administration is mainly responsible. Indeed, it is under pressure from fellow Republicans to become even more ruthless in its disregard of the international community, as in the proposed 'American Service Members' Protection Act' which exempts US citizens from rulings of the International Criminal Court which prosecutes war crimes and crimes against humanity. Indeed, this act authorizes the US President to use military force for liberating US citizens and allies held in custody by the Court in The Hague. Therefore, the act has already been dubbed 'The Hague Invasion Act' (Tucker 2001).

Finally, such a strategy would paradoxically fulfil one of the key intentions of the attack. It was meant to reinstate violence as the main means of international affairs, undermining liberties at home and peace processes abroad. It was meant to make the world centre accept that international affairs is not about conflict resolution, democracy and freedom, but only about money and military might. A mainly military response without any vision of world order would produce what they were supposed to avoid: an attack on democracy. It would be a terrible irony if, by our reactions in accepting the militarization of our thinking about world politics, in accepting the building of a fault-line around identities exactly where the terrorists wanted us to see it, we would realize this intention better than the perpetrators of these attacks could ever have done themselves. No single attack, however violent, can defeat democracy and a world politics that attempts peaceful change – only we can.

The second scenario, which is increasingly voiced by US and international observers would start from the understanding that a military posture will hardly suffice to avoid future attacks. At the same time, the military alone is considered no longer sufficient for achieving security; US foreign policy must more decidedly embed itself into international society. It would imply a change towards real multilateralism, and not just coalition-building.

The most traditional move would be the multilateralization of the military side by restrengthening arms control. There is a widespread consensus, including former Reagan officials like former Assistant Secretary of Defense Lawrence Korb, that the Bush administration has gone too far in unilaterally renouncing or challenging major treaty commitments of the arms control era, like the Anti-ballistic Missile Treaty, the Comprehensive Test Ban Treaty (already rejected in 1999 and left there by Bush), the Biological Weapons Convention (rejected in 2001), and the recent reduction of funds for the Cooperative Threat Reduction Initiatives (to hinder the proliferation of former Soviet nuclear capacities).

But arms control alone is simply a crucial means for a further end. As Kissinger writes, besides the element of power, legitimacy is necessary to build a more peaceful international order, since an order 'which is not considered just will be challenged sooner or later' (Kissinger 1994: 79). Hence, whether or not there will be real change in US foreign policy will only become visible later when those points of the international agenda reappear which have been overshadowed by the tragic deaths. The decreasing legitimacy and obvious lack of any vision in the G8 will make itself felt even more in the future. At this point, it should be clear to the US administration that the attack is not a problem for US foreign policy alone, but also for international governance. These are huge problems, for which the US cannot bear sole responsibility and which it certainly cannot resolve alone. But, as Kenneth Waltz once wrote, while we might be all sitting in the same leaking world boat, one of us wields the biggest dipper (Waltz 1979: 210). The present administration might have the chance to address these problems anew. It will be judged on how wisely it will use this 'opportunity', as Bush called it.

'Primacy or world order'

During the cold war, the US administrations faced the 'American dilemma' between 'primacy or world order', as Stanley Hoffmann so aptly described it in the late 1970s (Hoffmann 1978). This Bush administration started as if its primacy was enough to ensure a world order of its liking. The attack has shown the vulnerability of the country and of this strategy: US primacy that is not embedded in a legitimate world order undermines US security. What remains to be seen is whether the changes in US foreign policy, including the pledge now to pay up to the UN, are but tactical moves, or if they could become the basis for a reorientation, a really 'defining moment'.

It remains to be seen whether the attack will have an effect on US policy similar to Matthias Rust's small private plane, which, towards the end of the second cold war, landed undetected on the Red Square in front of the Kremlin (imagine if he were a suicide bomber). Made aware of its vulnerability, this is a moment in which the US, only apparently protected by its geography, can more fully understand that security is something that can neither be achieved alone, nor with military might.

All necessary attempts to narrow the window of vulnerability cannot replace an international policy that renders its inevitable vulnerability less dangerous.

9

ROBERT GILPIN

A realist quest for the dynamics of power

A crucial date in recent international political economy (IPE) was 15 August 1971, when the US administration decided to suspend the Bretton Woods monetary system. Not only did this unilateral decision change the way the international monetary system was run, but the USA was perceived to have officially declared its power position as challenged. After the 1973 crisis, observers began to link the erosion of US power with the recession and the increasing protectionism. US academics began for the first time to apply analyses of the decline of power to their own country. The oil shock and the accrued influence of economic weapons moved economic issues to the level of 'high polities', i.e. to questions of diplomacy and war.

A scholar relatively well prepared to respond to these issues was Robert Gilpin. One reason was that he had *not* specialized in the core of International Relations with its emphasis on narrowly defined security, strategy and traditional diplomacy. Gilpin specialized in the role of science and technology both for domestic and foreign policies. At the time of the 1971 watershed, his most recent book was a detailed analysis of the social and political responses of one former great power (France) to the challenges of the after-war period (Gilpin 1968b).

In an article in which he presented some of his book's central theses, he focused on industrial and technological policies which different European countries had devised to close the so-called 'technology gap' between them and the USA (Gilpin 1968a). In answer to T. Levitt's critique that the 'gap was not technological', but managerial, Gilpin responded that this was true, but beside the

---

Earlier versions were presented at the inaugural conference of the Nordic International Studies Association, Oslo, 18–19 August 1993 and at an author workshop at the European University Institute in 1994. I would like to thanks the participants of the two meetings for comments on the previous drafts of the chapter. Moreover, I am indebted to Monika Berkman for language-editing the text.

point. The 1968 text is worth quoting at length because it spells out much of Gilpin's later research programme.

> The point is that the technology gap is much less an economic than a political problem. This is true in several senses. In the first place, what is at issue for Europeans is their political position *vis-à-vis* the great powers and their capacity for long-term national independence. Whereas, beginning in the latter part of the nineteenth century, control over petroleum resources became essential once naval ships shifted from sail to diesel, so today an independent aerospace and electronics industry, along with the supporting sciences, is seen to be crucial for a nation to enjoy diplomatic and military freedom of action. Second, the intensity of the European reaction to the technology gap must be understood in the context of the profound economic and political developments which have engulfed western Europe since the end of World War II. . . . First, there has been the trauma for France, Great Britain, and several other European countries of decolonization; seldom in history have proud and ruling peoples been reduced to second-class status so fast. Second, for the first time in history the political and industrial leaders of western Europe have experienced and must come to terms with a full-employment market economy.
> *(Gilpin 1968c: 125–6)*

Gilpin's research programme, as will be claimed here, is an attempt to understand the historically changing nature of 'power' and the rise and decline of great 'powers'. In other words, it is about the *dynamics of power*. Gilpin wants to understand when and which resources provide power, and why and how the hierarchy of powers changes. For him, two historical shifts are central to answering these concerns at the end of the twentieth century, namely the increasing prominence of technological and economic sources of power, and the qualitative change from states to welfare states. More particularly, his research programme can be characterized by three central puzzles:

1. *The basic driving forces of change*: on the level of the actor, the quest for power and wealth; on the system level, market mechanisms and technological change. In the modern age, technology/efficiency and power have become inextricably linked. The result is a global, i.e. national and transnational, 'struggle for efficiency'.
2. *The domestic response to this struggle* in which many governments find themselves often sandwiched between international requirements and a domestic social contract whose legitimacy increasingly rests upon material well-being for the majority of the society. Gilpin's judgement on the welfare state is therefore twofold. On the one hand, he values it for its capacity to stabilize democracies. On the other hand, he is aware of the protectionist, at times also nationalist, tendency to shift the costs of resolving domestic problems abroad.

3. *The international management of power shifts*, especially great-power decline, where competition risks degenerating into technological and other wars.

When Gilpin in 1987 recalls his crucial turn in 1970 to what would later be called the discipline of IPE, he refers to his experiences in France where the US multinational corporations would have been kicked out had General de Gaulle been able to convince the German government to follow suit. According to Gilpin's analysis the German refusal was linked to a wider bargain in which the US military guarantee to Germany was 'traded off' for the multinationals: only the *Pax Americana* made transnationalism of this kind and speed possible.

> Although I did not fully appreciate it at the time, I had returned to a realist conception of the relationship of economics and politics that had disappeared from postwar American writings, then almost completely devoted to more narrowly conceived security concerns.
>
> *(Gilpin 1987b: xii)*

This research programme about the dynamics of power makes it difficult to fit Gilpin into the boxes available in IR/IPE. He is normally referred to as a neo-realist, mainly for two reasons: his use of utilitarian (economic) methodology and his apparent ahistorical assumptions. This interpretation focuses primarily on his book *War and Change in World Politics* (1981), and in particular Chapter 6, where he develops a utilitarian theory of war, expansion, hegemony and decline. Ever since Gilpin declared that Thucydides 'would [following an appropriate course in geography, economics, and modern technology] have little trouble in understanding the power struggle in our age' (Gilpin 1981: 211), he has been considered one of the most ahistorical realists who put their faith in the profoundly unchanged and unchanging character of the international system. Yet, seen from the, rather simplistic, dichotomy between historical and scientific forms of Realism, he represents a curious mixture at best. Although he tries to systematize a theory of (hegemonic) action, based upon generally unchanged utilitarian assumptions, he derives the present system and its ordering principles historically.

Indeed, and this is the second major claim of this chapter, Gilpin's Realism is profoundly at odds with several central tenets of neo-realism, at least if Kenneth Waltz's *Theory of International Politics* (1979) is understood as its paradigmatic text. He does not derive conflict solely from international anarchy. His theory draws a historical and qualitative difference between international systems. His international theory necessarily requires a theory of the state. For Gilpin, Realism needs to be broadened so as to become a form of neo-mercantilism. The treatment of change might perhaps best exemplify this central difference between Gilpin's neo-mercantilism and neo-realism. Gilpin's approach sees both more and less change than neo-realism. On the one hand, he analyses at length the changes that have occurred in the international system since the Peloponnesian War – with the coming of capitalism, its globalization, the rise of the nation-state and the welfare state. On the other hand, if applied to the understanding of the end of the Cold War, Gilpin's approach would systematically relativize those changes emphasized by neo-realist analyses. Whereas neo-realist theories would identify the change in terms of shifts in the balance of power (see also Mouritzen 1997), Gilpin's neo-mercantilism stresses the profound continuity of the international political economy and the increasing difficulties in managing an international liberal order – which are partly independent from the effects of strategic polarity.

The following discussion will, in more detail, deal with these two central claims of this chapter, namely first that Gilpin's research programme is best understood as a realist quest for the understanding of the dynamics of power, and second that he does not fit the neo-realist category well. The first section examines Gilpin's underlying assumptions. Although his link between human nature and group conflict is slightly unclear, his approach is certainly closer to Morgenthau than to Waltz. Second, his academic project will be identified as a plea for a necessary updating of realist IR as neo-mercantilist IPE. The third section presents Gilpin's design for rendering the realist approach more dynamic. It will be spelled out as a research strategy around three basic theoretical 'dialogues': between Clausewitz and Lenin, between Marx and Keynes, and between Lenin and Kautsky. This is followed by a short discussion of his empirical and normative assessment of the present global political economy, which according to him requires, but lacks, a hegemon. The final section indicates some limits in this neo-mercantilist approach, in particular Gilpin's state-centrism.

This chapter argues that Gilpin's main contributions lie in the updating and development of realist theory, and in the redirection of IR towards IPE. Before the detailed analysis of Gilpin's ideas begins a last preliminary remark is warranted. The following discussion is built around central tensions in Gilpin's thought, often acknowledged by Gilpin himself. His work is characterized by an attempt to do justice to a wide variety of approaches. Sometimes this results in a rather accrued sense of indecision. Gilpin once referred to himself as a 'liberal [with regard to his moral values] in a realist world and frequently also in a Marxist world of class struggle' (Gilpin 1986 [1984]: 304). Given the established categories of our disciplines, such or similar passages can be considered as confusing, and thus a major weakness of his work. I think they should rather be read as an indicator of academic transparency. Gilpin makes no effort to hide or cover uncertainties which, to be sure, are not only his. This is another, perhaps not minor, contribution to the discipline. In our times of hasty disciplinary closures his work stands for an attempt to offer the possibility of mutual learning.

Assumptions:
Ontological ambiguities and methodological individualism

Gilpin's assumptions represent a singular realist mix of permanence and change. His ontology posits the permanence of human drives, group organization and intergroup conflict. Yet his analysis of international systems stresses historical changes. To this, he adds a methodological individualist approach which expands the utilitarian realist tradition. The goals are threefold: security, power and wealth. They are given. The actors, however, are historically defined. Today's main social group is the nation. The changing international systems define the constraints within which these actors can pursue their goals. This section will, in turn, take up these ontological and methodological assumptions.

Moral pessimism and the permanence of human nature

Pressed to define what he understands by Realism, Gilpin refers to Rosecrance's description of political Realism not as a systematic theory, but 'as an attitude regarding the human condition'. Gilpin bases his interpretation of political Realism on three assumptions: the essentially conflictual nature of international affairs; the essence of social reality being the group, which, in modern times, means the nation; and the primacy in all political life of power and security in human motivation (Gilpin 1986 [1984]: 304–5).

For this last item, the unchanging human motivation, Gilpin quoted Thucydides with approval. And indeed, at many points he refers to a sceptic view of human nature as the underlying criterion to distinguish Realism from both liberalism and Marxism; because liberalism believes in the possible harmony of interests and Marxism insists that socialism will overcome the propensity to social conflicts.[1] Whereas changing contexts might make conflicts less likely, human conflictual nature remains constant.[2] The incessant attack on the realist story as a never-ending repetition and rehearsal on the stage of world politics has its core here. This ontological assumption is also consequential for Gilpin's methodology. If one can perceive a permanent basic motivation in human beings, then this is the place to start theorizing. Gilpin's turn to a utilitarian, or as he, following Brian Barry, calls it, an economic approach, is inextricably linked to this realist assumption.

The utility function of security, power and wealth

The economic approach to Realism and IR is not exactly new. In microeconomic theory, agents try to maximize their utility functions. That is, given a set of preferences and for a particular set of resources at hand, agents will choose to allocate their resources in order to maximize their return. Neo-classical economic theory cannot determine exactly what utility means for a particular agent. Yet the concept, and historical fact, of *money* allows the economists to commensurate the variety of aims on a common scale.

When applied to international relations, utility is interchangeably identified with 'security' or the 'national interest'. Once again, there is no way of knowing exactly

---

1 To what extent it makes sense to present IR/IPE in three opposing schools will be treated later in the second section.
2 So also for the advent of nuclear weapons; see Gilpin (1988b: 613).

what this means for any international agent (generally the state or government), but power is often conceived as functionally analogous to money in economic theory. Utility maximizing in IR means the maximization of security expressed in power.

This approach has been severely criticized by a few writers, either because the power–money analogy is said not to exist at all,[3] or because the analogy is only of limited use due to the incomplete transferability of power resources from one issue area to another, i.e. due to the lacking 'fungibility' of power (Baldwin 1989). Whereas an individual agent is able to 'cash in' labour in money and use money to buy something else, states cannot necessarily 'cash in' atomic weapons (strategic issue area) for lower tariffs (trade issue area).

Gilpin uses this approach in an unorthodox way. His main interest is the understanding of change. Besides his inquiry into the changing bases of power, he wants to understand the origins of power shifts and expansion. He transfers the analogy of marginal economics to the phenomenon of territorial expansion. Territorial expansion will occur as long as the marginal return outweighs the incurred costs. When the two are equal, expansion will stop. This idea of equilibrium is, of course, an economic translation of the balance of power. Similarly, it alludes to the classical realist argument about a 'power vacuum' which inevitably will be filled. As will be discussed in more detail later, Gilpin's major variance with the traditional realist approaches is that he applies this utilitarian theory of action not to strategic theory but to the order of world political economy: from deterrence theory to the theory of hegemonic war.

This redefinition of utilitarian Realism is a consequence of Gilpin's historical situating of today's international political economy. For Gilpin, the international system has been profoundly changed by the mutual feeding dynamics of the rise of the global market economy, and the emergence of the territorial state. Its ordering principle refers not only to strategic characteristics, as, for instance, the distribution of power, but to the global political economy which, in the present historical context, is either a (liberal) hegemony or in a state of anomy. As we will see later, for Gilpin Realism today necessarily means neo-mercantilism; to be an IR scholar requires one to be an IPE scholar.

Individual or group permanence?

Gilpin does not follow those who have tried to 'rescue' Realism from Morgenthau's 'dark' assumptions of human nature and who derived international conflicts from the nature of the international system. Gilpin is here particularly at odds with Waltz's neo-realism. But nor does he adopt a Hobbesian view, which likens the international realm to a pre-societal state of nature. His starting-point is the social groups in which humans organize themselves.

---

3 For this early and trenchant critique, see in particular Raymond Aron (1962). For a late and insufficient response to this critique, see Kenneth Waltz (1990).

> The building blocks and ultimate units of social and political life are not the individuals of liberal thought nor the classes of Marxism.... Realism, as I interpret it, holds that the foundation of political life is what Ralf Dahrendorf has called 'conflict groups'.... This is another way of saying that in a world of scarce resources, human beings confront one another ultimately as members of groups, and not as isolated individuals.... True, the name, size, and organization of the competing groups into which our species subdivides itself do alter over time – tribes, city-states, kingdoms, empires, and nation-states – due to economic, demographic, and technological changes. Regrettably, however, the essential nature of intergroup conflict does not.
>
> (Gilpin 1986 [1984]: 305)

This poses a theoretical problem. Scholars like Gilpin whose Realism rests on a strong assumption about human nature, should logically start their analysis on the level of the individual. Instead, the privileged unit of analysis is the state – for Gilpin, the nation; that is, a collective actor. There exist different solutions to this old problem.

Morgenthau (1948: 17) posits three basic drives of 'all men': to live, to propagate and to dominate. In a world of scarce resources, these different drives must result in a struggle for power. Hence, domestic politics is mainly about the collective attempt to control the individual struggle for power. But this lust for power cannot be eradicated. As a result, power drives frustrated within societies are projected abroad, a phenomenon that Morgenthau calls 'nationalistic universalism' for the universalization of nationalist drives – as opposed to a foreign policy which is both primary to, and isolated from, domestic politics. Morgenthau sees a close relation between social disintegration, personal insecurity and the ferocity of modern nationalistic power in international affairs. Methodologically speaking, this also implies that the analysis of IR can start at the national level, by reapplying the arguments derived from human nature now to another political environment, the international system, where the struggle for power is not checked by an overarching authority comparable to the state.

Gilpin has a similar view on human nature. He does, however, leave unanswered exactly how the link between the individual level and the national one should be conceived. If human nature and motivation are the permanent factors (as he says in the last of three characteristics of Political Realism), and intergroup conflict a permanent (or even 'essential') feature, then this aggregation should be spelled out. It seems that Gilpin presupposes that since everyone shares the same motivation, the group in which they are embedded will just do the same. But this begs the question, and we will return later to the issue of whether there is anything like a unified national interest. The economic model Gilpin uses must actually assume this, although he himself appears to question it.

Realist IR as necessarily neo-mercantilist IPE

On the basis of these assumptions, Gilpin proposes an academic project which tries to overcome the military emphasis of international studies and which redefines the borders of the discipline of IR. Particularly different from Waltz's form of neo-realism is his sensitivity to historical changes in the forms of intergroup conflict. For him, with the evolution of the groups' *internal* organization, the nature of conflict among groups also changes. The advent of the nation-state and market economy make a difference to realist theory: they require a neo-mercantilist conception of Realism. The welfare state in the twentieth century leads him to plead for a study of IPE around themes that synthesize neo-mercantilist and Marxist concerns.

The changed modern international political economy

Ever since his initial studies of technology and industrial policy, Gilpin believes that with the rise of the nation-state and market economy, power cannot be understood independently from the economic base. This basic insight of mercantilists and Marxists alike is the driving force of his theorizing: wealth and power, and the agent's pursuit of these, are inextricably linked. Thus, Gilpin provides a historical picture of today's IPE.

Gilpin believes that the rise of an international market economy had a major impact on state security, because it constituted a more or less autonomous sphere within and across borders, due to its independent dynamic and its aims, which were separate from the state or society at large.[4] This extraordinary development was possible for three reasons: the invention of a monetarized economy; the rise of a merchant middle class; and the avoidance (or postponement) of a unifying empire in Europe. The European balance of power allowed the merchant class to develop its strength in an environment where competition for wealth and power was pushing societies to adopt the modern state organization. Since the modern nation-state had an unchallenged fiscal and war-making capacity, it became from then on the major group organization whose expansion has lasted until today (Gilpin 1981: 123).

From the advent of the European state system (city-states) until the *Pax Britannica* is the phase of *mercantilism*; the first attempt of the modern world to organize a market economy on a global scale. Technological and organizational innovations in warfare bolstered the rise of mercantilism – as a form of political economy and concomitantly as a theory. Both the production of gunpowder and the rise of professional armies depended on the merchant trading system (to assure the provision of powder) and wealth (to pay the armies). In return, the sovereign guaranteed property rights.

---

4 For this and the following, see Gilpin (1977: 21ff.).

But only Britain's victory in the Napoleonic wars, the industrial revolution, and new means of communication brought together all the conditions necessary to create an interdependent world. The nineteenth-century balance of power (balance for the continent and power for Britain) allowed the competitive leader to manage the international economy financially and commercially. Britain's comparative advantage and national security interest demanded a 'liberal' approach based on an open market strategy. In short, the *Pax Britannica* provided the political framework for the emergence of a liberal international economy and concomitantly for (economic) liberalism as a doctrine.

This doctrine was soon criticized by economic nationalists like Hamilton or List who argued for a dynamic theory of comparative advantage where endowments might be created by conscious policies and must be protected in their infant phase, and later by socialists and in Lenin's theory of imperialism.

For Gilpin, the First World War was the test for the shift in power that occurred with Britain's decline and the rise of Germany and the USA. The absence of strong leadership in the interwar period produced the breakdown of the system.[5] Only with the *Pax Americana* after 1945 could a new liberal international order be established.

Gilpin generalizes from this historical account the factors that affect the incentive structure of actors and thus the stability of an international system. In his utilitarian theory of war, instability arises whenever a state calculates that it will be rewarding. This calculus is affected by changes in transport and communication, and military technology, and by demographic and economic factors that distinguish our period from the premercantilist ones.[6] Thus, although neo-realist theory might refer to the eternal return of power politics, Gilpin's necessarily mercantilist approach introduces as endogenous factors many otherwise neglected features. The causal chain of his approach starts with organizational, technological and economic change, often induced by the international competition of states. This affects the distribution of power in the system, and the incentives for agents to change their behaviour. Actual policies finally determine the specific international system (liberal or not).

Finally, Gilpin places today's IPE in the context of an international system which does not start in 1648 with the Westphalian Treaties, but which has existed only since 1815 with the advent of a British-led international liberal order. 'First in the European system and then on a global scale, successive political and economic hegemonies have supplanted the pattern of successive empires as *the fundamental ordering principle of international relations*' (Gilpin 1981: 144, italics added).

---

5 Gilpin (1971) interpreted the interwar period as a period where one leader was not strong enough and the other not willing to play the leader for the establishment of a liberal international order. This thesis got its authoritative formulation by Kindleberger (1986 [1973]) to whom Gilpin later often refers.
6 For this and the following, see Gilpin (1981: 55–84).

If neo-realism has been criticized for not being able to differentiate the change from the medieval to the modern system, Gilpin's historic and more dynamic account cannot be attacked on this charge.[7] A neo-mercantilist realist finds the major ordering principle of IR in the hegemonic governance of the international political economy, whether liberal or not.

Definition and ideologies of IPE

The historical development of IPE in the last few centuries also informs Gilpin's (1975b) typology of approaches to IPE: economic nationalism (or neo-mercantilism), liberalism (called, with reference to Raymond Vernon, the 'Sovereignty at bay' model) and neo-Marxism (or dependency). Later the same 'models' for the understanding of Foreign Direct Investment have been expanded into three 'ideologies' of IPE in general (Gilpin 1987b: ch. 2).

Since he repeats this tryptic at a time when the components have become common wisdom also in IR, Gilpin gives the impression that he wants to conceive IPE as a sister discipline of IR ('the economic approaches of Realism, Pluralism, Marxism').[8] Yet, as we will see, his view of IPE *de facto* attempts to overcome the limits of IR by a wider approach based essentially on the integration of ideas derived from neo-mercantilism and neo-Marxism. If, for historical reasons, it is impossible to preserve a purely political understanding of the state in realist theory, Realism must, according to Gilpin, be based on an approach which integrates politics and economics on the same footing. Similarly, the discipline of IR should become IPE.

Together with the threefold typology, Gilpin provides a rather succinct focus of the subject-matter that IPE is supposed to cover (and that defines its scientific research programme). His definition is often repeated in the standard literature:[9]

> political economy in this study means the reciprocal and dynamic interaction in international relations of the pursuit of wealth and the pursuit of power. In the short run, the distribution of power and the nature of the political system are major determinants of the framework within which wealth is produced and distributed. In the long run, however, shifts in economic efficiency and in the location of economic activity tend to undermine and transform the existing political system. This political

---

7 For its classical statement, see John Gerard Ruggie (1986 [1983]). For a discussion, see Wæver (1997b).
8 To cite just some of the innumerable triads in IR, see K.J. Holsti (1985) and Michael Banks (1985). In IPE, see R.J. Barry Jones (1981), Nazli Choucri (1980), and finally Stephen Gill and David Law (1988).
9 See, as an example, already ten years later: Martin Staniland (1985).

transformation in turn gives rise to changes in economic relations that reflect the interests of the politically ascendant state in the system.

(Gilpin 1975b: 40)

This definition claims to be broad enough to integrate the three 'models of the future' into one discipline. This is also what he attempts in the later textbook. Yet the three ideologies do not seem to be entirely satisfactorily integrated. The difficulty lies in the 'liberal model'. There is, at least, a tension in the solution he provides us.

In his book on multinational corporations (MNCs), the liberal model was subsumed under the interdependence literature. The essential claim of this literature was that increasing economic interdependence and technological advances in communication and transportation are making the nation-state an anachronism and shifting the control of world affairs to transnational actors and structures (e.g. the Eurodollar market). To this framework is added a world-view of voluntary and co-operative relations among interdependent economies, whose goal consists in accelerating economic growth and all-round welfare by means of the MNC as transmission belt of capital, ideas and growth.

This presentation superimposes insights from the interdependence literature on the liberal economists' or neo-functionalist credo. In other words, Gilpin links the transnationalist framework of analysis, which privileges non-state actors and dynamics, with the old-established, and simplified, idealist creed, which says that more commerce breeds harmony. By fusing these two ideas, his category of a 'liberal' school bridges the gap between transnational politics and the idealism of economic liberalism. As a result, Gilpin runs into a problem for his general definition of IPE. For political economy, political or power-analysis is an endogenous variable of the explanation. Liberal international economics, however, treats power as *exogenous*. By the force of his definition (where power and wealth are integrated), Gilpin seems pushed to exclude liberal international economics from the body of theory.

Maybe this is why he adjusts the definition in the 1987 textbook to what seems to be the present orthodoxy for the definition of IPE, the 'state–market nexus':

> The parallel existence and mutual interaction of 'state' and 'market' in the modern world create 'political economy'. . . . In the absence of the state, the price mechanism and market forces would determine the out-come of economic activities; this would be the pure world of the economist. In the absence of the market, the state . . . would allocate economic resources; this would be the pure world of the political scientist. . . . For the state, territorial boundaries are a necessary basis of national autonomy and political unity. For the market, the elimination of all political and other obstacles to the operation of the price mechanism is imperative. The tension between these two fundamentally different ways of ordering

human relationships has profoundly shaped the course of modern history and constitutes the crucial problem in the study of political economy.
(Gilpin 1987b: 8, 11)

This definition allows an integration of liberal economic theory as the model for the study of markets – even if power is treated as an exogenous variable. Nevertheless, he cannot but later admit that therefore 'liberalism lacks a true political economy' (Gilpin 1987b: 45). This squaring of the circle (how to integrate the liberals, even if they are, as defined here, of no use) leaves one rather perplexed. The stress on *political economy* (as in his first definition) was a reaction against the compartmentalization of the subject-matter in two different disciplines which often treat the other as exogenous to the subject. The field of economics was considered insufficient, because it did not integrate power analysis in its explanatory models. In its turn, political science often treated economics as exogenous to, or sometimes only dependent on, the political setting: the autonomy of market *forces* was missed. To alter the definition which stresses the 'organization' of the pursuit of power and wealth, rather than the 'objective' of this activity (Gilpin 1987b: 11), is to fall back on a conceptual and disciplinary split that political economy was supposed to overcome.

Dynamizing neo-mercantilism: three dialogues

In coherence with his earlier view, Gilpin in fact tries to overcome this split by elaborating an approach which is a mix of the two 'real' theories of political economy: mercantilism and Marxism. They will be articulated here in the form of three 'dialogues'.

State dynamics: the dialogue between Lenin and Clausewitz

An economic approach whose basic unit is the state necessarily requires a 'theory of the state'. Gilpin offers one that can accommodate both Marxists and the elitist theorists of the state (thus, also realists). The state is an 'organization that provides protection and [welfare] . . . in return for revenue' (Gilpin 1981: 15). This corresponds to the above-mentioned historical bargain between the political system and the rising middle class when the nation-state developed in concomitance with the (global) market economy. The primary function of states is to provide protection/security against foreign threats, establish property rights and distribute wealth domestically.

Aware of the long-lasting problem of assuming a national interest, or a state's utility function, he states that, of course, no such thing exists, and that strictly speaking only individuals have interests. This brings us back to the initial ontological question: is the individual or the state the 'essential' unit? Gilpin does not really discuss this, but refers to the national interest, in a manner not entirely unsimilar to elitist or radical theories of the state as determined 'primarily by the interests of their dominant members or ruling coalitions' (Gilpin 1981: 19).

Yet when he goes on discussing the so-called national or foreign policy interests, he falls back on a 'universalist' position, the interests being security and welfare, that are the logical consequence of the permanent motivation at the individual level. Thus, he remains undecided whom to side with in what Raymond Aron has called the 'dialogue between Clausewitz and Lenin':

> Le premier ne mettait pas en doute la notion du bien de la communauté (ou de l'intérêt national, dans le vocabulaire d'aujourd'hui).... Lénine répliquait à Clausewitz qu'il admirait, que dans un Etat de classes, il ne pouvait y avoir de bien commun. L'action extérieure des Etats exprimerait la volonté d'une classe ou d'une autre. Les événements, depuis la revolution de 1917 réfutent simultanément, me semble-t-il, les théories extrêmes. [He (Clausewitz) did not question the notion of the common good (or the national interest, in today's vocabulary).... Lenin answered to Clausewitz, whom he admired, that in a class society there could be no common good. The foreign action of states would express the interests of one class or another. It seems to me that the events since the 1917 revolution simultaneously refute the extreme version of both theories.]
>
> *(Aron 1984: 30; my translation)*

If for the external function and motivation there has been little change, at least on the domestic side, Gilpin sees in the type of 'social formations' (the concept is taken from Samir Amin) a major source of international change. Social formations determine how the economic surplus is generated, transferred and distributed both within and among societies. The change from one social formation to another determines the change from one international system to another.

> The distinguishing features of premodern and modern international relations are in large measure due to significant differences in characteristic social formations. The displacement of empires and imperial-command economies by nation-states and a world market economy as the principal forms of political and economic organization can be understood only as a development associated with the change from an agricultural formation to an industrial formation.
>
> *(Gilpin 1981: 110)*

It is important to note here that for Gilpin the former socialist countries and the western liberal countries have, of course, many differences, but they share the aspect that the economic surplus is generated by industrial production and this affects their foreign behaviour. It is, however, probably not only the similar industrial social formation but its insertion into a common international market system that creates a pressure for similar behaviour. If for a Waltzian neo-realist, states in a self-help system behave similarly, independent of their political system, neo-mercantilism redefines both the unit and the system level, as well as their effect on the behaviour of states. The shift to welfare states implies a redefinition of the 'self' of the state; a new identity which needs to be protected and for which states do compete. The international political economy, which results *also* from the character of the political economy of individual social formations, means that the international system is not just a configuration of power, and that states have to find means to conform to the pressures of a world market economy.

Socioeconomic dynamics: the dialogue between Marx and Keynes

More recently Gilpin has come to specify a change that might in fact correspond to another major historical shift, although he does not characterize it as such. As Gilpin describes the global political economy after 1945, it is characterized by a hegemonic liberal international order, the *Pax Americana*. Yet this hegemony is different from the British one. The key to the difference lies precisely in the link between the social formations and the international system they create. The change that has occurred and that was institutionalized after the First World War is the change to mass societies in which legitimacy derives from their capacity to enrich their people and to do it on a more equal basis. The *Pax Americana* is based on a special kind of the liberal state, the welfare state, which under US leadership collaborates in an international system of 'embedded liberalism'.[10]

Gilpin analyses the Keynesian revolution as a response to the inherent problems of nineteenth-century capitalism that Marx had more or less rightly recognized (Gilpin 1987b: 59). For him, the welfare state has 'nullified' three Marxist laws of the internal contradictions of capitalism. The 'law of disproportionality' has been overcome by the welfare state's demand management through fiscal and monetary policy. The 'law of accumulation' could be countered through income redistribution, support for trade unions, and regional and small business policies. Government support for education and research can increase the efficiency of all factors of production so as to upset the 'law of the falling rate of profit'. Yet capitalism is intrinsically expansionist. With the end of territorial imperialism and consequently the diminished capacity to export the burden of capitalist adjustments, the contradictions of capitalism ricochet back on the leading economies. As the world has been recognized as finite since the end of the nineteenth century, capitalism becomes inherently conflictual on the international level. Whereas capitalism can be supplemented by a welfare state to overcome its contradictions on the domestic level, the question arises if it can work on the international level where no world welfare state exists. Gilpin believes that

> the logic of the market economy as an inherently expanding global system collides with the logic of the modern welfare state. While solving the

---

10 The concept and the analysis to which Gilpin refers are from John Gerard Ruggie (1982). See also Wæver (1997b).

problem of a closed economy, the welfare state has only transferred the fundamental problem of the market economy and its survivability to the international level.

(Gilpin 1987b: 63)

The result is a system where states compete over the international division of economic activities, by using and creating comparative advantages, and by attracting production into their countries. The domestic welfare legitimacy makes states more nationalist than before. For Gilpin, only a hegemon can impose a liberal order in this competitive environment. Only the hegemon can provide the necessary public goods to allow the 'compromise of embedded liberalism', i.e. to run a multilateral system by allowing autonomous national economic policies.

IPE dynamics: the dialogue between Lenin and Kautsky

If the present international system has been the second in a series of liberal hegemonies (and not just empires), then the rise and decline of hegemons are the major research focus at the international level. The research is part of what has come to be called 'hegemonic stability theory'.[11] The latter can be characterized by three theses:

1. the emergence of a hegemon is necessary for the provision of an international public good (Hegemony thesis);
2. the necessary existence of free riders (and thus the unequal distribution of costs) and/or a loss of legitimacy will undermine the relative power position of the hegemon (Entropy thesis);
3. a declining hegemon presages the declining provision of an international public good (Decline thesis).

Such a hegemon normally arises after a rearrangement of power shifts, which is most probably violent. The reason is that power (and efficiency) shifts are quicker than the political reactions and thus produce an incentive structure for the rising powers to go to war in order to change their status in the system.[12]

The particular public goods that Gilpin finds the hegemon providing are roughly those that Kindleberger analysed as lacking in the interwar period:

---

11 This section owes much to Anna Leander.
12 The same logic applies to Krasner's (1982a: 498–500) image of the 'two tectonic plates', which might produce an earthquake (major conflict), if the shifts in one (distribution of power) are not reflected in the other (international regimes).

1. the stabilization of monetary and trade relations via
   - rediscount mechanisms for providing liquidity during international crises
   - lender of last resort function
   - management of the international monetary system (Kindleberger would add the maintenance of a structure of exchange rates and coordination of macroeconomic policies)
   - openness of markets for distressed goods
   - a steady, if not countercyclical flow of capital;
2. redistribution of income through foreign aid; and
3. regulation of abuses (sanction mechanisms).[13]

Thereby, Gilpin gives a two-sided account of hegemony in general, and the international liberal order in particular.

On the one hand, he follows the typical realist account that hegemony breeds order in the sense of limiting (and deterring) conflicts.[14] He does not, or at least does not want to, subscribe to the idealist turn which speaks of the US 'sacrifice' for a liberal order.[15] Quite to the contrary, he follows Carr's critique of the British ideology of a harmony of interests:

> Once industrial capitalism and the class system had become the recognised structure of society, the doctrine of the harmony of interests acquired a new significance, and became ... the ideology of a dominant group concerned to maintain its predominance by asserting the identity of interests with those of the community as a whole. (. . .) No country but Great Britain had been commercially powerful enough to believe in the international harmony of economic interests.
>
> *(Carr 1946: 44, 46)*

He states explicitly that the hegemon must perceive it in its own (perhaps long-term, or enlightened) interest to provide the public good. Only this is consistent with the underlying economic approach (Gilpin 1986 [1984]: 311–12).

On the other hand, Gilpin shifts from the focus on the utilitarian calculation to a domestic analogy: the hegemon takes over the same functions in the international society as the government has in domestic society, namely providing the

---

13 For the original statement, see Kindleberger (1981: 247, 1986 [1973]: 288–93). For Gilpin's initial formulation, see 1971; for his more developed formulation, see 1987b: 368.
14 For instance, Kenneth Waltz (1969: 312) says: 'Extreme equality [among states] is associated with extreme instability.'
15 For this unexpected idealism in a staunch Realist, see Charles P. Kindleberger (1976: 10).

public goods of security and protection of property rights in exchange for revenue (Gilpin 1981: 145). This is linked to the basic assumption of the ubiquitous nature of conflict in politics *tout court*. It is in this vein that he follows Keohane's (1984) argument against the Hegemonic Stability Theory which rejects the decline thesis, that regimes (Keohane's public good) once established can take on a dynamic of their own and subsist, although the hegemon that issued the system may decline in power. In that respect, Gilpin translates the common norms that realists have found necessary for the functioning of a (political) concert system into IPE. The concert has to be run not just by the major powers, but, in order to allow a liberal order to function, by all the major *liberal* powers. Their common code integrates domestic political and international economic issues.

This having been said, Gilpin believes that the decline of the hegemon definitely weakens the international liberal order. It weakens the first of the three political foundations of such an order, which are a dominant liberal hegemonic power or powers able to manage and enforce the rules; a set of common economic, political and security interests that binds them together; and a shared ideological commitment to liberal values. Here, he refers to the classical socialist debate between Lenin and Kautsky (Gilpin 1987b: 38–40). Lenin stipulated that the 'law of uneven development', i.e. the necessarily differential growth of national capitalist economies, would undermine any attempt to establish an international multilateral order. The expansionist drive of monopoly capitalism at the imperialist stage would necessarily provoke wars. Kautsky, on the other hand, argued that the capitalist countries would not be so stupid as to go permanently to war with one another if a collaboration in international exploitation would be more lucrative. This is his doctrine of 'ultra-imperialism'. Consequently, Gilpin's empirical question has become the future of the liberal order after the decline of the *Pax Americana*.

International liberal order after the decline of the *Pax Americana*

The crisis of 1971/3 has been aggravated by recent developments. The first major change came when the US capacity to handle both the international political economy and its own society became visibly strained. This was, according to Gilpin, the consequence of a massive redistribution of world economic power away from the United States towards first Europe and then the Pacific around Japan and Southeast Asia. The USA has become deeply indebted and needs foreign, in particular Japanese, help to run international monetary relations. Furthermore, the monetary system's change to a flexible system has removed the former discipline and induced the phenomenon of global inflation. This risk factor heavily constrains traditional Keynesian policies. The monetary system is by now nearly out of control due to the revolution in the financial sector. The management of industrial production in a firm has become vertically integrated, and is now genuinely transnational. Finally, Gilpin speaks of a change to a third phase of the industrial revolution, with the coming of knowledge-intensive industries, which has 'undermined the basic assumption of the Bretton Woods trading system that comparative advantage was a "given" of nature and could not be altered by the policies of corporations and/or governments' (Gilpin 1991: 16–17).

Consequently, the present system is characterized simultaneously by the transnationalization and integration of markets *and* by increasing nationalistic impulses. At the same time, the 'struggle for the world product' (a Helmut Schmidt quote Gilpin likes to use) will be decided with the victory of one hegemon, because, for Gilpin, economic efficiency and political power have become increasingly linked. The identity of this hegemon will largely determine the character of the next international order.

The pressure has already led to many adjustment programmes, both domestically (supply-side economics, education, industrial policies, and so on) and externally (protectionism in different forms, the use of political power for markets or investments). The biggest of these adjustments was certainly the Soviet one. For Gilpin, Gorbachev's policies were induced from abroad. Aware of the increasing 'technological gap' to the G7, the Soviet Union decided on the most liberal reforms since the Bolshevik Revolution.[16] But domestic restructuring also took place in Japan and Europe started a new initiative to regain some macroeconomic instruments via an accelerated political and economic integration (Maastricht). The Third World has given up its demands for a New International Economic Order (NIEO) and competes for the attraction of Foreign Direct Investments (FDIs) (the worst is not to be exploited, but to be neglected by the international division of production). Finally, even the USA seemed to be reconsidering its policies after years of 'mask[ing] the profound developments that have occurred and the challenges they have posed. The United States has lived on borrowed time – and borrowed money – for much of the last decade' (Gilpin 1987a: 33). Many of Gilpin's later writings are filled with policy recommendations in which he also incorporates his studies on technological policies.[17]

But the major risk of the system is the threat not only to the liberal order inside or outside individual countries, but to the very existence of this present international system as a whole. This theme appears twice. First, the increasing transnationalization of production exposes not only industries, but entire social formations, to competitive pressures from abroad, which can disrupt existing social consensus and, in turn, spill over conflict to the international level. This partly explains Gilpin's repeated concern with Japan–US (or Western) relations. Second, the decline of the *Pax Americana* seems to be accompanied by a decline of the legitimacy of the principles on which it was built. 'Inter-civilizational conflict' (his term) looms on the international scene.

16 For Gilpin, the fundamental change in recent world politics is an inextricable link between technological and power competition. This provides the background against which the end of the Cold War must be understood.
17 For an account of the most efficient technology policies, see Gilpin (1982).

Gilpin's solutions correspond to a typically realist solution, both pragmatic and normative. On the pragmatic level, he is rather critical of the attempts to impose changes on the social structure of specific states from abroad. Hence, he does not endorse the 'cultural' turn US–Japanese mutual reproaches sometimes take. To salvage at least a partial version of embedded liberalism and reduce the impact of possible trade wars, Gilpin follows the general idea of a 'benign mercantilism' organized through the partition of the world into three hegemonic orders (USA–Europe–Japan) with respective economic spheres of influence (Gilpin 1987b: ch. 10). His normative answer to forms of inter-civilizational conflict is once again separation, this time not geographically into world regions, but axiomatically between internal and external relations. Gilpin hereby reiterates a recent theme of the Rawlsian liberal political philosophy. Taking seriously the 'plurality of incommensurable conceptions of the good',[18] legitimate collective choices are possible in liberal orders only by means of a private (values)/ public (space of tolerance) distinction. Incommensurable values are confined to the private sphere, as religion, for instance, to preserve a public sphere of debate and compromise, indeed of justice. Liberalism claims therefore to be neutral or to provide a 'higher order theory' compared with all other political theories or ideologies. Gilpin, who finds himself a Grotian realist in this respect, uses this liberal distinction and procedural solution as his maxim for the establishment of order at the international level. States (should) understand that the best way to avoid major conflicts lies in the sharp division between domestic value-systems and international politics and in the reciprocal acceptance and moderation of national interests. Hence, for Gilpin 'in contrast to liberalism and Marxism, realism is a universal political theory which every society can understand' (Gilpin 1990: 137). To state and hopefully reduce the confusion between the disciplines: Grotian *Realism* in IR relies on a public–private distinction which permits it to claim to be neutral or potentially universal, just as recent (domestic) political *liberalism* does.

It also shares the problem of political liberal theories: how to 'persuade' an actor to follow such a universal maxim, when the latter's underlying value-system cannot accept the private–public distinction. In IR the problem is more consequential. Although major conflicts are to be avoided, war in its limited form is at times a justified instrument of realist politics. Revolutionary powers who want to export their ideology are checked by force. After so many attempts to update Realism, we are back to the basic dilemmas as posed by Classical Realism. As long as neither human nature nor the conflictuality of the international system varies, neo-mercantilist IPE is certainly a valuable advance in order better to apprehend the dynamics of the system and the possible widening of the

---

18 The formulation refers to John Rawls. See in particular his turn of the 1980s (Rawls 1985: 248–9; and 1987: 4 ff.). One of the potential differences is that realism says to accept any (national) value-system, whereas Rawlsian liberalism requires the necessary acceptance of principles of justice for a conception of the good to be admitted.

cracks in the wall of the existing order. When asked how to react, however, its instruments do not differ from those of realist normative theory.

The limits of neo-mercantilist IPE

Gilpin's initial interest is double: it concerns both the capacity of societies to react and adapt to a changing international environment and the possible spillovers of societal dynamics on to the international order. It is guided by a liberal concern for the welfare state and for a liberal international order, which is, as we will see, not always clearly defined.

Therefore, Gilpin cannot indulge in the purely structural turn of neorealism, because this approach neglects the societal level. As we have seen, Gilpin's approach needs the latter to historicize the international structure, as, for instance, the present link between the welfare state and the international liberal order. In fact, whereas Gilpin integrates Waltz's structure as one of the elements of the systemic level into his model, the latter does not integrate a theory of the unit-level, although Waltz (1986: 331) admits that 'international-political theory at times [sic!] needs a theory of the state'.

Gilpin's attempt to dynamize Realism problematizes the co-determination of the two levels. It can be understood as a way to overcome two major problems in balance of power theories. First, a focus on changing power bases and actors' power dynamics should help to prevent the risk of tautological reasoning where any outcome can be explained *ex post* by a reassessment of the initial distribution of power. To avoid tautology, balance of power theories in fact require an actor-based relational rather than a structural-positional power approach.[19] Second, this approach allows for *competing* unit and system-level explanations of international events (see also Mouritzen 1997). To give up the mechanical view of the balance of power has more implications than is usually acknowledged. If international politics is articulated along unpredictable patterns of the actors' amity and enmity (Wolfers 1962) or of the 'homogeneous or heterogeneous' character of the international society of states (Aron 1962: 108f.), then no extrapolation can be done from the distribution of power. The balance of power theories are indeterminate (Wolfers 1962: 86). Or the other way round: a structural analysis based on the anarchy assumption might exclude security and behavioural options that features of amity and homogeneity create at the level of interaction.

As we have seen, Gilpin's neo-mercantilist project is a somewhat ambiguous mix, or an 'ambivalent juxtaposition'[20] of a scientific (choice-) theoretical ideal on an historical approach – at first hand a puzzle for those used to classifying him

---

19 Since the 1970s, this point has been repeatedly advanced by David Baldwin. See his articles collected in Baldwin (1989).
20 For the critique of this Realist strategy to overcome its inherent tension between structuralism and historicism in general, but applied to Gilpin, see R.B.J. Walker (1987: 78f.).

into the scientific corner of Realism. The mix should rather be read the other way round. Gilpin is a historicist realist who tries to clarify the assumptions that underlie many traditional empiricist accounts of international politics, namely utilitarian thinking and consequentialist ethics. Unfortunately, he dismisses debate about these assumptions with a single reference to an underdiscussed liberal political theory and to choice-theoretical approaches, both acceptable to the main canons of IR/IPE. His first and only reaction to meta-theoretical critique is telling in this regard.[21]

This is also the general thrust of the following critique of this neo-mercantilist project: in a sense the later writings of Gilpin restrict the interdisciplinary exchange to which his own approach had initially contributed. On the one hand his project consisted in a more general critique of how IR should be analysed (namely as IPE), i.e. in an attempt to overcome Realism by integrating some of its insights. On the other hand, the turn to a more systemic hegemonic stability theory and the state/market nexus provided no more than an update of Realism. Being one of the forerunners of IPE as a redefinition of IR, Gilpin might unwittingly have 'normalized' it to an unchallenging subcategory of international and increasingly US politics.

By insisting on the necessity of a theory of the state, he opens the door to both 'comparative political economy' and historical sociology, disciplines that have became increasingly isolated within IR. Both approaches study the articulation of the particular state–society nexus in the changing global political economy, either by in-depth studies of one case or by more macro-level comparisons.[22] In stressing both the transnationalization of production and the adaptation processes at the societal level, Gilpin should logically proceed to analyse transnational blocking groups and lobbies and integrate the study of domestic dynamics with transnational ones.[23] In short, seen from this perspective transnational actors and networks cannot be reduced to the outside environment of state action, but must be regarded as participating in a single realm of world politics.

Yet Gilpin repeatedly shifts back to a policy-making level. An example is his discussion of Third World development, where he rightly points to domestic reasons for underdevelopment, but in fact bypasses them. 'Those less developed societies that have put their houses in order and have created efficient domestic economies have succeeded in achieving very rapid rates of economic growth' (Gilpin 1988a: 205). This explanation begs the question: how can a country with a specific social formation, a particular position in the global political economy, and specific transnational links put its house in order? What are the systematic

---

21 'The Richness of the Tradition of Political Realism' is a response to Ashley's (1984) critique of neo-realism in which Gilpin does not even mention the meta-theoretical level on which Ashley's critique is pitched.
22 Representative of others, see Peter Katzenstein (1985) and Theda Skocpol (1987 [1979]).
23 This is one of the tenets of more radical political economy, as, for instance, in Robert Cox (1987).

and what the contingent constraints and opportunities, including the domestic history of social groups and the collective memory that patterns political debate and the active understanding of issues?

Despite his own analysis of the vertical integration via firms, of the increasing globalization of political economy, it is as if politics were conducted only by states. This could be due to the central role of hegemons in the theory and thus the concentration on great power policies. Or maybe it is because the role of the (realist) writer to provide counsel to the prince (Gilpin 1986 [1984]: 320) requires a state-policy oriented perspective.

Yet returning to a national (or state) perspective has consequences for the very identification of the problems of the present global political economy. There is first of all a reduction of liberalism to a free-trade order (Gilpin 1986 [1984]: 311ff.). Protectionism therefore represents the main evil to be avoided. This appraisal is influenced by the historical lesson of the interwar period, with competitive 'beggar-thy-neighbour' policies, or more aggressive ways to export the burden of domestic adjustments abroad. In this reading, the welfare state is as much a liberal domestic solution as an international problem. Gilpin is, however, well aware that today's technological and economic change has brought about a system of international production where international trade is decreasingly important and the major flows either are goods exchanged within firms (also across different states) or are in the form of capital, know-how or other forms of what is called the 'New Foreign Direct Investments' (patents, licences, domestic savings used for FDIs, and so on). In other words, it seems clear that, contrary to Gilpin's opinion, the 'health' of the global market system can hardly be satisfactorily measured with the thermometer of its free-trade conviction.

This signifies that the liberal international order has to cope with a transnational agenda, where national reversals to more neo-liberal policies, which Gilpin at times notes with tentative approval, only increase the fiscal crisis at the state level, not on the expense, but on the income side. Far from preparing a return to a less national (because less state-interventionist) order, neo-liberal policies, in fact, constitute a kind of nationalist strategy in the new global competition for foreign investment and market shares.

Gilpin's focus on trade might induce one to think that if only multilateral management of national trade policies were introduced, the liberal order could be saved. Yet the novelty is not hegemonic decline and rising protectionism, but the global stage of production. The difficulty is not the rising use of national economic policy means, i.e. an affirmation of national sovereignty that could be negotiated with others, but the increasing powerlessness of these very means at the disposal of individual states.[24] Even if we had a hegemon, in today's world, the hegemon could hardly enforce a liberal order as before.

---

24 In her recent writings, Susan Strange (1988, Stopford and Strange 1991) is stressing the diffusion and 'disappearance' of authority.

It is difficult not to have the impression that Gilpin's very legitimate interest in the adaptation of his own society eventually plays a trick on his neo-mercantilist approach: it becomes increasingly not only state, but US-centred. The link to social formations, elsewhere neglected, reappears in the implicit (and sometimes explicit) US agenda. Although Gilpin has helped to open many new routes in the study of politics, widely conceived, he may thus have contributed to making IPE just a particular subfield of the 'American science' IR.

Conclusion

Informed by a historical analysis of different orders in the international political economy, Gilpin has challenged established realist IR and proposed to renew it as neo-mercantilist IPE. The basic questions in his research concern the dynamics of power and powers. Gilpin set out a research programme which can be divided into three sets of problems: the identification of state dynamics, socioeconomic dynamics and the tensions in global governance. As the preceding chapter attempted to show, this research programme incorporates many more historical and conceptual facets than the official version of neo-realism made the discipline believe. His intellectual breadth makes him a classical realist who plays with the potential of utilitarian analysis, rather than one of those rational choice scholars who want to discipline IR/IPE on the basis of economic methodology.

Maybe the development of the nation-state and of the last phase of global productive integration requires a further step outside the neo-mercantilist logic. Maybe the opening to the historical sociology of social formations demands a greater sensitivity towards meta-theoretical and theoretical critiques of utilitarian approaches. Gilpin provides some hints, he openly acknowledges theoretical and normative tensions and yet he remains undecided. Apart from his many historical, conceptual and theoretical insights, it is this honesty which honours his work and still provides needed thinking space for the discipline.

10
SUSAN STRANGE'S OSCILLATING REALISM

Opposing the ideal – and the apparent

Introduction

Writing about the relationship between Susan Strange and realism is like trying to make two moving targets meet. This is because there are nearly as many forms of realism as there are realists. Moreover, Strange consistently shifted the direction of her scholarly and non-scholarly work. Hence, if this chapter claims that Strange can be well understood as a realist, this has to be a realism of sorts.

This chapter argues that Strange's version of realism has been systematically oscillating between two poles: opposing the ideal and the apparent. This oscillation, which can also be found in E.H. Carr, produced perhaps her most important conceptual contribution, namely 'structural power'. At the same time, it is responsible for two important internal tensions in her work: it clashes with her encompassing materialist position with which she wanted IR to become IPE and, eventually, it renders her views on (political) agency incoherent.

The two poles of Strange's realism

Strange's realism displays a central duality. Traditionally, the discipline of International Relations conceives of realism in opposition to idealism, to utopian thinking. Without wanting to deconstruct the long lists of dichotomies that have been spurred by this distinction (see Walker 1987, 1993a) or the fictitious presentation of inter-war debates as idealist (for this critique, see Schmidt 1998), this chapter will show that Strange fits rather well with some of the central tenets of realism, so understood. She did not spare her criticism of those fellow realists who did not seem to appreciate what she considered to be major shifts in the

I would like to thank Anna Leander, Tom Lawton and Amy Verdun for helpful comments on an earlier draft. All disclaimers apply.

nature of global affairs. Strange, the anti-idealist realist, was the champion of a power-materialist discipline of IPE, which subsumes, if not swallows, classical IR and its more narrow-minded scholars, as she would see them. However, political theory distinguishes a second facet of realism, understood in opposition to yet another phenomenon: the real is the opposite of the apparent (see the characteristically astute discussion in Bobbio 1996 [1969]: xiv–xvii). This facet has frequently been the main motivation of Strange's work, in particular when she scorns the self-celebration of the 'American Century'.

This double heritage of political realism, opposing both the ideal and the apparent, is ripe with tensions. Realism as anti-idealism is status quo-oriented. It relies on the entire panoply of arguments so beautifully summarized by Alfred Hirschman in his *The Rhetoric of Reaction* (Hirschman 1991). According to the *futility* thesis, any attempt at change is condemned to be without any real effect. The *perversity* thesis would argue that, far from changing for the better, such policies only add new problems to the already existing ones. The central *jeopardy* thesis says that purposeful attempts at social change will only undermine the already achieved. The best is the enemy of the good, and so on. Anti-apparent realism, however, is an attitude more akin to the political theories of suspicion. It looks at what is hidden behind the smokescreen of current ideologies, putting the allegedly self-evident into the limelight of criticism. With the other form of realism, it shares a reluctance to treat beautiful ideas as what they claim to be. But it is much more sensitive to their ideological use, revolutionary as well as conservative. Whereas the anti-ideal defends the status quo, the anti-apparent questions it. It wants to unmask existing power relations.

International Relations (IR) has known many scholars who have shifted back and forth between these two conceptions of realism, often without noticing it. The most obvious example, perhaps, is E.H. Carr's (1946) *The Twenty Years' Crisis*. In the initial chapters, he sets up a typology of realism as opposed to utopia and argues for a discipline of IR, which now has to settle down, and get rid of its early history of hopes and wishes, as necessary as they had been to launch the discipline. Yet, at the same time, Carr takes visible delight from bashing his fellow Britons who, in the name of liberalism, were so amazingly blind as to believe that what was good for Britain was good for the world. The famous critique of the apparent 'harmony of interests' strikes the reader as obviously realist; but it is a realism of a very different kind. Far from defending the real against a utopia that will never come, it unmasks a utopia dressed up as real. Being aware of the historical character of any ideology, Carr later logically delves into the study of history, indeed into the history of change *par excellence*, the history of revolutions. For the same reason, he relies on Karl Mannheim's (1936) historical sociology of knowledge (for a trenchant exposition of the intellectual origins and internal inconsistencies of Carr, and the usually one-sided reception, see Jones 1998). It comes as no surprise, then, that many radical writers, such as, for instance, Robert Cox (1986 [1981]), see themselves in the tradition of the realist Carr.

Strange's realism does not feel comfortable with either strand for too long, being no absolute defender of prudence misunderstood as immobility, and no proponent of change illuminated by the grand vision. It is as if her work reversed its direction whenever it risked getting too close to one pole. Again, this oscillation is necessary for such a type of realism. As Carr had remarked a long time ago, '[t]he impossibility of being a consistent and thorough-going realist [understood as anti-ideal] is one of the most certain and most curious lessons of political science' (Carr 1946: 89). The anti-ideal position, if reified, becomes itself an ideology that needs to be undermined.

By the same token, this double realist inspiration does not in itself provide a framework for understanding the world – a theory, as it were; realism so understood is merely an attitude towards the world (for this argument, see also Gilpin 1986 [1984]: 304–5, referring back to Rosecrance). Consequently, Strange's work is torn by internal tensions that she was at pains to reunite.

Yet perhaps it is exactly the tension and intellectual challenge of this oscillation which inspired some of her most important conceptual particularities, many of which are important contributions to both IPE and realist thought. As the next section will attempt to show, anti-ideal realism is the source for her wider materialist conception of politics as expressed by the necessary shift from IR to IPE. In order to make this argument, Strange develops a new approach to power, including prominently 'structural power', perhaps one of the more important contributions to IPE and realism. At the same time, her discontent with the present 'ungovernance' of the international system, and the role the United States plays therein, introduces her anti-apparent realism. She criticizes the present ruling of the global political economy, which comes in the disguise of a necessity, to which we cannot but adapt. For her, such a view is nothing but a new version of an apparent 'harmony of interests' embodied by the international business civilization. Instead, she sees it as a global order, which the collectivity of states, and in particular the United States, chooses not to control.

This oscillating reliance on the two sides of realism produces two internal tensions, as the third section will try to show. On the one hand, her structuralist understanding of power includes a structure – knowledge – which basically contradicts her realist materialism. On the other hand, her assessment of the diffusion of power eventually clashes with her very critique of US policies.

The necessity for a realist to be a political economist: Taking power materialism seriously

While studying the politics of a currency and the decline of a former global actor, Strange (1971) commenced a long series of publications that examine the interrelationship between power and finance. This is the one continuous inspiration for her research. She drew two lessons, that might appear obvious today but were quite contentious to many of her colleagues in IR at the time, particularly to realists.

The first lesson was that international politics could not be reduced to what states do. As well as in her later study on the Bretton Woods system (Strange 1976), state policies, even if nicely designed and with all the best intentions, have 'realistically' to take into account the force of private actors, such as firms. To put it more generally, they have to cope with market forces. In her career, Strange made no secret of her contempt for the British Foreign Office which was still too much attached to a view of the world long since obsolete. The insistence on a classical definition of international statecraft, classical war and classical diplomacy could not, according to her, produce anything but political blindness in world affairs.

Her academic colleagues in IR were not spared either. Exasperated by her own collaboration with Schwarzenberger at University College London, she insisted that if IR did not incorporate political economy, it was doomed to produce useless analysis. She never shared the strategic focus of many of her colleagues during the cold war. Whereas, in her earlier work, she maintained a focus on the state system, even that focus would give way to the triangular diplomacy between states and firms in her co-authored *Rival States and Rival Firms* (Stopford and Strange 1991).

The second lesson, more directed against economists – whether politicians or academics – was that the driving force in international economics was not trade, but finance and production. In fact, in her world view, the most important factor in the political economy was the control of capital (credits and production). With the need to keep good ratings on stock and debt markets and the need to hedge against currency rate fluctuations, capital markets of all sorts became the driving forces of modern capitalism. Trade, despite its prominence in mainly US studies, was largely a secondary indicator following these more profound forces. In a move similar to her critique of IR security specialists, Strange criticized the discipline of economics as basically irrelevant. Instead of abstract modeling, her approach to political economy was always more historical and progressively shifted to insights from political geographers, and business and banking economists.

As a result, her approach can be said to be very critical of realism. Ever since Waltz's *Theory of International Politics* (1979) was used to redefine the agenda in IR, Strange's type of analysis appeared fundamentally at odds with contemporary realism. Confronted with a crisis of the realist school, Waltz resurrected a disciplinary wall, which defined the subject-matter (international politics, not foreign policy), a method (based on an analogy with neoclassical economics) and a specific approach (systemic realism, or outside–in, based on the balance of power, as the only theory of IR). His success exasperated all those who had been trying to open up the research agenda.

Yet if some scholars were exasperated by what realism had done to the discipline of IR, some realists were increasingly wary of what the discipline of IR had done to realism. Hence some realists who wanted to open up the research agenda, rather than to move it to other disciplines, opposed Waltz's narrow definition of both IR and realism. Although doing so in a different vein, Robert Gilpin also tried to shift realists away from the classical security agenda. The works of both Gilpin and Strange stand out as attempts to break loose of the neorealist straitjacket imposed on international research (see also Guzzini 1998: ch. 11). As such, they are not much interested in reproducing the paradigmatic distinction between domestic and international politics, so cherished by neorealists. Nor are they interested in keeping politics apart from economics. Indeed, all the disciplinary walls so meticulously erected by Waltz would come tumbling down. A realist IPE in the vein of Strange and Gilpin is a critique of the role realism, both old and new, played in defining a narrow agenda for research – and for politics.

At the same time, this move, as critical as it became to much of the traditional realists who populated IR in Strange's early career, is a move that does not fit the classical realism–idealism divide. Strange did not criticize realism for its cyclical vision of history, for its obsession with conflict, for its emphasis on power and hierarchy. Instead, she criticized it *for not taking these issues seriously enough*; that is, for assuming a very static environment, as if the historical development of capitalism had no effect on power politics. The history of conflict might repeat itself, but not its nature.

In fact, Strange argues for a revision of realism, in which its basic power materialism is redefined. Matter matters, but not only the strategic one. The control of finance, that is currency, capital and credit, is the matter of the day. As a good realist, she will admit that the security structure is predominant 'in the last resort' (Strange 1988), but for the time being we have to deal with the other ones. Her IPE, similar to Gilpin's version, is one possible but logical outcome of an attempt to update realism in an age of the welfare state and global capitalism. Behind the apparent materialism of the balance of power lurks a more encompassing one in a realist political economy.

Being both a critique of disciplinary realism and a renewal of realist materialism, it comes as no surprise that her approach centers on the old realist obsession with the concept of power. But given her understanding of what moves global politics – her redefinition of politics itself – she has to develop a view on power that differed from the classical realists. For her, power is more diffused both in its sources and effects. In order to better apprehend its present sources, she conceptualizes international hierarchy as the effect of the interrelation of four power structures: security, finance, production and knowledge. The control of these basic resources – arms, credit, capital and technology/culture – defines who is top dog or under dog in international affairs. Obviously, these power resources are not limited to state agents. In fact, firms might be prominent in the last three, many states irrelevant in all. The second part of her concept of power, the diffusion of power effects, is based upon the increasing globalization of politics. Here, Strange is essentially concerned with the effects of actions which, whether intended or not, crucially affect others. It is this second aspect that eventually produces tensions in her realism, moving from the anti-ideal to the anti-apparent.

A critique of the apparent decline of US power: Taking soft power and the diffusion of power seriously – eventually

The basic tension in Strange's approach can be summarized as follows: how is it that in a world in which power is increasingly diffused and the capacity to control events is said to evaporate, some actors are still criticized for being basically responsible for the situation and able but not willing to resolve it? The answer lies in a shift from the anti-ideal critique of our view of the world, stressing its base on material power redefined, to the anti-apparent critique of the top dogs, the 'international business civilisation' with its headquarters in the United States (Strange 1990: 260–5), that makes us believe that not much can be changed (Gramscian undertones are not fortuitous). Yet this shift produces internal tensions: to uphold the anti-apparent critique of the United States, Strange has to rely on a concept of structural power whose two ingredients, the diffusion of the sources of power, including ideas, and the diffusion of its effects, contradict both her anti-ideal materialism and eventually her critique of the United States itself.

The idealist streak in soft power

As long as Strange does not refer to the diffusion of power, there is not much of a tension. Hence her earlier critique of regime theory (Strange 1982) argues that international organizations, allegedly important in these international regimes, have no impact whatsoever. This, as she says herself, is the clearly (anti-ideal) realist streak in her argument.

But then an anti-apparent realist part creeps in. For her, the new focus on regimes and IOs should not blind us to the 'non-territorial empire' of the United States (ibid.: 482). In this piece, Strange basically argues that the United States is setting the research agenda, and that it has a vested interest in presenting the world run by regimes. Furthermore, she argues that regime theory is biased in assuming that everyone wants regimes, and more of them. This point is perhaps better phrased when she refers to 'order' as being the main aim of some states and not of others. This recalls Carr's typical realist criticism of the apparent harmony of interest in the status quo. Moreover, it is overly state-centric, leaving out important bargains and distributional issues below and across state frontiers.

The basic tension starts to develop when her critique of US policies, that is policies by a state, clashes with a world view which is less and less statist. The solution, or at least so it seems, lies again in the reconceptualization of power: the US empire is non-territorial, its power is structural. Hence one could have the cake and eat it: the United States is still *at* the center of world power, its policies could make a difference – and yet all this is part of a more diffused international power structure. But does it work?

The debate about the decline of US power in the aftermath of the Vietnam War, a debate that took on a political economy spin in the 1980s, provided

Strange with a welcome foil for developing her thoughts on the changed nature of international power and politics. According to her, far from being a symptom of US decline, the demise of Bretton Woods was a testimony to US might: the United States was able to destroy the most important international regime on its own conditions – and got away with it (Strange 1986). In other words, although not necessarily controlling all outcomes, the United States still controlled the rules of the game and could bend them in its favor. This is a conscious choice. This part of her concept of structural power could be called 'indirect institutional power' (Guzzini 1993).

A second aspect of structural power is conceptually more daring. It insists on the study of unintended effects as part of power analysis. Instead of taking them as a kind of fatal mishappening, the anti-apparent realist rebels and argues that such effects are perfectly conscious by now. Moreover, those effects that are important for the international power structure are the result of the actions of only a few international actors. Their place in the respective power structures is such as to systematically (structurally) affect others. Perhaps it would be better therefore to refer to this part of her concept of structural power as 'non-epistemic power', as Morriss (1987) does, or as 'non-intentional power' (Guzzini 1993).

To have used the concept of power as a hinge for her critique of the United States is not fortuitous. Here Strange plays with a central characteristic of the concept of power. Power is a concept which has a variety of purposes (Morriss 1987: 37–42). To mention two: power is used in practical contexts in which we are interested in what we can do to others and what others can do to us. It is also important in moral/legal contexts where it functions as an indicator of effective responsibility: if actors could not have carried out an act (if they had not the capacity to do so), they cannot be found guilty for it. The first indicates the realm of action, power as an indicator of politics as the 'art of the possible'; the second assesses possible blame. By limiting the practical context to only those actions with which we intend to affect others, we rule out any moral judgments on those actions that affect others, whether intended or not.

Hence, to have redefined power is necessary for a realist of the anti-apparent inspiration. Leaving out non-intentional power mobilizes a status quo research bias and blinds us to the tacit power of the strong. It is useful to look at power from the side of the power holder and not, as non-intentional power does, from the perspective of the actors affected by it.

This reconceptualization, meant both to attack US power and policy and to display a vision of a diffused power system in international relations, does run into trouble, however. It eventually must relax the materialist understanding of power. This becomes visible when Strange likens her critique of the US decline debate to Joseph Nye's *Bound to Lead* (1990a). The similarities are remarkable indeed. In a later article, Nye (1990b) specifies why he sees no decline in US power. First, rather than having any other country picking up US power, the world is characterized by a 'general diffusion of power' (Nye 1990b: 155). Second, given the rise of political interdependence and modern technology, power is becoming 'less transferable [from one issue area to another], less coercive, and less tangible' (ibid.: 167). In such circumstances, it turns out to be a cost-efficient strategy to get other actors to do what you want them to do, not by ordering or imposing (command power), but by getting them to want what you want (co-optive or soft power). For the latter, increasingly important, form of power, intangible resources are crucial, such as cultural attraction, ideology and international institutions. Here the United States is by far the most influential actor, whose power is growing rather than receding. This combines well with Strange's understanding of the knowledge structure, which is not only about technology, but also about belief systems, ideologies, fashions and ideals (Strange 1988). This concept smuggles the issue of culture into her political economy approach.

Consequently, her critique of the US decline school produces some tensions with her critique of the apparent continuity of the classical IR agenda, as mentioned above. In the first critique, she argues for a thoroughly materialist account of international affairs. In the second, she makes an important concession to less materialist conceptions of politics. The knowledge structure has two components, technology/know-how and culture. Whereas the first can be accounted for, the second looks like an idealist cuckoo in the realist nest.

For a realist, the use of language and ideology is no problem, as long as it can be shown that actors are in control of it: ideas are factors of power when they are manipulated by actors. Strange does see the ideological use of much US theorizing that systematically tends to shift blame abroad. If the US government could not keep its house in order, and had to leave Bretton Woods, it was because of the USSR/cold war (in Vietnam), the US government's generosity towards its allies, the liquidity problem of the international monetary system, the oil shocks, and so on: 'American theorising has thus become an elaborate ideology to resist sharing American monetary power' (Calleo and Strange 1984: 114).

Unfortunately for a coherent realism, Strange does not assume that the ideology embedded in the business civilization, or the advantages occurring to English-speaking countries by the use of their mother tongue and their cultural products, are necessarily manipulated or channeled in a specific direction: they have a life of their own (they form a structure). Denying their existence and importance for the worldwide hierarchy would be 'unrealistic' for the anti-apparent realist, even if its account is at odds with the materialism underlying Strange's anti-ideal realism. The implication is candidly spelled out by Nye: 'when ideals are an important source of power, the classic distinction between *realpolitik* and liberalism becomes blurred' (Nye 1990b: 170).

'Ungovernance' by the non-territorial empire as a critique of the United States:
Taking the diffusion of power seriously

This subsection explores the second part of the tension between the diffusion of power on the one hand, and the critique of US action on the other. Whereas we discussed earlier the mismatch of soft power and materialism, we now refer to the mismatch between the increasing non-territoriality of power, its diffusion – if not evaporation – and US control and responsibility. This section claims that Strange's concept of power cannot really overcome the tension. It is a tension that builds up gradually in her work when she refocuses away from US control and onto international 'ungovernance'. The tension subsists later in another source of strain: her Keynesian urge for international regulation and her realist pessimism that anything like this will actually happen (see Leander 2000b).

The initial motivation of Strange is her drive to demystify US decline, that is to question the only apparent truth. One of Strange's best known articles on the 'myth of lost hegemony' has a very symptomatic title (1987). Her demystification aims at the real existing *Pax Americana* as the best of all possible worlds, or, a slightly weaker claim, as a world which could not have been avoided – ordained, as it were, 'by God or History' (Strange 1975: 215).

She uses her concept of structural power to reveal the hidden might and responsibility of the United States. This is already visible in her famous analysis in *Casino Capitalism*, where she shows that a series of decisions and non-decisions by the US government (mainly) were responsible for the present system, whether intended or not. Finally, she alludes to the fact that it suits the US government to keep it as it is, a statement made more strongly in *Mad Money* (Strange 1998).

She is most explicit in later pieces, where she dissects the power of the United States to set the rules of the games to be played in the four basic power structures. Starting with the production structure, she argues that, although TNCs control the largest part, this does not mean that the United States has lost control over the world economy. Most TNCs are based in the United States. The others, wanting to be profitable worldwide, have to conduct business on US territory. It follows that the structural power of the United States is not to be measured in US GNP but 'as the total value of goods and services produced by large companies responsive to policy decisions taken by the US government' (Strange 1989: 167). The same applies to the financial structure, where the United States has lost power to the banks or to the foreign exchange markets, but can take it back: 'As the experience of the Roosevelt administration in 1930s showed clearly, bankers like everyone else (even insider traders) are subject to the law, and the law can be changed to bring them back under the control of the states' (ibid.: 168). 'In every important respect, the United States still has the predominant power to shape frameworks and thus to influence outcomes. This implies that it can draw the limits within which others can choose from a restricted list of options, the restrictions being in large part a result of US decisions' (ibid.: 169). Put more bluntly, 'it is the world economy that is the anvil and the United States the hammer, in Lenin's apposite metaphor' (ibid.). As a result, power, no longer being territorially defined, is still concentrated in the United States, which is the core of the non-territorial empire. Its capital is Washington, but its control over people (not over land) extends to all aspects of its 'international business civilization'.

Given this assessment, it is obvious that Strange believes some new form of international regulation has to be found. Since she does not much trust international institutions, she keeps her faith, somewhat ironically, with the United States itself, which would be the most benign hegemon (ibid.: 173). Her critique of the United States's structural power is meant to make the country conscious of, responsible about and thus responsive to the effects of their action: the usual excuses will not do. But this faith is also the result of her realist inclinations that not much will be done without getting the consent of the powerful. If the United States is indeed as powerful as she describes, then all depends on it. Therefore she does not fail to lambaste, provoke and ridicule US policies so as to provoke directional change.

In her last writings, this assessment starts to be undermined by her own vision that all governments, including the US, have lost control over the world economy. It is not at all sure that she would repeat the confident assessment of US power after 1989. It might have been the choice of the United States, and not some technical necessity, to 'lift the lid' of globalization, but it is not clear that the process can subsequently be reversed.

This analysis finally produces a typical realist dead-end: the optimism of the will is persistently checked by the pessimism of the intellect. Strange's inclinations cannot envisage any other solution than one guided by the most powerful actors, and yet she says this will not be forthcoming. Although she maintains her attack on US unilateralism, she is then at a loss to conceive of any solution to the general problem of ungovernance. Her realist inclinations cannot conceive of regimes or world governments as solutions – and she offers little other alternative to this classical dichotomy. Strange's entire approach leads her repeatedly to ask for a recreation of the Keynesian control over the world economy, in particular its finance (1989: 175–6; 1996: 194), a move her realist vision of IR cannot conceive of happening.

As a result, her concept of structural power has played a trick on her argument. At the start, it allowed her to unravel US influence where it might not necessarily be seen. But insisting on the diffusion of power inevitably led to an analysis, where also the control of the still most powerful state can no longer be assumed to guarantee world stewardship. Far from resolving the problem, the concept of structural power embodies it. Once controlling for its two facets, however, it can be fruitfully used to analyze social hierarchy and control in the global political economy. It opens up one promising track for analysis in IPE.

Epilogue: retreat or reform of realism?

This chapter has argued that Strange's version of realism can be best understood as oscillating between a (conservative) opposition to the ideal and a (critical) opposition to the apparent. This oscillation pushed her to make perhaps her most important conceptual contribution – structural power. At the same time, it forced her into internal tensions concerning her underlying materialism and her views on (political) agency.

After presenting the two types of realism, Bobbio proceeds by saying that there is a third one, attempting a synthesis of the first two. Such a realism would scorn both the catechism of the utopian and the cynicism of the reactionary. Indeed, realism can be understood as the attempt to steer through a middle-ground between the realm of necessity and the realm of freedom (Berki 1981). As such, 'real' realism, one not confounded with any of the poles, would necessarily come mainly as a negative attitude, always reversing direction, speedily oscillating (see also Griffiths 1992). Strange might seem to fit this bill. While doing so, she makes an achievement of no small proportion by rescuing a more credible, 'realistic' version of realism through a structural analysis of power which goes beyond any other realist writings – and which can be fruitfully used also by non-realists.

But, at the same time, this realism can produce a very stale, if not sterile, political agenda. It gives discussions this priggish taste so typical of the realist scholar who 'has always been there already' – not by moving forward, but by shifting to the right and left. The one solution perhaps best suited to keeping this type of 'real' realism alive was proposed a long time ago by the realist who had struggled most with this double heritage of realism, E.H. Carr. His idea was not to oscillate between the two poles at any single point in time, depending on which audience one chose to address. Instead, he oscillated between the poles over time, meeting head-on the truth of the day, whether reactionary or revolutionary (Carr 1961: 177). In *Mad Money*, her political testament, Strange may have come closest to this (temporarily) one-sided stance when she knew that her oscillation could no longer continue.

PART III
Constructivism

11
A RECONSTRUCTION OF CONSTRUCTIVISM IN INTERNATIONAL RELATIONS

What a success story! Hardly known a decade ago, constructivism has risen as the officially accredited contender to the established core of the discipline (Katzenstein, Keohane and Krasner 1998). 'The social construction of . . .' is littering the title pages of our books, articles and student assignments as did 'the political economy of . . .' in the 1980s.

The success is at least partly due to constructivism's alleged 'middle ground' position (Adler 1997). Taking a constructivist stance allows us to be critical towards, or at least innovative with regard to, the mainstream. And yet it does not succumb to the sirens of poststructuralism, which critics have turned into a radical idealist position, increasingly emptied of any intelligible meaning. Put more positively, constructivism promises to make significant contributions to the theoretical debate in International Relations. For some time already, and including many mainstream scholars, this debate has aimed at avoiding the pitfalls of the extremes of empiricism and idealism, of individualism and holism, or of single truth and relativism. Hence, rather than 'seizing' a middle ground

---

This chapter has been written under the auspices of an international project funded by the Volkswagen-Stiftung on 'New Curricula for Teaching International Relations: A Task for Regional Institutions in Central and Eastern Europe'. Its first versions were presented at workshops in St Petersburg (February 1999) and Nida, Lithuania (September 1999). I want to thank the participants and in particular Christopher Daase, Andrey Makarychev, and Klaus Segbers for their comments on an earlier draft. Moreover, I have greatly benefited from suggestions and comments by Lóránd Ambrus-Lakatos, Alexander Astrow, Jeffrey Checkel, Jef Huysmans, Markus Jachtenfuchs, Peter Katzenstein, Anna Leander, Michael Merlingen, Cas Mudde, Heikki Patomäki, Ulrich Sedelmeier, Davide Sparti, Alexander Wendt, Colin Wight, Friedrich Kratochwil and two anonymous referees of *EJIR*. The usual disclaimers apply. After six years of teaching at the Central European University, I would like to dedicate this chapter to my students from whom I learnt more than they could imagine.

in theoretical debates left vacant, constructivism was allowed to become its legitimate tenant.

The new prominence of constructivism comes at a price, however. It is only one step to reverse the relationship between constructivism and the middle ground – although constructivist positions are part of this middle ground, not all theorizing on the middle ground is constructivist. In other words, the success was paid for by a neglect of some of the basic ideas of constructivism.

As a result, 'the social construction of. . .' is often either eclectic or redundant. Eclecticism shows up when constructivism has become a general category out of which many researchers pick and choose their particular version without necessarily looking at the theoretical coherence of the final product. Redundancy applies when a constructivist touch adds some face lift to already existing approaches. This happens, for instance, when constructivism is said to refer to the claim that ideas, besides material matters, have an impact on politics. As such, it would differ from 'rationalism' in that this impact is not necessarily reducible to calculated strategic action. It would differ from pure 'idealism' in that these ideas do not come about in a vacuum (see the well-coined title by Risse-Kappen 1994a) – they are embedded in a historical context and need an institutional support to be effective. Moreover, ideas and their institutional support can affect the preferences and interests of actors. If that were all, Stephen Krasner's (1982a) analysis of the feedback of regimes on actor preferences would make out of him an early constructivist (not that he might care much about labelling). But if that were all, why bother to study constructivism? Life is short.

Against this tendency of eclectic or redundant use, this chapter looks for theoretical coherence, and tries to rebuild bridges to empirical research. What follows offers a systematic rethinking of constructivist tenets. It will hence not provide yet another survey of constructivism. It does not look for a basic common denominator of constructivism shared by all scholars who so call themselves. This undertaking has undoubted merits as a first step for gathering information about a new research programme. But more recent attempts have also shown its limits. The sheer diversity seems to make the category of constructivism explode. Consequently, the plethora of recent survey articles decided to give constructivism a better coherence either by emphasizing a single particular view (Adler 1997), by picking out particular approaches for discussion (Checkel 1998) or by providing typologies (Hopf 1998). Although this chapter shares some of these endeavours, it more explicitly wants to offer one coherent, although not the only possible, *reconstruction* of constructivism, understood solely as an explanatory meta-theory.[1]

The present *reconstruction* emphasizes two major inspirations of recent 'middle-ground' theorizing, namely the interpretivist and the sociological turns in the social sciences. Taking the interpretivist turn seriously means to start from the

---

1 Hence, the following is not directly concerned with moral questions which are of central concern to some constructivists (Kratochwil 1989b, Onuf 1989) and to postmodern approaches (for an assessment of poststructuralist ethics in IR, see Guzzini 1997).

idea of meaningful action, and hence from the difference between social sciences which need to interpret an already interpreted world, and natural sciences who need not (Schutz 1962 [1953]). Theorizing must therefore conceptualize the level of common-sense action apart from second-order action (or, observation). Most importantly, it must analyse their relationship. Again setting the social world apart from the natural, our understandings of people and their action can make a real difference to the latter. For instance, being identified as an opportunist state representative influences options in future negotiations. Moreover, human beings – but not natural phenomena – can become reflexively aware of such attributions and influence their action in interaction with them. This 'looping effect' (Hacking 1999: 34) is one of the reasons for the importance of 'identity' in constructivist writings, theoretically and empirically.

Taking the sociological turn seriously implies that meaningful action (and hence also the knowledge of both agent and observer) is a social or intersubjective phenomenon. It cannot be reduced to cognitive psychology or to choice, based on interests. Instead, the sociological turn emphasizes the social context within which identities and interests of both actor and acting observer, are formed in the first place. Finally, it means that the relationship between the two has in itself to be problematized, i.e. the relationship between the social world and the social construction of meaning (including knowledge).

In other words, the present reconstruction understands *constructivism in terms both of a social construction of meaning (including knowledge), and of the construction of social reality*. It proceeds in two steps. A first section aims at contextualizing the recent sociological and interpretivist turn in the social sciences. I will argue that the recent success of constructivism can be linked to the double context of what Ulrich Beck has called 'reflexive modernity' which affected all social sciences, as well as of the end of the Cold War which touched more particularly on IR. The main second section presents three central tenets of constructivism, coherently reconstructed from the double turn in the social sciences. The chapter argues that constructivism implies first a double hermeneutical position at the level of observation and, second, an intersubjective theory of action. It must avoid mixing an intersubjective theory of knowledge with an individualist theory of action (for a related critique of regime theory, see Kratochwil and Ruggie 1986).

Third, and given the 'looping effect', the relationship between observation and action proper needs to be problematized in a 'reflexive' way. This reflexivity raises questions about the relation between meaning/knowledge and power which nearly all recent constructivist approaches, in contrast to their poststructuralist predecessors, tend to neglect. Hence, the central issue of power stressed by just one analyst (Hopf 1998) is, as I will argue, not so much a question of research taste as of theoretical logic. For, if social constructivism is fundamentally stating that the present is not determined by the 'nature' of things, then it is analytically akin to power analysis which is always about a counter-factual and how things could have been different (Baldwin 1985: 22). If meaning attribution and the social world are in interaction, then the political status quo and the legitimacy of public action fundamentally depend on this interaction, on this construction.

Reflexivity is then perhaps the central component of constructivism, a component too often overlooked. This chapter is, to some extent, an attempt to show how constructivism in IR is harking back to some ideas expressed earlier by Keohane (1989 [1988]) in his distinction between rationalism and reflectivism (for all its shortcomings in providing only a residual category for the latter), or by Neufeld (1993) or, outside IR, in the social theory of Ian Hacking (1999) or of Pierre Bourdieu (see in particular Bourdieu 1990, Bourdieu and Wacquant 1992).[2]

Origins of constructivism in IR: Reflexive modernity and the end of the Cold War

New intellectual developments within an academic community, such as constructivism in IR, can always be seen as the product of a double conjuncture. On the one hand, they are embedded in historical developments outside of the academic community. On the other hand, they reflect the structure and content of the debates that define the identity of an academic community itself. Shifts in theoretical attention are the reaction and adaptation of (at least a part of) the academic community to intellectual fads and achievements, inside and outside the discipline, as well as to peer pressure and to employment patterns for the professional academic.

In the following, I will first attempt to delineate several 'external' lineages, before the next section will discuss the tenets of constructivism against the disciplinary background within which it developed. A caveat is needed, however. I cannot establish whether these lineages were indeed the ones that have influenced all or a certain number of constructivists, directly or indirectly, because this would require other empirical work on the production of knowledge in International Relations. Consequently, my reading is as much a possibility of understanding the historical and intellectual background of constructivism.

Two historical developments merit to be mentioned for the understanding of constructivism in IR. First, I would relate the emergence of constructivism to what Ulrich Beck (1986: 14, and passim) calls 'reflexive modernity'. This refers to the increasing awareness of the inherent limits and ambiguities of technical and social progress, an awareness dating back to the beginning of the 20th century. The second important historical context was intrinsically tied to the internal debates in IR, looking here at an incomparably shorter time-span – constructivism has undoubtedly profited from the *certitude of possible change* that swept over Europe, in particular during the second détente and the end of the Cold War.

2 Being particularly important for constructivism does not mean that reflexivity is specific to it. It is present in any more advanced sociological theory, be it in the individualist tradition (Coleman 1990: ch. 23), or in Niklas Luhmann's system theory.

Reflexive modernity

For some it might sound far-fetched to invoke long-term historical changes or, as for the second origin, a prevailing *Zeitgeist* as a background for the understanding of a specific meta-theoretical shift in a social science. But then, despite claims to the contrary, scientists are no isolated lot. Moreover, there is an internal connection between a more hermeneutical, indeed 'double hermeneutical' (see later) move in scientific explanations, and the understanding that modernity has become reflexive to itself. Both render problematic the self-awareness of the scientist, and of modern (wo)man, respectively.

Societies, mainly in Western Europe and North America, have known a resurgence of pessimistic ideologies or moods during recent decades. This shift in attitudes is characterized by a critique of modern industrial societies, if not of modernity as such. For many of its critiques, modernity is understood as the belief that, with its technical capacities, humankind can assure never-ending progress. Moreover, modernity is taken to be a basically individualist project where the rational ego is the sole protagonist of history. Or as Raymond Aron (1969: 287) once put it, the disillusion with progress stems from the very source of modernity, 'the Promethean ambition', that he finds exemplified in Descartes – the ambition of becoming masters and owners of nature, including human nature, through science and technology.

The origins of the demise of this faith in progress can, among other things, be found in recent ecological disasters, famines with ever increasing death rates, or the threat of a nuclear Armageddon. If rationality cannot solve these plights, if technocratic action is indeed often the cause of these disasters, then, so the argument goes, the Enlightenment project, or rationalism *tout court*, is no longer a way forward. Postmodernity refers to this kind of hangover after the ebriety of progress. It also alludes to the attempt to 'think the unthinkable', since it is compelled to think in categories mainly borrowed from the Enlightenment; and yet it must invent new ones to show us a way 'beyond' them.

This civilizational pessimism is not exactly new. Its roots are to be found at the turn of the century, when Max Weber already had to struggle with humankind's 'disenchantment'.[3] (Wo)Mankind was both producing incomparable riches and the iron cage of bureaucracy. The increase of individual and social power was not matched by any increase in moral certitudes. On the contrary, we have lost both the mysteries of the for ever unknown, and the comfort of the all-encompassing gospel – different Gods are fighting each other.

But whereas most critiques of modernity never envisaged leaving modernity itself, today some claim to do so. This claim, in turn, has been opposed by many who, in principle, would share the same assessment of present dangers. For the

---

3 One could, of course, argue that the conservative counter-movement to the beginning Enlightenment expressed civilizational fears, too. But these are of a different type than the ones of Nietzsche/Weber who certainly do not profess a way back to the unity of faith.

latter, however, the call to postmodernity is not the empirical and moral consequence of a bankrupt project of technological progress, but the internal and logical consequence of a mistaken understanding of modernity itself. For the Enlightenment is not about Reason with a capital R, but about reasoning. Reason, to be coherent with itself, must undermine itself in a dialectical movement, in which the truth of today will be replaced by another tomorrow, as in particular early members of the Frankfurt School have reminded us (Adorno and Horkheimer 1969 [1947]). Indeed, as Jürgen Habermas (1985) has repeatedly pointed out, this critique of a reason that no longer allows criticism of itself – a reason which has become a dogma – this very critique is the modern project *par excellence*.

Ulrich Beck has investigated the reason for which modernity could be mistaken for an already accomplished project. According to him, it is due to a fatal conceptual conflation of modernity and industrial society. We have come to believe in the myth that modernity has reached its apogee in the industrial society of the 19th and 20th centuries, 'with its schemes of labour and life, sectors of production, its thinking articulated in categories of economic progress, its conception of science and technology, its forms of democracy' (Beck 1986: 15, my translation). Consequently, we have started to think that the problems of this form of social organization, as well as any critique of this society, must equal a critique of modernity.

By redefining modernity as an open project, by de-linking again industrial society from modernity, Beck proposes a different view of our present state. When modernization has overcome its traditional opponent, it turns against itself. We are living in a world in which modernity has reached a new stage – it has become reflexive.

Constructivism in IR can be understood within this context of reflexive modernity. Particularly relevant for International Relations has been the sudden self-awareness of the (European) international society that it is only a particularistic one despite its global expansion during the 19th century. It could no longer assume or impose its rules as being universally shared.

After World War I, the relatively taken-for-granted diplomatic culture showed signs of a crisis which was later taken up by those realists with a more classical understanding of International Relations, more historical and practical, than scientific and technical. A main concern lay in the recruitment of a foreign policy elite different from what Hans Morgenthau called the 'Aristocracy International'. Diplomacy was no longer in the hands of this transnational class, which shared a similar socialization and rules of conduct, and which would be in control of diplomatic recruitment. 'While the democratic selection and responsibility of government officials destroyed international morality as an effective system of restraint, nationalism destroyed the international society itself within which that morality had operated' (Morgenthau 1948: 189). Also Henry Kissinger worried about the survival of the European international society in this context of a rise of particularism, nationalism in Europe and then decolonization elsewhere. 'When domestic structures – and the concept of legitimacy on which they are based – differ widely, statesmen can still meet, but their ability to persuade has been reduced for they no longer speak the same language' (Kissinger 1969: 12). The lack of such a common language could jeopardize the very existence of a shared diplomatic culture and hence the possibility of Concert diplomacy.

More profoundly, decolonization reminded Western powers that the rules of this international society were not only made *by* them, but *for* them (Bull 1984). The arrival of the 'Third World' on the international scene made it impossible to overlook the fact that the international system was ruled in a way which had little to do with liberal principles, and that the story of economic progress had forgotten several parts of the world. Indeed, as some early dependency theoreticians argued, the wealth of the 'North' could be systematically based on certain conditions of backwardness in the 'South'. Early writings by R.B.J. Walker (1980), a scholar only later labelled poststructuralist, insisted on the relationship between the Western crisis of confidence and the difficulties of the West to talk in the name of a universe it was told it no longer represented.

Being put in front of a mirror which showed a rather unflattering picture of itself, Western philosophy and social science engaged in discussions and redefinitions of its own and hence others' identity (for a recent discussion on identity, see in particular Sparti 1996). In democratic theory, this shows up in the discussions about multicultural societies (C. Taylor 1992, Kymlicka 1995). More generally, it reverberates in the debates about the social construction of collective identities in the form of *Imagined Communities* (Anderson 1991), and our construction of others, like Edward Said's (1979) *Orientalism*. In International Relations, poststructuralists deconstructed the practice of sovereignty as the historical solution to the problem of cultural pluralism and universalism (Walker 1990, 1991, 1993a, Bartelson 1995). The importance of identity, and its analysis, became central issues for the empirical analysis of the social construction of others – be they labelled poststructuralist (Campbell 1992) or constructivist (Neumann 1995, Kratochwil and Lapid 1996). Identity is also central for the sociological critique of rational choice approaches, which assumes that this socially constructed identity is causally prior to the definition of interests (e.g. Jepperson, Wendt and Katzenstein 1996, Ruggie 1998).

The end of the Cold War

It seems probably less debatable to relate the development of constructivist theories to the immediate historical background of the end of the Cold War, and not only because the most quoted article of constructivism has been explicitly referring to it (Wendt 1992a). For constructivism refers to a (social) 'World of Our Making' (Onuf 1989). And a politically geared change of a stalemate that had lasted for half a century seemed to show that international structures were not objective. If, as Hacking (1999: 6) contends, social constructivism is basically about questioning the inevitability of the social status quo, then the unexpected fall of the wall gave new legitimacy to such claims, in particular since the change seemed to have been effected by actors who have become self-consciously aware of the dilemma situation in which the Cold War had trapped them.

Again, it was definitely not a new point that the international system could be understood as a social artefact. It is the basis of the English School of International Relations.[4] In a different vein, it had been hammered out by peace researchers all over the world for some time already. But during the 1980s, different versions of determinist and materialist approaches to understanding international affairs had taken the floor. In the aftermath of the Afghanistan invasion/Euromissile decision, East–West relations looked grim again and seemed to comfort all those who had said it from the start – détente was a way to sell out national interests (a category that could be filled by virtually everything) which, in turn, would be better served by rearmament. For them, there was no way out of the security dilemma. In the absence of a forceful arbiter, state actors have to face the dilemma of choosing between two equally costly options – do not arm and you risk defeat (insecurity); arm and you risk escalation (insecurity). The Second Cold War of the 1980s tipped the balance in favour of the second choice.

With the end of the Cold War, the European continent moved beyond the security dilemma, at least for the time being. Disarm and you get de-escalation. Gorbachev's 'New Thinking' showed that although states can meet instances of the security dilemma, this was no necessity. Nor was any single bilateral relation doomed to stay within it. This possibility of change is basic to the constructivist understanding of the international system.

Yet, there are two basic misunderstandings about the relationship between the understanding of change in world politics and constructivism in International Relations. The first misunderstanding reduces the constructivist challenge to a mere critique that international theories had been unable to predict the dramatic changes (Wohlforth 1994/1995). That a single event is difficult to predict is something which could be expected. What spurred the constructivist critique was, rather, that prevailing theories did not even recognize the possibility that it would happen in the first place (for this critique, see Patomäki 1992, Kratochwil 1993, Koslowski and Kratochwil 1994). For, according to constructivists, the end of the Cold War showed that the world of International Relations is not fixed like the natural world, a world which exists independently of human action and cognition (including here the social phenomena of language and communication). The international system, usually described as being anarchical because it lacks a central government, is still a system whose rules are made and reproduced by human practices. Only these intersubjective rules, and not some unchangeable truths deduced from human nature or from international anarchy, give meaning to international practices.

---

4 Therefore, some constructivists return to representatives of the English School for inspiration, or even try to read a constructivist agenda into their work. This last move, however, is more problematic given the empiricism of the English School. For such a reading, see Timothy Dunne (1995).

The second misunderstanding consists in saying that constructivism is a form of pure voluntarism. It would imply that we can construct any social world, simply by wanting it. As the previous argument indicated, however, rules and norms guide the behaviour of actors, and they are intersubjective, not individual. Change is to be conceptualized on this normative level, the legitimacy crisis in the USSR, not on a volontarist base, say Gorbachev's or Shevardnadze's vision, although individual volition obviously can play a role, and did so in this case.

Tenets of constructivism in IR

If neither the reference to reflexivity of modernity, nor the awareness of the social nature of the international system were new, why all that fuss about constructivism? The reasons can be found in the internal debates of the discipline. Whereas previous schools of similar content fought their battles on the level of policy analysis, this time the struggle was drawn into the meta-theoretical field. Constructivism combines many old hats with a willingness to challenge the scientific project of Mainstream International Relations, in particular in the version which became dominant in the 1980s. This assessment seems, at first hand, to contradict the statements of its most well-known representatives in the USA (Jepperson, Wendt and Katzenstein 1996, Ruggie 1998). But then, the disagreement is only apparent, since those scholars tend to sideline the problem. Jeffrey Checkel's (1998) reception is symptomatic of that stance. There, the Mainstream understanding of science is so widely defined that it begs actually the significant questions. Checkel defines it as a commitment to empirical research (and not pure philosophy) and a commitment to scientific criticism (and not relativism); two commitments easily shared by many who would yet ask for a departure from a more positivist understanding of science. For we need first to know which kind of empirical analysis and which type of scientific criticism we are talking about. These are typical middle-ground questions – not only for constructivists.

In the following I would like to discuss three central tenets of constructivism which, if taken together, depart from established theorizing and empirical research by taking the interpretivist and the sociological turn in the social sciences seriously. Given the twofold interpreted character of the social world, these tenets refer to the level of observation, the level of action and their relationship. There is, at the level of observation, first and foremost the very core of *epistemological constructivism* which developed out of the critique of empiricism and positivism. Second, there is the closely related tenet of methodological intersubjectivity, or what one could call *sociological constructivism* which developed out of the critique of rational choice approaches. And finally, there is the central *concept and the analysis of power* in constructivism which functions as the reflexive link between observation and action. If the present status quo was not inevitable or naturally given, the very world-view of Mainstream IR, its definition of politics, and consequently the 'art of the possible' to cope with it, are challenged. The 'art of the possible' is a central theme of the concept of power. Constructivism is part of a wider definition of the international political agenda. Meta-theories do matter both empirically and politically.

The level of observation: Epistemological constructivism and double hermeneutics

Epistemological constructivism

Scholars who had so laboriously opened IR to new frontiers during the 1970s, had to watch how the success of Waltz's *Theory of International Politics* locked up the discipline again. It was a classical balance of power theory. Its success was due to the fact that it said much rehearsed things in a scientifically acceptable manner.[5] Waltz's book not only resurrected a very narrow definition of what was international, a very materialist conception of politics, but provided also a welcome 'scientific' definition of how to conduct theorizing and research (for a more detailed critique, see Guzzini 1998: ch. 9).

The critique therefore aimed at the meta-theoretical foundations of Waltz's new disciplinary wall. Indeed, one can say that Waltz's critiques used the debate around his book to force an inroad of meta-theoretical discussions into IR. Since Waltz's defence of scholarly criteria was taken from the standard methodology of economics, the critique focused on the potential shortcomings of this methodology – its positivism and empiricism (for its individualism, see the next section). Empiricism and positivism were understood in the following way. Empiricism meant that scholars could have direct access to empirical data, or, to put it more casually, 'data speak for themselves'. Positivism referred to the meta-theoretical position which, at least in principle, would adhere to methodological monism, that is, the idea that social and natural science are of the same kind; a position which includes a model of explanation where explanatory hypotheses are deduced from general probabilistic laws and tested empirically.

Curiously enough for all the ink spilled to denounce it, Waltz, as all true positivists, always rejected an easy empiricism. He certainly endorsed the notion that knowledge is not based on the extrapolation of empirical facts alone, but on concepts which define which fact is a fact. As Immanuel Kant, a philosopher much honoured by Waltz, had put it, categories are the condition for the possibility of knowledge. The task of a theory is a construction of *significant* data, which yield results for our understanding of, and action in, the world out there. Why then this recurring reference to empiricism?

---

5 Waltz is really not very innovative there. Morton Kaplan had already used balance of power theory in a scientifically acceptable manner, mixing, like Waltz, system theory (or a holistic approach) and game theory (an individualist approach). See respectively Kaplan (1957, 1969 [1966]).

Waltz's empiricist trait stems from his position on testing. He embraced Milton Friedman's (1953) pragmatic defence of testing – assumptions could well have nothing to do with reality; all that counted was that the explanations deduced from them had an empirical fit (weakening his own case, Waltz did explain at some length, though, why this turns out to be difficult even for his theory). And here an empiricist position creeps in by the back door – although we have no direct access to the outside world, and although our theories are only heuristic models with no claim to represent reality 'as it is', the testing procedure can be done on the neutral ground of empirical reality. When it comes to theory-building, data are theory-dependent, but when it comes to theory-testing, data are data. (The interpretivist critique of this dilemma echoes Kuhn's classical critique of Popper.)

But then, having opposed (this version of) falsificationism in the social sciences, does constructivism not fall into the trap of relativism and idealism? This question might be fruitfully assessed by relating it back to one of the main defenders of epistemological constructivism who is also well known in IR, Thomas Kuhn. Kuhn (1970 [1962]) had criticized the positivist view of science with an empirical analysis which showed that major scientific advances in the natural sciences were not the result of cumulation and rational debate where the theory with the better empirical fit had won, but incidences of what he called paradigm shifts (for the following, see in more detail Guzzini 1998: 3–5, 119–20). New world-views or paradigms were accepted even before they explained something more than the formerly leading school of thought, to recall Lakatos' (1970: 116) definition of scientific progress. Even without necessarily addressing all the explanatory strength of the old one, new paradigms were accepted as potentially resolving central anomalies of the established research.

Indeed, for Kuhn, it seemed inappropriate to say that the shift to a heliocentric view of the world, for instance, explained simply more phenomena of the same kind. Rather, phenomena changed their meaning with each new school of thought. 'When Aristotle and Galilei looked at swinging stones, the first saw constrained fall, the second a pendulum' (Kuhn 1970 [1962]: 121). Kuhn referred to this shift as a 'gestalt-switch'. In this case, two major schools of thought were relying on such different ontological assumptions that they were incommensurable, i.e. no neutral measure could be found to assess one against the other. Some major theoretical breakthroughs could imply the shift from one world-view to another, from one paradigm to another.

Kuhn's understanding of the production of knowledge requires, hence, an analysis of the social realm in which it takes place. According to Kuhn, paradigms fulfil two central functions (see also Gutting 1980: 1–2). The first is the already mentioned epistemological function of providing a coherent set of assumptions, a world of meanings, that define legitimate research questions and significant research puzzles. Since paradigms provide the basic tools of researching and understanding the world, of science, that is, science, in turn, cannot correct the paradigm (Kuhn 1970 [1962]: 122). Paradigms come as a whole and must be replaced as such. Furthermore, this already implies the second function of paradigms – they define the social subsystem of disciplines and what counts as legitimate research; they define the shared values and boundaries of a scientific community. Indeed, as Kuhn (1970 [1962]: 80) wrote, 'a paradigm governs, in the first instance, not a subject-matter, but a group of practitioners. Any study of paradigm directed or paradigm shattering research must begin by locating the responsible group or groups.'

Such a conception has been, erroneously I think, criticized for being relativistic, reducing science to 'mob-psychology' (Lakatos 1970: 178). If paradigms, so the argument goes, with their holistic theory of meaning, are incommensurable, no rational deliberation is possible and hence 'anything goes'.

It is, of course, correct that Kuhn denies that there is a neutral language with which we can compare observations produced by different paradigms (Kuhn 1970: 265). But only from a naturalist understanding of science does this result in the statement that no communication and debate, no reasoned rebuff, is possible (Bernstein 1983). Kuhn himself likens scientific communities to language communities, and paradigm debates to (hermeneutical) language translations. The latter are open to the informed judgement of the community of scientific observers (Kuhn 1970). We might accept that there is more than one correct translation, depending on the purpose and historical context of the translation. But, surely, some translations will be considered less well done or will not meet the consent of the observer. Indeed, they might be unintelligible to the respective audience. Hence, Kuhn and epistemological constructivism, for all their resistance against a naturalist conception of science, are not relativist, but conventionalist (although the stress between the two poles might be different in other constructivist approaches, see Merlingen 1999).

Still does this not imply an ontological poverty, an idealist mirage? What does the real world mean for the constructivist? This criticism does not come from the more empiricist side, but from critical realism which suspects that putting epistemology in front of the meta-theoretical cart ends up in a shallow, mainly implicit ontology (Patomäki 1996, Patomäki and Wight 2000). In a sense this mirrors the criticism made against those constructivists, like Wendt, who do weigh ontological concerns more heavily, but are faulted for being shallow on the understanding of language and intersubjectivity cherished by more epistemology-focused constructivists (Zehfuß 1998).

Constructivism does not deny the existence of a phenomenal world, external to thought. This is the world of brute (mainly natural) facts. It does oppose, and this is something different, that phenomena can constitute themselves as objects of knowledge independently of discursive practices. It does not challenge the possible thought-independent existence of (in particular natural) phenomena, but it challenges their language-independent observation. What counts as a socially meaningful object or event is always the result of an interpretive construction of the world out there. 'We construct worlds we know in a world we do not' (Onuf 1989: 38). This construction is, however, not a kind of idiosyncratic will to knowledge. Our interpretations are based on a shared system of codes and symbols, of languages, life-worlds, social practices. The knowledge of reality is socially constructed.

At the same time, constructivism, being in the hermeneutical tradition, distinguishes between the natural and social world. Ontologically speaking, it is a theory about the construction of social reality. Besides brute facts, there are some facts which exist only because we attribute a certain function or meaning to them. Searle (1995) relies heavily on the example of money which besides being a metal coin or a piece of paper becomes 'money' only through an attribution done by actors. In other words, if everybody ceased to believe that this piece of paper was money, it would no longer be (although it would still be a metal coin or a piece of paper). Searle calls these facts 'institutional' – they depend in their very existence, and not only in their observation, on an intersubjectively shared set of meanings.

Now, one reason why constructivists in IR, with the exception of Wendt perhaps, tend to be less concerned with ontological questions is that all they are concerned with are institutional, not brute facts. To this extent, constructivism claims either to be agnostic about the language-independent real world out there, or simply uninterested – it often is irrelevant for the study of society (the argument will get a bit more complicated later in the section on intersubjectivity).

To sum up, constructivism recalls against empiricism that observation is no passive recording or purely subjective perception, but that objects of knowledge are constructed. It would oppose epistemological idealism on the grounds that the principles of knowledge construction are not entirely internal to discourse, but socially constituted through practices (Bourdieu 1980: 87). Finally, it holds against positivism that there is a qualitative difference between institutional and brute or natural facts, and it is the former, in their fundamental social quality, which command the interest of the social scientist. In a nutshell, constructivism, as understood here, is epistemologically about the *social construction of knowledge*, and ontologically about the *construction of social reality*. It is to the latter that we turn now.

Double hermeneutics

The previous discussion on constructivist epistemology showed the intrinsic link between the epistemological and sociological level of analysis in constructivism. As Barry Barnes (1982) has argued, it is not particularly telling to look at how social sciences fit into Kuhn's scheme, but rather at what Kuhn's approach has to say about the social sciences. Constructivism does exactly this. As we will see in this section, it argues that any theory of action must be coupled with a theory of knowledge.

Basic to the interpretative or hermeneutical understanding of science is that the very human action which counts as significant in the social world, cannot be apprehended without interpretation, that is, without understanding the meaning that is given to it (Weber 1988 [1922]). When social scientists analyse a red traffic light, they are not interested in the electric circuit and technology that finally produces something we recognize as light with a certain colour (the natural world). They focus on its meaning for the actor and on its role and function within society. In other words, meaning is not limited to the actor itself, but must comprise the significance given to it by other actors, and also observers (Sparti 1992: 102–3). Meaning is not something idiosyncratic to be studied through empathy. Moreover, when interpretative social scientists analyse the red light, they would resist the behaviouralist understanding of such an action. There, action is seen in a stimulus–reaction chain, similar to Skinner's rat experiments, in which the human decision-making is a black-box, a 'through-put'.

Imagine the following caricature. The traffic light turns red and a car stops while a person crosses the street. Whether one observes such an action in Italy or Germany, the explanation in terms of behaviouralism is always the same. But, as those traffic users combat proven in both countries can testify, the apparently equal actions might be profoundly different. In Germany, both persons were following certain rules, here the traffic code. In Italy, the red light is not necessarily a strong indicator of the driver's intention. In this particular event, the person crossing the street, a German tourist, had neither looked right nor left simply because his/her traffic light turned green. Having no eye-contact, which is the Italian convention for double-checking the car driver's usual priority, the driver was forced to stop to avoid a traffic accident (a good example for brinkmanship strategies, too). Interpretative scholars would argue that the apparently equal actions meant something very different and that this difference is crucially relevant for the social sciences. Without retracing the actual meaning of social action, this scientifically significant difference would be overlooked.

Those interpretative approaches interested in social rules would, instead, be interested in the context of the society within which traffic comes to be regulated, and would try to understand why this convention of a red light was chosen, or out of what it developed, in the first place. The analysis would centre on the social and cultural context within which this rule or convention suggests a certain behaviour to individual actors. An actor coming from another society where such a convention does not exist would at first be at an utter loss to understand the meaning of the red traffic light. Hence, correct behaviour presupposes a type of background knowledge. Yet, even persons who do not understand the sign, still make sense of it within their world of understandings, their background knowledge. It is this interpretation which is crucial for understanding their action, independently of whether the action fits the context or not.

In both cases, the actor's capacity to attach the 'right' meaning to a social event depends on the capacity to share a system of meanings within the society. Hence, 'interpretation', as used here, does not necessarily imply an act of conscious or intentional understanding, but the sharing of what Searle (1995: 127–47) calls background abilities or what Bourdieu calls a *habitus* (see later).

This gives a double hermeneutical twist to the analysis. We have to think about the two levels of action involved in a scientific explanation – the level of action proper and the level of observation. In both instances we interpret, at one time making sense within the life-world of the actor, and at another time making sense within the language shared by the community of observers. We interpret an already interpreted social world (Schutz 1962 [1953]). Furthermore, Giddens's (1984: 249–50) concept of *double hermeneutics* problematizes exactly the relationship between self-interpretations and second-order interpretations. For not only do observers rely on first-hand interpretation, but their interpretation, in turn, can itself have a feedback effect on the former (for this point, see also Jaeger 1996: 325, fn. 25).

This double interpretation differentiates social science from the natural sciences, and therefore also interpretivist approaches from naturalist approaches, like neoclassical economics, within the social sciences. Interpretivists cannot therefore unconditionally collapse the level of action proper into the level of observation as done in naturalist approaches to the social sciences.

The level of action: Sociological constructivism, intersubjective units of analysis, and Bourdieu's field theory

Again referring to Barnes's claim that one should think what Kuhn's approach means for the social sciences, constructivists need to take seriously that if science is just another form of human action, both theories of knowledge and theories of action have to be understood in connection. 'Basic concepts of social action and the methodology of understanding social action are fundamentally connected' (Habermas 1985 [1981]: 152, my translation). As a result, constructivists must assume scientific and common-sense knowledge to be socially produced. Furthermore, to the extent that the social world is made of institutional facts, they must be able to analyse these institutional facts without reducing them to individual cognition. They need to combine a social theory of knowledge with an intersubjective, and not an individualist, theory of meaningful action.

Intersubjectivity vs. individualism

To clarify what is meant by intersubjectivity, let us develop one individual theory of action, as presented by rational choice. Rational choice, similar to constructivism as defined here, is not a theory proper, but a meta-theoretical framework of analysis. Rational choice entails an individualist theory of action. It makes two main assumptions about human behaviour. First, humans are self-interested utility maximizers; and second, humans are choosing rationally on the basis of a consistent (transitive) preference ranking. If A is preferred to B and B to C, A should be preferred to C.

A straightforward and parsimonious theory of action derives from this basic depiction of self-interest and rationality. Once we know the *desires* of individuals (their preferences), as well as their *beliefs* about how to realize them, we can deduce their rational *behaviour*. Indeed, as Keith Dowding has succinctly put it:

> The three go together in a triangle of explanation and given any two of the triumvirate the third may be predicted and explained ... This is a behaviouralist theory of action, since it is studying the behaviour of individuals that allows us to understand their beliefs (by making assumptions about their desires) or their desires (by making assumptions about their beliefs). We may understand both by making assumptions about different aspects of each.
>
> *(Dowding 1991: 23)*

It is hence the situation, or the set of incentives, which suggests behaviour to the individual and, besides the two behavioural assumptions, carries the major weight in the explanation. Although rational choice does not necessarily entail such a behaviouralist theory of action, it has become prominent in IR (e.g. Waltz).[6]

There are two problems with this type of individualist analysis, namely the very assumption of egoistic value-maximization and the misunderstanding of the nature of norms and rules. First, the assumption of value-maximization seems either erroneous, if purely egoistic, or of little use (for positivist studies), if not. It has been an old charge against realism in International Relations that its assumption of egoistic behaviour was contradicted by many instances of world politics. The classical realist answer consisted in saying that, in the absence of an arbiter in world politics, non-egoistic behaviour was certainly possible, but that it would not be wise to base one's behaviour on it and that 'ultimately', 'in the last resort', egoism materialistically understood, would obtain. Worst-case thinking meant exactly this – preparing for the case that people did behave according to purely materialist egoistic desires.

This charge that egoism is an erroneous assumption has also been levelled against rational choice theories. In response, proponents of rational choice in International Relations insist that the formula 'value-maximization' does not at all exclude altruistic preferences (Keohane 1984: 74). Although this is strictly speaking not wrong, it does strip theories based on rational choice of their predictive power and possibly more. For, if behaviour can be either driven by egoism or altruism, by one thing and its opposite, then human action becomes indeterminate (Schmalz-Bruns 1995: 354). Indeed, rational choice inspired theories then risk becoming mere taxonomies, a system of concepts which simply reformulate any behaviour into terms of rational action. Then, as with Waltzian realism, the biggest problem of rational choice inspired approaches would not be that they are wrong, but that they can never be wrong.

The second problem with this individualism is that it is unable to have a proper understanding of norms and rules. If regime approaches rely on an economic model of explanation, the ontological and the methodological levels

---

6 I am grateful to one anonymous referee for drawing my attention to the possible non-behaviouralist approaches in the rational choice tradition.

contradict each other. For rules and ideas are ontologically intersubjective, not individualist as an approach based on economic methodology would have it (see the classical critique by Kratochwil and Ruggie 1986). As a result, the structural level becomes reduced to a set of naturalized or objectivized constraints, the institutionally sedimented strata of previous strategic and collective action.

This approach is hence unable to conceive of an independent status of the structural level in intersubjectivist terms.[7] Intersubjectivity is best understood through an analogy with language. Language does exist and cannot be reduced to the simple material support for communication (voice or other). It does not exist independently from its use, but its rules cannot be reduced to individual choices — language cannot be reduced to meanings that individuals attach to it. Or, to use a Wittgensteinian phrase, there is no private language. Hence, languages are neither reducible to objective materialism, nor to subjective individualism — they are intersubjective. They exist in the shared meanings of their users and are reproduced through their practices. These practices, in turn, are patterned by the rules embodied in the language. In order to avoid individualist reductionism, structural change cannot be conceived as being the simple aggregation of individual action, but must be conceived as the open reproduction of intersubjective practices following rules on their own.

An example of a social theory sensitive to the double turn and intersubjectivity: Bourdieu's field theory

This is the crucial point at which constructivism should insist on a logical analogy — if meaning is socially constructed at both levels of action and observation, then we need a conceptual apparatus which can cope with a non-mechanistic, but interpretivist intersubjective level of analysis. Some writers have used Giddens's structuration theory (Wendt 1987, Jaeger 1996), others the socially thicker theory of communicative action (Müller 1994, Risse-Kappen 1995, Risse 2000). In the following, I will illustrate my point by referring to Bourdieu (see also Schlichte 1998) because of the wealth of empirical studies in sociology which have been influenced by it (for Bourdieu-inspired IPE, see Leander 2000a).

Bourdieu explicitly tries to avoid different reductions inherent in rational choice approaches or functionalist approaches, by offering a theory around the concept of a *field*, a social subsystem. A field stands both for a patterned set of practices which suggests competent action in conformity with rules and roles, and for the playing (or battle) field in which agents, endowed with certain field-relevant or irrelevant capital, try to advance their position. This social subsystem

---

7 Alexander Wendt has pointed out to me that 'common knowledge' as theorized in rational choice can take on board some, yet not all, of the mentioned requests for intersubjectivity (see also Wendt 1999: ch. 4), although it must theorize them as a purely interactionist phenomenon.

is not mainly defined by its functionality as compared to the entire system, but relies intrinsically on a historically derived system of shared meanings which define agency and make action intelligible. Being historical, fields are open and change over time. It is this concept, together with the concept of *habitus* (see later), which is the intersubjective core of the theory.

The starting point is the relationship between structure and field (*champ*). In Bourdieu, *structure* is conceived as the product of collective history. In the widest sense, structures are social, not natural phenomena, although they certainly have a material character and, this being the sociologically most important question, are often taken as self-evident. Being interested in (domestic) social systems, structure is a concept linked to the system of 'social difference' or stratification, in other words, to the generative context for the establishment of status groups, for the establishment of (social) power.

Bourdieu's theory of stratification is based on his theory of capital. He distinguishes between economic, social and cultural capital (symbolic capital being a fourth but slightly different notion). Agents are endowed with different amounts of these capitals. Conversely, their capital has not always the same efficacy depending on the context in which it is used. Having much economic capital might not be of much use in being well positioned as an artist, although it certainly influences the way the artistic field is structured. Indeed, to some extent the very identity of these subsystems is closely connected to the particular mix of the relevant capital. Bourdieu, when referring to these differentiated social subsystems, calls them *fields*. This argument is wider, but reminiscent of Baldwin's (1979: 167) insistence that power instruments are issue area specific, or, to express it in a more technical language, that power is not necessarily fungible from one policy-contingency framework to another (you usually cannot force devaluations with a nuclear weapon).

Within the overall structure, and depending on the level of differentiation of a society, different fields exist within a society. Fields, like the artistic field, the academic field, are the specific contexts within which *practices* take place. Fields correspond to a network of positions, a set of interactions with a shared system of meaning. They give meaning to agency. They are the playgrounds where agents realize individual strategies, playing within, and thereby openly reproducing, the rules of a given game (as defined by the specific set of capital most valuable for holding power within the field).

The practices of agents in these fields are inspired by taken for granted beliefs, the so-called *doxa*, which Bourdieu defines also as the very presuppositions of the field. *Doxa* refer to the quasi-perfect correspondence of a socially constructed, yet objectified order (structure and fields) and the subjective principles of its organizations that agents share. It is in this spontaneous sharing of the common-sense in which the natural, but also the social world appears as self-evident (Bourdieu 1977: 164).

Such an analysis relies heavily on the study of field-specific sets of *dispositions*, called the *habitus*. Bourdieu defines the *habitus* as a product of history which in itself (through effecting certain practices) produces history. It guarantees the active presence of past experiences through providing schemes of perception, thought and action which tend to reproduce practices in conformity with the field throughout time (Bourdieu 1980: 91). The *habitus* functions like the materialization of collective memory. Comparable to Kuhn's 'paradigm', it is a disposition to act, perceive and think in a particular way.

The logic of the field also implies that the dispositions are not themselves perceived as the result of a particular history; they are, as Bourdieu says, the 'forgetting of history that history produces', or, in other words, collective memory that appears as the 'natural' way of doing, perceiving and thinking things. Dispositions lead to the smooth reproduction of exactly those assumptions that define the autonomy of the field. This is Bourdieu's *sens pratique* which means both meaning/sense (of action and practices) and drive/direction (of the open reproduction of fields). It is important to note that this 'reproduction' is neither closed nor mechanistic.[8]

This conceptualization is a sociological translation of socialization processes that take place not on the individual level via competition and strategic learning, but on a social level where the agent's identity is related to groups. It is a revised version of a Weberian status group approach. Cooperation or common action is hence not necessarily the result of choice. Practices are (also) the result of the orientations given by the *habitus* and the structure of the field as a system of authorizations and punishments (Bourdieu 1982: 14). In other words, identity (agency), interests and strategies are field-specific and can be understood only after a prior analysis of the field itself (for a short discussion of how Bourdieu redefines these usually economistic concepts of interests and strategies, see Bourdieu 1990: 87–93, Bourdieu and Wacquant 1992: 91–5). For a synopsis of this approach, see Figure 11.1, adapted from Guzzini (1994: 244).

Some examples from the second Gulf War might serve as an indicative illustration of the conceptual apparatus (for a more detailed analysis, see Guzzini 1994: Part V). In this case, constructivism-inspired approaches would be interested in the way the understanding, and therefore also the agendas of policies

---

8 Fields are not there for ever, and dispositions even less. Besides changes in the overall social structure, there are different internal barriers through which the mechanical reproduction of the field can be inhibited. There is, first, the very passage from collective memory to the schemes of thought and action. Like language which shows the generation of much new thought and understanding, even the strongest adherence to established practices cannot determine the use individuals make of their past. Second, the dispositions are realized in a context which is different from the one in which they were formed. The bigger the perceived difference, the greater the possibility that dispositions may change. Finally, there are all the interferences that can exist because the same agent is part of different fields. Here, it depends very much on the 'discipline' the field (as, for instance, an academic discipline) succeeds in imposing on its participants not to 'steal' and transpose dispositions from other fields (arts or politics, for instance). Hence, it depends on the degree of 'autism' of the field's ability to refract the influence of other fields. These questions can only be established empirically.

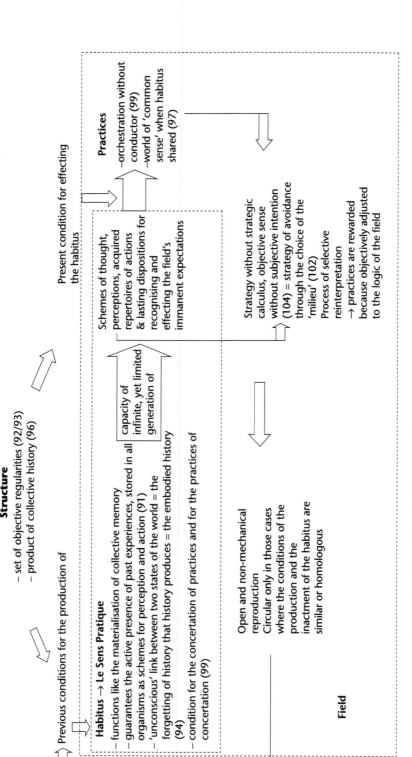

FIGURE 11.1 A conceptual synopsis of Pierre Bourdieu's *le sens pratique*

which are deemed possible and necessary, both of the policy-makers and their observers were shaped. Such an analysis would have first to specify the relevant fields to be studied.

The most obvious field for IR is diplomacy. Here the field's *habitus* is rich in a collective memory of the lessons of the past which provide the background abilities for understanding and acting in foreign affairs. So some politicians looking at the Gulf War through the lenses of World War II, on the basis of an analogy of Adolf Hitler and Saddam Hussein, would understand the Gulf conflict as a further incident of an anti-totalitarian war in which the allied forces had to anticipate Hussein before he got weapons of mass-destruction (Lakoff 1991, Luke 1991). Such a script in which several metaphors are bundled, has an inbuilt logic in the story which could explain, for instance, why the US public did not really understand why the allied forces did not go all the way to Bagdad (to remove Saddam Hussein). The former President Bush was at pains to point out that the allied forces had no mandate to do so – when his public justification for the intervention in terms of the World War II script would have made him go for unconditional surrender.

Another field which is of particular interest to constructivists is international media (Jaeger 1996: 333–5). The study of media would have to include its relationship to political and economic fields which have been heavily shaping the selection and production of footage, indeed the very prevalence given to live footage as opposed to the written press (P.M. Taylor 1992: 272). The organization of the media coverage where journalists were dependent for their security on the allied forces, obviously had a similarly biased effect.

More precisely, the study would need to analyse the dispositions (*habitus*) of journalists. A practice particularly prominent during the Gulf War was self-censorship which again features the distinction between an individualist and an intersubjective approach. An individualist account of self-censorship sees it as an anticipated reaction of an imputed sanction, should compliance not happen. An intersubjectivist approach would not deny those instances but makes it possible to conceive of self-censorship in a non-individualist way. Such an analysis would look at the *habitus* of the agents in the media field and establish whether their competent behaviour according to the rules of the field, their very being a (competent) journalist would result in such a self-censorship.

> It is this sense of acceptability, and not whatever form of rational calculus oriented towards the maximization of symbolic profits, which . . . determines corrections and all forms of self-censorship. These are concessions granted to a social world by the fact of having accepted making oneself acceptable.
>
> *(Bourdieu 1982: 75–6, my translation)*

This sociological approach also shows why it is probably incompatible to link constructivism up with cognitive psychology (Checkel 1998). Checkel asks for such a link to remedy the supposedly weak concept of agency in constructivist approaches. Although the macro–micro link is no easy thing, and claims about its final solution are premature, theories like Bourdieu's do at least provide concepts, like the *habitus*, which are rich enough to account for the regulated part of agency without necessarily relying on cognitive rules of behaviour. Constructivism does not need to deny the possible importance of psychological factors. Some psychological approaches, like scheme theories and similar approaches in the belief-systems literature, are compatible with it. Yet, it must deny a concept of agency which would not include some socially thick components like the *habitus*. That would be hardly coherent within the constructivist framework. Hence, Checkel's call for the missing agency is slightly misplaced – it is only an individualist understanding of agency which is missing.

Once one accepts the existence of intersubjective units of analysis, their study must become a research agenda on its own. It means that research not only addresses the nexus between material and ideal inputs and individual behaviour, but must first understand this agency in a more embedded way, understanding the historically evolving schemes of thought, perception and action, as well as the distribution of capital, including the social, in carefully defined fields where agents meet. Many of the important questions for a social scientist are located at this wider level. Indeed, being related to social stratification, as in Bourdieu's approach, the analysis is concerned not only with questions of action, but with social power.

'Power' and the constructivist linking of the levels of action and observation

Absolutely crucial for understanding constructivism is the turn power analysis has taken during the 1980s in International Relations. For the concept of power provides a link between a coherent constructivist understanding of the level of observation and the level of action proper. As mentioned earlier, constructivism sees the international system as socially constructed through practices, in particular diplomatic practices. Similarly, on the level of observation, action is understood in terms of the practices of the scholarly community (although not that alone). Since both levels are levels of action, a coherent constructivism must approach them in the same way. The very basis of double hermeneutics means that constructivism must theorize the relationship between them. The concept of power has emerged as one of the most prominent ways to link the two, i.e. the interaction between the social construction of meaning (including knowledge) with the construction of social reality.

Given the usual understanding of power in IR, it is not self-evident why power would be able to provide this link. For a long time, the discipline has been happy living with a fairly narrow and usually materialist conception of power as capacities. Yet this understanding has produced a series of anomalies that fundamentally vitiate the usefulness of this type of power analysis in IR (for a short assessment of contemporary power analysis in IR, see Guzzini 2000c). First, with the opening of the international agenda, sources of capabilities expanded; military might did not necessarily prove useful in other sectors. This lacking 'fungibility' implied that general national power indexes, not to speak of their aggregation as general balances of power, are fairly useless for particular empirical analysis (Baldwin 1979: 193). Related to this, it implied that some of the issue areas might be heavily influenced by the skilful use of non-material capabilities, as Susan Strange's (1987) insistence on US 'structural' power in the knowledge structure, and Joseph Nye's (1990b) related 'soft-power' bear witness. Indeed, power concepts increasingly referred to the production of systematic effects, whether they were intended or not, whether their sources could be pinpointed at some agents or not – they tried to include non-intentional or impersonal power approaches (Guzzini 1993). This went beyond the only partial exception to the rule of intentional power concepts, namely the famous 'law of anticipated reactions' (Friedrich 1963: 199–215), in which actors changed their behaviour by imputing intentions to another actor.

But why call non-intentional or impersonal influence power? Indeed, many scholars within the tradition of methodological individualism resisted the inclusion of non-intentional power for its apparent randomness, and impersonal power for the so-called 'benefit fallacy'. First, although economic approaches can include non-intended effects (Elster 1989) in their analysis, within this framework, it does not make sense to include them in their concept of power, or their power analysis. Second, impersonal power approaches have been criticized for deducing power from rewards, something which has been called the 'benefit fallacy' of power (Barry 1989 [1987]: 315). Nelson Polsby (1980: 208) explicitly mentioned the case of the free-rider who certainly profits from a certain systemic arrangement, but who basically remains at its mercy. One would not necessarily ascribe power to the free-rider. In other words, expanding the concept meant confusing power with randomness or luck.

I think that both arguments are falling short by excluding non-intentional and impersonal effects from a power analysis. More importantly, the reason for this also helps us to understand why power (I would add: power *analysis*) can serve as a link between the level of observation and the level of action.

For seeing the importance of power, we have to shift our conceptual analysis from the question what power *means* to what the use of the concept power *does*. And here we are at the core of a political debate. Power is a concept which has a variety of purposes (Morriss 1987: 37–42). To mention two, power is used in practical contexts in which we are interested in what we can do to others and what others can do to us, whether intentionally or not. It is furthermore important in moral/legal contexts where it functions as an indicator of effective responsibility – if actors could not have done an act (if they had not the capacity to do so), they cannot be found guilty of it. The first indicates the realm of agency and change. Power is a counter-factual which implies that things could have been otherwise. Hence, power is an indicator of politics understood as the 'art of the possible'. The second purpose assesses possible responsibility. As William Connolly (Connolly 1974: 97 ff.) noted some time ago, attributing power to an agent implies an attribution of responsibility and hence a potential need for justification.[9]

In such a context it is quite understandable that dependency scholars have been stressing non-intentional effects. For by limiting the practical context to only those actions with which we intend to affect others, we rule out from political action and moral judgement those actions with which we affect others, whether intended or not (as explicitly done by Knorr 1973: 77–8). Leaving out non-intentional power mobilizes a status quo research bias and blinds us to the tacit power of the strong (Guzzini 1993: 476).

Similarly, the 'benefit-fallacy' is linked to a power holder-centred and causal understanding. To say that a system benefits certain people does not mean that they caused that benefit or that they control it. 'All one need do is note that a status quo that systematically benefits certain people (as Polsby agrees it does) is relevant in itself . . . Yet if the social system performs in such a way as systematically to advantage some individuals or groups, it certainly seems odd not to take account of this' (Morriss 1987: 105–6). And although scepticism about the links between power and benefits are warranted, it seems a reduction not to allow for a conceptual apparatus which can take account of systematic benefits in any other terms as 'systematic luck' (Dowding 1991: 137). Because again, as a consequence, since power is not involved, we 'have no alternative' but to live with this fateful state of affairs. Power, understood as an indicator of the 'art of the possible', is ruled out. By reducing a systematic bias to a question of luck, this approach leaves out of the picture the daily practices of agents that help to reproduce the very system and positions from which these advantages were derived. For this reason perhaps, Dowding (1996: 94 ff.) now rephrases his approach and explicitly includes systematic luck into power analysis which he correctly then links to normative debates.

Now, if the concept of power functions as an indicator of the 'possible', it is obvious that constructivist theoreticians who spent their time in unravelling 'worlds of our making' had to be interested in it. Morever, it is this particular function of power analysis which made it that power, and not another concept, theoretically appealed to scholars interested in bridging the reflexive relationship between the level of action and the level of observation. For this to happen, however, power needed (again) to be approached in a way which allowed it to

---

9 To be more precise, the issue of justification involves both questions of responsibility (justifying through the absence of abilities and alternatives) and liability. The latter includes cases where missing alternatives or intentions do not exclude being charged with the costs of remedies. I am indebted to Friedrich Kratochwil who has drawn my attention to this distinction.

view socially constructed knowledge as a constitutive factor of social power and which, relatedly, made it possible to conceive of the relationship between power and consensus.

In other words, the concept of power provided a central, because sociologically pertinent, link between the construction of knowledge and social order. It does so basically in two ways. First, people are attributed labels or 'kinds' as Hacking calls them. When the IMF puts a country in the category of insolvent, that country has been disempowered in its social relations. Other international financial actors will change their behaviour accordingly. The country itself will react towards this being perceived as of a certain kind, either by trying to ignore or remedying it. Similarly, giving some immigrant citizens the status of permanent residents empowers them to do things they could not have otherwise done (again, people can become aware and conscious of these kinds and interact with them). Second, power analysis emphasizes the link that exists between the social production of knowledge and collective action. Here the focus is on those social groups empowered to provide the authoritative vision of the world. Both types of power analysis which are profoundly intersubjective, link, on each level, the theory of knowledge with social theory, 'because the specific symbolic power to impose the principles of construction of reality, in particular, social reality, is a major dimension of political power' (Bourdieu 1977: 165).

To offer again a conceptual illustration of both power links, one could recall Richard Ashley in his communicative and then his Bourdieu-inspired phase. He is the one scholar who most contributed to further thought in IR of the centrality of power in providing the link between the two levels of action.[10] His starting point is the understanding of the consensual aspect of power. This aspect was traditionally handled through the concept of *legitimacy* which, in the Weberian reading, demarcates authority (*Herrschaft*) from power (*Macht*). The more radical hermeneutical twist can be seen in the meta-theoretical redefinition where the significant concept of power has to be placed, namely not at an individual, but at an intersubjective level.

Ashley starts out with what one could call a *communicative* approach (Kratochwil 1988: 272, Little 1989). Here, it is worth quoting him at length, because, although dating from 1984, this section could have been written by today's constructivists. Ashley (1984: 244, 245, 259) writes that for neorealism,

> [t]here is no concept of social power behind or constitutive of states and their interests. Rather, power is generally regarded in terms of capabilities that are said to be distributed, possessed, and potentially used *among* states-as-actors ... Such understandings of power are rooted in a utilitarian understanding of international society: an understanding in which a) there

---

10 For an analysis of the agent–structure problem in power analysis in International Relations and International Political Economy, see Guzzini (1993).

exists no form of sociality, no intersubjective consensual basis, prior to or constitutive of individual actors or their private ends, and hence b) the *essential* determinants of actors' relative effects on one another will be found in the capabilities they respectively control. ... Yet such a position strictly rules out a *competence model* of social action. According to a competence model, the power of an actor, and even its status as an agent competent to act, is not in any sense attributable to the inherent qualities or possessions of a given entity. Rather, the power and status of an actor depends on and is limited by the condition of its *recognition* within a community as a whole.

In a later piece, Ashley (1987) tries to give a name to this international subject. He finds it in the community of Realist statesmen and their 'heroic practice' – starting from the idea of an anarchical realm, the shared understandings, hence community, of realist statesmanship must deny its own very existence. Realism is not only about power, but the realist discourse is a power exercise itself. It works through ritualized empowerment as exemplified by the 'double move' of realist discourse, that is, the conception of a universalist abstract rational community on the one hand, which has, on the other hand, a historical (because spatial and temporal) margin – the frontier between the domestic and the international. The rituals of power

> administer a silence regarding the historicity of the boundaries it produces, the space it historically clears, and the subject it historically constitutes ... [International politics] appears as a realm of necessity existing independent from knowledge, will, and practice ... the double move excludes from active political discourse the strategies and procedures by which the margins of the domestic and the international society are produced, the sphere of international politics is constituted and normalized, and the prevailing subjectivity of modern statesmanship is empowered ... [These strategies] are appreciated, if at all, not as rituals of power participating in the production of order but as necessary responses to a truth already given.
> (Ashley 1987: 419)

Instead of understanding international cooperation as the result of strategic interaction, Ashley (1984: 236) adopts 'the posture of an ethnomethodologist of a diplomatic community' (and certainly more so than the classical and empiricist Realists he quotes), a position which he will (unfortunately) reject in his later writings.

Consistently, and necessarily for a double hermeneutical approach, Ashley applied such an intersubjective approach to the level of observation, to the academic community. This strong epistemological outlook is the result of two necessarily related issues. It is a symptom of the realist paradigm in crisis, which prompts debates about fundamentals. But it is also the logical result of an explanatory framework that focuses on disclosing the legitimating routines in the community of diplomats and observers alike.

In a nutshell, the central concept of intersubjective power completes the sociological and interpretivist turn in constructivist International Relations – knowledge is a social construction; international politics is not simply a series of individualist choices in a naturalized environment, but a social construct defining and constructing identities; the reflexive relationship between the two levels of action is central for any intersubjective power analysis.

Conclusion

Given the increasingly inflationary and at times woolly use of constructivism, the main aim of this chapter was to clear the ground for a better communication within constructivist research as well as between it and competitive approaches. Instead of looking for middle positions or lowest common denominators, it has tried to make sense of constructivism by looking for a coherent meta-theoretical position from which it can be reconstructed.

Its main claim is that constructivism is best understood by carefully distinguishing between its position on the level of observation, on the level of action, and the relationship between the two. With regard to the first, it argues that a coherent position of constructivism implies a constructivist epistemology (the social construction of reality) and double hermeneutics. It argues that constructivism is epistemologically about the social construction of knowledge and ontologically about the (social) construction of the social world. On the level of action it assumes an intersubjective unit of analysis. And since constructivism relies on a problematization of how reality is constructed, it must theorize the link between these two levels, which usually comes in one or the other version of intersubjective power analysis.

The basic underlying thrust was to increase reflexivity in both theoretical and empirical studies in IR on the basis that analysis of the social world is not only a very part of the real world but might also affect it. This intrinsic link from social science to power and politics might be rejected by some scholars for it seems to imply that all social science is ideological. But this seems to be an unnecessary deduction from the position of this chapter. I simply stated a truism, namely that social sciences interact with the social world. It asks us to see us as scholars and social actors at the same time. But saying that social science has political implications does not imply that social science is *nothing but* politics. Inversely, as already mentioned, it does not mean that although the social world is constructed, it is simply a matter of will to reconstruct it in order to get it changed. Although some scientists might have preferred access to political power, this is by no means a general position, nor one with necessary effect.

I was told a story which I cannot verify, but *se non è vero, è ben trovato*. In a keynote speech to an Association of Economists, the chairman criticized the discipline for the little impact it had on actual politics. His speech was met with outrage. The audience recalled numerous examples of policies influenced by the discipline's thoughts or main protagonists. After listening to these examples, the chairman addressed the floor by asking how it could be then, that so little research has been done on this link, why the discipline was not reflecting on its eminently social role. Constructivism would have helped to avoid the embarrassed silence which followed.

12
THE CONCEPT OF POWER
A constructivist analysis

It has become more commonplace to stress the centrality of the concept of power for constructivist meta-theory and theorising (see, in particular, Hopf 1998, Guzzini 2000a). Moreover, constructivism has put some order into its own power concepts, which usually come as variations on the theme of 'Lukes-plus-Foucault' (Guzzini 1993, Barnett and Duvall 2005a). Therefore, this chapter will take a slightly different tack. Rather than exploring once again what the concept of power can mean for constructivists, it analyses the implications of constructivism for doing a conceptual analysis, here of power.[1] It will try to show that besides an analytical assessment ('What does power mean?'), a constructivist conceptual analysis also includes a study of the performative aspects of concepts ('What does "power" do?'), which, in turn is embedded into a conceptual history or genealogy ('How has "power" come to mean and be able to do what it does?'). Indeed, by stressing the reflexive relationship between knowledge and social reality, such a conceptual analysis is itself part (but only part!) of a more general constructivist power analysis.

After a short preface on my take on constructivism, this chapter exposes in some detail the results of such a threefold analysis. Turning to the classical focus of conceptual analysis on the meaning of power, the first section disputes the

---

This is a slightly revised version of Guzzini (2005). For many incisive comments and criticisms, I am indebted to Jens Bartelson, Ludvig Beckman, Andreas Behnke, Felix Berenskötter, Olya Gayazova, Janice Bially-Mattern, Linda Bishai, Walter Carlsnaes, Raymond Duvall, Jef Huysmans, Anna Leander, Aaron Maltais, Jörgen Odalen, Charles Parker, Heikki Patomäki, Vincent Pouliot, Gerard Toal and, not least, to Steven Lukes, on whom I first tried out some of these ideas more than a decade ago. I am only too well aware that many criticisms could not yet be satisfactorily answered. The usual disclaimers apply.

1 For a similar strategy applied to the concept of security, see Huysmans (1998).

viability of attempts to find a neutral meaning across meta-theoretical divides. Although such attempts clarify thought, and would undoubtedly facilitate scientific communication, as well as enhance our capacity for the construction of variables, the meaning of most central concepts in the social sciences is dependent on the theoretical or meta-theoretical context in which they are embedded. When applied to concepts in explanatory theories, this results in explanatory perspectivism. As long as we have to live with our meta-theoretical dilemmas, such as the agency–structure debate, concepts cannot be neutral.

Moving to the performative analysis of the concept of power, the second section discusses how conceptual analysis, instead of digging deep in order to find a neutral meaning of a concept, starts from the usage of concepts and from there moves backwards to their meaning. From there, constructivist analysis asks what the concept of power 'does'. Following William Connolly and Steven Lukes, it is possible to show that using 'power' has a certain role in our political discourse (Connolly 1974): it tends to 'politicise' issues. Connected as it is to the idea of the 'art of the possible', attributing 'power' to an issue immediately implies that 'we could have done things otherwise'. In other words, attributing power to an issue immediately raises the stakes for political justification of action or non-action. Hence, the plethora of newer and wider power concepts in international relations (IR) reflect the attempt to draw more aspects of international life into the realm of politics – and its resistance has the opposite effect. The definition of power thus becomes part and parcel of politics itself (Guzzini 1994).

Finally, a short, indeed too short, third section deals with the historical or genealogical component of how 'power' has come to mean and to do what it does. Such an analysis in its entirety is of course well beyond the scope of this chapter. Yet, if the argument of the second section is accepted – namely, that the use of power discourse tends to be connected with a certain definition of politics (its realm and its justification) – a genealogical analysis would investigate under which definitions of power and politics such an effect has become historically possible. Here, one could hypothesise that only in contexts where politics is defined in a way to privilege manipulative features in the 'art of the possible', rather than the notion of a common good, does 'power' have this effect in political discourse. I will argue that, historically, this more manipulative definition of politics has moved from domestic politics to IR.[2]

---

2 A final caveat: in what follows, there will be ideas perfectly acceptable to non-constructivists. IR debates being often about turf wars, this could be seen as an unwelcome attempt to bring other schools into the constructivist fold. But that would be to misread the intention of this piece. It does not seek to establish a turf of the type: 'only if you are a constructivist can you do this type of analysis.' Rather, it wishes to impose some coherence onto constructivism itself when applied to a type of research which is crucial to it, namely conceptual analysis. Something necessary for constructivism is, however, not necessarily unique to it.

A preface on constructivism

Constructivism is perhaps best understood as a meta-theoretical commitment (see also Kratochwil 2000a: 101). I assume that constructivism is based on three characteristics (for this definition, see Guzzini 2000a, Adler 2002). First, it makes the epistemological claim that meaning, and hence knowledge, is socially constructed. It is constructed, since concepts are the condition for the possibility of knowledge. Our senses are not passive receptors of 'given' facts. The very identification of facts out of the ongoing noise is dependent on pre-existing notions that guide our view of the world. 'When Aristotle and Galilei looked at swinging stones, the first saw constrained fall, the second a pendulum' (Kuhn 1970 [1962]: 121). This knowledge is, moreover, socially or intersubjectively constructed. Concepts are part of language. Language can neither be reduced to something subjective nor objective. It is not subjective, since it exists independently of us to the extent that language is always more than its individual usages and prior to them. It is not objective, since it does not exist independently of our minds and our usage (language exists and changes through our use). It is intersubjective.

Second, constructivism makes the ontological claim that the *social* world is constructed. As in Searle's famous example about a money bill, it is only our shared beliefs that this piece of paper is money which 'makes' it money (Searle 1995). As all people who have had to go through periods of hyperinflation would recognise, the moment that this shared belief ceases to exist, the bill is literally no more than a piece of paper. This assumption does not entail that everything is constructed, but it covers that part of reality in which the social sciences are usually interested. Hence, the physical type of support for money (paper, plastic, etc.) is usually not the most relevant for social analysis. What is most relevant is the social or institutional fact; the ontological result of 'our making'.

Third, since constructivism distinguishes and problematises the relationship between the levels of observation and action, it is finally defined by stressing the reflexive relationship between the social construction of knowledge and the construction of social reality. In other words, it focuses on reflexivity; that is, on how the social construction of knowledge can itself affect the construction of social reality and vice versa. On the micro-level, reflexivity has to do with what Ian Hacking (1999: 34) calls the 'looping-effect'. Categories we use for classifying/naming people interact with the self-conception of those people. Whereas it makes no difference to stones how we classify them, it makes a difference to people. Identification and identity thus become crucial terms for constructivism.[3] Max Frisch's novel *Stiller* opens with the sentence: 'I am not Stiller!' (Frisch 1954). It tells the story of a Mr White who travels to Switzerland and is taken to be a Mr Stiller who had left that same country many years ago. Although he tries to shrug off this identity in which the environment casts him, the main character

---

3 Crucial, but not therefore unproblematic. See Maja Zehfuss (2001a).

does increasingly come to accept a new (or rediscover a previous) identity of his. He becomes 'Stiller' (and the other way round).

On the macro-level, reflexivity refers to 'self-fulfilling prophecies'.[4] As earlier peace research insisted, whether or not the 'law of the jungle' best describes the international system, if we all believe it does, it will quite certainly come to look like one (or be impervious to social learning).[5] The concern in the response to Samuel Huntington's (1993a) 'Clash of Civilisation' thesis had much to do with this reflexive relationship between knowledge and the social world. Whether or not the main fault lines of conflict really have to be thought in this way, if all people assume they do and act accordingly, the world would indeed become one of inevitable clashes of civilisations. Assuming the claim to be true, our actions would tend to produce the very reality the claim was only supposed to describe. But the relationship between social reality and the social construction of knowledge also works from social facts to knowledge, a component perhaps less touched upon in recent constructivist writings. This involves the questions about the sociology of knowledge which have arguably pushed Thomas Kuhn to his constructivism (Kuhn 1970 [1962]). It also involves wider questions about the political economy of expertise or knowledge production (e.g., the organisation of learning and education, or the role of think tanks, just to name two); questions which are not specific to constructivism, but which it too needs to account for.[6] With this understanding of constructivism in mind, the remainder of the chapter assesses what constructivism implies for conceptual analysis.

Analytical conceptual analysis: what does 'power' mean?

The first characteristic of a constructivist conceptual analysis becomes visible by contrasting it with an ideal type of positivist conceptual analysis. In the latter, conceptual analysis is but a means to an end. It should allow better and stable communication. If we never shared at least similar meanings about words, no pertinent discussion would be feasible. In turn, clear understandings of concepts permit the exact definition of variables, which can then be used in scientific explanations. In this context, conceptual analysis is a crucial first step for variable construction and for the transferability of analytical results. Drawing on examples of such conceptual analyses of power, this section will argue that they are useful tools for clarifying thought but eventually fall short of doing justice to the richness of conceptual analysis and, if their methodology is not revised, of even elucidating the meaning of the concept they look at.

---

4 Among recent constructivists, Alexander Wendt (1999) has stressed this point when discussing the possible stickiness of his cultures of anarchy.
5 For the relationship between peace research and constructivism, see Guzzini (2004a).
6 For instance, it is a crucial component of Pierre Bourdieu's social theory which is compatible with constructivism. See Bourdieu (1984, 1989).

Conceptual analysis as a means:
Descriptive neutrality for better explanation and communication

In its most common version, an instrumental approach to conceptual analysis aims at reconstructing a 'descriptive', i.e. theoretically neutral, meaning of a concept(s) in order to avoid incoherent usage and misunderstandings. This reconstruction is meant to make the concept(s) usable for philosophical discourse and/or scientific inquiry. Since Felix Oppenheim explicitly applies this approach to a conceptual analysis of power, his work provides an appropriate inroad for us into this kind of approach.

For Oppenheim, precisely because social sciences lack a full-fledged theoretical system, academics are put before the choice either to leave political concepts unexplained, a choice of little appeal, or 'explicating them independently of any theories with the purpose of clarifying whatever isolated generalizations have been made or may be asserted' (Oppenheim 1981: 189), thus preparing the day when a theory in the stronger sense will be developed. To construct such a neutral term, Oppenheim wants to carefully include the findings of earlier conceptual analysis so that his proposal be widely shared and acceptable. In the end, he sticks to an understanding of power close to causation (as in the work of Robert Dahl 1968, 1976), without necessarily including the idea of intentionality (as already proposed by Dennis Wrong 1988 [1979]). As a result, Oppenheim's definition of power refers to the causal relation between one action and another. Oppenheim is careful to define action widely – it includes also 'not doing an action' – so as not to be caught in a behaviouralist fallacy. He also avoids any reference to preferences, intentions or interests, which, in the wake of Lukes's (1974) discussion, have been shown to be contestable and not neutral concepts. He shows cases where none of them is needed. As a result, he approaches power in terms of a probabilistic causation. '[T]o assert that R's action x was influenced by some action y of P is not merely to describe what R did, but also to provide at least a partial explanation of P's conduct. (Why did R do x? Because P influenced him to do x)' (Oppenheim 1981: 33).

The probabilistic causation of power is expressed in conditional sentences. Concepts of power can differ in the extent to which Action X is either sufficient, or necessary and sufficient, for Action Y to happen or to be prevented. For instance, a possible condition for the coercion of an Actor B is that Actor A possesses a revolver and the skill to use it. Acquiring both does not yet cause anything, and hence it is not an exercise of power. If Actor A points the revolver at Actor B (Action X), and the latter is induced (1) to do an action which B had not thought of doing before, or (2) to refrain from an action B had thought of doing (Action Y), we have a causal nexus. Here, we have an exercise of power. Action X is a sufficient condition for Action Y. If one can presume that there are other ways to cause B to do Y, this condition is not necessary for causing Action Y.

There are obviously good arguments for being neutral in the construction of concepts. Indeed, it comes as no surprise that the most widely used approach in empirical theorising is to see concepts as synonymous with 'variables' whose content needs to be fixed in order to allow for a rigorous and reproducible analysis. This conception of an artificial, almost mathematical, language is in the tradition of positivism and the condition for the possibility of the quantification of hypotheses.

Yet, whenever the analysis is concerned with the richer concepts of our political vocabulary, this instrumental strategy faces a dilemma. So do concepts like democracy and development, for instance, hardly offer an uncontentious definition in need of only just a bit more careful phrasing. A result of this indeterminacy is that corresponding variables may not always fit from one analysis to another, and communication is impaired (Rueschemeyer 1991). Since discussions about democracy keep on using different meanings which are not easily reducible to each other, the analyst is tempted to replace or narrow the concept with something less contentious (cf. Collier and Levitsky 1997). Hence the dilemma: faced with the difficulties of pinning down a concept, scholars decide to go for its more easily operationalisable aspects, but they thereby incur the risk of neglecting its most significant aspects, which would void the concept of the very significance for which it had been chosen in the first place.

Trying to keep a certain conceptual coherence despite lacking neutrality, a slightly different tack consists in presupposing that the different usages have a common core, which does not necessarily imply a full-fledged taxonomic definition, nor even a neutral one. Steven Lukes, for instance, uses a distinction, taken from John Rawls, between a concept and its different conceptions:

> What I propose to do instead is to offer a formal and abstract account of the concepts of power and authority respectively which inhere within the many conceptions of power and authority that have been used by particular thinkers within specific contexts, in development from and in reaction to one another. Any given conception of power and of authority (and of the relation between them) can be seen as an interpretation and application of its concept.
>
> *(Lukes 1979: 634)*

Here, all concepts must ultimately have a common core.[7] Otherwise, communication would not work. A term like 'anarchy', for instance, might mean the 'law of the jungle' in one context, in another 'rule without government', and in another still 'social organisation without hierarchy'. Yet to be able to refer to all as interpretations of anarchy presupposes a common core. Although this move ensures communicability on a very general level, Lukes's approach is not intended to and does not solve the dilemma for the positivist. By having climbed up the 'ladder of abstraction' to such daring heights, these concepts no longer function as 'data-containers' viable for positivist analysis (Sartori 1970; see

---

7 In her comments, Janice Bially Mattern has suggested a more pragmatic reading of this passage: a scholar might infer such a common core knowing that it is only an interpretative exegesis. This might allow a contextualised use of concepts as variables.

also Collier and Mahon 1993). Hence, scholars in this tradition of conceptual analysis face a dilemma (at least when some concepts are concerned): they can either assure communicability or more rigorous variable construction, but not both.

Impossible neutrality and the meta-theoretical dependence of explanatory concepts

Showing the dilemmas of a conceptual analysis conceived in terms of variable construction is but a first step in undermining the positivist understanding of conceptual analysis. As I will try to show in the following section, it is often impossible to isolate concepts from the theories in which they are embedded and which constitute part of their very 'meaning'. As a result, the analysis of concepts such as power cannot be used as a mere means for explanation, wherein they would neutrally assess the salience of competing theories. When Max Weber (1980 [1921–2]) put a lengthy introduction to 'basic sociological concepts' at the start of his *Economy and Society*, this was not just a technical and definitional basis for his theory but already part of it, the result of much of his earlier analysis. The relation between these concepts provided the framework of his sociological work. As Martin Bulmer writes, 'concepts such as the "protestant ethic" or "marginal utility" derive their meaning from the part they play in the theory in which they are embedded, and from the role in that theory itself' (Bulmer 1979: 658). As a result, a conceptual analysis which isolates one concept necessarily slides into the task of assessing a whole theory.

I will illustrate this point by discussing the positivist attempt to produce a neutral or descriptive concept (Nagel 1975). That any definition of power can be neutral or descriptive has been contested in mainly two ways. First, some scholars have argued that 'power' belongs to a family of 'essentially contested' concepts. I will take up the discussion of this in the next section, since it will serve as a springboard for a more pragmatic understanding of conceptual analysis. Second, any neutral definition of power seems elusive, precisely because one can make sense of concepts only in their meaning world; a claim with 'strongly holistic implications' (Skinner 1989: 13) which became prominent in the aftermath of Kuhn's analysis of paradigms. This applies as much to the relationship between concepts and social philosophies as it does to the more narrow purposes of explanatory theories, where concept formation and theory formation stand in a mutually constitutive relationship.

Oppenheim opposes this view. He claims that his definition of power does not exclude particular ways of conceiving a social theory. He rests his case with the persuasiveness of his definition: 'I have no better justification than to point to the results of this study' (Oppenheim 1981: 189). And yet, that such a meta-theoretical dependence eludes the search for a neutral concept across the individualist–intersubjective divide can be shown by briefly comparing Oppenheim's claim of a neutral concept with a radically holistic theory and its embedded concept of power; namely Niklas Luhmann's system theory.[8] Luhmann defines power as a symbolically generated medium of communication which reduces complexity and allows calculus. Power resides in the communication, not in action. It is not causal, but functions by attributing causality to a particularly steered communication. I will explain this definition step by step.

Luhmann's social theory is a theory of systems and their autopoietic (internally self-generated) reproduction, not a theory of action. Communication plays a major role in this theory: it consists in the linking-up of systems (coupling) wherein the 'external' is included into the internal reproduction processes. This process can be conditioned by particular media of communication. A medium of communication is a code of generalised symbols that steer the transmission of inputs into the respective selection processes of systems. Power is such a medium of communication.

Media of communication, like power or money, are seen by Luhmann to have developed as a response to the rising complexity of modern societies. As throughout his entire theorising, Luhmann is interested here in the ways systems have been able to cope with (and, in turn, generate) increasing complexity. With the development of written communication and the greater complexity it allows, symbolically generated media of communication became necessary in order to reduce complexity, i.e., to reduce the uncertainty of selection processes (Luhmann 1975: 12–13). They create tacit incentives for the acceptance of certain meanings, thus avoiding the communication to become too complicated, or even impossible.[9] Communication exists only if the reproduction of systems is affected in its ongoing 'selections' – what an individualist approach would perhaps call 'choices' or 'decisions', but which lack the conscious or explicit component of the latter two concepts. Media of communication steer communication and, through this, transmit 'selection impulses'. Power as a medium of communication organises alternatives so that it becomes clear to the communication partners which are those to be avoided. For Luhmann, the code of power communicates an asymmetrical relation, a causal relationship, and steers the transmission of selections from the more powerful to the less powerful system (Luhmann 1975: 22, 1990 [1981]: 157).

At this point, it might be helpful to pull out the differences between Luhmann's and Oppenheim's concepts of power. For Luhmann, power is not in action, but in communication. 'Will' and motives, i.e., traditional attributes for the explanation of action, are not important for the assessment of action or for power. 'Will' is not prior to power, in the sense that an act of power would overrule a pre-existing will. In a code-steered communication, expectations can be such that the will of an actor for a specific action never arises. Will is neutralised by power,

---

8 For a more detailed analysis and critique of Luhmann's concept of power, see Guzzini (2004b).
9 This view is constant throughout Luhmann's work. See Luhmann (1990: 179).

not broken. Power-steered communication constitutes the will of one partner by *attributing* to his actions successes, expectations and respective motives. 'Power does not instrumentalise an already present will, it constitutes that will and can oblige it, bind it, make it absorb risks and uncertainties, can tempt it and make it fail' (Luhmann 1975: 21, my translation). 'Motives' are not an origin or cause of action. In the execution of power, the communication process itself attributes motives to systems. This allows the communicative system to socially understand action. In a nutshell: power does not cause an outcome, but communicatively regulates the attribution of causality for understanding that outcome (Luhmann 1990 [1981]: 157).

As this short discussion shows, Luhmann's concept of power cannot be accounted for within Oppenheim's conceptual frame. It is a form of power which has an agent referent, but the causality of power does not in fact derive from the agent as such but is attributed to it by the communication process. Luhmann's holistic epistemology and system theory has no place for an action-concept of power like Oppenheim's.[10] Some of our central concepts – in particular if, like power, they have an explanatory value for social theories – cannot escape a basic meta-theoretical dependence: they make sense within their respective meta-theories, which are not always compatible.

John Gray, for instance, compares individualist (voluntarist) and structuralist (determinist) frameworks of explanation and concludes that 'since judgements about power and structure are theory-dependent operations, actionists and structuralists will approach their common subject-matter – what goes on in society – using divergent paradigms in such a fashion that incompatible explanations (and descriptions) will be produced' (Gray 1983: 94). He argues that these are incommensurable views of man and society which elude a rational choice. In a similar vein, in reference to the difference between a classical Weberian and a Foucauldian understanding of power, Peter Miller (1987: 10) concludes that a 'considerable distance separates a notion of power understood as the exercise by A of power over B, contrary to B's preferences, and a notion of power as a multiplicity of practices for the promotion and regulation of subjectivity'. Concepts of power necessarily reflect meta-theoretical divides. This calls for a position of explanatory perspectivism in conceptual analysis.[11]

Summing up, two points are worth repeating. First, it has to be noted that, although conceptual analysis is important for variable construction, variable construction is not all there is to conceptual analysis.[12] Second, taking seriously Kant's dictum that categories are the condition for the possibility of knowledge (shared also by positivists), also means that one needs to look at the way these

---

10 Except for conceiving it as itself a construct of communication.
11 For my earlier statement on this, see Guzzini (1993). This view is more widely shared across different approaches, see e.g. Barnes (1988), and Merritt and Zinnes (1989: 27).
12 As it tends to be even in King, Keohane and Verba (1994).

categories are meta-theoretically embedded. Scholars need to control the assumptions upon which they make their variable construction, and this will inevitably lead them to question concepts in themselves. For, as the following sections are going to show, these concepts are a means to re-embed our knowledge into its social or political context.

A note on constructivist understandings of the meaning of power

Since constructivism is a meta-theoretical commitment, there is not one single conception of power which would be shared by all approaches. However, given its general interpretative commitments and attempts to overcome methodological individualism, constructivist theories tend to understand power as both agential and intersubjective (including non-intentional and impersonal power), and they are also more attuned to questions of open or taken-for-granted and 'naturalised' legitimation processes.[13] Indeed, some recent power approaches tend to add Foucault to Lukes's three dimensions of power (Barnett and Duvall 2005a; see outside IR, e.g., Clegg 1989).

This does not mean that the conceptual work is already accomplished. For this is just one step in unfolding the dialectical relationship between concepts and theories. Clarifying meanings of power within a constructivist understanding requires us to relate the meanings arrived at back into a coherent social theory; this is something even comprehensive taxonomies or typologies cannot do. Such comprehensive approaches risk overloading the concept, which is still too closely related to ideas of effective cause (for a discussion of this fallacy and a proposal how to coherently combine Lukes and Foucault within a wider Bourdieu-inspired power analysis, see Guzzini 1993: 468–74). Hence, just adding up facets of power is analytically insufficient and all depends upon into which kind of framework this power analysis is re-embedded; an undertaking that is far from self-evident, as Lukes's own cautious treatment of Foucault suggests (Lukes 2005).

Performative conceptual analysis: what does 'power' do?

The foregoing discussion has looked at conceptual analysis when used as a means for understanding. Although a necessary, if limited, tool in any analysis, it leads towards a conceptual analysis for which the better understanding of a concept arrived at is itself an aspect of that which is being explained.[14] This type of

---

13 For a presentation of a wider analysis of power compatible with constructivism, which stresses the need to include non-intentionality and a structural component, see Guzzini (1993).
14 For a discussion of the role of such conceptual analysis in IR theory and its teaching, see Guzzini (2001c).

conceptual analysis is not so much about what exactly is meant by the concept, but what it achieves in communication. In a move stemming from pragmatic linguistics, it does understand the meaning of a concept by what its use *does*. This section will argue that the concept of power plays an important role in our political discourse in that it indicates realms where political action could have been different; or indeed where against apparent odds, it would have been possible in the first place. It defines the realm of political action and its justification. As such, attributing power is not innocent, but implies that things could have been done otherwise. Because they define the realm of politics, attributions of power are themselves part of politics. This performative effect illustrates a reflexive link typical for constructivism.

The effect of 'power':
From essentially contested concept to the definition of political space[15]

Peter Morriss's (1987) book *Power: A Philosophical Analysis* has been rightly celebrated for including the first systematic study of the question: why do we need 'power'? Asking backwards from the purposes of power (its usage), Morriss finds three contexts of power (practical, moral and evaluative) as a way to show that we are not always interested in the same subcategory of power concepts. In the practical context we might be particularly interested in non-intentional power, since we want to guard against any adverse effects, whether intended or not. In the moral context, intention plays a more important role. Hence, according to Morriss, power debates would be less heated if only we clearly contextualised them. Yet perhaps this is not quite as easy as Morriss presents it. I will use a detour through a discussion of the concept of power as an 'essentially contested' concept to open up another way of addressing the 'purposes' of power, one which takes the role of language more seriously. The most-often-repeated reason for the essential contestability of power is the value-dependence of social theories. According to this view, if power is to play a role in social theory, its definition and interpretations will inevitably be value-laden.

> [I]ts very definition and any given use of it, once defined, are inextricably tied to a given set of (probably unacknowledged) value-assumptions which predetermine the range of the empirical application. [. . .] Thus, any given way of conceiving of power (that is, any given way of defining the concept of power) in relation to the understanding of social life presupposes a criterion of significance, that is, an answer to the question what makes A's affecting B significant? [. . .] but also [. . .] any way of interpreting a given concept of power is likely to involve further particular and contestable judgements.
>
> *(Lukes 1974: 26; 1977: 4–5, 6)*

---

15 This section draws heavily on Guzzini (1994: Part II).

Unfortunately, Lukes's (and Connolly's) argument was both too easily embraced and too hastily rejected. On the one hand, value-dependence quickly became synonymous with being 'ideological'. From there it was only one step to analyse Lukes's three dimensions as the expression of our well-known Anglo-American ideological triad of conservatism, liberalism and radicalism (as, for instance, in Cox, Furlong and Page 1985). Just as in IR, questions of value dependence have been translated into well-known, yet all too facile theoretical triads (for a more detailed critique, see Guzzini 1998: ch. 8).

Another faction of the discipline reacted with contempt upon being told that academic enterprise is politics (although nobody ever said, 'nothing but politics') and being offered this well-known menu from which to choose. Moreover, since the implication of this argument seemed to be a form of radical relativism, the argument was judged incoherent.[16] Still others argued that value dependence is nothing which distinguishes power from other concepts in the social sciences. Thus, if the determination of an evaluative character was meant to establish a particular category of concepts in the social sciences, it fails. If it aims at describing a characteristic of all social-science concepts, it is not 'enlightening' (Giddens 1979: 89–90). Although this debate therefore seemed to open up conceptual analysis to political contexts in particular, it did it in a way which is ultimately not very fruitful for conceptual research.

Yet, the attempt to limit the issue to value dependence is to underrate some other important facets of Lukes's and Connolly's argument. Connolly explicitly refers to the necessary connection between the idea of power and the idea of responsibility. This seems to fit nicely into one of Morriss's contexts, the moral one. Yet, whereas for Morriss, this closes the analysis, for Lukes and Connolly, it does not. For they are not only interested in what the concept means and where it is used, but what it does when it is used.

> When we see the conceptual connection between the idea of power and the idea of responsibility we can see more clearly why those who exercise power are not eager to acknowledge the fact, while those who take a critical perspective of existing social relationships are eager to attribute power to those in privileged positions. For to acknowledge power over others is to implicate oneself in responsibility for certain events and to put oneself in a position where *justification* for the limits placed on others is expected. To attribute power to another, then, is not simply to describe his role in some perfectly neutral sense, but is more like *accusing* him of something, which is then to be denied or justified.
>
> (Connolly 1974: 97, emphasis in original)

---

16 For this position, see Oppenheim (1981: 185). David Baldwin's position reads like a critique of essentially contested concepts, but seems close to the latter's precepts. See Baldwin (1989: 8).

Connolly's position here is not about why we look for power, as Morriss does, but why we *call* something a phenomenon of power, as Connolly and Lukes do. Put into this context, I think the latter two authors made a very important point. 'Power' implies an idea of counterfactuals; i.e., it could also have been otherwise. The act of *attributing* power redefines the borders of what can be done. In the usual way we conceive of the term, this links power inextricably to 'politics' in the sense of the 'art of the possible'. Lukes rightly noticed that Bachrach and Baratz's (1970) conceptualisation of power – which included agenda-setting, non-decision-making and the mobilisation of bias – sought to redefine what counts as a political issue. To be 'political' means to be potentially changeable; i.e., not something natural, God-given, but something which has the potential to be influenced by agency. In a similar vein, Daniel Frei (1969: 647) notes that the concept of power is fundamentally identical to the concept of the 'political'; i.e., to include something as a factor of power in one's calculus, means to 'politicise' it (for a similar point, see Hoffmann 1988: 7–8). In other words, attributing a function of power to an issue imports it into the public realm where action (or non-action) is asked to justify itself.

In return, 'depoliticisation' happens when by common acceptance no power was involved. In the conceptual analysis of power, this depoliticisation has been taking place through the concept of 'luck'. The starting point for the discussion is the so-called 'benefit fallacy' in power analysis (Barry 1989: 315). Nelson Polsby (1980: 208) explicitly mentions the case of free riders who may profit from something, but without being able to influence it. Keith Dowding (1991: 137) extended the discussion with his refusal to include 'systematic luck' under the concept of power. And since there is no power, so the argument implies, there is no politics involved and no further (public) action needed. Yet, although scepticism about the links between power and benefits are warranted, it seems reductive not to allow for a conceptual apparatus and a social theory which can account for systematic benefits in terms other than 'systematic luck'. By reducing a systematic bias to a question of luck, this approach leaves out of the picture the daily practices of agents that help to reproduce the very system and positions from which these advantages were derived. Making it conscious raises questions of responsibility, and finally also issues of political choice.[17]

Such a performative analysis of concepts is not new in IR, in particular with regard to the concept of security.[18] Jef Huysmans has worked on security as a

---

17 For this reason perhaps, Keith Dowding (1996: 94ff.) has later rephrased his approach and now explicitly includes systematic luck into power *analysis*, although still not calling it power.
18 Some readers might wonder why I do not use the concepts of 'speech act' or 'illocutionary force' here but a more generic term. The reason has to do with the contested usages of those terms, which would warrant a longer discussion. With regard to speech acts, some might argue that the performative character of 'power' is not yet a speech act, since it is not as equally ritualised and institutionalised as 'I do' is

'thick signifier' with performative effects for ordering social relations (Huysmans 1998). Barry Buzan and Ole Wæver have proposed a performative analysis of security suggesting an approach to 'securitisation'. According to them, security is to be understood through the effects of it being voiced. It is part of a discourse which, when successfully mobilised, enables issues to be given a priority for which the use of extraordinary means is justified. In its logical conclusion, 'securitisation' ultimately tends to move decisions out of 'politics' altogether (Wæver 1995; Buzan, Wæver and de Wilde 1998). Curiously enough, therefore, the performative effects of these two concepts are connected: 'politicisation' is a precondition for a possible later 'securitisation', which, if successful, again puts issues beyond 'politics' (understood here as bargains within regular procedures). Whereas 'power' invokes a need for justification in terms of a debate, 'security' mobilises a pre-given justification with the effect of stopping all debate.

Reflexivity loops in IR:
Conceptual power analysis as part of (power) politics

A conceptual analysis which focuses on the performative character of some concepts implies a series of reflexive links. A conceptual analysis of power in terms of its meaning is part of the social construction of knowledge; moreover, the definition/assignation of power is itself an exercise of power, or 'political', and hence part of the social construction of reality. As the following two illustrations will indicate, the very definition of power is a political intervention.

This reflexive feature of power has been at the origin of some of the newer power conceptualisations in IR. It does, for instance, help to account for two components in Susan Strange's concept of structural power (Strange 1987, 1988).[19] First, Strange created this concept in the context of a perceived US decline. Thus the incapacity of the USA to keep the fixed exchange-rate system or to manage the international economy better found justification in a perceived decline in power. In other words, the US government may have been willing, but no longer able, to provide the public goods it used to provide.[20] Strange tried

---

during a marriage. On the other hand, 'power' seems to mobilise a convention in our political discourse and seems therefore akin to that which is described in Austin's or Searle's analysis. As to the type of speech act, I would see this performative effect rather as perlocutionary than illocutionary, although the concepts can slide into each other. On this last point, see, for example, the discussion in Habermas (1985 [1981]: 388–97). For speech-act theory in IR, see Onuf (1989), Fierke (1998) and, most akin to the present view, Kratochwil (1989b). For an attempt to ground the performative aspect not in speech-act theory but in Derrida, see Zehfuss (2002).

19 For a more detailed discussion of Strange's 'structural power', see also Guzzini (2000b); and for its link to the purposes of power, see Guzzini (2000c).
20 The language of public goods is typical for the debate around hegemonic stability theory.

to argue that the declining provision had less to do with declining power than with shifting interests unconnected to power. To do this, her concept of structural power casts a wider net (her four structures) that encompasses areas in which the USA is not clearly seen to be declining. As a result, the USA has to justify its action with means other than the 'excuse' of lacking power. Second, Strange's concept of structural power also includes non-intentional effects. Whether the Federal Reserve intended to hurt anyone is less important than that it did. By making actors also aware of the unintended effects of their action, they are asked to take this into account next time. They become potentially liable to the question of why, now aware of the effects, action had not changed. Having a broader concept of power asks for more issues to be factored into political decisions and actions (exactly as in Connolly's analysis).

The link between knowledge, power and politics is also visible in the daily practices of diplomacy. Here it is less the performative aspect of language than the relationship between knowledge and conventions which directly intervenes into politics. Despite claims to the contrary, power is not especially fungible; i.e., resources effective in one area might not necessarily be so elsewhere. In more technical terms, power does not do for politics what money does for economics since it does not provide a standard measure with which a particular resource can be exchanged with another one.[21] Yet, given the special role great power status plays in international affairs, diplomats need to 'make up' indicators for overall power. Given the need to trade gains and losses so as (not) to upset the ranking of power (also achieved through politics of compensation), diplomats have to come to agree on what counts before they can start counting. Taking this link for granted, Daniel Frei (1969) had early on urged scientists to help politicians in this task.

Yet, there is still no neutral solution in sight. Indeed, the very definition of power is so contentious precisely because of its political consequences. During the Cold War, the Soviet Union resisted those definitions of power whose stress on non-military factors would imply a decline in its status. Similarly, in the recent controversy about soft and hard (coercive) power, deciding what power *really* means has obvious political implications. Focusing more on the military side and hence stressing an unprecedented preponderance of the US military made it possible to ask the USA to push its advantages further (since it is 'possible'), and at times even stress the duty of the USA to intervene given its capacities (which relates back to the performative argument above). Or, stressing US soft power and its potential decline, analysts could advocate a much more prudent and varied foreign policy strategy sensitive to claims of legitimacy and cultural

---

21 The best place to read about power fungibility is still the work of David Baldwin. See in particular Baldwin (1989). For a recent assessment of the fungibility debate, see Guzzini (2004c: 537–44).

attraction (whether or not the legitimacy crisis is simply an effect of poor public diplomacy or of a more fundamental origin).[22] Or, as I have shown elsewhere (Guzzini 2006), insisting on the unipolarity of the present international system, such a power statement mobilises a justification for leadership and responsibility which, in turn, can justify the 'inescapable', and hence excusable, nature of unilateralism (and a consensus on multipolarity does the opposite).

As this section has tried to show, a constructivist conceptual analysis must, by its very assumptions, include an analysis of the possible performative effects of concepts. These are not addenda to the meaning of the concept, but an integral part of it. Hence, a constructivist analysis of power necessarily re-embeds the concept into the explanatory theory and the political discourse to which it belongs.

Conceptual analysis as conceptual history and genealogy: How has it become possible for 'power' to mean and do what it does?

The above examples show both the contribution, but also the limits, of constructivism-inspired conceptual analysis for the study of power. Indeed, as much as these reflexive loops are important, they are in themselves only understood through the political context in which they take place. Hence, although they make a conceptual analysis of power part of the definition of politics and hence a component of a wider analysis of power, it is emphatically not all that there is to a constructivist power analysis.[23] Such an analysis would look at the institutionalised systems or fields in which these performative acts are played out and which highlight the role general practices and authority positions therein play to affect the social construction of knowledge and their effect (for an application in the field of security, see Leander's (2005b) study of the 'epistemic power' of private military companies). Indeed, who is authorised to speak in the first place and which authority (roles, institutions and the taken-for-granted understandings) supports the claims?

So, one could argue, here is where the reflexive loop back to actual power, hence the relevance of constructivism for a conceptual analysis of power, stops. Not yet. Since constructivism denaturalises the status quo, the performative effect of conceptual analysis must also open up to further analysis: does the effect apply to all contexts; is it always the same, over different time horizons? Precisely because constructivism shares a pragmatic approach towards concepts (i.e., it works back from their usage) and because such usage follows a certain path dependency, it seems consonant for constructivists to ask themselves how such

---

22 On soft power, see also Janice Bially Mattern (2005).
23 For such a wider power analysis in IR, see, for example, the different studies now collected in Barnett and Duvall (2005b).

meanings and performative effects have historically been constituted and evolved. The concept of power is not only put into a political context but is also placed in a wider historical one. If it is true that invoking power often has an effect of 'politicising' issues, when, where and how has this become possible? This leads to conceptual history, but of a kind. It is not the type of analysis that simply takes a concept and looks for its usage over time. Here, the constructivist argument runs parallel to the previous sections: meanings are derived from the pertinent contexts in which the concept has been used. If there is conceptual history, it must be one which is strongly embedded in the different historical meaning contexts of the audience its use wanted to address (this obviously points to Quentin Skinner's approach, now collected in Skinner 2002). It would include a sociology of knowledge. Moreover, it must be a conceptual history which includes the performative aspects of political language and, hence, the interplay between social history and conceptual history.[24] Finally, taking seriously the claim that 'it could have been otherwise', such a conceptual history would be akin to a Foucault-inspired genealogy.[25]

Such an analysis is obviously beyond the scope of this chapter. Still, I would like to use the findings of the Bielefeld approach to conceptual history to give the reader an idea of what such a historical contextualisation of 'power' in IR might look like. For this purpose, the following sketches one hypothetical lineage from eighteenth-century statecraft via German political theory to political realism as it developed in IR.[26] The starting point is that the use of 'power' as a 'politicising' act was premised on the definition of politics as the 'art of the possible' (or feasible). Yet, this naturalised understanding is of rather late origin. Volker Sellin argues that with early modernity, the Western conception of politics became dual: a neo-Aristotelian lineage stressing the common good and a Machiavellian tradition based on the reason of state (Sellin 1978). Only in the eighteenth century did an increasing reduction of the understanding of politics to *Machtkunst* (roughly the 'art/craft' of 'power/governing') appear.

---

24 See, for example, Koselleck (1979: in particular 107–29), Skinner (1989) and Farr (1989). Indeed, these analyses which show how rhetoric, targeting concepts, can be used to unravel historically sedimented and taken-for-granted patterns of legitimacy is congenial to the way Lukes's three dimensions have been operationalised and sequentialised in Gaventa (1980).

25 For an argument on the similarities in Skinner's and Foucault's approach, see Tully (1988). For a genealogical study in IR and a general discussion which has inspired this section, see Bartelson (1995).

26 For the present purposes, the following is simply meant as an illustration of how such an analysis could get started in the context of IR. It neglects many analytical difficulties, such as the variety of competing past schools of thought in different cultural contexts or the possibility of actually translating concepts from one context to another (even within Europe, now that the 'classic' and common understanding of what it is no longer exists, let alone a common language).

To some extent, this reductionist reading was countered in liberal (and some conservative) political theories, mainly with regard to domestic constitutionalism. Yet, so Sellin, within the German context of the nineteenth and early twentieth century – the shift to positive law, and especially the idea of the reason of state and of power as the chief ingredient in *Staatskunst* (roughly 'statecraft') – had attracted an important group of followers not only interested in internal affairs. Members of this group also belonged to, or were influenced by, the German Historical School. Starting with von Ranke, and leading up to von Treitschke, von Rochau's Treatise on *Realpolitik*, Friedrich Meinecke and Max Weber – they were all strongly, at times primarily, interested in the *international* status of Germany, nascent or newly unified. At the same time when politics became defined in an increasingly narrow way, *Macht* became increasingly decoupled from the political sphere/state and diffused onto other social spheres (Faber, Ilting and Meier 1982). In other words, precisely when politics and power got conceptually coupled in the German context of the second half of the nineteenth century – in particular, but not exclusively, when applied to international affairs (which included German unification, after all) – power lost its exclusive attachment to the sphere of the state. Now moving conceptually together, with this diffusion of power, 'politics' diffused too.

Such a look at the quite recent conceptual history in Germany allows us to establish some hypotheses for answering the question of why the use of 'power' somewhat naturally 'politicises' issues and yet, why this should not be seen as a sole matter of the state. On the one hand, the 'politicisation' is but the logical consequence of a historical development of tying power so closely to politics. On the other hand, the increasing diffusion of power throughout society implies the increasing 'politicisation' of different social spheres. This tendency is well established in social history, accounting for both the increasing enfranchisement of larger portions of the society and the political struggles over the public control of previously 'private' or 'civil society' spheres like education or the economy. This, in turn, connects the political back to the state. Therefore, de Jouvenel (1972) retraces the history of *pouvoir* as one of steady state expansion. Yet the reconnection is only part of the story, and de Jouvenel therefore neglects all counter-'powers' that liberal societies have developed in the face of an ever-increasing state.

Such conceptual analysis, besides providing the historical context for studying the origins of the performative content of 'power', allows for the possibility to develop hypotheses for possible tensions in existing usages. Applying the foregoing argument to IR, it was noted that there has been a strong German tradition working with the notion of 'power politics'. Even a cursory reading of the early Morgenthau (1933, 1946) shows the importation of this actually often (German) idealist thinking (cf. Palan and Blair 1993) onto the new environments of his emigration and later also onto a particularised field, IR. Yet, Morgenthau's explicit intention was to isolate a particular 'morality' of the national interest – a reason of state, different from national morality – so as to establish the independence of the international realm in the first place. The reconceptualisations of power today – i.e., today's 'politicisations' in IR – instead undermine this specificity (Guzzini 1993). What has come under the name of 'structural power' signifies, in a certain sense, a return to the unitary vision of the political which existed in the nineteenth century and which was partly abandoned by its followers in the realist tradition in IR. Doing so, these politicisations not only expand the realm of the 'art of the feasible', inviting for more public agency, but simultaneously lay the ground for a return to notions of the common good, now thought at the international level.

Hence the return and broadening of the 'political' in IR comes at a price for more traditional power-oriented conceptions of international politics. Power and politics have a strong mutually defining link, in particular in realist theory, so much so that they are often used together as a single concept. For realists, politics is about the individual (national) pursuit of power and its collective management. Or, expressed the other way round: outcomes in international politics are decided by power differentials and their distribution. Broadening the research agenda implies a critique of this approach or, at least, exposing some of its limits. In this critique, politics is seen to be done by actors other than states. States, in turn, have international policies which in the time of 'embedded liberalism' (Ruggie 1982) encompass more than strictly military or diplomatic security. This implies new forms of collective management of international politics, from regimes in new policy areas to the new public–private arrangements in the 'global compact'. Meanwhile, the transnationalisation of politics specifically undermines the control capacities of states and other international actors, or so it seems. A first look at the power differentials no longer explains the outcomes. It seems as if 'structural' factors are increasingly shaping and moving world events.

This leads to the following hypothesis: it is this context of both an expansion of 'politics' as a potential field of action and a perceived contraction of 'politics' as real room for manoeuvre that informs and is addressed by the new power research programmes (Guzzini 1994: 14). These concentrate both on the new direct and indirect ways to control knowledge, agendas and regimes and on the increasing perception of an impersonal rule of the international scene. In today's IR, power analysis has become a critique of classical 'power politics'.

Conclusion

As I have tried to argue, a constructivist conceptual analysis of power stresses the theory-dependent meaning of concepts, the performative effects some concepts can have (and which are an important component of their meaning) and the historical and social context of the conventions which underlie this effect. Doing so, it exposes a reflexive interrelation between the concept of power, conceptual analysis and political power, which is not always that easy to disentangle. Only in the first step and claim of the conceptual analysis is there a simple link: a conceptual analysis of power is tied to the underlying social theory, such as those inspired by constructivism. The second claim includes a direct link, when the inherently performative role of power is specifically related to questions of political legitimacy. But, and this adds a reflexive twist, this performative aspect shows how the acceptance of certain usages of concepts can have an effect on social reality – an effect which as such is part of our understanding of political power, independently of the particular concept at hand. In other words, the constructivist way of understanding conceptual analysis is itself consequential for the understanding of power in the social world. For 'the theory of knowledge is a dimension of political theory because the specifically symbolic power to impose the principles of the construction of reality [. . .] is a major dimension of political power' (Bourdieu 1977: 165). In this context, the stress on the constitutive effects of knowledge typical for both post-Lukes power analysis and constructivists, makes power analysis and constructivism share a family resemblance.[27]

Finally, by opening up how concepts have come to mean and do what they do, this type of conceptual analysis further connects the idea of power and constructivism via their common connection to counterfactuals. Power analysis and constructivist analysis are structurally akin (Guzzini 2000a: 150, 154). By revealing how the social world is of our making, constructivism tends to question the inevitability of the status quo (Hacking 1999: 6). In an analogous way, power is usually conceived in terms of dispositions and capacities which suggest how things could have been different (Baldwin 1985: 22). Given then this particular role conceptual analysis has for and within constructivism, it was obviously not innocent to have chosen power as the concept with which to illustrate a constructivist approach. It allowed a focus on power from the very start, before this similarity between power analysis and constructivist theorising was even introduced. Yet, using 'power' to illustrate also makes the final analysis more complicated insofar as the many reflexive relations have to be thought in parallel. This chapter hopefully contributed to opening up this path.

27 I am indebted to Vincent Pouliot for this reminder.

13
'THE COLD WAR IS WHAT WE MAKE OF IT'

When peace research meets constructivism in International Relations

This chapter argues that one of the lineages of present-day 'constructivist' research in International Relations is peace research. Indeed, the ease with which constructivism-inspired research has swept over Western and Northern Europe cannot be understood otherwise. Constructivism provides the meta-theoretical support and furthered the classical peace research criticism that the Cold War was no necessity, but politically 'constructed'.

Peace research, as well as constructivism, insists that international 'anarchy' does not exclude the existence of an international society. In its view, anarchy has no unbreakable logic: its effects are a construct of that international society. It does not exclude that agents can learn in international society, that its rules can be amended and that these are, in turn, related to the constitution of the roles these very agents can play in that society. In other words, International Relations are the effect of political processes, not structural or historical necessities. Peace research/constructivism does not deny that 'power politics' can exist. This power politics is, however, not the result of invariable laws of politics, but is the compounded effect of agents who believe in such pessimistic invariable laws of politics caught in structures reflecting these beliefs. In terms of research, this meant that the Cold War lock was at least partly a 'self-fulfilling prophecy' whose extent needed to be empirically established and not axiomatically excluded from

---

An earlier version of this chapter was presented at the joined CEEISA/NISA/RISA convention in June 2002, Moscow and at COPRI, Malmö and Uppsala Universities. For helpful suggestions and criticisms, I am indebted to Emanuel Adler, Alexander Astrov, Chris Browning, Barry Buzan, Tarja Cronberg, Olya Gayazova, Mats Hammarström, Pertti Joenniemi, Dietrich Jung, Peter Katzenstein, Anna Leander, Sonia Lucarelli, Bill McSweeney, Andrey Makarychev, Heikki Patomäki, Alexander Sergounin, John Vasquez, Christoph Weller and Ole Wæver. The usual disclaimers apply.

research. In political terms, the potential for détente policies was to be sorted out step-by-step, with controlled confidence-building measures and arms control, not excluded through a policy which mistook the sometimes necessary *means* of containment and deterrence with the *ends* of foreign policy.

Arguing for this point of encounter, even if central, comes with a series of caveats, however. First, it should not be mistaken to mean that everything there was and is to peace research can be subsumed under constructivism, or vice versa. Rather, it wants to remind constructivists that some of their political argument creates a sense of 'déjà vu' for peace researchers, and that they might be well advised to also look at the rest of peace research, in particular its emancipatory tradition (Alker 1996). Inversely, peace research would gain from taking some of the particular constructivist or indeed post-structuralist insights seriously. For constructivism has been inspired by a series of developments in the philosophy of social sciences which have undermined the faith in 'data'. Since the recourse to the 'real world' to question the validity of realism was *alone* not enough, it needed to provide an ontological base for the claim of a self-fulfilling prophecy; it needed to provide a general approach which could conceptualise learning and process in a more coherent manner. If constructivists should be more aware of the analytical, practical and normative agenda of peace research, peace research, in turn, should not take the 'déjà vu' as an excuse to neglect the theoretical and meta-theoretical turn in the social sciences which is necessary to their own defence.

The second caveat has to do with the presentist presentation of the main claim. I will try to address mainly IR scholars, which means, as a result, that peace research is primarily seen through the lenses of the discourse in IR, of 'realism and its critics'. Although this makes the lineage around self-fulfilling prophecies more visible, it also does some violence to the very self-conception of much peace research. I hope that this shortcoming is at least partly offset by the advantage of opening up for this encounter, and by Heikki Patomäki's (2001a) article, which, written from within peace research, can be read parallel to much of the following.

The early critique of the logic of anarchy and the realist opening for process

Realists insisted that whereas politics in a domestic setting was able to show instances of progress, international affairs could not (Wight 1966; for the most forceful critique of this dichotomy, see Walker 1993a). There, history was bound to return. For all his own scepticism about science, Morgenthau was read as a protagonist of a determinist realism insisting, as he was, on the balance of power, the 'self-regulatory mechanism of the social forces which manifests itself in the struggle for power on the international scene', which was there out 'of necessity' (Morgenthau 1948: 9, 125).

The first important step in reclaiming ground from realism consisted in showing that politics can make a difference, that realpolitik was no necessity.

Two conceptual critiques have been particularly important. Inis Claude's (1962, and again 1989) and Ernst Haas' (1953) analyses of the balance of power had to conclude that, far from being a 'necessity' as in Morgenthau's treatment, it was void because tautological, and hence rather a normative appeal for its implementation, a 'prescription' or 'ideology'. Similarly, Morgenthau's concept of the national interest was scrutinised – with much the same result, as the young Robert Tucker's (1952) sober and all the more cruel dissection of Morgenthau's self-contradictions shows. Later, and on a more theoretical level, Raymond Aron (1962: 97–102) tried to show that a utilitarian theory of politics cannot hold where the national interest (security) in terms of power would be analogous to utility (wealth) expressed in terms of money in neo-classical economics. For power is not analogous to money. Hence, national interest assessments are intrinsically indeterminate.

The implications of this indeterminacy did not escape all 'realists': they had to open up for the understanding of process and not just necessity. Wolfers (1962) proposed an approach which was not saying outright that realism was (always) wrong, but that realism was simply *a special case* which applies at one pole of the international continuum between power and indifference. Crucially, one had to find out what makes some systems drive towards the pole of power and some towards the pole of indifference. And with all but the name, Wolfers analysed the risk of power politics as a self-fulfilling prophecy. For there were situations in which power politics was the right strategy and some where strategies of re-assurance, as we would call them now, would be the correct ones. Power politics/escalation before the First World War was as fatal as appeasement before the Second World War. In some cases, it is the effect of worst case thinking which only produces the very worst case it is supposedly trying to avoid.

Peace research as the study of process pathologies

Starting with a section on realism exemplifies the IR lenses of the present chapter. Although presenting realism as peace research's 'other' is not uncommon in the literature (Vasquez 1983), it is more correct to say that, for early peace researchers, the 'other' was war, not realism.[1] Yet there is a crucial link between war and realism which is also central for the argument about 'self-fulfilling prophecies'. For early peace research was interested in finding out the systematic reasons for being locked in the Cold War posture. In doing this, it focused on material impediments to change, such as the imperialist structures of the international system (Galtung 1971) or the military–industrial complexes in both superpowers (for a critique of the Western model, see Galbraith 1978 [1967], especially chapter XXIX). More consequential for the link to present-day constructivism was, however, the focus on the role of realpolitik ideas in reproducing Cold War politics and the 'worst case'. As put by Herbert Kelman (1978: 166), one of the

---

1 I am indebted to Emanuel Adler for this idea and formulation.

founders of peace research in the USA (and the *Journal of Conflict Resolution*), '[i]n the search of a settlement, however, the dangers to be avoided are self-fulfilling prophecies that a satisfactory settlement is unattainable. . . .'

When détente seemed possible, enemy-images and systematically biased understandings of world politics were perceived to blind high politics. Yet, in contrast to classical deterrence analysis, early peace researchers tended to see this blindness not as a kind of collective action problem, i.e. as the irrational outcome of strategic interaction due to the adverse condition of anarchy. Instead, they relied heavily on insights from social psychology (Kelman 1958) and studied what appeared to be *systematic learning pathologies* and irrationalities.

For the economy of this short reconstruction, Karl W. Deutsch will play a doubly pivotal role (for the lineage of Deutsch, and Ernst Haas, to constructivism, see also Adler 2002). On the one hand, Deutsch and his associates (1957) launched a research agenda on amalgamated or pluralistic 'security communities'. Rather than being fixed on the bipolar divide and the conditions for a simple Concert, they looked back at the conditions under which former zones of war have become zones of peace. For their focus on process, it is not fortuitous that such studies were then related to the analysis of international organisation (Claude 1956) and integration (Haas 1964). Since much of this experience is based on the lessons of European integration, and in particular the 'anomalous' Scandinavian/Nordic peace (Wiberg 1993, 2000), accordingly much of the security community model was ingrained in European peace research, indeed providing an important part of its identity.

Deutsch, the scholar of cybernetics, that is the science of information, plays a second pivotal role. For systems theory and more particularly cybernetics was to provide peace research with one crucial theoretical underpinning. Indeed, it allowed peace research to systematically analyse learning pathologies in terms of perverse effects of self-referentiality. Cybernetics allowed the connection of two crucial research agendas, namely the self-referentiality of military build-up/deterrence on the one hand, and of psychological processes on the other. It looked at the systematic effects of political economy on foreign policies, as well as at the possibility of *systematic* misperception, either because of the systematic bias in decoding information (coherence versus cognitive dissonance) or because of the functional needs for upholding *Feindbilder* (enemy-images), for example, to rally domestic support and national/group identity.

It is in particular this *Feindbild* literature (the concept stems from Dieter Senghaas), very prominent in Europe, which is a forerunner of present constructivism-inspired scholarship in IR, and in its insistence on self/other politics also of post-structuralist IR. Similar to those studies of 'belief systems', which focus more explicitly on social components (Little 1988), this literature is more encompassing than the literature on sheer misperception (Jervis 1976), which tends to be more cognitively oriented (see also Frei 1985). Yet, by focusing on the ideational components of social constructions, it has a less materialist ontology than Marxism-inspired peace research approaches.

'Autism' and the social learning pathology of deterrence practices

Deutsch's communicative approach starts from the self-referential characteristics of systems and looks for the way information is processed within a system to respond to disturbances (Deutsch 1966). As such, the approach, although not being 'functionalist' in an IR sense, has a theoretical functionalism to it.

When applied to international politics during the Cold War, this way of looking at politics in terms of complex information management has important consequences. The usual way of presenting the Cold War consisted in an action–reaction scheme. Whether intended or not, the security dilemma pushed international 'powers' to be on their guard and react to any advance of the other side. Whether intended or not, such relentless 'being on guard' produces a spiral in the arms race. It is a process which is basically outside–in driven.

Instead, basing politics on the structure of communication process produces a different result. Dieter Senghaas, a student of Deutsch, called an extreme closure 'autism' (Senghaas 1972: 38–62), i.e. a pattern of communication which is not only self-referential, as practices generally are, but has an inbuilt logic which makes adaptation to the environment extremely difficult. Expressed the other way round, when dispositions, both institutional and perceptual, clash with the context of their application, it is not the dispositions, but the processing of reality that is adapted. In cybernetics, this would be considered a learning pathology.

Deterrence theory survives only via the expectation of the worst-case. Deterrence policies *predispose* to a particular stereotyped understanding of the world which reproduces autonomously the perceptions of threats. Thus, the arms race is not an action–reaction between perceptions/actions of agents, but the product of self-generated moments of inertia and autonomously produced threat-perceptions. Escalation is less a collective action problem of individually rational agents and more an inertial effect of two autistic systems. Superpower relations were decreasingly the product of their interaction and increasingly the result of the juxtaposition of their internal dynamics. In other words, deterrence thinking is connected to a process pathology which risks locking the international system into a self-fulfilling prophecy of a worst-case perception relentlessly reproduced.

Feindbilder *and individual learning pathologies*

This pathological self-referentiality was also understood at a more individual level which concentrated on social groups linked with and dependent of the practices of deterrence, such as some politicians, academics and military lobbyists.

Feindbilder provide the analytical link between the social and the individual level. From the literature, Weller (2000: 87–93) has distilled five basic approaches to the understanding of 'enemy-images' in peace research, which are not mutually exclusive: (1) stereotypisation, (2) selective perception, (3) dichotomisation of the social world (reduction to friend–foe relations), (4) an effect of psychological projections from oneself onto others, and (5) socially functional in so far as they allow, for example, the strengthening of unity of a population to legitimate government, arms race and diversionary warfare.

All five enemy-image approaches link up with the study of social pathologies, the first three methodologically, the last two in terms of the collective level of action. The first three derive their explanation from the cognitive economy of mental processes usually understood in cybernetic terms (Steinbruner 1974) just as much as Deutsch and Senghaas used it on the social level. The last two refer to social psychology and a functional theory of society, respectively. Hence, whereas enemy images refer to both the individual and the social level of explanation, they share an interest in a functional/system analysis of mental and social processes respectively.

This link of peace research to social psychology and the study of prejudice and stereotypes has also been very important in shaping its normative component (for the following, see also Weller 2001). For it allowed perceptions to be criticised as 'distorted' and not 'reality-suitable' (*realitätsunangemessen*), inertial to change or cognitively dissonant with 'real' politics.

Finally, assuming the interrelationship of the material and ideal world, it hence allowed the more forceful and open criticism of the tendency to create self-fulfilling prophecies of such enemy-images, as done in the programmatic statement of the project at the *Hessische Stiftung für Friedens- und Konfliktforschung* (Nicklas and Gantzel 1975).

Constructivism and reflexivity on process

As this last section will show, many of the constructivist empirical insights come as little surprise to peace researchers (and many liberal writers in IR). Yet constructivism provides for the first time a meta-theoretical and social theoretical anchorage. It can show how self-fulfilling prophecies are something always present in the social world, not the villain result of intentional conspiracies. Because for its reflexivity, all social actions and processes tend towards self-fulfilling prophecies (McSweeney 1999: 140ff. and passim). In this way, constructivism provides the basis for theoretically more varied and, arguably, more refined explanations.

The paradoxical success of peace research-cum-constructivism

There is a certain paradox in this sweet, if silent, success of peace research through its new constructivist host. For its quantitative wing dominant in the USA had been put on the defensive, and appears at odds with present-day constructivism. Yet the less quantitative traditions, such as much of Galtung's writings and the German tradition, could argue that the end of the Cold War confirmed both peace research approaches and the détente policies they inspired (Wiberg 1992).

Some peace research faced a series of critiques. The quantitative nature of much peace research in the USA, like the famous 'Correlates of War' research project, and its imitators came under scrutiny again in the 'methodological turn' (Little 1991) of the 1980s. Although quantitative peace researchers have been much less simplistic than often decried (for a balanced defence, see Vasquez 1987), the very assumptions underlying huge cross-historical comparisons met with increasing incredulity in some parts of the scientific community (Suganami 1996). In parallel, the early peace research tradition, also including part of Galtung's writing, was relying on behaviouralist assumptions – the diminution of violence through social justice based on objective human needs (see in particular Burton 1985, 1986) – which were being increasingly challenged (Patomäki and Wæver 1995), albeit perhaps not the idea of a utopia itself. Finally, the normative peace research tradition, so strong in Europe, seemed to rely on a clear picture of what 'reality is really like', as compared to distorted perceptions others have, and how a more peaceful history could evolve if only we followed certain recipes – all of which belied a certain empiricism and West(Euro)-centrism. Hence, the varieties of peace research came under combined attack for their positivism, their empiricism and their unreflected normative character.

Yet the end of the Cold War worked as a catalyst. It seemed to give an immediate plausibility to the critiques of realism: peaceful change was possible. The starting point for understanding the meeting of peace research and constructivism in an IR perspective lies in the critique that neorealism was actually unable to even conceive of this type of peaceful change (Koslowski and Kratochwil 1994; Kratochwil 1993; Patomäki 1992). This critique relied on the rehearsal of the 1980s by writers who would be called post-structuralists today. Ashley (1984) and Walker (1987) had started the critique by showing the biases of neorealist theorising, Ashley (1987) later arguing that realism itself has been the (status quo) culture of an international society of diplomats.

Such a critique explicitly connected the level of observation with the level of action and hence comes to one of the crucial parameters of constructivism. For, in my understanding (Guzzini 2000a), constructivism is a meta-theory that can be characterised as:

1. being particularly sensitive to the distinction between the level of action (proper), the level of observation and the relationship between the two (usually theorised in terms of power);
2. having an epistemological position which stresses the social construction of meaning (and hence knowledge);
3. having an ontological position which stresses the construction of social reality.

Such a position emphasises two major inspirations of recent theorising, namely the interpretivist and the sociological turns in the social sciences. Taking the interpretivist turn seriously means starting from the idea of meaningful action and hence from the difference between social sciences, which need to interpret an already interpreted world, and natural sciences, which need not (Schutz 1962 [1953]).

Theorising must therefore conceptualise the level of common-sense action apart from second-order action (or observation). Most importantly, it must analyse their relationship. Again setting the social world apart from the natural, our understandings of people and their action can make a real difference to the latter. For instance, being identified as an opportunist state representative influences options in future negotiations. Moreover, human beings – but not natural phenomena – can become reflexively aware of such attributions and influence their action in interaction with them. This 'looping effect' (Hacking 1999: 34) is one of the reasons for the importance of 'identity' in constructivist writings, theoretically and empirically – and for the study of self-fulfilling prophecies (McSweeney 1999).

Taking the sociological turn seriously implies that meaningful action (and hence also the knowledge of both agent and observer) is a social or intersubjective phenomenon. It cannot be reduced to cognitive psychology or to choice based on interests. Instead, the sociological turn emphasises the role of the social context within which identities and interests of both actor and acting observer are formed in the first place. It also focuses on language as the model case of intersubjectivity, both on the epistemological level and in its practical performative function (Kratochwil 1989a; Onuf 1989; for a discussion, see Zehfuß 1998). Finally, it means that the relationship between the two has in itself to be problematised, i.e. the relationship between the social world and the social construction of meaning (including knowledge).

Hence, when Alexander Wendt (1992b) published his 'Anarchy is what states make of it', he dressed up a basic peace research idea in new and arguably more coherent theoretical and meta-theoretical clothes (Wendt chose Giddens' social theory for this). Wendt provided a predominantly, but not pure, idealist ontology to base the 'social construction of reality' on, something not done in earlier peace research (for an assessment of his approach, see Guzzini and Leander 2001). It comes as no surprise that he then conceived of the international system as a society with different 'cultures of anarchy', including Hobbesian Realpolitik, which have a tendency of a self-fulfilling prophecy (Wendt 1999). Again, the realist case was special in a wider approach, and again research was to centre on questions of process, such as moving from the least to the most peaceful cultures (on change and process in Wendt, see Drulák 2001, 2006; Sárváry 2001, 2006), identified, again, in security communities.

Sketching the variety of IR research inspired by constructivism and peace research

Taking the interpretivist and the sociological turn seriously opened up many more paths for IR research than just Wendt's, some of them constructivist and close to peace research themes and claims. What follows cannot be an exhaustive list. The underlying theme of all approaches is how to create the conditions for a de-escalation or de-militarisation of conflicts, removing the inertial obstacles of predominant constructions of social reality.

Emanuel Adler's constructivism (Adler 1997) has had two interconnected research interests which, almost textbook-like, link up the emphasis on the social construction of knowledge with the construction of social reality. In his earlier work (Adler 1987), he studied the influence of political entrepreneurs and their ideas in shaping the policy process and initiating change (see also Checkel 1997). This theme was picked up in a study together with Peter Haas on epistemic communities, more resolutely asking questions about the power of ideas-entrepreneurs, reflexively applied to all knowledge producers (Adler and Haas 1992). To complete the picture, Adler together with Michael Barnett (1998: chs 1–2) explored the concept and the policies around 'security communities', trying to get it out of its originally objectivist and Euro-centric formulation.

Related to the last item, some constructivists have been concerned with the role of language in the process of change. Coming from a critique of instrumental rationality, Harald Müller (1994, 1995) has emphasised the role of communicative rationality in negotiation processes (see also Risse 2000). Such an approach can also be connected to questions of rhetorical action (Schimmelfennig 2001) and their potential for entrapment, which might force actors to change policies, as part of more general studies on norm-diffusion and socialisation (representatively, see Klotz 1995).

In a related manner, the 'Copenhagen School' of security studies has concentrated on the performative function of language for understanding processes of 'de/securitisation'. It does not understand security as an 'objective' phenomenon which could be deduced from some power calculus, nor as an arbitrary 'subjective' phenomenon. By concentrating not on what exactly 'security' means and is, but rather on what invoking 'security' does (Buzan, Wæver and de Wilde 1998, Wæver 1995), it argues that whenever security (or the national interest) is invoked, i.e. when issues are 'securitised', particular issues are taken out of regular politics and made part of a special agenda with special decision-making procedures and justifications attached to it. '(National) Security' mobilises intersubjectively shared dispositions of understanding, political action and legitimation. In reverse, and this shows the initial puzzle which prompted the conceptualisation, if issues are taken out of national security, if they are 'de-securitised', then politics can return to its place. Wæver's initial case study was German *Ostpolitik* as a conscious de-securitisation strategy. It accepted the post-45 border for changing their political meaning. Several issues were actively 'de-securitised' by being taken out of high politics, to allow more exchange between the two German states and to allow a possible change in the GDR.

Finally, the symbolic construction of social reality, which peace researchers had handled with the analysis of enemy images, has been picked up by another type of constructivism-inspired discourse analysis. The latter focuses on the construction of collective identities, be it national identities and 'other'-identities (Neumann 1995, 1999), or on the role of 'security imaginaries' in the construction of the national interest (Weldes 1999). It does not look as much at whether or not enemy images fit reality, nor whether they are reducible to lacking empathy, but on how they get inscribed into existing discourses/scripts and hence into patterns of understanding and legitimation. Campbell's (1992) earlier study, although self-avowedly not constructivist, seems related, exploring the relationship between foreign policy and identity construction, reversing the idea that foreign policy follows an already constituted identity.

14
ALEXANDER WENDT'S CONSTRUCTIVISM

A relentless quest for synthesis

Stefano Guzzini and Anna Leander

Alexander Wendt's work has rapidly become one of the main reference points of the theoretical debate in International Relations (IR), at least in Europe (for an early assessment, see Ringmar 1997). It is part of a recent trend in IR to acknowledge that meta-theoretical and theoretical reflections are necessarily connected. In his long-awaited book *Social Theory of International Politics*, Wendt consequently first develops his position in the philosophy of science and social theory, before establishing an IR theory of inter-state politics.

The book was acclaimed and contested even before it was published in 1999. It has been the issue of special panels at ISA (International Studies Association) and other conferences, of a Forum (2000) in the *Review of International Studies* and in *Cooperation and Conflict* (Behnke 2001, Jackson 2001), and of an interminable series of book reviews, including even – an event perhaps unique for any theoretical treatise in IR – in *The Economist* (2001).

As this chapter will try to show, the reasons for the book's standing in the discipline can be found in both the very conception of the work within the disciplinary tradition and in more particular substantial points. For Wendt pursues a daring project whose main endeavour is accumulating knowledge for IR in a 'relentless quest for the essence of international relations' (Doty 2000: 137). In the world of scholars, Wendt is not a hunter out to shoot others but a gatherer, albeit

---

We are grateful to the many people who have generously provided us, on short notice, with comments, suggestions and criticisms – namely Emanuel Adler, Alexander Astrov, Andreas Behnke, Milan Brglez, Chris Browning, Barry Buzan, Lars-Erik Cederman, Petr Drulák, Ania Jetschke, Peter Katzenstein, Mette Lykke Knudsen, Friedrich Kratochwil, Richard Little, Ian Manners, Michael Merlinger, Heikki Patomäki, Frank Schimmelfennig, Trine Villumsen, Jutta Weldes, Colin Wight, Ole Wæver and Maja Zehfuss. The usual disclaimers apply.

not a passive one since he uses philosophy of science and social theory to connect loose ends within IR. He combines his theoretical challenges with a desire to 'maintain unity, stability, and order within the discipline' (Doty 2000: 137).

This results in a perhaps unusual mix of orthodoxy in terms of discipline-identity and heterodoxy in terms of the theory that should flesh it out. In other words, he consciously stays within the identity defining parameters of the discipline, including its reference to states as the main organising principle, to more legitimately undermine two key theoretical positions in IR, methodological and ontological individualism and materialism. He bases his theory on two ontological choices hitherto uncommon in IR theories: idealism and holism. But it is not as simple as that.

In fact, Wendt's ultimate project is to gather, synthesise, indeed sometimes 'assimilate' (Wendt 2000: 180) apparently antagonistic meta-theoretical and theoretical positions within a wider framework. Hence, he is not making a purely idealist argument; for him, the world includes a residual, 'rump materialism' (see below for an explanation). Wendt links this, in turn, to a meta-theoretical position called 'scientific realism' which fundamentally says that there is a world independent of our thought. Finally, he advocates a social science that accepts traditional causal analysis, but is not reduced to it. He also qualifies his holism by arguing for a dual ontology in which both agency and structure have an autonomous standing. This dual ontology eventually leads to his constructivist theory of IR that encompasses, but is not reducible to, rationalist (and individualist) approaches in IR.

In this sense, it is less pertinent to talk about a 'via media' as Wendt himself does (Wendt 2000), or about Wendt as a bridge-builder (Palan 2000). Perhaps more than anyone else, he exemplifies constructivism's 'almost frightening potential as meta-theory subsuming all others' (Wæver 1997a: 25). Like in a synthesis, Wendt wants to overcome and preserve existing contradictions. Hence, he abstracts them within one (his) social theory of IR. That is where the strong emphasis of 'reflexivity' in constructivism comes into play since it allows a second-order, a meta-solution. It resembles the way Einstein embedded Newtonian physics: for much of our daily life the latter is perfectly good enough. Yet, at the same time, Wendt is uncomfortable to use this higher level to actually 'dissolve' the tensions into a new unitary thought. He instead plays with an idea of complementarity which one could liken to the dualism of particles/waves in twentieth-century physics: in some moments light behaves like particles, in others like waves, without there being an overriding idea which could synthesise it (for this idea in a normative IR context, see Guzzini, Patomäki and Walker 1995: 427–30). In this context, it comes as no surprise that Wendt's present project is to use the idea of complementarity in quantum theory – a post-positivist natural science, as it were – as a basis for his social theory (Wendt 2006).

However, as canny as it is for being able to legitimately speak to and attack the mainstream of IR research, such a choice of an opening grand synthesis comes paradoxically with risks of closure exactly because it is done within this disciplinary orthodoxy. For Wendt accepts the narrow confines for the discipline erected by Waltz (1979), as well as the narrow borders of the classical self-understanding of international society. He knows there is no way back for a social theory of IR to a time where the languages of the practitioner and the observer, the theoretician and empirical researcher, entirely coincide. Knowing that one can no longer talk the same language, Wendt decided to at least talk about the same and hence unchanged topic.

The risk of this strategy is that by openly endorsing the old borders, Wendt's grand opening synthesis could become hijacked by this orthodoxy: his theory must reproduce it. He updates the self-understanding of the discipline exactly at a time when it is again challenged. Through his statist theory, he reproduces the embedded understanding of politics of a narrowly defined international society – which might look out of touch with world politics. In other words, his synthesis, as opening and challenging as it is within IR, runs the risk of reifying a specific historical stage of both the discipline and international politics.

This chapter will show how one can make sense of Wendt's approach as a synthesis combining disciplinary orthodoxy and theoretical heterodoxy. In a first step, we analyse how Wendt's project is self-consciously inscribed into the disciplinary identity of IR, a choice which makes the constant reference to (neo-) realism necessary. Then, we examine three different synthesising moves within his meta-theory and his theory. On both levels, it allows him to encompass different versions of rationalist approaches and of realism and liberalism respectively, as special cases of his own. Here we argue that, however Wendt or his defenders and critics want to call his final synthesis, it has little to do with 'positivism' as it is commonly understood in the discipline. Finally, we spell out some of the tensions of Wendt's project, when his theoretical synthesis has to function within the disciplinary identity from which he starts.

Wendt's orthodoxy in the disciplinary identity of IR

Throughout its history, the discipline of IR has been plagued by a problematic identity. War and peace formed the early subject matter but, except for political reasons, it was not self-evident why this would need an extra discipline. Conflicts, whether armed or not, have been of interest to lawyers, psychologists and sociologists alike. The domestication of violence was crucial for all sciences of the state, as political science often used to be called (and in some places still is). Nor was there any special methodology to set IR aside, as marginal utility calculus did for economics.

The first demarcation happened with regard to international law, in whose backyard IR used to be. Morgenthau (1936), himself a lawyer, argued that one needed to radicalize legal positivism and based its argumentation not on the internal logic of law, but on its context. This tension between law and reality became an evergreen for IR debates. This move, however, placed IR (and Morgenthau) squarely within political science. To allow for a second demarcation not only from law, but also from political science, the IR discipline had to insist that there was a significant difference between domestic and international politics. The notion of 'anarchy' satisfied this quest. Whereas domestic politics had indeed domesticated violence through the state, the international realm was experiencing a form of the 'state of nature' before the Leviathan. According to Aron, had states escaped this state of nature in their relations, there would no longer be a theory of international relations (Aron 1962: 19).

Whereas politics at home can look at a variety of purposes, International Relations, so the story goes, were caught in a security dilemma (for the classical statement, see Herz 1950). Without an arbiter above the parties who could enforce order, actors have to look after themselves (including cooperation and building coalitions). Having no guarantees when trust is not reciprocated, they have to be on guard. Everybody being relentlessly on guard might end up in an arms race whose security effects could be negative.

The starting point of anarchy and the security dilemma can be found in all sections of the classical tradition. It does not demarcate 'realism' from 'idealism', but IR from political science. What distinguished 'realism' is a further assumption: its cyclical view of history. Whereas, in principle, an 'idealist' position would not exclude the possibility of the international system becoming 'domesticated' (although not necessarily in the same way as in domestic politics), realism would insist that, whatever improvement there is, it can only be temporary. We are bound by and will inevitably return to the security dilemma in one guise or another.

Adding the assumption of a cyclical view of history had the invaluable side-effect of cementing the differences of IR and hence at least temporarily 'resolving' the identity problem of IR. At the same time, it made the self-definition of realism and the legitimate boundaries of IR coincide.

The overlap of the self-identification of a discipline and the assumptions of realism had two logical consequences. First, any attempt to redefine the borders of the discipline was immediately seen as an attack on realism. Vice versa, there has been the tendency to see the many attacks on realism as attacks on the legitimate independence of the discipline as such, which would call for significant reactions by IR scholars more widely. In the so-called second debate waged in IR, realists mistook an attack on the methodology of the discipline, part of its identity so far, as an attack against realism. Bull's (1966) defence of a more traditionalist approach was based exactly on the substantial difference which set IR apart. However, later studies seemed to show that the majority of 'scientific' writers had never given up basic realist assumptions (Vasquez 1983). When the transnational paradigm was launched, it again undermined the classical boundaries of IR – and was therefore perceived as a critique of realism, although Keohane and Nye (1977) had repeatedly pointed out that their approach did not invalidate realism in all, or even necessarily the more significant, circumstances.

Waltz's *Theory of International Politics* (1979) acquired its status in the discipline not because it said anything new or because it had a theoretical sophistication unparalleled elsewhere. Waltz's work has become paradigmatic for the new (reductionist) twist he gave to the self-identification of realism-cum-IR. Challenged in its boundaries by the emerging liberal or transnationalist research, the *Theory of International Politics* redefined what the subject matter of an IR theory could be. It was a balance of power theory under anarchy that set the international system apart from hierarchical systems. This again made IR coincide with a very restrictive (and materialist) view of realism, now dubbed neo-realism (for a more detailed discussion, see Guzzini 1998: 125–41). For Waltz, other approaches could well be perfectly legitimate, but were a form of 'reductionist' theorising or foreign policy analysis – that is, not International Relations proper.

Wendt is aware of the possible conflation of the boundaries of IR and realism. Indeed, he comes close to making the same conflation when he writes that 'there should continue to be a place for theories of anarchic inter-state politics, alongside other forms of international theory; to that extent, I am a statist and a realist' (Wendt 1992a: 424), as if the two last things were necessarily connected.[1] Yet, one can perfectly well be a statist without being a realist, as some institutionalists would be quick to point out; and a realist and not a statist, as testified by realist scholars in international political economy (IPE) such as Susan Strange.[2]

With good knowledge of this potential confusion, Wendt chooses to embed his theoretical challenges against the mainstream of IR (including realism) within a very orthodox definition of the subject matter of IR. This choice is cunning. Given that earlier debates were haunted by the conflation of realism and the identity of IR, assuming disciplinary orthodoxy might be a more effective way of making realists understand that their theory is wrong. And, for Wendt, realism must remain the main target since it is closest to the self-definition of practitioners and hence most prone to damaging self-fulfilling prophecies in international politics. Seen in this way, it is perhaps less surprising that he uses the last paradigm of realism-cum-IR, Waltz's *Theory of International Politics*, as a foil, although by this time this enterprise entailed a serious effort of 'reanimation', as it were. Indeed, the real interlocutor often seems to be Buzan, Jones and Little's reworking of neo-realism, which shares with Waltz and Wendt a similar spirit of looking for 'a wide-ranging and integrative general theory of international relations' (Buzan, Jones and Little 1993: 65).

Wendt's disciplinary boundaries are set in a narrow and orthodox way. He has little doubt that international politics is first and foremost about inter-state relations. He tells us that this is so because 'states are still the primary medium through which the effects of other actors on the regulation of violence are channelled into the world system' (Wendt 2000: 174). In response to critics who point to this state-centrism, Wendt simply answers that accusing a theory of international politics of state-centrism is like accusing a 'theory of forests for being tree-centric' (Wendt 1999: 9). Moreover, in orthodox realist fashion Wendt assumes unified action capacities of states and even anthropomorphises states by giving them purposes and intentions.

1 But observers also react in this way. In an early typology (Jaeger 1996), Wendt's statism earned him the label of a realist constructivist, as opposed to 'liberal-institutionalist constructivists' such as Müller (1994, 1995) and Risse-Kappen (1995).
2 For an assessment of Strange's idiosyncratic mix, see Guzzini (2000b) and Leander (2001a).

Wendt's state-centrism and his essentialising of states have been among the most contested issues of his theory, as he anticipates in the book himself. Suffice it to say at this point that, by giving Waltz such a central place in his disciplinary reconstruction, Wendt makes Waltz's narrow definition of the IR discipline stand for classical IR at large. In other words, Wendt's starting point in Waltz reads Waltz's narrow understanding of IR backwards onto the IR tradition.[3] Waltz's theory has the place of the 'previous synthesis', although Waltz's project was a completely different one from Wendt's, namely defining IR by narrowing it down. Instead of starting with defining politics first, as arguably some (including Morgenthau) in the classical tradition did, Wendt finds his subject (matter) already made up for him. As we discuss in the last section, this feature will inevitably produce tensions with his constructivist approach. Before moving to this discussion, we want first to show how his synthesis proceeds to embed contrasting meta-theories and theories as special cases of his own.

Wendt's heterodox social theory of IR: A project of manifold synthesis

Within this disciplinary orthodoxy, Wendt situates his theoretical challenges. He gives theoretical predominance to inter-state relations and anarchy – but only in order to redefine both. Whereas the security dilemma seems a logical necessity, Wendt argues that anarchy is foremost a social construct. Instead of having a logic of anarchy, he establishes cultures of anarchy. Once states are understood as sharing a culture, their very identity is open to conceptualisation, and not only their utility calculus.

For it is here that Wendt places his two most daring challenges to the discipline. He criticises existing theories for being too individualistic. He wants a theory to include a truly holistic component. He argues for a dualist ontology that takes both agency and structure seriously (Wendt 1987), and he proposes an idealist understanding of structure, and of politics (Wendt 1992a). His version of constructivism is the encompassing framework within which this takes place.

Wendt consciously bases his theory on the primacy of ontological choices. In his opinion, the excessive focus on questions of knowledge and truth has contributed to the big schisms in IR. According to him, these antagonisms have led to many mutual misunderstandings and eventually to a block on communication. For Wendt, this is a threat to his entire project. For if theoretical debates are again relegated to the realm of 'ideology', of unbridgeable assumptions, theoretical debate can never command a cross-paradigmatic audience. Wendt's ambition to 'wrap up' IR by offering an encompassing approach would be killed at its inception. Indeed, the very need for further theoretical discussion would be

---

3 We are indebted to Alexander Astrov for this point, which will be taken up again in the concluding section.

undermined. And, however difficult it might be to classify Wendt, he is surely a convinced theoretician.

In other words, for his project Wendt must avoid a return to the days when the 'Third Debate' (Lapid 1989) or the 'rationalist–reflectivist' divide (Keohane 1989 [1988]) was said to be a non-starter since, to put it in Kuhnian terms, paradigms were 'incommensurable' (Holsti 1985; Krasner 1985b). This superficially received argument about incommensurability legitimised 'business-as-usual at the price of a pre-defined pluralism' (Guzzini 1993: 446), since it was a welcome excuse not to bother too much about what other people had to say (Wight 1996). A specific stage in the development of IR debates was reified (Guzzini 1998: 108–22), cutting short a self-reflection in the discipline which would upset existing research programmes and scientific cultures. Hence, in his own understanding Wendt needed to 'rewire' IR debates to make his ambitious theoretical enterprise possible.

Moreover, putting two fundamental ontological choices first was to permit him a strategy of synthesising apparently contradictory positions on both the metatheoretical and the theoretical level. There are three syntheses, two within his social theory, one within his IR theory. For his social theory, as we will develop in some detail, he opts for an idealist approach with a 'rump materialism'. This allows for brute material forces to have some effects on the constitution of power and interest, even if always mediated by ideas (Wendt 1999: 96, 109–13). In turn, this will eventually lead him to accommodate causal and constitutive theorising within a version of 'sophisticated positivism', as he later calls it (Wendt 2000: 173). In a way, he tries to assimilate (natural) science within a qualified scientific realism as a base for a social science. For his IR theory, it is the basic dual ontology of agency and structure, irreducible to each other, which ultimately allows him to assimilate rationalism/individualism within his wider constructivism.

'Rump materialism', scientific realism and 'sophisticated positivism'

Although Wendt reserves a predominant place for philosophical idealism and culture in his theory – otherwise it would hardly qualify as constructivist – he also includes a rump materialism: it is 'not ideas all the way down', as he writes. This rump materialism is the residual category of what is 'effective' in our social world and yet not based on culture, that is, shared beliefs. It includes human nature, a weak version of technological determinism, and geography/natural resources (Wendt 1999: 130–1, 136).

From this assumption of rump materialism, Wendt sees a logic running through scientific realism, which fundamentally says that there is a world independent of our thought, to reach eventually his synthesis, namely a sophisticated positivism which, in his reading of the hard sciences, allows a juxtaposition of causal and constitutive theorising. This logical path has been at the centre of a theory-internal criticism by other scientific realists. Although the first step, a certain link between materialism and scientific realism, is usually acknowledged, the second step is not: positivism is necessary neither for scientific realism, nor for having the possibility of a social science (Patomäki and Wight 2000; Brglez 2001).

We would frame this critique in a different way. If we carefully follow Wendt on his logical path, the final destination which Wendt calls positivism has little to do with positivism as commonly understood in the discipline. For laying out this discussion, we will bracket the question of scientific realism and concentrate on the other steps in Wendt's argument, namely rump materialism, Wendt's conception of science, and finally his dual mode of theorising.

Starting from a mainly idealist ontology, Wendt's residual or rump materialism is, as Wendt (1999: 136) himself acknowledges, relatively inconsequential for the social scientist. The acceptance of rump materialism neglects the question of where the significant problematique for social scientists qua social scientists is to be found (Guzzini 2000a: 160, Kratochwil 2000a: 94–6). If we watch a red light as a social scientist, we are not interested in the residual matter of electric circuits but, for instance, in the norms which the interpretation of this sign mobilises.

For a constructivist, it is not the existence of a world independent of our thought that is at stake, but whether we can have unmediated access to it. Wendt does not hold this position any more than do post-positivists. In his response to Doty (2000), Wendt claims the position of sophisticated positivism to be his own, where all observation is theory-laden and theories cannot be tested against the world but only against other theories, and that, as a result, knowledge can never have secure foundations (Wendt 2000: 173). This is most probably not the positivism Krasner (2000) speaks of when endorsing Wendt's move.[4] It is in fact a version of constructivism which, albeit begrudgingly, accepts the necessary epistemological component besides the basic ontological one: constructivism is most coherently about the construction of social reality and the social construction of knowledge (Guzzini 2000a, Adler 2002).

In other words, Wendt can make a claim for positivism only because he has voided the concept to such an extent that it becomes synonymous with a commitment to scientific work, broadly understood as making analyses to allow us a better understanding of the world. This Wendtian criterion does not distinguish positivists from non-positivists, but scholars from non-scholars. And since the scientific enterprise is defined with weak discriminatory criteria, it largely coincides with the way interpretivists have conceived of social science, in opposition to traditional natural science, in the first place.

This tension in Wendt's approach might best be illustrated by another claim he makes when responding to Doty's critique. He says that Doty 'proceeds more or less as any positivist would – amassing data and developing the best narrative she can to make sense of them' (Wendt 2000: 173). His charge is that

---

4 Also, as Kratochwil (2000a) notes, this last move creates a tension in his position insofar as he needs to combine his idea of scientific realism and the fact that one cannot test against an outside world.

post-positivists, far from being radical, are basically very conventional when they do empirical work.

Wendt's response creates a paradox: if post-positivist empirical analyses were so conventional, why is the discipline so adamant in refusing them a 'scientific' stamp of approval? When universities (prominently in the United States but also elsewhere) offer 'scientific method' courses, concept or discourse analysis does not exactly figure prominently in the syllabuses (see also the critique by Alker 2000). The reaction within the discipline is not to say that post-positivism is respectable and nothing new, but that it leads to bad science or no science at all. In other words, if Wendt's positivism is content with an empirical analysis done as a narrative approach which makes sense of the world as well as possible, then he joins company with post-positivists, not positivists, as usually understood in the discipline. Thus, we have travelled together with Wendt in the direction of his roadmap sign 'positivism', but we reached 'a non-positivistic social science of international relations' (Smith 2000: 152, n. 8). The real issue at stake is not positivism versus post-positivism, but what exactly this non-positivist 'social science' is all about.

Wendt's vision of a social science again displays his synthesising attitude by offering a dual mode of theorising. Wendt tries to assimilate some features of classical positivism into his wider approach (whatever the name) by insisting that, besides causal theorising, there is 'constitutive' theorising more interested in the 'what' and 'how possible' questions. By showing that there is also constitutive theory in the hard sciences, Wendt tries to get interpretivists to look at what the no-longer-so-hard sciences really are, before dismissing any attempt to integrate the scientific endeavour, here and there. Using the same argument, he tries to get 'positivists' to understand that exactly because their vision of science is outdated they need to give up the idea that only causal theorising is science.

This opens up the final question about the relationship between causal and constitutive theorising. Here, it is not entirely clear where Wendt would position himself. One possibility is a refined version of the classical division of labour between concept formation, understood as variable operationalisation, and then (causal) analysis. In this scheme, constitutive theorising would be basically no theorising on its own but the first step of more positivist research designs, as argued by King, Keohane and Verba (1994) and feared by Smith (2000): first take Wendt and then add KKV and stir.

Although Wendt chooses not to rebut this way of seeing it, it seems to contradict the thrust of his argument. He insists quite strongly that constitutive theorising is an equally important source of knowledge in its own right, not just a means to another end. When Weber (1980 [1921–2]), after decades of research, put his framework of central concepts at the beginning of his *Economy and Society*, this already included a major part of his social theory, as the often quoted definitions (understandings) of the state and power/authority bear witness. Hence, concept formation is not simply the operationalisation of variables but an important part of our knowledge in itself. For Wendt, the choice between the two fundamentally depends on the questions one chooses to ask which, in turn, are not independent of meta-theoretical commitments (Wendt and Duvall 1989).

Moreover, Wendt not only introduces constitutive theorising as equally legitimate, he also qualifies which type of causal theorising is acceptable today for a self-regarding scientific realist. It is not the covering-law model usually taught in our textbooks. The subsumption under a covering law does not explain anything, but simply states a regularity. In other words, the famous 'if . . . then' explanations, purged of spurious correlations, are just another set of data (regularities), nothing more. Causality lies in process-explanations which go beyond Humean causality. This places Wendt close to the causality concept in relationism (for IR, see Jackson and Nexon 1999), in critical realism (Patomäki 1996, Patomäki and Wight 2000, Brglez 2001), in qualitative comparative sociology, such as Charles Ragin's (1987: 88–119) multiple conjunctural causation (see also Ragin 2000: 88–115) and also in historical sociology (Tilly 1995). This part of the argument seems to exclude an unqualified division of labour between constructivists on one hand (constitutive theory) and KKV's research design on the other.

In this reading, Wendt's synthesising strategy is indeed much more harmful to established positivist research designs than to post-positivist ones. His sophisticated positivism keeps one single element of positivism, namely that there is in principle no difference between natural and social sciences, but qualifying it to such an extent that his social science looks pretty similar to the type of qualitative research advocated by those post-positivists who have asked for more methodological self-awareness (Milliken 1999, Neumann 2001).[5] Hence, the implication of his assimilating strategy, and the flip-side of his reply to Doty, is that it is not fortuitous if he finds post-positivist empirical research fairly conventional, since this, and not established positivism, would correspond closely to the convention of *his* social science.

A dualist ontology and the assimilation of individualism/rationalism

Upholding the autonomy of a holistic component in his conception of the agent–structure debate is Wendt's second basic ontological decision. Wendt strongly supports the sociological turn in the social sciences. In this move he is the most different from much of what counts as middle-ground constructivism since he refuses to have his theorizing restricted to a theory of action – even a 'thick' one, such as that inspired by Habermas's communicative action (Müller 1994, Risse 2000).

The choice of a dualist ontology, respecting both agency and structure, is carried out through a threefold conceptual split (see Figure 14.1): at the level of action (between identity/interests and behaviour), at the level of structure (between a macro- and a micro-structure) and in their feedback relation (between

---

5 For a discussion of constructivist research which looks at what they call 'positivist-leaning' and post-positivist research designs, see Klotz and Lynch (2007).

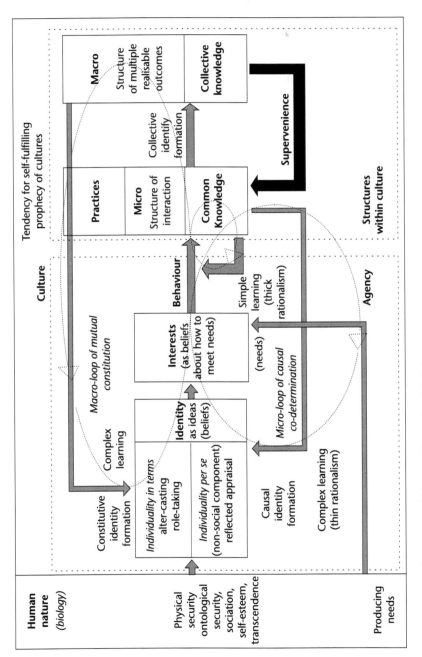

Figure 14.1 Wendt's synthesis in *Social Theory of International Politics*

constitutive and causal links). In turn, this conceptual apparatus then allows him to assimilate no fewer than three other social theories ranging from the most limited one, behaviouralist rational choice, to his own all-encompassing synthesis.

The origin of the threefold conceptual split is to be found in Wendt's plea for a dual ontology. In 1987, Wendt argued that discussions in IR tended to conflate research design with methodological and ontological questions, levels of analysis with the agent–structure debate.[6] There was a tendency to trivialise important questions. For it is trivial to say that there are agents who find themselves in a wider context which imposes systematic constraints and privileges on them. Any analysis worth its name will combine a micro- and a macro-level, even if only by assuming one constant.

Hence, the level of analysis gives no indication of meta-theoretical choices. Waltz's theory was called structuralist because his level of analysis was systemic; but the underlying logic of explanation was derived from the individualist level (for this argument, see Ashley 1984). His structure is also not more than the interaction of states. In other words, Waltz's so-called structural realism focuses on the macro-level of a methodological and ontologically individualist approach.

The more important issues lie elsewhere. For one, it is consequential whether or not a scholar accepts that things we do not see, including structures, can have effects and therefore can be said to exist. Denying this follows the path of empiricism, but also of methodological individualism where all social facts are, in the long run, to be reduced to the effects, intended or not, of individual actions. Supporting the statement, as Wendt does, leads to a social theory that includes a holistic ontology.

At the same time, Wendt wants to keep certain insights from individualist approaches. He agrees with Giddens's (1984) influential analysis which tries to show that neither agency nor structure can be reduced to the other. His attraction to Giddens's structuration theory lies in its dual ontology, both individualist and holistic.

Yet, once having chosen a dual ontology, Wendt faces the problem of how to theorise the relationship between the two. That is so because the classical inclusion of the factor of time into the scheme simply 'stretches out' but does not resolve the reductionism. According to this solution, today's structures are the sedimented effect of yesterday's actions and interactions; and they constrain or make possible tomorrow's actions and interactions. But, as long as this leaves no independent status to the structure, it is ultimately individualist.

With time being no sufficient solution, since it does not guarantee dualism, i.e. the thinking of two independent yet connected dynamics, a dualist approach leads to the conceptualisation of two overlapping circles, to a 'dyadic' approach. The point of overlap could be thought of as the moment or level of interaction as proposed by, for example, Guzzini (1993: 471–4) and Daase (1999: 259–68) in

6 See also the exchange between Wendt (1991, 1992b) and Hollis and Smith (1991, 1992).

following up the early agent–structure debate in IR (Wendt 1987, Dessler 1989, Hollis and Smith 1990, Carlsnaes 1992).

Wendt follows this idea of an in-between level by doubling his structure into a micro-structure (the interactionist level) and a macro-structure (see Figure 14.1, right half). The relationship between the two is one for which he borrows the concept of 'supervenience' from the debates on the philosophy of mind. Supervenience means 'that macro-structures are both not reducible to and yet somehow dependent for their existence on microstructures' (Wendt 1999: 155–6).

This fundamental distinction immediately sets the stage insofar as it makes visible the difference between the structural level in individualist and holistic approaches. For the micro-structure is the only structure individualism can conceive of, the only structure 'seen' from a purely individualist standpoint. Yet for Wendt individualism cannot explain 'multiple readability'. By this, Wendt means that certain unit- or interaction-level states of affairs are sufficient for the existence of a macro-state – but their existence is not necessary for producing that macro-state. This contradicts individualism since in individualism any structure must necessarily be derived from the lower level, that is, a certain pattern of interaction will always produce a certain macro-structure. If it is possible that a certain macro-structure can correspond to a number of interaction-level practices, each of them or their combination being sufficient for its existence, while none of those is necessarily producing it, then something escapes an explanation which goes bottom–up.

This pair of structures is further specified through the parallel distinction between common and collective knowledge (Wendt 1999: 160–5). Common knowledge stands for 'interlocking beliefs', which implies not only shared beliefs but the mutual awareness of these. Common knowledge is the background assumption in individualist intentional theories of action which make (tacit) coordination possible. Yet this is not enough to capture cultural structures for which Wendt refers to collective knowledge. As an illustration, Wendt refers to collective memory:

> As long as individuals see themselves as having an allegiance and commitment to the group, collective memories will be available as a resource for mobilising collective action even if they are not believed, in a phenomenological sense, by individuals, and in this way they can help to explain patterns in aggregate behaviour.
>
> *(Wendt 1999: 163)*

He notes a similarity to Foucault's concept of discourse (Wendt 1999: 164).

Having made out of collective and common knowledge the lynchpin of culture and of his theory, two further distinctions logically follow. First, since he conceives of idealist structures, Wendt argues that important effects of cultural structures are similar to language, i.e. not causal, but constitutive. 'Thinking depends logically on social relations, not just causally. Human beings think through culture. And since the structure of shared beliefs is ultimately a linguistic phenomenon, this means that language does not merely mediate thinking, it makes thinking possible' (Wendt 1999: 175). In other words, it is not possible to see the relationship between agency and structure only in terms of pre-existing entities which would *co-determine* each other, as causal explanations would. Instead, they are always also 'entities in the making', in a loop of *mutual constitution* of their very properties (for the causal and constitutive loops, see respectively the lower and upper half of Figure 14.1). Based, in turn, on this distinction between causal and constitutive effects of cultural structures, Wendt's theory must eventually specify the different places of this constitution. This leads Wendt to distinguish between agent *properties*, namely identity and interests, and agent *behaviour*.

With these three distinctions – between micro-(interaction) and macro-structure, causal and constitutive effects of cultural structures, and agent properties (identity/interest) and behaviour – Wendt has his conceptual grid in place to play out his assimilating strategy. His theory will, in fact, assimilate no fewer than three other theoretical enterprises (see the three dotted loops in Figure 14.1). We will present them in terms of their comprehensiveness.

The narrowest theory to be assimilated is rational choice, or what Wendt calls thick rationalism. In this theory, the agent–structure link is understood as a very small loop between the micro-structure of interaction and the agent's behaviour, excluding identity. This approach, despite its materialist setting while expressed in utilitarian terms (value maximisation), does include an ideational component to the extent that behaviouralist rational choice is based on the triad of desires (interests/preferences), beliefs and action. In case the micro-structure changes (via the intended or unintended effects of action), it can also affect future action through a change in the beliefs used for the calculus. Wendt calls this simple learning. Yet, this approach divorces beliefs from desires in the first place, a stance which Wendt shows to be highly contestable. And it entirely neglects identity formation. As nicely put by Ruggie (1998: 19, emphasis in original), 'a core constructivist research concern is what happens *before* the neo-utilitarian model purportedly kicks in'.

A slightly wider agent–structure approach to be incorporated into Wendt's constructivism is, in fact, the full rationalist action theory programme, called thin rationalism for its less constraining assumptions as compared to behaviouralist rational choice. This includes the possibility to think of ways in which desires are causally affected by cultural structures. Hence, what is crucial here is Wendt's identity/interest vs. behaviour distinction (see Figure 14.1). To some extent, Wendt constructs this thin rationalism which is not yet much theorised in the literature. According to him, the causal effects of micro-structure on identity-interest formation correspond to 'reflected appraisals', that is actors learn identities and interests as a result of how significant others treat them (Wendt 1999: 171). The link between identity and common knowledge allows for the larger micro-loop of causal co-determination.

A third agent–structure approach which Wendt's constructivism can include is the classical (holistic) sociological approach. Here, Wendt can play out the other two distinctions. First, he prolongs the structural loop by including the macro-structure. Then, his approach can include complex learning through the constitutive effects of cultural structures on agent identities. Identities are seen as roles which are internally related to role-identities of other actors, in the form of role-taking and alter-casting: 'By taking a particular role identity Ego is at the same time "casting" Alter in a corresponding counter-role that makes Ego's identity meaningful' (Wendt 1999: 329). This link of identity formation at the collective and individual levels constitutes the macro-loop of mutual constitution (see Figure 14.1).

And, finally, in his own view, Wendt's constructivism goes beyond a purely cultural approach insofar as his rump materialism, more precisely human nature, has a double impact. First, the autonomy of mental states is the non-reducible biological component of individual identity formation. Second, the five basic characteristics of human nature which Wendt develops give rise to needs which are part of interest formation.

This last addition achieves an ambitious meta-theory which, after all has been said and done, is still heavily idealist. Hence, for the social scientist the important claim is 'that power and interest have the effects they do in virtue of the ideas that make them up' (Wendt 1999: 135). Indeed, Wendt repeatedly stresses the pivotal importance of shared beliefs, that is, culture. Culture influences behaviour, constitutes the meaning of behaviour and even constructs identities and interests. His conception of language (see above) does exclude any type of biological reductionism. In principle, it could be made more compatible with more language-based constructivists such as Onuf (1989) and Kratochwil (1989b), but Wendt never really develops it (Zehfuß 1998; Zehfuss 2001b). His conscious downgrading of epistemological issues on the meta-theoretical level and his less hermeneutic IR theory produce this curious type of constructivism where language is very much out of the picture, despite his repeated reference to its centrality.

A cultural theory of the state-system: Assimilating the 'neo–neo' synthesis

Once the meta-theoretical deck is stacked this way, Wendt is free to derive a theory of IR in Part 2 of the book. Here, his general strategy of combining disciplinary orthodoxy with meta-theoretical heterodoxy produces a theory of IR which, despite the heavy holistic idealist component, looks quite familiar to IR scholars. As already mentioned, being an orthodox in terms of disciplinary self-understanding, Wendt came up with a theory of the state-system, adding a cultural component. But Wendt's theory looks familiar for two further reasons. First, Wendt again uses a strategy assimilating already known theories. Indeed, in his embrace, he does to institutionalism what institutionalism did to realism.

Second, the three cultures he describes have a clear English School ring to them. As will be argued below, Wendt not only has an orthodox view on the discipline, he also holds an orthodox view of international society.

As in the meta-theoretical field, Wendt tries to encompass already existing approaches within a wider framework. He does this by combining two methods. The first one is an offshoot of the meta-theoretical enlargement beyond rationalism. In other words, Wendt simply translates the need for a theory of structure/culture and wider theory of action into a framework of analysis which swallows the rationalist component of the 'neo–neo' synthesis between institutionalism and realism (Wæver 1996). The other method is connected to this general idea: Wendt takes over the strategy of complementarity which was used by institutionalists in their critique of realism.

Neo-institutionalism, despite much academic politics, never claimed that all of realism was wrong. It harked back to classical critiques of realism, often realists themselves, such as Wolfers (1962) and Aron (1962). Wolfers tried hard to show that a one-sided realism, which would understand state behaviour strictly in terms of power maximisation, got it wrong. Politics was to be thought of in a continuum between the pole of power and the pole of indifference. At the latter pole, thinking in terms of power would have unintended effects. Indeed, although it might be correct to think in terms of preventing the worst case, sometimes it is the effect of this worst-case thinking which is the very worst case to be prevented. Although this might now sound 'constructivist' to some ears, it is not exclusively so. Wolfers simply drew together the different lessons from World Wars I and II.

The result of such a critique of one-sided realism was that all theories needed to accommodate cases or (scope) conditions where realist power politics could be expected to prevail, and those where they could not. In the heyday of the transnationalism/interdependence literature, the influential statement of the paradigm in Keohane and Nye's *Power and Interdependence* (1977) never said that realism was always wrong. Politics was conceived on a continuum between power politics and complex interdependence. The more we were facing the latter conditions, the less realism would apply. Therefore, there has actually never been a 'neo–neo' debate but rather an attempt of one neo to gobble up the other. The neo-institutionalist pole always embraced neo-realism as a special case of its own approach.

Using this strategy of assimilating complementarity, Wendt, in turn, embraces the neo–neo synthesis within his wider 'constructivist' framework (Wendt uses 'constructivism' for both his meta-theoretical and his theoretical level). He comes up with a matrix of 3×3 boxes (Wendt 1999: 254) with one side of the matrix defined by the degree of cultural internalisation (coerced, self-interested, norm-internalised) and the other side defined by the degree of society (which corresponds to the Hobbesian, Lockean and Kantian cultures). Having based the theory on the relentless (re)construction of collective identities, Wendt needs a process component. For this, he uses three different degrees of cultural internalisation of roles ranging from coercion via self-interested calculus to identity change. The more internalised the roles, the more the culture will have a self-fulfilling tendency. This holistic component of the third level is beyond the neo-institutionalist synthesis which can accommodate the first two levels. Having thus based the theory on an idealist structural level, Wendt proposes three different collective identities of the inter-state system – the Hobbesian, Lockean and Kantian cultures – which function as the broad scope conditions for understanding the agency role-identities (from enemy to friend), and hence the behaviour of states. Again, the third (Kantian) culture, as exemplified by security communities, tends to go beyond the neo-institutionalist synthesis of Hobbesian and Lockean cultures typical of classical writers such as Wolfers or the regime approach in IR, at least if more than opportunist calculus is assumed (see also the discussion in Hasenclever, Mayer and Rittberger 1997).

Besides this strategy of assimilation, his theory looks familiar since it is couched in terms reminiscent of the English School's triad of realism (Hobbes), rationalism (Grotius) and revolutionism (Kant) (see also the discussion in Suganami 2001). Indeed, given Wendt's constructivism, and hence commitment to reflexivity, this similarity is an even stronger endorsement than is usually acknowledged. For the three traditions of the English School can be understood at the level of the observer and of the actor. At the level of observation, Wendt is perfectly right to say that his theory has a richer meta-theoretical and theoretical framework. At the same time, it is perfectly possible to read the English School as an attempt to 'understand' the languages of international society at the level of the actors themselves. In other words, the fact of the three cultures is not necessarily imposed by an observer who cannot possibly think of other options. Rather, it reflects the self-understood range of political cultures within the diplomatic field of international society itself. Since his is a reflective theory, Wendt sees himself bound by what he understands to be the self-understanding of international society. Wendt is orthodox not only in the self-understanding of the discipline, but also in the self-understanding of international society.

Yet, reading Wendt's theory as having merely added some new drawers to the expanding wardrobe of IR misses perhaps the most important contribution: its crucial process character. This theory, even more than institutionalism, is out to establish the scope conditions under which we might be able not only to recognise certain agent and collective identities, but to understand when we are where, and how we move from here to there. Having insisted that his theory is basically about process, the static matrix recedes somewhat into the background and questions of change and historical dynamics come to the fore. As Ringmar (1997: 285) had noted earlier on, Wendt wants to return history to neo-realism, to put the neo-realist (static) picture into motion (see also Wendt 2003).

It is therefore not fortuitous that critics have concentrated on exactly this dynamic component. They focus on Wendt's theory of structural change and collective identity formation, as well as on his vision of politics and progress (respectively, Drulák 2001, 2006, Sárváry 2001, 2006). In their own way, they all deal with the politics of structural change in Wendt's theory – and find either 'history' or 'politics/diplomacy' still wanting.

When disciplinary orthodoxy fails to meet theoretical heterodoxy?

This chapter has argued that Wendt's social theory of International Relations mixes orthodoxy in terms of the discipline's self-understanding with heterodoxy in terms of the theory itself. Wendt makes a very ambitious attempt to assimilate existing knowledge in IR and in social theory in a relentless quest for preservation, accumulation and synthesis. Indeed, by blending a theory of scientific progress with a theory of historical progress (see Sárváry 2001), his theory displays this quest in terms not only of science but of nothing less than world history.

This is an enterprise of tall proportions. It explains a series of reactions towards his work. First, although widely quoted, there is a general neglect of the issues Wendt raises. Since the theory weaves all its parts together, it is not all that easy, and certainly not always correct, to 'pick and choose'. Although written in a perfectly accessible way, it builds up an argument where the pieces fall into place bit by bit. It needs the patience of a consumer used to the incremental stages of old cooking recipes, 'slow food', as it were. And it also explains the immediate suspicion of those, as perhaps best expressed by Behnke (2001), who are wary of grand theoretical enterprises in general, and about the strong liberalism which comes through his vision of progress.

But perhaps another way to read Wendt is to do to him what he does to the discipline. He is self-consciously positioning himself in present debates about the self-understanding of the discipline. He sees a need to get social theory into IR without losing too much of an oversight of what IR is actually about. As a good holist, he does not want us to lose sight of the wood for the trees. He asks the discipline to think big and to think big things together. In his view, he must therefore synthesise. But such a synthesising approach only makes sense if scholars eventually depart from it. No discipline worth its name survives if made up by a community of only synthesisers. In the very self-understanding of a reflective science, any synthesis can only be temporary. It is a means, not an end in itself. In the self-consciousness of the discipline, a synthesis can only be 'assimilated' if it is explored and eventually exploded, again.

Hence, rather than dismissing Wendt for the big questions he dares to ask, and to which his answers will ultimately be judged insufficient, one might take his attempt at synthesising simply as one way, among others, for probing the many 'wires' in contemporary IR theorising. Doing so points to many instances in which the different aspects of his ambitious project might undermine each other. Since this chapter concentrated on the mix of disciplinary orthodoxy and theoretical challenge, we will highlight some tensions in this particular synthesis.

The tensions arise out of the clash of two orthodox choices, crucial perhaps for the self-understanding of much of the discipline, but which substantially restrict the impact of his theoretical challenges. The first choice is to define IR out of the self-definition of its dominant discourses, which gives primacy to tradition and, in particular, to statism. The second, related to it, is the choice to let the self-understanding of the traditional society of states define international politics. Neither of these choices is necessary for Wendt's constructivism since his, like any, meta-theory allows for a series of compatible approaches.

Our criticisms fundamentally derive from the implications of the role given to the state in Wendt's theory. By this, we refer not only to his state-centrism but also to the conscious essentialisation of the state: for Wendt, states are also people, a move which allows him to use symbolic interactionism as his theoretical backbone.[7] The two main implications are that his *Social Theory of International Politics* opens up IR for social theory, but not sufficiently, and restricts our understanding for the always contested borders of international politics.

A first criticism would start by saying that, even if we take the society of states as the given focus, there is no need to give the state such an under-sociological essence. There are at least two ways to make a thicker social theory of it. One way out would have been to herald Ashley's idea for a social theory of IR, to which Wendt explicitly refers. Ashley (1987) argued in support of looking at the community of realists to locate the intersubjectivity of the international society. This move, which is reminiscent of the English School (see also Cronin 1999), would require a more interpretative analysis of (transnational) political elites, rather than its black-boxing under the heading of corporate or role-identity. In a processual and constructivist theory, role-identity formation has a locus in particular life-worlds, such as the diplomatic field for international society. We would think that sociological institutionalism, and in particular Bourdieu's field theory (Bourdieu 1980), would offer some avenues for a necessarily more microsociological underpinning of a constructivist theory (Guzzini 2000a, Leander 2000a, 2001c).

In fact, even if we take the focus on states for granted, one would also need to unpack the slot Wendt left for corporate identity. Wendt openly says that he is not writing a theory about (state) identity formation in a move similar to Waltz (1979) when the latter refused to write a theory of foreign policy. But this assumes that the two can be unconnected, which has been shown as erroneous for Waltz (Guzzini 1998: 125–41) and is arguably so for Wendt (Zehfuss 2001a) who is asked also to endogenise corporate identity formation (Cederman and Daase 2003).

The second criticism involves Wendt's understanding of international 'politics'. It draws on the implications of a brief remark in the book where Wendt (1999: 194) acknowledges writing a theory of the inter-state system and not of

---

7 This seems to clash with his scientific realism for which states cannot have the same properties as humans (Wight 1999).

international politics at large. Now this might open up another of Pandora's boxes, as much as his blending out of agent-identity formation. It makes the title of Wendt's book as much a misnomer as the title of Waltz's. Waltz might be excused since he might actually believe that his theory is all there is to international politics. But Wendt is aware of the wider field, and yet closes that path down.

The underlying reason for this narrow definition of politics is that Wendt, like Waltz, tends to start from agents to define their practices (Jackson and Nexon 1999). Having settled on states, and unitary ones, Wendt's theory necessarily reduces the nature of politics to what states think of it, actually something a structurationist should not do. For it is not states that define 'politics', but political processes that define their agents (and structures). Starting, like the English School (see the critique in Guzzini 2001a), from the agent end, Wendt does not address the always contested border of the political (for this critique, see also Kratochwil 2000a: 96), of what is of a public and not simply a private concern in International Relations, of what is part of international governance and what is not – perhaps the political question *par excellence*. Instead, he takes it for granted and subsumes it under the progressive domestication of violence under the different stages of collective identities.

This narrow view of politics has quite limiting consequences for the international theory Wendt can come up with. To some extent, the book is not a theory of international politics but, seen from a reflexive angle, a theory of how international politics is understood within the classical diplomatic field. Since the borders of international politics are already set there, his theory does not touch on questions of the redefinition of polities in some of the processes bundled under the label 'globalisation' (Leander 2001b, 2006b).

Indeed, following a disciplinary orthodoxy informed by Waltz, the borders between politics and economics, so painfully torn down by some scholars in IPE, are simply re-erected. Political economy disappears and hence even the question of whether international society is still best understood as the pure society of states and not, for instance, as a hybrid including the 'international business civilisation' with New York, Chicago and Los Angeles as its capital (Strange 1990) and Davos as its meeting point.

Tying the definition of politics to the state undermines even the understanding of the inter-state system, that is, the very core of Wendt's definition of politics. When he assumes the successful domestication and monopolisation of violence by states, he excludes from his view how this field has been reorganised, indeed 'privatised' away from the state (Leander 2005a, 2006a).

In other words, Wendt's orthodoxy in terms of the self-understanding of the discipline, along with his orthodoxy in defining politics in terms of the self-understanding of the international society of states alone, undermines the very processual character his theory should in fact have and limits the heterodox challenges of his theory of international politics. It produces a blind spot in his constructivism which one can, in turn, observe.

Conclusion

This chapter has argued that Wendt's project is best understood as a grand synthesis rather than a via media. This synthesis makes divergent positions in IR complementary by reconfiguring and assimilating them under a new encompassing framework. Such a synthesis is much less innocent to other theories than a via media. We find that, despite its references to materialism, rationalism and positivism, the overall picture is one heavily tilted towards holism, idealism and an understanding of science which has little to do with positivism as usually understood in IR. In this context, it comes as no surprise that Wendt's present project is to use the idea of complementarity in quantum theory – a post-positivist natural science, as it were – as a basis for his social theory (Wendt 2006).

Moreover, we argued that Wendt's theoretical challenge uses a strategy of sharing (or simply assuming) a very traditional self-understanding of the discipline. At a time when the languages of the practitioner and the observer are drifting apart, Wendt finds a base for his theoretical communication not in a renewed practical language, but in the conventions of disciplinary identity. Knowing that one can no longer talk the same language, he decided at least to talk about the same and hence unchanged topic. Rather than stressing tensions within his synthesis, this chapter thus emphasised the (reflexive) implications which this taking for granted of the self-understanding of both the discipline and international society has for his theoretical project: it tacitly reifies both self-understandings at a time when they are challenged.

15

IMPOSING COHERENCE

The central role of practice in Friedrich Kratochwil's theorising of politics, international relations and science

Introduction

In 1986, Friedrich Kratochwil and John Gerard Ruggie wrote an article on the evolution of the study of international organisations. They diagnosed that research had decisively moved forward since the 1960s, away from the studies of formal institutions as locus *of* international governance to the study of political organisations widely understood and their informal effects *within* a larger system of international governance. Such move was epitomised by the then-recent literature on international regimes. In this 'state of the art' article, they however claimed that the existing theories of international regimes were systematically problematic. For they ran on a fundamental self-contradiction: their intersubjective ontology flatly contradicted their positivist epistemology, that is, their 'model of explanations and the presumed relationships among its constitutive analytical constructs' (Kratochwil and Ruggie 1986: 771). More precisely, defining regimes in terms of converging expectations assumes a realm of shared understandings which, in turn, implies that there is a significant – indeed for the very definition of regimes, central – component of the real world which is based on intersubjective meanings. And whereas regime theory thus assumes an interpretivist

For comments and critique, I want to thank all the participants of the author's workshop for the *Festschrift* in honour of Friedrich Kratochwil, 14 February, 2009, Columbia University, in particular Nicholas Onuf and Friedrich Kratochwil himself. I also wish to thank Andreas Behnke, Barry Buzan, Piki Ish-Shalom, Colin Wight, *JIRD*'s three anonymous referees and Patrick Jackson. The usual disclaimers apply. A shorter version will appeared in the *Festschrift* edited by Oliver Kessler, Rodney Bruce Hall, Cecilia Lynch, and Nicholas Onuf, eds (2010) *On Rules, Politics and Knowledge: Friedrich Kratochwil, International Relations and Domestic Affairs* (London: Palgrave).

position for the actor in the real world, the assumption of a positivist epistemology denies such interpretivism for its observer.[1]

With assumptions about the real world contradicting those for its analysis, regime theory was stuck. Its theory and meta-theory were incoherent. The only way forward was to impose coherence. And for Kratochwil and Ruggie, there was little hesitation when put before the choice between abandoning the subject matter (regimes or international governance) since it would not fit positivism, or abandoning at least some facets of positivism since it did not fit the understanding of regimes. Problem-driven research was surely preferable and consequently they advised that the thorough consideration of interpretivism, 'more closely attuned to the reality of regimes . . . be delayed no longer' (Kratochwil and Ruggie 1986: 766).

It was quite new to find this type of critique on the central stage of the discipline of international relations (IR). Theories were usually assessed for their fit, sometimes also whether the theoretical assumptions were plausible (external critique) or consistent (internal critique). But for IR, only very rarely had such a comprehensive internal critique been done by checking the coherence of its philosophical assumptions (here hermeneutics), its underlying philosophy of science (the *Verstehen-Erklären* debate), and the empirical-ontological and conceptual assumptions of the theories themselves (for an exception of these days, see e.g. Ashley 1984, Kratochwil 1984a). Moreover, that assumptions about politics, philosophy and science had to be thought in a coherent manner met the discipline largely unprepared. After all, it had spent quite some time establishing its credentials as an empirical science with empirical theories. But the implication of the argument was that precisely for being a consistent empirical science, meta-theory and philosophy were unavoidable. As their discussion showed, it was indeed fundamental for a theoretical enterprise meant to grasp a core theme like international governance.

And so, despite the reference-article it was (critically surveying the publications in *International Organization* since its beginning) and for all the fame of an argument so busily footnoted later, its main thrust was not so quickly accepted in the field, whether the actual critique of an incoherent regime theory, or its underlying approach of a need for such overall coherence in the first place. Different strategies caused this delay. One, already anticipated by Kratochwil and Ruggie, was simply to deny the contradiction. That was an evident strategy for researchers who did not follow the first part of their argument. Here, the fact that there were convergent expectations and norms may simply not imply intersubjectivity at all; instead, even norms were to be conceptualised as ideational 'resources' in a rationalist theory of action, akin to other type of resources: this denied intersubjectivity by effectively objectifying it. Much of the neo-realist-neo-liberal synthesis followed this line. But

---

1 Moreover, such intersubjective phenomena like norms, central to the definition of regime theory, cannot be reduced to external variables which would work independently of the actors themselves; and therefore norms cannot be said to 'cause' their behaviour. Hence, although norms may be crucial to understand human action, they cannot be reduced to an independent causal variable in a positivist model of explanation.

the denial also appeared with what then became dubbed 'soft', 'thin', or 'modernist' constructivism (in a discipline too easily prone to attach labels and define turf) when scholars stated that they combined a postmodern/intersubjective ontology with a (soft) positivist epistemology increasingly diluted to mean a commitment to science and (a loose conception of) causality (e.g. Checkel 2001: 554).[2]

Redefining it within the agency-structure debates was another way in which the argument was blunted and the call for coherence redefined. This is visible in Alexander Wendt's reading of the underlying self-contradiction. Whereas Kratochwil and Ruggie saw an implicitly intersubjective ontology clash with an objectivist epistemology, Wendt summarises it as: 'its individualist ontology contradicted the [implicit, S.G.] intersubjective epistemology necessary for regime theory to realise its promise' (Wendt 1992a: 393). Both versions are in themselves correct, but the first one asks the theory to re-assess its philosophy of science, whereas Wendt's formulation suggests a solution that concentrates solely on the theory of action, neglecting the philosophy of science. Going beyond the individualist ontology in regime theory was all it takes to fix the problem.[3]

The background for this chapter is that, for some time now, the discussion in IR has caught up with this delay. Increasingly, theorists have accepted the challenge to impose coherence on their assumptions from philosophy to politics. Although perhaps less perceived in this way, this is visible in the enormous success of 'qualitative methods', now having a section in APSA. True, not all qualitative approaches are interpretivist. But, as shown in some of the new methodological (and not just method) treatises coming out of IR (Lebow and Lichbach 2007, Klotz and Prakash 2008), scholars are increasingly reflective of the ways in which the specificity of the social world may ask for a methodological pluralism which is not reducible, if not antithetical, to textbook positivist research design. There is an increasing concern that phenomena which are perhaps not analysable with strict positivist criteria need nevertheless to be studied, and then studied differently, so that the methodology/epistemology conforms to the ontological specificity of the social world (Hall 2003).

But this concern with overall coherence is obviously more visible in IR theorising as such. In fact, theorising this coherence from the conception of politics, IR, science, and philosophy is one of the last great frontiers of IR theorising. And the gauntlet has been picked up, including by scholars who had

2 The trouble with the concern about such labels is that it does often no justice to the scholars involved. In my reading, Emanuel Adler, usually put here, does not fit. But having titled a core article as constructivism 'seizing the middle ground' (Adler 1997) made many readers overlook that he had redefined that middle ground effectively in a quite interpretivist manner to start with. Inversely, Goldstein and Keohane's approach (1993), usually put into a rationalist (neo-institutionalist) category, would fit better that particular argument here.
3 Although Wendt tried to sideline the philosophy of science debate – not to allow the mainstream a quick way out of the debate – and concentrated on the critique of rationalism and individualism instead, his defence of positivism ended up having almost nothing in common with its usual understanding in IR but the name (and a commitment to the monism of natural and social sciences, yet profoundly redefined).

earlier been professing a division of ontological and epistemological concerns, but are now seeing the two in parallel (e.g. Checkel 2007). Some recent examples must suffice (there are not many). At first, Wendt's *Social Theory of International Politics* 'only' provided a coherence between meta-theory and a constructivist macro-theory, by trying to show how politics of prudence and self-restraint and a politics of change and learning are best understood within a constructivist meta-theory which takes intersubjectivity and collective knowledge seriously (Wendt 1999). His later writings added several philosophical layers to it. He added an explicit theory of history in terms of a 'struggle for recognition' (Wendt 2003), echoing contemporary Frankfurt critical theory (Honneth 2003 [1992]). And he eventually embedded his meta-theory into a meta-physics derived from quantum theory (Wendt 2006). Whatever Wendt's final destination will be, it is clear that the main impetus of his work is to ground the analysis of actual world politics in a coherent meta-theoretical and philosophical setting. Emanuel Adler (2005, 2008), opening up for a more clearly moral philosophical agenda, has recently proposed a 'communitarian constructivism' which includes a rapprochement to communitarianism in an attempt to provide his first sketch of a constructivist theory of politics. And, to refer to a different approach, Heikki Patomäki (2001b, 2002, 2008) has consistently tried to move in his work between the realm of politics, political theory, the philosophy of science and normative theory from a critical realist position, be it in his writings on critical realism, causality and future scenarios, in his peace research, or in his interventions into world politics, as, for example, the Tobin Tax and other issues for global governance.

It is the aim of this chapter to further our thinking about how one can create such coherence in our theorising. Yet since the linkages between the different levels are complex, and can be managed in different ways, it would easily go beyond the limits of a single article to discuss them in a non-superficial manner. Therefore, I have chosen to show the travails of imposing such coherence by reconstructing the thought of a single scholar, one with whom this chapter started: Friedrich Kratochwil.

My approach is a reconstruction of Friedrich Kratochwil's theoretical edifice. A reconstruction is a hermeneutic enterprise which provides a specific interpretation, not a summary. If the re-interpretation 'works', it appears as a self-evident way of presenting a theory, thought or thinker. Or, put differently, a successful reconstruction, while not being a summary, seems one. To the reader unacquainted with the subject matter (here Kratochwil's work), it must provide a consistent view; for the acquainted, the specific interpretation must fit.

This reconstruction makes a series of claims. The first is connected to the very setup of the article, the logic of the reconstruction: Kratochwil stands out as one of those very few thinkers in IR whose work tries to understand the implications of thinking assumptions about ontology, social theory, and scientific discovery (and, indeed, ethics) in parallel. My reconstruction presents this quest for coherence as Kratochwil's underlying theme and the role of practice as the bridge between the different layers of his theorising. According to my interpretation,

Kratochwil ultimately refers back to human or social practices as the fundament upon which the different fields can be thought in parallel.[4] As a result, for him, there cannot be Realpolitik without politics, theory without reflexivity, science without judgement, ethics without a humanist sense of responsibility.

This fundamental claim has a series of significant implications. By making the analysis of practices the pivotal point for understanding politics, theory and science, his theorising works from 'politics' upwards to philosophy, and not from meta-theory downwards to empirical analysis, as it is often assumed.[5] It is because of his interest in and understanding of political practice, and for the need to achieve coherence of thought between political, theoretical, and scholarly action, that Kratochwil takes his understanding of practice to develop his positions in IR theory, the philosophy of social sciences, and eventually to ethics. Therefore, I will show that Kratochwil's more recent 'pragmatist' turn in meta-theory is ultimately connected to his earlier writings on politics during the Cold War. As such, this interpretation puts politics, rather than norms, back into the centre of Kratochwil's work.[6]

Moreover, I argue that the proposed solution is less different from some versions of scientific realist thinking than usually acknowledged. Hence, this reconstruction exemplifies how theoretical coherence (here in constructivist thought) can be achieved in a way which may not necessarily correspond to easy textbook descriptions or received wisdom. Finally, I prolong the thread to an analysis of the underlying ethics in Kratochwil's project. Far more than the other points, this is an interpretation which needed to be done between the lines. I see in Kratochwil not only a humanistic scholar, but also a humanist commitment.

In short, this chapter reconstructs the thought of Kratochwil to exemplify the necessary coherence of thought from politics to science to ethics, a project which is truly important for the development of theorising in IR, whether constructivist or not. And at the same time, it uses this very reconstruction of his multilayered coherence, imposing indeed, with the aim of portraying a significantly different understanding of a central thinker in IR. By retracing the link between

---

4 For a discussion of his multifaceted conception of 'practice' or 'practices', see below.
5 For instance, Checkel (1998: 337) sees Audie Klotz's (1995) work as 'empiricising' Kratochwil and Ruggie's approach, bringing the theory down to touch empirical ground. But then, their approach is grounded in their understanding of (empirical) international political change in the first place. In fact, in my reading below, Kratochwil's major theoretical book (Kratochwil 1989b) is not the start of his work, the theory from which then all the rest derives, but the first theoretical result with the insights gathered from his study of the Cold War.
6 In some sense, this is the opposite take to that of Maja Zehfuss (2002: ch.3), who puts norms (and Kratochwil 1989b) at the centre of the analysis and then criticises Kratochwil for missing 'politics'. In my understanding, Kratochwil's core focus on practices, which she also clearly sees (Zehfuß 1998: 119, Zehfuss 2002: 94) allows for a more reflexive and critical role towards politics than in her reading.

the different layers in his thought, the chapter defends the need for imposing coherence, but it neither comes as an external critique, nor a defence, of Kratochwil's solution. Its aim is to muster his work for a plea to challenge ourselves more often to search for coherence in our views in politics, science, philosophy, and ethics.

The chapter will proceed in those four main steps, dealing with the relationship between the nature of political practices, their theorisation, and the philosophy of science in the work of Friedrich Kratochwil, in that logical order, before ending on its ethical implications.

International politics: Symbolic communication and the problem of order

What is politics? Very early Kratochwil was disenchanted with the way leading political theorists understood and conceptualised politics. He quickly moved beyond the futile attempt to define what politics really 'is', since almost anything can, depending on the situation, be considered 'political'. Hence, the conceptual analysis has to start the other way round and approach 'the political' from its usage, the way it is expressed in practice.[7] Having thus ruled out the typical positivist conceptual analysis,[8] Kratochwil's quest draws also little succour from prevailing political theories which reduce politics to some version of utilitarianism or an authoritative allocation of (scarce) values. Whereas the first tradition errs by reducing politics to maximising behaviour, the second suffers from an assumption of scarcity of values which is not necessarily appropriate. Moreover, the 'authoritative allocation of values', already an ideal-type for political systems in their domestic environment, ends up excluding the international altogether from the understanding of politics.

Instead, Kratochwil has taken the international realm as his frame of reference, in which the 'political' is most visible. For the study of politics is, as he will later write, an 'attempt at illuminating the problem of order' (Kratochwil 2000b: 53). And the specifically political emerges when action takes place in a situation in which no reference to a *common* value system can be established, but a choice is made (Kratochwil 1971: 121).[9] This is reminiscent of Max Weber's eternal clash of Gods (Weber 1988 [1919]: 605). Let me use it to introduce the fundamental role of practice in Kratochwil's thought.

Weber and Kratochwil share a sense for, and fear of, the totality of conflicts since the turn of the 20th century. But Kratochwil is not essentialising 'value systems'. In fact, for him, or so I would argue, it is just as thinkable that no

---

7 For these ideas, see Kratochwil (1971: 114). More generally, for a discussion of the pragmatic and not semantic, understanding of language and concepts, see, for example, Kratochwil (1989b: 28ff.).
8 For an example of such an analysis, see Oppenheim (1981).
9 Kratochwil takes this understanding from Bertrand de Jouvenel.

common reference system evolves between actors, despite allegedly common values,[10] as it is that apparently diverse actors can find a common language. Indeed, this is the guiding idea for his analysis of the Cold War. He furthermore avoids essentialising the role of value systems, because, according to his understanding of politics, they are not to be defined in theory, but by the way they work themselves out in human practices. However abstract the level of his thought, it is the way practices unfold to which his analyses almost inevitably return. Hence, to approach the abstractly put question of politics (how to deal with collective choice with no common value system), an abstract answer would not do – be it the liberal philosopher's quest for some general neutral position from which agreement would rationally follow,[11] or the alleged need of some Schmittian decisionism to impose a solution, a position to which Weber was tempted at times (see the discussion in Walker 1988–9, 1993b). For Kratochwil, both ways eventually eschew the 'political', either by reducing it to an eschatology of reason or to the determinacy of a reified enmity.

Instead, Kratochwil has no closed and fixed history in mind; all is played out in practice. For him, practices are fundamentally characterised by the human capacity of creating symbols and

> symbols create meaning by structuring our universe, building up images far removed from the immediacy of sense perceptions. Because symbolic structures cannot be unequivocally tested against reality – reality itself being a creation of the symbolizing activity that endows perceptions with certain meanings – deception but also persuasion are possible.
> *(Kratochwil 1978: 20)*[12]

Hence, exactly because of this creativity and open development of symbolic systems, the encounter of different value systems neither guarantees nor excludes the possibility of a mediation between them. Even if such systems might seem logically unbridgeable, political practice can create bridges. The 'world political process is an ongoing "conversation"' (*ibid.*: 39), and diplomacy is about establishing and using a common language (Kratochwil 1971: 122), or, perhaps more precisely, of commonly accepted translations.

At this point, it may be important to add a word on the ambivalence of the term 'practice'.[13] On the one hand, and then mainly used in the plural, 'practices'

---

10 The point was explicitly made by Raymond Aron (1962: 111).
11 It is in this sense that Kratochwil invites philosophers to 'forget Kant'. See Kratochwil (1998b).
12 NB: it is the social and interpretivist ontology which drives a certain understanding of science here, not the opposite. To this, see below.
13 I am indebted to one of the referees who succinctly pointed out this ambivalence and its need to be addressed within the thought of Kratochwil.

tends to be equated with the habitual or the typical actions which are shared by a group of people. It is in this sense that much of Bourdieu used to be received in IR (e.g. Ashley 1987, which Kratochwil quotes favourably). When used in the singular, however, 'practice' can refer to the contingent, 'actual', and therefore possibly creative part in human action where things are played out case by case. In my previous quote, it would seem that this second reading is the closest to Kratochwil. And it surely plays a crucial role. But for Kratochwil, practice and practices are connected, as they are for other constructivist writers like Emanuel Adler (see his essays in Adler 2005).[14]

Starting from an intersubjective ontology and focusing his analysis on shared understandings, norms or rules, Kratochwil's approach does include an important role for social practices. For such norms and rules, for instance, inform and indeed characterise typical or routine behaviour of groups such as diplomats or social scientists. But concentrating on such routines does not imply sheer repetition or lack of creativity. Indeed, it is consistent with Bourdieu's understanding of practices, as visible in his analysis of the way the *habitus* is linking structure to practice. Bourdieu wants to overcome the stale opposition of 'determinism and freedom, conditioning and creativity', and conceives of the *habitus* as having the ability to generate an infinity of new schemes of perception and understanding, new expressions and appropriate actions, an ability that is however limited within the historically and materially thinkable and doable (*'capacité de génération infinie et pourtant strictement limitée'*, Bourdieu 1980: 92). Taking its inspiration from Habermas, Kratochwil's approach does probably allow more than this by focusing on the interaction that takes place within communication and within which new symbols and meanings can come to the fore and be agreed to.

Fundamental for this connection between shared meanings and understandings that inform typical action and the creativity of practice is hence the role of language. Just as with our use of language (and the rules implied in it), the starting point must be intersubjectivity and hence habitual or routine action, like in 'social practices'. But just as language adapts, and is therefore no historically fixed framework, so practices do. For this change to happen, a certain individual practice must first have evolved (a new word invented, its meaning altered). But for it to take effect, it must have become accepted. In that regard, novel or creative practice is socially bound both in its origins (it comes out of the given language or *Lebenswelt*) and its effects (it needs to be recognised and accepted). Language rules circumscribe the realm of the new; but at the same time, there is a generative capacity in language which allows proposing new twists again and again, as in Kratochwil's repeated use of the analogy with a game of 'scrabble'.

14 Indeed, Adler's research programme is arguably about the relationship between intersubjective structures and political practices for the understanding of social learning in terms of cognitive evolution. Adler goes beyond his mentor Ernst Haas, but does surely not leave him altogether.

'Practice' in its more contingent and creative part is hence always intrinsically connected to 'practices' and vice versa. Routine and typified behaviour is not to be confused with changeless repetition. To use the words of Barnes' critique of Kuhn, 'once more we are led to the conclusion that Kuhn's insistence upon the "necessity" of scientific revolution is misplaced ... It is worth pointing out that major cultural change can be brought about ... by activity earned out in meticulous conformity to routine' (Barnes 1982: 86). Or in Kratochwil's own words:

> Actors ... reproduce and change by their practice the normative structures by which they are able to act, share meanings, communicate intentions, criticize claims, and justify choices. Thus, one of the most importance sources of change ... is the *practice of the actors* themselves.
> (Kratochwil 1989b: 61, original italics)

Kratochwil developed this role of practices in his understanding of the world politics of the time, that is, against the background of the Cold War and its diplomacy. Here, he used Kissinger's study of international order and gave it an intersubjective-symbolical and linguistic twist. Kissinger (1957: 1–3) had argued that a stable order requires shared rules of the game ('legitimacy' is Kissinger's term), and an equilibrium, 'both moral and physical' (*ibid.*: 12). These two aspects can be teased out to mean far more than the usual textbook realism which is often applied to Kissinger. First, shared rules of the game imply that inter-state relations are analogous to social relations. There is a kind of international society, not only when the rules of the game are tacitly shared, but also when they are debated. From this it follows that most of realist politics – for instance, the balance of power – appears not (just) as a cause of order, but as its effect, deriving from 'a framework of shared conventions with normative status' (Kratochwil 1984b: 347);[15] the balance of power thus becomes an institution of the society of states.[16] In their symbolic interaction, practitioners generate conventions and symbols, which, if successfully shared, stabilise meanings and hence enable decisions. Before diplomats can count, they must first agree on what counts. International politics has a social ontology.

Secondly, Kissinger's peculiar definition of the equilibrium adds a historical and cultural dimension to this order. He repeatedly castigates a mechanical understanding of equilibrium, that is, one which is purely based on force and not a 'reconciliation of historical aspirations' (Kissinger 1957: 147), as noted by

---

15 See in particular Claude (1962, 1989) for the classical treatment of the paradox that realists need a balance of power to establish an order, which in turn is necessary for the balance of power to function in the first place.
16 For the classical account of the institutions of international society in the English School, see Bull (1977). Bull (1980) also notes the similarities in his book review of Frederick (*sic!*) Kratochwil (1978).

Kratochwil (1978: 201). In a passage mined by more than one constructivist, Kissinger wrote that

> ... an exact balance is ... chimerical, above all, because while powers may appear to outsiders as factors in a security arrangement, they appear domestically as expressions of historical existence. No power will submit to a settlement, however well-balanced and however 'secure', which seems totally to deny its vision of itself.
>
> *(Kissinger 1957: 146)*

Although Kissinger does not pursue much on this opening on identity ('vision of itself'), in Kratochwil's hands, it adds a further layer to the social ontology of international order. Such identities reveal themselves and evolve through historical analogies and collective memory, through 'myths' and 'metaphors', which actors mobilise when trying to make sense of a situation (for 'the link between historical reconstruction and identity', see Kratochwil 1978: 61). Together with legal rules (later: norms) and actual doctrines, these are part of the 'rule-like inference-guidance devices' which form the background knowledge of international order.[17] Diplomacy is called upon in this ongoing conversation of international politics to find shared translations, eventually establishing a common system of references, while accommodating diverse historical identities. It is helped by the fact that political practice comes with an added, and crucial, time factor through which principled disagreements *can* be bridged in the course of iterated 'conversations'. And it is to this political practice that Kratochwil returns when showing how shared background knowledge developed through the Cold War between the two superpowers.

Kratochwil's early insistence on the role of practice and on the evolution of common references during the Cold War prepared him well for coming to terms with the end of the Cold War. Not that he would have 'predicted' it.[18] However, by having focused on the origins of norms and their possible changes in the practices of actors, and expecting such a change only to happen when a more shared reference system had come into place, 1989 cannot just stand for some balance of power shifts or sanction-induced change of the Soviet incentive structure. Just as with the change that took place after the Cuban Missile Crisis,

> a redefinition of the game on the basis of mutual role-taking was sought ... Putting oneself into the shoes of the other leads to sharing of aspirations,

---

17 This is then the basic theme of Kratochwil (1978). The quote is from p. 4.
18 See Kratochwil (1989a) for his discussion about how to understand Gorbachev's openings, which is surely not written with the expectation that things will change so quickly.

fears, and weaknesses that not only reassures the opponent but makes a rediscovery of a common sociality possible.

(Kratochwil 1989b: 50)[19]

Contrary to disenchanted lawyers like the early Morgenthau (1933, 1935), Kratochwil was not impressed by an allegedly ultimate role of sanctions – and the analogy to criminal law – for the understanding of how law (and rules) impinges on actions (Kratochwil 1978: 46, 1998a: 200–1). A purely capability-based understanding of how the Cold War came to an end therefore appears profoundly misleading (Koslowski and Kratochwil 1994).[20]

Kratochwil's earlier studies also provide an important basis for understanding the problem of how the international order would play out after 1989. There is the basic problem that the diversity of historical aspirations and understandings held by the multiple actors who take part in ordering the world inhibit the development of a common language. But that diversity itself is not static. Although there is no guarantee that common translations will be found (and even disagreements can be on common terms), solutions are not foregone *by definition* because of alleged civilisational or other differences. Only political practice will tell. Diplomats are surely well advised not to rule out the possibility of unbridgeable value systems or life-worlds, not least to refrain from conceiving or imposing one's own system as the universal one, and so preventing the curse of self-righteousness and hubris. But diplomats are equally well advised to assume the existence of a common background knowledge (which can anyway not be ruled out), since such assumption, or indeed pretence, feeds into the ongoing conversation which can recursively produce it as a social fact. Human practices are shot through with institutional facts; they are performative.

Theory: interpretative practice and reflexivity

This central role of human practices has clear implications for the kind of social theory that is possible and the role of the theorist in it. Social theory cannot predominantly be of the positivist kind in which efficient causality applies. Theorising must start from the social ontology of human practices, which feature prominently the role of language and interpretation, background knowledge and symbolic communication, open systems of meaning and an open history, one that is non-teleological and non-cyclical. Theory must be reflexive. Let me take

---

19 For the role of 'alter-casting' in Wendt's account of change, see Wendt 1999: 329.
20 Kratochwil's critique of capability-based approaches is ostensibly alluding to the realist tradition, but should not be taken as a general critique. Besides his usage of Kissinger's early writings, Kratochwil's work on containment had shown him that the more diplomatic wing of realism, as represented by George F. Kennan, offered a useful starting point for understanding actual politics (Kratochwil 1993).

up here the so far less touched issues of causality, as well as systemic and historical openness.

Kratochwil repeatedly condemns the attempt to turn ideational phenomena (such as ideas, norms, values, regimes) into antecedents which 'cause' behaviour. According to him, this misconstrues the intersubjective nature of these phenomena and wrongly fits them into an objectivist explanation where they are assumed to exist independently of an actor's interpretations. Such efforts also misunderstand the nature of the antecedent in the explanation of human behaviour which is the actors' motives, not an external cause. And so the motive, that is, the antecedent, is not independent of its effect. In fact, 'the causal arrows run from our (or the agent's) understanding to the world and not from "the world" to our understanding or theory' (Kratochwil 2006: 14). Hence social causality, even when it is an insufficient but non-redundant part of an unnecessary but sufficient condition, is profoundly different from natural (efficient) causality (Kratochwil 1984a: 316–17, 2008: 94–7).[21]

But the problems of causality in the social world go even further. Social reality is influenced by human understanding. Institutional facts, such as conventions, are actually dependent on it. Hence, a crucial part of any social theory must be the understanding of this *recursiveness* between understanding and reality, whether for the macro level of institutional facts or for the actor's identity which is profoundly shaped by what others make of it.[22] This focus on the evolution of background knowledge (and culture) and identity formation is necessary for all social theory, IR theory included (Kratochwil and Lapid 1996). At the same time, the content and coherence of background knowledge has to be 'discovered and understood, not assumed and inflicted' (Hopf, Kratochwil and Lebow 2001: 12887). Nor can recursiveness be understood in terms of causes; rather, it is about co-constitutive relations. Here, the 'why' question, already redefined above in terms of meaningful action, is replaced by 'how', 'how possible' and even 'what' questions.

This understanding of social reality also affects science at yet another level. There is no reason to see the social field of scientific observers as being qualitatively different from the fields of other social groups. Rather than conceiving of scientific observations as taking place at a meta-level, an Archimedian point from which to look down on the social world, science is just another social field which (horizontally) interacts with the social reality it interprets. As a result, truly constructivist theorising must include this *reflexivity*, that is, the relationship between observation, social reality and the actors' understandings.

When applied to the study of politics, Kratochwil's solution is to invoke practical reasoning as the common element in all social spheres in which the political

---

21 This does allow however for the treatment of reasons as causes, as done by many scientific realists. For a treatment in many ways congenial to Kratochwil (as acknowledged in Kratochwil 2008), but by a critical realist, see Patomäki (1996).
22 Kratochwil's standard references go here to speech act theory. For the interaction effect on the personal (identity) level, see Hacking (1999).

can be analysed. Not just language in general, but also law is to be understood in pragmatic, not semantic terms, and so are politics and science. Hence, Kratochwil's effort of thinking through assumptions about ontology, social theory, science and politics in parallel is not a question of choice, but an implication of and resource for his way of thinking.

This has a series of corollaries. One is that all these social practices are open. Whereas semantic, deductive or teleological logic asks for closure already at the level of our theories, a pragmatic approach sees closure occurring only in the actual application (Kratochwil 2005: 117), or, put differently, in practical, not pure reason. Reason is what reason(ing) does. For this very openness, the attempt to reach universal theories of action may be appealing but is eventually futile, if not counter-productive: it is the '*fata morgana* of a transhistorically valid theory' (Kratochwil 1998a: 195, fn. 9). Instead, Kratochwil reserves a special place for conceptual history as a way to reveal the collective memory of international politics and its evolution: 'precisely because social reality is not simply "out there" but is made by the actors, the concepts we use are part of a vocabulary that is deeply imbricated with our political projects' (Kratochwil 2006: 11). Last, but not least, reflexivity has also implications for the theorist because it cuts short the debate about whether or not the language of science should be closer to the language of practice from which it has become increasingly divorced, or vice versa. Scientists, just like political practitioners, should not choose languages; they need to be multilingual and translate between those languages. Only this provides the necessary hermeneutic bridge, allowing understanding for the scientist and reflective distance for the politician.

Science and judgement

The fundamental role of language and human practices define also Kratochwil's approach to science in what is a non-foundationalist or conventionalist position, one which has been regularly challenged for its alleged relativism. For Kratochwil, anti-foundationalism is the idea that our knowledge claims cannot be ultimately justified within reason itself, or by recourse to method, ontology, or even the world (Kratochwil 2007a: 28). That does not mean that reality does not exist. It means only that the fact of its existence has limited implications for our understanding of what it is.

The reason for this stance lies with the idea that language is not representational, but constitutive: our knowledge of the world is not a passive registration, impossible outside of language; it is an active conceptualisation. And this, in turn, makes our observations theory- and concept-dependent: all scientific laws contain theoretical terms (Kratochwil 1984a: 314). Consequently when we conduct research by asking the social world a question, the answer cannot be provided independent of the system of meaning (language in a wider sense) in which we have asked the question. There is no direct access to the world. Therefore truth cannot be a property of the world, and we cannot test the validity of our claims against reality. 'Things or entities cannot be true, only assertion

Kratochwil: imposing coherence **281**

about them can!' (Kratochwil 2007a: 45). This involves doing away with a classical correspondence theory of truth, not to mention the infamous but fashionable instrumentalism attributed to Milton Friedman (1953), which claims that the plausibility of theoretical assumptions does not matter as long as the explanations have an empirical fit. Instead, we can only 'test' against other theories, which we can use to uncover blind spots, or provide a different perspective (Kratochwil 2008: 82).

At the same time, it is not the case that 'anything goes'.[23] Scientists have to be analysed as a group of practitioners. We need 'an epistemology that does justice to the *practical* aspects of human interaction' (Kratochwil 1984a: 310, original emphasis). Science is a practice and, as such, organised according to its own conventions – conventions which have a history and that indicate which kinds of theories might be more appropriate in particular contexts. Kratochwil uses the analogy of a game of scrabble for showing the path dependence and yet open evolution of this practice (Kratochwil 2007a: 49–50). For here the progress in our understanding is not so much understood as an accumulation of more and more facts, but as the newly acquired capacity to 'formulate new questions that *could not even be asked previously*' (Kratochwil 2007c: 12, original emphasis).

Therefore, Kratochwil's use of Kuhn is not so much on the possible incommensurability of paradigms, but on the behaviour of its practitioners and hence the context-dependent criteria for the appropriate judgement of validity (Kratochwil 1984a: 314).[24] Indeed, like Kuhn himself (Kuhn 1970), Kratochwil does not see incommensurability as an insurmountable barrier to debate or proofs, since, as scientific practice shows, translation between paradigms/theories is possible (Kratochwil 2007a: 52, en. 12). But then, he needs to qualify what exactly goes on in these deliberations, and how best to think of the discourse of scientific proofs. And here, Kratochwil uses the Kantian metaphor of a court in which rules of appropriate proofs provide the basis for judgement. A court's judgments establish what is 'right', not true. Just as legal practice shows, such judgements can be determinate, but they need not be unique, in that cases can be judged differently, albeit not arbitrarily so (Kratochwil 2007c: 12).

And so Kratochwil proposes a (Pascalian) bet. Just as with the political practice where actual interactions show a possibility to uncover and establish common background knowledge which informs individual acts, scientific practice can achieve something similar. In other words, it would be premature and imprudent to give in to 'Cartesian anxiety' (Bernstein 1983) which is, in any event, a positivist blackmail: something is either true according to positivist standards or it

---

23 One should perhaps add that these words taken from Feyerabend are frequently used out of context when trying to attack constructivists. Feyerabend was rather more a disciple of Popper than sometimes acknowledged. Concerned with the way methodological strictures could pre-empt the critical and open spirit necessary for scientific debate, so dear to Popper, Feyerabend preferred some 'going'.
24 The central reference for Kuhn can be found in Kuhn (1970 [1962]: 180).

must be denying the existence of any truth whatsoever. Rather, scientists do make scientific judgements to the best of their knowledge by applying the appropriate rules, and indeed should be doing so. Whether or not this brings us closer to 'truth' in any positivist sense is perhaps less important than its capacity to achieve increasingly more appropriate judgements for understanding and dealing with the world.

Hence, science is what scientists do. But this opens a possible breach. If science looks like 'convention all the way down', then does, in principle, still anything go, even if in practice scholarly communities have come to agree on conventions which rule that out? Inversely, why does scientific practice come up with conventions which impose limiting conditions on scientific debate and empower reasoned argument? Is there not a reality constraint which, however indirectly, is responsible for the development of such conventions?

Scientific realists have asked these questions, among them Colin Wight most forcefully in a debate with Kratochwil. But, as I see it, the difference between these precise two positions is actually not that great. First, both Kratochwil and Wight agree that there is an indirect contact with reality, both social and material, which influences the scientific process. Neither of them sees the material as ultimately foundational for social explanations. Nor can Wight say precisely how much the material matters, if at all, and in what way (Wight 2007b: 302). This means that one needs to have a better sense of how this 'indirect contact' is to be understood.

My guess is that Luhmann's (1990) solution could be agreeable to both sides: scientific systems build up expectations which the environment answers. This means that the questions scientists ask, as much as the decoding of the response, are driven by the system or scientific discourse – and not by the environment. Yet, the environment does influence the system's reproduction by answering to the expectations built up by the system. In that regard, constructivists can rightly claim that it is theory-dependent observation and interpretation, truth not being a property of reality. At the same time, the existing feedback from reality would be validating Wight's critical realism. This view also implies that the important word for Kratochwil in the phrase 'theories are not tested against reality, but against other theories', is not 'reality', the ontological vacuity feared by Wight, but 'tested'. And here their epistemologies meet: there *is* contact to the world, but that contact is insufficient to provide a final 'test', as Wight also confirms, since it is driven by an interpretation in the light of competing interpretations.

Second, social facts have often a material substratum. Again, this is something on which both seem to agree, although perhaps they weigh the consequences differently. For Kratochwil, since this 'rump materialism' is most of the time of little interest to the social scientist, it can be dispensed with (Kratochwil 2007b: 74). Wight might leave a bigger role to a (usually biological) rump materialism.[25]

---

[25] Wight also mentions Marxist materialist concerns that would be excluded by fiat from Kratochwil, or so he claims. But these are social, not natural, facts, and hence their being considered normally 'material' by Marxists and others, should not exclude them from Kratochwil's scheme.

Indeed, the role of the material may need to be established case by case, suggesting that its actual significance is an open question. Here again, I think both would agree.

Third, Wight charges that a constructivist epistemology, in which it is the rules of the scientific community which ultimately define the truth value of an explanation, will lead to relativism. In the face of several such scientific communities, and with no cross-community meta-language or criteria (and no ultimate check by reality), either the more powerful community obtains, or we are left without possible judgement, hence relativism (Wight 2007a: 49). But this is hardly self-evident. Oddly enough, it is not entirely clear whether Wight's own solution is any different from Kratochwil's. Since the world is not the ultimate arbiter for either, and since both agree on the interpretivist turn, Wight's endorsement of Habermas' (2004) more recent statement could well be acceptable to both. In this, Wight agrees with the idea that the humans' practical engagement with the world (for their daily problem-solving) is a further criterion. Since we have all experienced the resistance of the world to some of our *actions* which were based on our interpretations of it, there is a 'pragmatic presupposition' of a language-independent world out there, although its meaning is not presumed to be language-independent. Hence, for Wight (2007a: 47), 'although the linguistically constituted intersubjective world has an epistemic priority, the language-independent reality that resists our activity has ontological priority' (Wight 2007a: 48). Yet we still do not know what that resistance exactly entails. Reality cannot speak for itself; there is contact with reality but no correspondence to truth. So, the solution of a 'pragmatic presupposition' of an ontology seems not too far from the Pascalian bet we started with, all the more since Kratochwil sees a social ontology working in all practices, scientific ones included. Indeed, he openly endorses Habermas' pragmatic argument.

Conclusion: a humanist ethics

In our meta-theoretical discussions, critical realists tend to reprimand constructivists for putting the epistemological cart before the ontological horse (Patomäki and Wight 2000). It is, so the story goes, this obsession with our understanding of knowledge which leaves them agnostic about the world out there, and this agnosticism cannot be sustained since ontological assumptions inevitably slip in. Kratochwil may then not be a constructivist, since this is surely the opposite of his approach. His very starting point is a social ontology. And it is because of this social ontology that he argues for a certain understanding of international politics, IR theory and the philosophy of science which is usually dubbed 'constructivist'.

Kratochwil's social ontology is based on human practice. His analyses almost inevitably return to the way practices unfold, at whatever level. Human practices are fundamentally characterised by the human capacity to create symbols (Kratochwil 1978: 20), and to engage in meaningful communication. Moreover, 'man is not determined by nature but transcends nature by transforming it' (Kratochwil 1981: 120). It is an ontology borne out both in diplomatic and scientific practice.

But underlying this view is an ethical commitment which Kratochwil has not really thematised. Kratochwil often refers to Popper – not only to tease those quoting him without having really read him. But besides some meta-theoretical sympathies with the late Popper, Kratochwil shares Popper's commitment to the idea of debate and communication, of critique and openness. A liberal anti-totalitarian ideal meets a poststructural sensitivity in a suspicion against all meta-narratives or grand historical designs. His plea that we look at practices is also a plea that we keep them open, lest an all-encompassing ideology, grand theory or grand method takes over. Kratochwil is a theoretical scholar who spends his time against the grand-theoretical scheme as much for its general impossibility (Behnke 2001), as for its normative undesirability. He resists both the teleological visions which quickly box new data into pre-existing schemes, whether functionalist, evolutionist or other, and the rationalist simplifications which reduce human behaviour to causal action. Both are but reductionisms that fail to further the understanding of actors' understandings and of their background knowledge, thereby killing any curiosity in the specifically human – and in the human other.

It is the defence of this ultimate curiosity about the diversity of the human, of the human encounter in practice which seems to drive Kratochwil's project. Here, *de gustibus est disputandum*, not necessarily to agree, but at least in the understanding that the terms of disagreement can be found. And this asks for a classical mind, able to translate, to be multilingual, in time and culture. It is a hermeneutic worldview for both scientific observation and diplomatic practice. It is a defence of politics against the social engineer (although in ways different from classical realists) in theory and politics, against the technocratic, and not humanist, vision of the world, as well as the misconception of responsibility such a vision fosters.

For it is nonsense to assert *a priori* that disputes between value systems are meaningless. For the translating and hermeneutic actor, they are not only possible; they are necessary for the practical establishment of a common horizon.

> What is needed is a different approach that investigates more closely the process by which people can adjust their differences without resorting immediately to violence. I maintain that the theory of communicative action is helpful in this respect. Within a normatively secured framework of communication, actors can air grievances and debate value-choices, even if such debates are no longer limited to instrumental questions only.
>
> *(Kratochwil 1989b: 16)*

But, of course, this process provides no guarantee. And still, Kratochwil places his bet on it. In this call for responsibility, there is some similitude to Camus' understanding of the absurd. For Camus (1942), the absurd does not lie in the fact that life is ultimately meaningless. Instead, it stems from the ongoing attempt to uphold simultaneously the human aspirations for harmony and meaning, and the understanding that it will never be achieved. Camus urges himself not to betray this tension of the absurd, not to start repudiating any side of it, either by denying humanity's aspiration for harmony, as cynics do, or by believing in the possible realisation of harmony through transcendence by Reason or God or any other leap of faith. Neither reductionism is admissible if we take our humanity and our historical responsibility seriously. Just like Sisyphus, we roll that stone up the hill, knowing it will never stay on top, but roll down again. But we do this of our own will, almost as the last credible sign of human dignity. Pretending to be a happy Sisyphus despite the absurd, trying again and again, may be the best bet we have got – and, for Kratochwil, making good on this bet is the scholar's vocation (Kratochwil 1995).

EPILOGUE

The significance and roles of teaching theory in International Relations

Introduction

With the increasing independence of the field of study called International Relations (IR) and the professionalisation of its teaching, theory courses have acquired a more prominent place in the newer curricula. Some observers have started to question whether this can be justified. Criticism against an overly theoretical nature of the studies typically revolves around one central theme. Theory is said to be most divorced from practice. Hence, for teaching to be useful in the real world of the future practitioner, it should recoil from (pure) theory courses and emphasise applied studies (Wallace 1996).

This chapter tries to show that such an argument is based on an erroneous understanding of the relationship between theory and practice, and of the specific roles theory can play in the education of practitioners. For it conflates the theory/practice distinction with the academia/politics distinction. Hence, theory seems to be coupled with the "ivory tower" of academia, whereas applied studies are linked to (diplomatic) practice. Although some theoretical work will undeniably be scholastic, and some empirical work of practical use, this is not necessarily so. A quick look at much of the empirical literature in IR in, for instance, *International*

This is a revised version of a paper presented at the training seminar 'Teaching European Studies and International Relations in East Central Europe' organised by the UNESCO Chair in International Relations and European Studies at the Institute of International Relations and Political Science, Vilnius University, 2–5 March 2000. For comments and suggestions, the author is indebted to the participants of this workshop, in particular Raimundas Lopata, Nortautas Statkus, and Gediminas Vitkus, as well as to Kateřina Borutová, Barry Buzan, Lene Hansen, Ulla Holm, Pertti Joenniemi, Işil Kazan, Anna Leander, Ian Manners, Michael Merlingen, Karen Lund Petersen, Ulrich Sedelmeier, Ole Wæver, Zlatko Šabič and two anonymous referees.

Studies Quarterly or the *Journal of Conflict Resolution*, bears witness to the remoteness of applied studies from any direct practical value. On the other hand, theoretical research is of great political significance and commands public interest as, for example, democratic theory or theories of globalisation.

This chapter will reveal the neglected roles that the teaching of theory in IR can fulfil. These roles support the claim that there is a strong need for teaching (and researching) theory in IR. Indeed, this article will argue that thinking in terms of these very oppositions between theory/practice and academia/politics is part of the problem for understanding the role of academic education in IR today. For they lure us into the illusion that empirical studies can ever be divorced from theory, and that university education is only there to serve the policy relevance of the day and not the intellectual breadth and maturity of future practitioners.

My first argument is logical: no empirical analysis is without theoretical assumptions, without a framework of analysis. There is no explanation that is simply a neutral selection of "data speaking to us". Related to this is the dual character of theoretical knowledge: it is both explanatory and constitutive (Smith 1995: 27–8). In its classical explanatory sense, social science theories are the result of knowledge giving a common, more general and coherent explanation for a variety of specified cases. But this does not exhaust the function of theories. Theories also have a constitutive function; *i.e.* a theory is the condition for the very possibility of knowledge. Without concepts that cut through the forest of empirical data, we would be unable to see the wood for the trees. Theories are not just the result but also the precondition for the possibility of empirical knowledge.

My second argument is educational: making future practitioners and observers aware of the constitutive function of theories fulfils the crucial role of a more time-independent intellectual education. As mentioned by Wallace (1996: 317), the diplomat in the United Kingdom used to be trained through classical studies that gave them the general and time-independent skills to decipher and respond to changing political situations. The point here is simply that today we need to update this approach. Besides the necessary factual training in international law, history, economics, and politics, future observers and practitioners in international affairs (who might not necessarily be public servants) need to acquire the skill of intellectual self-distance, reflexivity as it were, to respond to changing challenges. Moreover, this ability and the related capacity to reflect on one's own and another's assumptions are crucial for the tasks of understanding and negotiating across national boundaries.

On the basis of these two arguments, I will consider the role that teaching and research in theory can play for entire academic communities. The chapter will try to show that the neglect of theoretical studies can cement the peripheral position in which the majority of academic communities find themselves today. If not opposed, the international division of academic labour tends to slot them into mere data providers and thought-takers. Theoretical expertise is, as some cases show, part of the way out.

Finally, I sketch out some of the implications this understanding of the roles of theory in teaching IR has on the type of theory teaching. I identify and discuss a non-exhaustive list of four types of courses where the constitutive function of theories is fruitfully addressed.

A logical argument:
The constitutive nature of theory and the necessarily theoretical nature of all knowledge

> There is sometimes an assumption that 'theory' is something that is suitable only for 'advanced' students. The fear is that students are not interested in theory, that they study IR with a practical orientation and become alienated if asked to think conceptually and abstractly, and, most damagingly, that students want to be told the 'right' answers and not to be exposed to the scandalous fact that authorities differ even on quite basic issues. These positions must be resisted. All understandings of IR and of the other social sciences are necessarily theoretical, the only issue is whether this is made explicit or not and most good students are well aware that this is so.
>
> (Brown 1997: vii)

How do we know what we know? This seems an arcane question and yet it is the basic question for establishing the fundamental identity of an observer or a scientist. For it allows us to justify why we believe something to be true. Teaching, in turn, has to do with the communication of this knowledge – both its content and its means of justification.

This position makes it very difficult to conceive of science and teaching in a simplistic, empiricist manner. By simplistic empiricism, I understand the position that "data speaks for itself", that is, that we can neutrally access empirical data. There is hardly anybody who subscribes to such a position in the philosophy of science, positivists included. Any empirical explanation relies on *a priori* concepts. The question then becomes whether the choice of such concepts, albeit necessary, can be neutral or innocent with regard to the event to be explained.

Going after the business of empirical research, some scholars, however, tend to bracket those questions. In IR, possibly the most famous research programme in this more empiricist tradition is the Correlates of War Project. This project is led by David J. Singer, who has succeeded in obtaining an almost incredible amount of resources over the last few decades, and seeks to find out which antecedent conditions correlate with war.[1] The project is based on a huge historical database of international conflicts for which we have enough information to code them. It is inductively driven in that it wants to derive knowledge from empirical correlations. In other words, our knowledge is based on empirical

---

1 For recent assessments of the findings, see Vasquez (1987), Geller and Singer (1998).

generalisations of which antecedent events correlate with war. In its self-understanding, this is the only possible way to get unbiased information.[2]

Apparently absent, theory enters twice into this type of explanation. First, as empiricists themselves stress, theory is needed since these correlations do not explain anything in the strict sense of the word. For they do not answer the question of why things correlate. Only an argument about causes can help us find out whether the correlations are spurious, or whether they are the social science equivalent of laws. It might be added that even economists, admittedly institutional ones, are not that certain whether social sciences can actually find these more general theories. Richter (1994), one of the *doyens* of institutionalist economics, has likened economics not to physics, but to medicine where we still do not know the causes, say, of rheumatism, but have (*via* trial and error) discovered ways to mitigate its effects.

More importantly perhaps, theories enter the analysis already before or rather for the establishment of these correlations. As already mentioned, we need concepts to code these events. Without concepts as meaningful data-containers (Sartori 1970), we cannot distinguish music (a meaningful fact) from sheer noise (the totality of information) in world history. In other words, pure induction is not possible. In turn, such concepts simply cannot be divorced from theoretical or pre-theoretical assumptions. This is also called the necessary theory-dependence of facts. How do we know, for instance, that the things we compare over the millennia, and which we label with the same concept (in this case, war) are actually the same? Did they mean the same to the actors then and now? The very possibility of "conceptual stretching" (Sartori 1970, Collier and Mahon 1993) is dependent on certain assumptions about history and/or human nature, for instance.

This criticism of empiricism does not necessarily imply that reality can be reduced to what we think about it. In the natural world, reality itself does impose limits on the way we can understand it. In the social world, which is more of "our" making, not every explanation will reach at least some intersubjective consent as being plausible.[3] Hence, if pure induction is impossible, if facts are always theory-dependent, this does not mean that the real world can be meaningfully described in a completely arbitrary way. The offshoot of the previous discussion is neither that there is only one true explanation for everything nor that "anything goes", but that there can be a series of plausible and theoretically founded explanations for

---

2 Indeed, one should not forget that empiricism is a highly sceptical position which was born out of the criticism to derive knowledge from preconceived ideologies, instead of what there "really is" which, in turn, is what our senses, and only those, tell us there is. In the context of heightened ideological debate, like the Cold War, it was only to be expected that peace researchers found empiricist research methods attractive. Unfortunately, no amount of data would have been enough to undermine the faith in *Realpolitik* (Vasquez 1983, 1998).
3 For a longer discussion, see Guzzini (2000a).

which, at any given time, we might not have enough evidence to decide between. Indeed, to put it more strongly, it cannot be excluded that these explanations will approach the apparently same project from very different angles, asking often incompatible research questions about it. In this case, there would be no common evidence against which we could make a final assessment.

This should not be confused with a related argument that ideologies imbue empirical research and that ultimately no justified choice between such ideologies can be made. This reading of the theory-dependence of facts is a very lazy attempt to stop any scholarly communication between, instead of just among, true believers (Guzzini 1988). Such a reading has been reinforced by the classical American way of framing IR/International Political Economy theories according to the triad of political ideologies in the United States (US): conservatism, liberalism, and radicalism. But such a confusion of (a particular national) ideological debate with meta-theoretical assumptions is not warranted. There is, for instance, no reason to assume that conservatives will necessarily link up with realism. Keohane (1989) was perfectly right that one can be both a realist (in IR) and a liberal (in political terms). More importantly, it is a matter for debate to establish whether ideologies really distort empirical analysis beyond a common ground. So-called realists and idealists in the classical IR tradition shared many of their assumptions about the international system; hence, they were able to analyse the state of affairs in a very similar way. They could differ about the question of whether or not this was a state of affairs to stay unchanged.

Instead, the importance of constitutive theorising and concept-formation better shows in the now inflamed discussion about what led to the end of the Cold War.[4] The interpretation of this event can already start with the exact dating.[5] Similarly to the debate on the origins of the Cold War, where scholars put the date at 1917 (Fontaine 1965) or 1945 or 1947, the end of the Cold War has been dated at 1985 (the rise of Gorbachev to power), 1987 (for some, the actual policy turn in the Union of Soviet Socialist Republics – USSR; e.g. MccGwire 1991), or more commonly 1989 (the fall of the Berlin Wall, either symbolising the end of the Eastern bloc or the commitment to change), and 1991 (the end of the Soviet Union). As with the nature of the Cold War, the dating here reflects whether the Cold War is seen as clash of ideologies or of superpowers, and whether individuals or structures play a role in world politics. The very interpretation of what the Cold War was becomes an issue which cannot be taken for granted when asking the question.

---

4 There are libraries written on this by now. Yet on the theoretical debate, see Lebow and Stein (1994), Wohlforth (1994–5, 1998), Lebow and Risse-Kappen (1995), Forsberg (1999), Lebow (1999), Patman (1999), Schweller and Wohlforth (2000), Brooks and Wohlforth (2000–1), as well as the exchange between Kramer (1999, 2001), and Wohlforth (2000).

5 In reality there is little debate about it, at least not in IR. Perhaps this simply shows the lack of trained historians in the field.

The answers to the question are similarly imbued by theoretical assumptions. Those who see the end in the final demise of the Soviet challenge to the US supremacy will have a materialist understanding of power, most saliently the new round of the arms race launched by the first Reagan administration. The USSR, so the story goes, was forced to give in. Apparently, the pure material power figures are, however, too vague to allow such an interpretation, even for realists themselves.[6] Therefore, some realists rescue themselves by saying that the USSR perceived a power decline and reacted accordingly, first stepping up efforts and then giving in (Wohlforth 1994/95), a claim now supported with a turn to political economy (Brooks and Wohlforth 2000/01). Still, this leaves a lot unexplained for understanding the extent of Soviet retrenchment (Kramer 2001), let alone about the origins of the Soviet legitimacy crisis in the 1980s. Another interpretation shared by those who conceive of the international system as a social construct in which governments behave on the basis of their self-identification will point to the non-material causes that pushed the USSR to change policy (Wendt 1992a, Koslowski and Kratochwil 1994). In fact, the "New Thinking" opened many diplomatic avenues, earlier forestalled, simply by ignoring the in any case illusionary military threat from the West. Still others will emphasise domestic politics, that is, the fact that it was only after the end of the Cold War, and not for any international anarchy or great power competition that the USSR disintegrated, but through the emerging Russian nationalism used by Yeltsin in his power competition with Gorbachev.

The assumptions which inform the interpretation are crucial for both the actual explanation of events and for policy advice. The interpretation of such crucial events constitute the "lessons" of history which then inform the judgement of many policy-makers. The example of the Great Depression might be useful here. For economic observers (Kindleberger 1986 [1973]), the Great Depression is mainly remembered because it showed the negative effect of closing markets off from international trade. Because countries did not work together to keep their markets open, their "beggar-thy-neighbour" policies only pushed the problem over to the next country from which, after a cycle, it would inevitably return in an exacerbated form. These lessons focus on the level of the international economy and on the efficiency of markets. More politically oriented observers will remember the Great Depression for the political turmoil which could only be stopped by inventive state strategies, such as the first Swedish social democratic experiments and the "New Deal" (Strange 1998). If not countered, countries were ripe to fall into the hands of populist regimes, some of the worst

---

6 The more profound argument is that "power" is an indeterminate concept which cannot play the same role as money in economic theory. For that argument, see already Aron (1962: 98), and Wolfers (1962: 196). See also Baldwin (1989: 25, 209) whose conceptual analysis shows that overall concepts of power, as used in classical balance of power theories are 'virtually meaningless'. For a discussion, see Guzzini (1993, 2000c).

sorts. Whereas the first vision, correctly, claims that state intervention in international markets deepened the depression, the second vision, equally correctly, would argue that state intervention was key in avoiding a turn towards authoritarian regimes in some countries (which would actually have been even more interventionist). These lessons still inform some of the debate about globalisation today. Defenders like Gilpin (Gilpin 2000) point to the risks of protectionism (as if globalisation were mainly about trade). Even moderate critiques like Strange (1986, 1998), however, point to the necessity to "cool the casino", to manage "mad money".

Indeed, these ideas might bring about the very things they wish to portray or avoid. For a long time, peace researchers have been arguing that realism was a self-fulfilling prophecy.[7] If all other governments assumed that Germany was prone to return to a more irredentist policy after its reunification, an argument forcefully defended by Mearsheimer (1990), then their policies might have isolated Germany to such an extent as to provoke a more assertive and aggressive Germany.[8] If all governments assumed that the next big conflicts are "clashes of civilisation" (Huntington 1993a), then their behaviour, opposing policies on the basis of a supposed threat to one's own culture, might well trigger ethnic/cultural conflicts which would not otherwise have appeared – besides justifying "ethnic cleansing" as the only rational way to solve the multicultural "problem".[9]

The educational argument: teaching future practitioners

Exactly because data does not speak for itself, because all observation is theory-dependent, and because observation can in itself have an effect on this very reality it is supposed to describe, it is fundamental that observers of international relations, whether practical or academic, be trained to become aware of their own and others' assumptions. As seen in the previous discussion on the end of the Cold War, these are highly significant questions for academia and politics. For this, they must understand both the explanatory and the constitutive functions of theories.

Nearly everybody agrees that teaching the explanatory or instrumental function of theory is important. For many scholars, this is basically the only path to theorising, its sole legitimisation. On the basis of case studies and comparative research, the discipline develops so-called middle-range theories. These are explanations for which one might be able to specify (scope) conditions under which they will with a certain probability apply to specified cases. They can also be used as tentative tools for policy advice. There, careful use of these models can

---

7 For a US version, see Vasquez (1983).
8 See the exchange collected in Lynn-Jones (1991).
9 Much earlier, geo-politicians heralded population exchange as a rational tool for conflict resolution. See, for instance, Mackinder (1944 [1919]) reflecting on the Turkish–Greek treaty in 1923.

produce a series of scenarios. It is through this ability of theories that science is usually considered "useful".

But IR is no different to any other social science: these explanations are often limited. Not only do we lack a general theory of international relations or foreign policy: we can give no "eternal advice" to the prince, as Aron (1962) already admonished. But given the amount of variables, and here the social sciences differ from the natural ones, we either tend to make reductionist explanations by concentrating on too few, or must refer to causal complexes without being able to disentangle the host of possible explanations. Forecasts are often nothing more than educated guesses. As Grosser (1972) once put it, political scientists are only able to tell afterwards why things had to happen that way (why a particular scenario was realised). Hence, if conceived similarly, and compared, to the natural sciences, IR theory frequently remains a very blunt instrument.

Nonetheless, there is another important utility in teaching theories in their explanatory function. It is a first step on the road to see the important constitutive function of theories. Insofar as this teaching emphasises the relationship between the event and its explanation, it helps to sharpen our mind on the way these very theories have been constructed. This is extremely important for learning to work theoretically, and to make this work more precise, a point on which again the majority of scholars would agree.[10] In other words, such teaching is meant to develop the capacity of students to train in clear thinking. As a first step, students must be made aware of the very difficult, but crucial, step of concept formation: why do we take which concepts for which type of empirical analysis? What is the cost of choosing one concept over another? Then, students could be made aware of how such concepts are used for the explanation of events. That is, they could get a sense of how interpretivist historians work, how they construct and defend their claims. Finally, they could try out making an inverted research design of other works before trying it out for themselves.

Looking at it in this way, we have already *de facto* reached the constitutive function of theories. This methodological understanding which stresses the problems of the crucial initial step of concept or ideal-type formation falls within the classical Weberian tradition.[11] Social science methodologies that skip this part, like King, Keohane and Verba (1994), tend to paper over the differences between naturalist and interpretivist approaches. By unproblematically using concepts, their positivistic research design takes for granted that which actually carries the most weight in interpretivist explanations.[12]

---

10 See the debate between Bueno de Mesquita (1985) and Krasner (1985b).
11 See the long development of a conceptual framework which precedes his *Economy and Society* (Weber 1980 [1922]).
12 For this argument, see also Wendt's (1999: 83–8) discussion about the difference between causal and constitutive theories and the importance of conceptual analysis.

One of the obvious merits of teaching the constitutive functions of theory underpins the above-mentioned qualification and was already covered in the previous section. There, we saw that concepts and conceptual frameworks are "the condition for the possibility of knowledge" as Immanuel Kant put it. Moreover, we met the basic social constructivist tenet that ideas about social events and those very social events can interact. Of course, students must be made aware of this.

But there is a second, apparently more far-fetched argument in taking the teaching of constitutive theories very seriously: its practical use for international politics. Learning theories is a means for acquiring skills that are crucial for diplomacy. Let me support this claim by making a little detour.

Any knowledge at any given time is bound to be limited. Our knowledge today is prone to change over the next couple of years, and certainly over the next decades. Yet, students as future practitioners will have to be knowledgeable over time. Hence, they must be trained in their capacity to assimilate and produce knowledge on their own. They must be intellectually independent by the time they leave university. Acquiring intellectual independence implies not merely practical knowledge about where to find information in the future, but the capacity to auto-correct one's knowledge. For this, being aware of one's assumptions, and how they relate to understanding, is absolutely fundamental. In other words, theoretical self-awareness is crucial for having the flexible and knowledgeable mind necessary to adapt to new and different practical circumstances. It is for this aptitude that traditional diplomacy often relied on classical education in the past and that many business firms in Western Europe have started to systematically recruit some of their staff from the so-called soft social sciences, and not only from law, economics or management. The same, of course, applies to public administration.

Yet there is an even closer link to diplomacy. Besides the necessary technical skills (law *etc.*) mainly necessary for the consular functions of foreign offices, other foreign office positions still have a touch of classical diplomacy. This applies in particular to the sections on information, some representational functions and, of course, all negotiations. There, diplomats are responsible for providing politically relevant interpretations about significant events in other countries, or for directly managing the relations between countries.

The classical education for these more diplomatic positions includes some training directly offered by the foreign offices, *i.e.* a form of in-house socialisation. Usually, accepted candidates undergo two years of courses and then qualify for their jobs. But such an approach presupposes the very existence of a foreign policy tradition. This is not an obvious option for new countries that often have to build up their foreign offices from scratch. Moreover, it assumes that socialisation is up to date with the way international diplomacy is run today or that it has strategies for correcting itself.

In countries with little in-house socialisation, universities take over part of this task. This happened in the US particularly after 1945, when the country's elite became even more self-conscious of its role in world politics, than during the days of the Princeton Professor turned President, Woodrow Wilson. The US academic solution after the World War II, as most forcefully represented by Morgenthau (1948), consisted of proposing a set of rules to follow in foreign policy-making which could be scientifically deduced from eternal laws (to be found in human nature). Science, not the clubby in-house socialisation was the answer. However, whereas in the past some might have believed that there is a science of foreign policy whose tools we simply have to apply, these certainties have withered. As a result, today we cannot simply propose a deductive science for the future diplomat, even if we have made progress in some domains.

Hence, some countries might find themselves facing the lack of both any history of their foreign office for socialising future diplomats, and of any deductive theory of diplomacy. So how do we train diplomats (not the consular clerks) and foreign policy specialists? Despite all the fuss about the science of foreign policy, the US experience shows clearly that another type of expertise has proved crucial. Faculties have developed huge area study programmes. The basic rationale was obvious. In order to better understand the world, people learnt the language and culture of other countries, coupled with some social science tools. Not some ready-made scientific laws, but some contextual knowledge was the answer.

Here, teaching the constitutive function of theories and, more precisely, teaching how different understandings might exist at the same time can fulfil a crucial learning function, similar to that in learning languages/culture: it prepares one for cross-cultural understanding and communication. To some extent, learning *via* philosophy/meta-theory different theoretical languages can substitute some of the heuristic functions of learning real languages in cultural studies.[13] Such an approach can have an economic appeal as well: in the absence of the means necessary to fund expensive international field studies and area specialisations, one simply needs some books – and mainly brains.

Moreover, teaching theory contributes to developing negotiating skills. For students are led to think as if they were explaining something from different points of view. They have to put themselves into a theoretical frame and produce explanations accordingly. Most importantly, when discussing with other students who might not share their interpretation, they have to learn how to make their own argument palatable to their opponent, to translate their ideas into the theoretical language of the other. It makes students able to decipher the other's position in terms of their assumption, and to respond by using this knowledge. They can therefore anticipate reactions more quickly.

---

13 Theoretical training can of course not entirely replace the exposure to different world-views and cultures. As such, it is relatively sad that many top politicians of the leading power of the day are not exactly known for their expertise in foreign languages and cultures. But theoretical training goes hand in hand with that exposure: being trained in the constitutive function of theories prepares the ground for a better understanding and use of the exposure to different cultures, exactly because there is a greater awareness of one's own values.

Such skills make for a more reflexive process of communication that should reduce misunderstandings. These are hermeneutical skills that are crucial for the observing and acting diplomat. If acquired, they are more time-proven and will be useful for any practitioner when some other form of knowledge has become outdated. In that regard, theoretical discussions are fundamental for developing the intellectual maturity of future actors in international affairs.

The golden rule of diplomacy is not to impose one's visions on the opponent but to change their preferences so as to make them compatible with one's own. This assumes good hermeneutical skills. Similarly, Kissinger used to complain about the recruitment of lawyers and business people to the State Department, exactly because they lacked this capacity to translate into different environments taking the world as one. Problems are treated *ad hoc* with little historical distance: 'Nations are treated as similar phenomena and those states presenting similar immediate problems are treated similarly' (Kissinger 1969: 33). Instead, Kissinger asked for more historical but also nation-specific knowledge. He called for acquiring a non-technical understanding of events, which requires an intellectual distance he himself achieved through his own M.A. thesis which was on the "meaning of history" (nothing less), that is, in political theory, if not philosophy.

A political/academic argument: getting out of the periphery

A final, more obvious yet perhaps less important argument in favour of teaching theory in IR has to do with the research agenda in IR. To put it crudely: IR (and increasingly more specialised studies on the European Union) has become a fully-fledged social science whose debates are basically driven by theory. Contributions are judged on their ability to advance more general knowledge that can be made accessible to a wider audience. Theory is part and parcel of all articles in the leading journals of the field: *International Organization*, *International Security*, *International Studies Quarterly*, and *World Politics* (for the US), as well as the *European Journal of International Relations*, the *Journal of Peace Research*, *Millennium*, the *Review of International Studies*, and the new *Zeitschrift für Internationale Beziehungen*. And this seems justified in the light of the arguments given above.

Theoretical strength has become an indicator of defining an academic core and an academic periphery. Let Germany and Italy serve as examples. Germany's academic IR community, although quite numerous, had no single anonymously peer-reviewed journal in its field until 1994. By that time, the IR section of the German Political Science Association decided to get rid of some of the classical feudal features of any purely cooptative, rather than meritocratic, academic system. It created the *Zeitschrift für Internationale Beziehungen*, which has met with an impressively quick and resounding success. Big shots see their articles refused. Lesser known figures become part of a more general debate. Whereas the traditional IR elite was already quite open to theoretical research (e.g. Czempiel, Senghaas,

Krippendorff),[14] by now the journal displays articles of a theoretical density fully competitive with any major international journal – a richness sustained by the mainly younger generations in the field. The German debate has moved out of the semi-periphery in which it found itself for quite a time. It did so by creating an internal intellectual dynamic and by connecting its findings to the core of research abroad. There was no way to do this without independent research on theory.[15]

This is not quite the situation of IR in Italy. In a recent study, Lucarelli and Menotti (2002) draw a rather critical picture of the Italian scene. There is, relatively speaking, little theoretical work in its widest sense, i.e. including those works which explicitly link theoretical models to empirical material. The most remarkable data is, perhaps, the number of Italian authors who have published in leading international journals. Defining an Italian scholar as one who works in Italy or is part of its academic community, there are only two people who have published in total four articles. For comparison, it would be easy to fill pages with German or Scandinavian names. Although there are journals of good, if mixed, quality like *Teoria Politica*, there is no really anonymously and internationally peer-reviewed journal. The debates go through the big names.

Now one could say that it is not necessarily a sign of being peripheral if the academic community does not publish in international journals. Some academic communities that used to happily publish at home only (given that their internal circles were big enough) were very much part of the international stage, because other communities referred to their work. French philosophy and sociology could serve as examples. Even if we grant that this could be a temporary possibility it is, however, quite natural to resume the link to the international level – a link which has passed necessarily *via* theoretical exchanges. Having no link for quite some time, in either direction, like in Italy, still seems to be a problem.

Still, one could reply that it is perhaps not disastrous if some academic communities do not torture their brains by following the latest intricacies of the "relative *versus* absolute gains" debate or similar theoretical research in IR. An academic periphery might serve as a good protective shield, in the way that poverty was often the best monument preserver during the European Baroque. There is undoubtedly some truth to this. Yet after so many years one needs

---

14 As an example for a much wider body of literature, see Senghaas (1972, 1987), Krippendorff (1975, 1977, 1985) and Czempiel (1981, 1989).
15 These theoretical contributions can be found (1) in the original debate between rational choice and communicative action in IR (a different take on the debate on rationalism and constructivism) by Meyers (1994), Müller (1994, 1995), Schneider (1994), Keck (1995, 1997), Risse-Kappen (1995), Schmalz-Bruns (1995) and now exported to the US by Risse (2000); see also the contributions to constructivism by Jaeger (1996) and Zehfuß (1998) and on action theory by Schimmelfennig (1997); (2) in the debate around democratic peace theory by Risse-Kappen (1994b), Czempiel (1996a, 1996b), Moravcsik (1996) and Schmidt (1996); (3) or in the debate about globalisation and post-national politics (e.g. Brock and Albert 1995, Zürn 1997, Jung 1998, Schmalz-Bruns 1999, and the special issue by Grande and Risse 2000).

something worth preserving, something up to the standards of later times. Moreover, moving out of the periphery does not imply that one has to imitate everything. As Zürn (1994) so nicely put it in the opening issue of the *Zeitschrift für Internationale Beziehungen*, 'We can do much better! *Aber muß es auf amerikanisch sein?*' Both the dynamic of the Scandinavian and German debates have rejuvenated a Continental debate which, although obviously neglected in the US (Wæver 1998), is now well alive and kicking (Jørgensen 2000). This renewal has been accompanied and reinforced by the establishment of a new (since 1995) and internationally peer-reviewed journal of very high quality, the *European Journal of International Relations*, first edited in Uppsala (Carlsnaes) and now in München (Kratochwil).

All of these points seem perhaps trivial to many, but these experiences are important for those countries which are still defining their place in the international division of academic labour, such as the new, and sometimes not so new, academic communities in Central and Eastern Europe. And here the picture seems often similar if not worse than in Italy. Whereas theoretical panels are very prominent in the Western European conference life, such as in the pan-European (well . . .) ECPR (European Consortium for Political Research) Standing Group on IR meetings, only the last conference of the CEEISA (Central and East European International Studies Association) included some theoretical research.

Some of the reasons mentioned for this remarkable lacuna are that young or poor countries must focus on their most immediate technical needs. It seems undeniable that some new technical expertise is warranted. I hope that the two earlier sections have shown that any neglect of theoretical work would be short-sighted, though. Moreover, since future teachers have to be trained, theoretical requirements are even more important since, without it, no academic work (including Ph.D.s!) of an international standard can be expected.

Indeed, there is a risk in the relative comfort the semi-periphery provides. Academic communities, for instance in Central and Eastern Europe, might simply accept the position in which the international division of academic labour will try to slot them, namely one in which they teach and research only on their particular region, passively relying on theories invented by somebody else (or worse, without even any theoretical background which would make them able to relate to other phenomena). The risk is great that scholars will be content with filling out those chapters where "regional expertise" is needed. "The view from . . ." litters book chapter headings like titles in United Nations reports. Ph.D. theses will be guided by these requirements mainly. Even in Germany, many Ph.D.s are financed through research projects that rarely extend to fundamental research. As a result, quite a few young Germans see little other way than to graduate in the United Kingdom or the US.

Such a position risks cementing the semi-periphery. Let us, for the sake of drama, express this in crudely economic terms. Knowledge follows, to some extent, a similar path as other products in international trade. Countries are, of course, free to specialise in raw materials, but the history of international trade has shown that there are limits to this. Exchanging their goods, these countries have come to know a dependence on international technology and tastes. Usually their prices are driven down compared to high value-added goods with a high knowledge component. In particular, Japan stands out as a country which found out that it is simply not enough to copy things, as one must also understand the logic of production. Instead of being a technology-taker, one should be a trend-setter in new technologies. Know-how also derives from basic science, hence the latter simply cannot be disregarded, neither in telecommunications, nor in academic production. Of course, that takes time. But it does not happen if one never starts. Without acknowledging the need for theory, and without developing the possibility for theoretical studies to develop, academic communities risk staying or becoming simple theory-takers (i.e. passive knowledge consumers) and mere data-providers.

A practical note on teaching IR theory

This conception of the significance and role of theories in IR is not inconsequential for its actual teaching. There are some obvious points. Since all empirical analysis, and all history, implies theoretical assumptions, one really cannot do applied studies first and theory later. Consequently, it makes little sense to wait for meta-theory/theory-content in courses of later semesters, although the type of course may differ. Also, since seminars are to be geared towards perspectivist thinking and theory-translation, the seminar leaders themselves must be competent in a variety of different approaches. In a similar vein, instead of a curriculum in which there has been a division of theoretical spheres of influence with little exchange in-between, it is preferable to have several courses which in themselves try to make people think on the basis of a variety of approaches, although the preference of the seminar leaders will differ.

Since the foregoing discussion has stressed the importance of the constitutive function of theories, I will not deal with the majority of courses that have a necessary theoretical content, but which are not specifically geared towards preparing students for theoretical thinking.[16] Instead, I will focus on those courses that more explicitly tackle the constitutive function of theories. These more theoretical courses are concerned with the way explanations are constructed. They must discuss the assumptions upon which middle-range explanatory theories are built. In other words, these courses must discuss meta-theories (of course not exclusively). There is no finite list for teaching the inter-relationship between meta-theories and theories in IR. Also, teaching should follow the needs of particular students and there is little generalisation that can be offered. Still, some patterns can be discerned.

There are perhaps four basic ways of combining theory/meta-theory in a course. The most classical way, at least on the European continent, would be *via*

---

16 For instance, in a course on conflict resolution, one can teach middle-range theories that specify the conditions under which attempts at third-party mediation might be more successful.

a history of thought. Strangely enough, this is rarely done. There are two basic strategies for such an approach. One can either refer to the philosophical forerunners of international theories, or limit oneself to the theoreticians that were prominent in the field that became institutionalised as a discipline after the World War I. In Western dominated IR, such a course then tends to be structured around the so-called four great debates (realism–idealism, scientism–traditionalism, realism–globalism, rationalism–constructivism), but that can be enriched by local references. The advantage of such an approach is that it introduces some of the peculiar IR language to students (security dilemma, balance of power, national interest), all its pitfalls, as well as some methodological issues in a "chrono-logical" manner. Moreover, if presented in a sociological way, students get some insight into the relationship between world political events and theoretical advances, i.e. they learn to put the production of knowledge into its social and historical contexts. The disadvantage is that the core will inevitable centre around realism in IR, and will hence not present the variety of approaches (as seen also in Guzzini 1998). Moreover, it can meet the incomprehension of students who might perceive this as an exercise in resurrecting mummified ideas, a kind of intellectual archaeology. Hence, it is important that links to contemporary affairs or debates be made throughout the course, something which is actually not that difficult.

A second approach, which works in a more straightforward analytical way, was prominent in the 1980s and 1990s, and not only in the West. It consists of presenting theory as a menu for choosing between clusters of assumptions bundled as schools of thought or paradigms. Let us call it the approach of the 'Inter-Paradigm Debate' (Banks 1985). There are some relatively famous books on realism, pluralism and globalism or similar titles.[17] This also applied to International Political Economy where, again, we were usually offered three choices: mercantilism, liberalism and structuralism/neo-Marxism (Gilpin 1975b, 1987b, Gill and Law 1988). Such a didactic approach has some obvious advantages. It is logical in that it takes first what comes first: the underlying assumptions of all theories and observation. Also, it immediately does some homework for the student in that it shows that assumptions usually come in a cluster. Finally, it trains students explicitly in method. The usual game consists of asking students to explain an event in any of the theories, which means that students must understand how hypotheses are formulated and put up for empirical scrutiny.

There are a series of caveats to this second approach, however. One is the above-mentioned and often encountered confusion of ideologies with meta-theories. In other words, there exists the risk of taking these clusters in purely ideological terms. Yet, one should be well advised not to confound realism/pluralism/structuralism with conservatism/liberalism/radicalism, as often done

---

17 For surveys of this triad, see Rittberger and Hummel (1990: 23) and Wæver (1996: 153).

especially in the US (Gilpin 1987b). If conceived in such an ideological way, the course might have the opposite effect: instead of opening up for thinking, it closes down the path to debate. If diverging values are all there is, then the debate can easily turn into a show of verbal fists. Worse, in some settings, the intellectual exchange might never start since everybody feels entitled to stick to what they think anyway (and professors are always right). At this point, theory courses simply add one more to the list of compulsory hurdles later quickly forgotten. Also, students do not necessarily get the link between knowledge and the social environment in which it is produced (the mirror argument to the advantage of the first more historical technique). So the "Inter-Paradigm Debate" was perhaps best understood as a historical phenomenon, *i.e.* as an indicator of the self-understanding of a discipline in crisis, and less as a logical clash of incommensurable paradigms (Guzzini 1988, 1998).

The present discussion between rationalism and constructivism is preferable to the classical Inter-Paradigm Debate in that it focuses very well on the meta-theoretical differences.[18] In other words, it does not reduce meta-theory to an ideological factor. The meta-theoretical matrix on which it is built has, however, inconveniences of its own. The two most important are the fuzzy borders of some categories and the general evacuation of all normative debates (Guzzini 1998: 190–235). Moreover, the disadvantage of teaching in this way is the "top–down" manner. Students previously unacquainted with the need to get some distance from the data presented to them will find it hard to make the theoretical-empirical link. Of course, teaching can help by using articles as examples, and so on. Similarly, small assignments that repeatedly ask to generate and compare explanations on the basis of different theories are helpful. Finally, newspaper articles can be used and compared to tease out the underlying assumptions. All this is relatively time-intensive, though, since the instructor has to give very thorough and frequent feedback to students. Hence, depending on the size of the class, the tasks of communication and learning control can prove difficult. To put it differently, such theory courses can hardly be lectures and do not work well in big settings.

A third way of teaching the constitutive function of theories is to take a central concept, like "power", "security", "world society" or "war", and then show how the meaning of such concepts, as well as their explanatory value, diverges from one meta-theoretical/theoretical context to another. For such central concepts, once they are made part of the vocabulary of an observer (applied or theoretical) they derive their significant meaning from the contexts in which they are embedded (Guzzini 1993). Also, depending on the concepts, this is a good way to refer to normative debates in IR.

The limits of such courses are similar to those met by the fourth type of enhancing the awareness of the constitutive function of theories, which explicitly

---

18 For the classical exposition, see Keohane (1989 [1988]) and Lapid (1989); for its present status, see Katzenstein *et al.* (1998) and Guzzini (2000a).

starts from the empirical end. One way, for instance, would be to take an important international event, as *e.g.* the above-mentioned "end of the Cold War". The seminar confronts different interpretations of the event. Then, it discusses the relative value of these interpretations on different levels: their empirical accuracy, their internal coherence, and finally the plausibility of the assumptions, both open and hidden, on which the explanation is based. The aim is to get students interested in exploring these assumptions, and hence to ask theoretical questions. This way works by motivating students to think theoretically starting from an empirical theme.

The drawbacks of this way of teaching are that assumptions are hardly seen in context or in a bundle. It leaves a certain taste of *ad-hoc*-ness to it. Again, the teacher can try to remedy this by referring to the larger theories to which particular assumptions tend to belong. Without proper preparation, however, this strategy risks moving the discussion too early to a higher theoretical level. Still, such a course could be good at the early stages of a student life, trying to stimulate the necessary theoretical awareness – and might then be repeated in a more advanced way at a later stage.

Conclusion

This chapter has sought to oppose the often-encountered conflation between theory and academia on the one hand, and politics and practice, on the other. Indeed, it has tried to show that these distinctions are themselves particularly damaging since they reinforce the illusion that empirical studies can ever be divorced from theory, and that education in international affairs is a purely "professional" exercise that stresses mere knowledge and not reflexive skills. In other words, these distinctions hide the specific contributions of theory training for practitioners in IR.

I advanced three arguments for better assessing the significance and roles of teaching theory in IR. First, all empirical analysis implies theory. Theory is not something to be added later. Its awareness is not an "academic" enterprise, but actual politics. Second, in times of changing knowledge, the teaching of theory can help foster a more time-independent self-reflexivity and cultural and contextual awareness, in short, a form of intellectual maturity particularly useful for cross-national understanding, communication, and negotiation. Finally, and perhaps also for this reason, teaching and researching in theory, including fundamental research, has been a major ingredient in moving academic communities out of the (semi-)periphery.

I ended with a short note on actual teaching by identifying four classical types of courses. This was not meant to exhaust all the possible ways to raise the hermeneutical skills deemed necessary for future practitioners (in academia, journalism, economics or politics). Also, they should not suggest that this kind of course is *all* there should be. To the contrary, as mentioned above, it cannot replace a good training in basic processes and issues in international history, law, politics and political economy. Yet, as I simply wanted to stress, neither can applied studies replace such theoretical courses, relying perhaps more on sociology and philosophy. Nor does it appear that they would be "more important" to the future practitioners who will, as academics should have no trouble admitting, necessarily learn a good part of their applied trade while doing it.

There is perhaps an even more far-reaching implication of the argument. The call for more applied studies betrays a longing for a time when academia and politics spoke basically the same language. In the past, realism, or more generally the classical tradition, has been the bridge between observation and decision. This bridge was taken for granted, the language was natural. There was an easy coming and going between scholars and politicians. Today, the impression is that the language of academia has increasingly moved away from that of practice. Hence, the call for re-importing the language of politics into academia.

But such a resurrection of the *old* united language is impossible to achieve in some countries by now. As practitioners have noticed themselves, there is no way back to the "natural" language of scholars and practitioners. It is this very self-awareness of needing competent translations that makes the return to a *status quo* very difficult. The realist or classical language and view of international affairs is no longer obvious in many countries. That is because realism or the parameters of the realist–idealist debate have in themselves become an object of study, exposing it as a set of practices which in itself influences the reality it is supposed to passively explain.

Therefore, it is also contestable whether this rapprochement should be done in this conservative way. Resisting this rising self-awareness and the exposure to academic distance with the excuse that the languages no longer fit is not an innocent move. It would have as an effect that the future elite, which might have been trained in these new professionalised academic environments, would itself stop speaking the old language of politics. For all the above does not imply that the link between academia and practice is lost forever. Rather, it has to be redefined. Practitioners can be self-reflective persons who are able to combine the old and new languages of practice and of observation, as diplomats have always been speaking different languages to different audiences. Academics should be able to include in the analysis the self-fulfilling effects that certain explanations can have. True, this implies a double socialisation. But instead of pursuing the conservative endeavour to paper over a unity lost, one might face the challenge of redefining it. It would not be difficult for constructivists to live with this commitment to self-reflexivity (Guzzini 2000a). The significance and roles of theory in teaching IR and researching international relations would be no matter for dispute.

BIBLIOGRAPHY

Adler, Emanuel (1987) *The Power of Ideology: The Quest for Technological Autonomy in Argentina and Brazil*. Berkeley: University of California Press.
—— (1997) 'Seizing the Middle Ground: Constructivism in World Politics', *European Journal of International Relations* 3(3): 319–63.
—— (2002) 'Constructivism and International Relations', in Walter Carlsnaes, Thomas Risse and Beth A. Simmons, eds, *Handbook of International Relations*, London: Sage, 95–118.
—— (2005) *Communitarian International Relations: The Epistemic Foundations of International Relations*. London and New York: Routledge.
—— (2008) 'The Spread of Security Communities: Communities of Practice, Self-Restraint, and Nato's Post-Cold War Transformation', *European Journal of International Relations* 14(2): 195–230.
Adler, Emanuel and Michael Barnett, eds (1998) *Security Communities*. Cambridge: Cambridge University Press.
Adler, Emanuel and Peter M. Haas (1992) 'Conclusion: Epistemic Communities, World Order, and the Creation of a Reflective Research Program', *International Organization* 46(1): 369–90.
Adorno, Theodor and Max Horkheimer (1969 [1947]) *Dialektik der Aufklärung: Philosophische Fragmente*. Frankfurt am Main: Fischer Verlag.
Albert, Mathias and Lena Hilkermeier, eds (2004) *Observing International Relations: Niklas Luhmann and World Politics*. London: Routledge.
Albrecht, Ulrich (1986) *Internationale Politik. Einführung in das System internationaler Herrschaft*. Munich: Oldenbourg Verlag.
—— (2000) 'On Learning from Wendt', *Review of International Studies* 26(1): 141–50.
Alker, Hayward R. (1996) *Rediscoveries and Reformulations: Humanistic Methodologies for International Studies*. Cambridge: Cambridge University Press.
Anderson, Benedict (1991) *Imagined Communities: Reflections on the Origins and Spread of Nationalism*. London: Verso.
Arendt, Hannah (1969) *On Violence*. New York: Harcourt, Brace & World.
—— (1986 [1970]) 'Communicative Power', in Steven Lukes, ed., *Power*, New York: New York University Press, 59–74.

Aron, Raymond (1962) *Paix et guerre entre les nations*. Paris: Calmann–Lévy.
—— (1967) *Les étapes de la pensée sociologique*. Paris: Gallimard.
—— (1969) *Les désillusions du progrès. Essai sur la dialectique de la modernité*. Paris: Calmann–Lévy.
—— (1976) *Penser la guerre, Clausewitz. II: L'âge planétaire*. Paris: Gallimard.
—— (1984) *Les dernières années du siècle*. Paris: Juillard.
Art, Robert J. (1996) 'American Foreign Policy and the Fungibility of Force', *Security Studies* 5(4): 7–42.
—— (1999) 'Force and Fungibility Reconsidered', *Security Studies* 8(4): 183–9.
Ashley, Richard K. (1981) 'Political Realism and Human Interests', *International Studies Quarterly* 25(2): 204–36.
—— (1984) 'The Poverty of Neorealism', *International Organization* 38(2): 225–86.
—— (1987) 'The Geopolitics of Geopolitical Space: Toward a Critical Social Theory of International Politics', *Alternatives* 12(4): 403–34.
—— (1989) 'Imposing International Purpose: Notes on a Problematique of Governance', in Ernst-Otto Czempiel and James Rosenau, eds, *Global Changes and Theoretical Challenges: Approaches to World Politics for the 1990s*, Lexington, MA: Lexington Books, 251–90.
Bachrach, Peter and Morton S. Baratz (1970) *Power and Poverty: Theory and Practice*. New York: Oxford University Press.
Badie, Bertrand and Marie-Claude Smouts (1992) *Le retournement du monde. Sociologie de la scène internationale*. Paris: Presses de la Fondation Nationale des Sciences Politiques & Dalloz.
Baechler, Jean (1978) *Le pouvoir pur*. Paris: Calmann–Lévy.
Baldwin, David A. (1971a) 'Money and Power', *Journal of Politics* 33(3): 578–614.
—— (1971b) 'The Power of Positive Sanctions', *World Politics* 24(1): 19–38.
—— (1978) 'Power and Social Exchange', *American Political Science Review* 72(4): 1229–42.
—— (1979) 'Power Analysis and World Politics: New Trends Versus Old Tendencies', *World Politics* 31(2): 161–94.
—— (1980) 'Interdependence and Power: A Conceptual Analysis', *International Organization* 34(4): 471–506.
—— (1985) *Economic Statecraft*. Princeton: Princeton University Press.
—— (1989) *Paradoxes of Power*. Oxford: Blackwell.
—— (1989 [1979]) 'Power Analysis and World Politics: New Trends Versus Old Tendencies', in David A. Baldwin, *Paradoxes of Power*, Oxford: Blackwell, 129–68.
—— (1993a) 'Neoliberalism, Neorealism, and World Politics', in David A. Baldwin, ed., *Neorealism and Neoliberalism: The Contemporary Debate*, New York: Columbia University Press, 3–25.
——, ed. (1993b) *Neorealism and Neoliberalism: The Contemporary Debate*. New York: Columbia University Press.
—— (1999) 'Force, Fungibility, and Influence', *Security Studies* 8(4): 173–83.
—— (2002) 'Power and International Relations', in Walter Carlsnaes, Thomas Risse and Beth A. Simmons, eds, *Handbook of International Relations*, London: Sage, 177–91.
Banks, Michael (1984) 'The Evolution of International Relations', in Michael Banks, ed., *Conflict in World Society: A New Perspective on International Relations*, Brighton: Harvester Press, 3–21.
—— (1985) 'The Inter-Paradigm Debate', in Margot Light and A. J. R. Groom, eds, *International Relations: A Handbook of Current Theory*, London: Frances Pinter, 7–26.

Barbalet, J. M. (1987) 'Power, Structural Resources and Agency', *Current Perspectives in Social Theory* 8: 1–24.
Barnes, Barry (1982) *T. S. Kuhn and Social Science*. London: Macmillan.
—— (1988) *The Nature of Power*. Cambridge: Polity Press.
Barnett, Michael and Raymond Duvall (2005a) 'Power in International Politics', *International Organization* 59(1): 39–75.
——, eds (2005b) *Power in Global Governance*. Cambridge: Cambridge University Press.
Barry, Brian (1989 [1987]) 'The Uses of Power', in his *Democracy, Power and Justice*, Oxford: Clarendon Press, 307–21.
—— (1989 [1975]) 'Power: An Economic Analysis', in his *Democracy, Power and Justice*, Oxford: Clarendon Press, 222–69.
Barry Jones, R. J. (1981) 'International Political Economy: Problems and Issues. Part I', *Review of International Studies* 7(4): 245–60.
Bartelson, Jens (1995) *A Genealogy of Sovereignty*. Cambridge: Cambridge University Press.
Bartlett, Randall (1989) *Economics and Power: An Inquiry into Human Relations and Markets*. Cambridge: Cambridge University Press.
Beck, Ulrich (1986) *Die Risikogesellschaft. Auf dem Weg in eine andere Moderne*. Frankfurt am Main: Suhrkamp.
Becker, Gary (1986 [1976]) 'The Economic Approach to Human Behaviour', in Jon Elster, ed., *Rational Choice*, Oxford: Basil Blackwell, 108–22.
Behnke, Andreas (2000) 'The Message or the Messenger? Reflections on the Role of Security Experts and the Securitization of Political Issues', *Cooperation and Conflict* 35(1): 89–105.
—— (2001) 'Grand Theory in the Age of its Impossibility: Contemplations on Alexander Wendt', *Cooperation and Conflict* 36(1): 121–34.
Berki, R. N. (1981) *On Political Realism*. London: Dent & Sons.
Bernauer, James and David Rasmussen, eds (1988) *The Final Foucault*. Cambridge, MA: MIT Press.
Bernstein, Richard (1983) *Beyond Objectivism and Relativism: Science, Hermeneutics and Praxis*. Philadelphia: University of Pennsylvania Press.
Bially Mattern, Janice (2005) 'Why Soft Power Isn't So Soft: Representational Force and the Sociolinguistic Construction of Attraction in World Politics', *Millennium: Journal of International Studies* 33(3): 583–612.
Bigo, Didier (2011) 'Pierre Bourdieu and International Relations: Power of Practices, Practices of Power', *International Political Sociology* 5(3): 225–58.
Bigo, Didier, Philippe Bonditti, Laurent Bonelli, Dario Chi, Antoine Mégie and Christian Olsson (2007) *The Field of the EU Internal Security Agencies*. Paris: L'Harmattan/Centre d'Études sur les Conflits.
Bigo, D. L., Bonelli, D. Chi and D. Olsson (2008) *Mapping of the Field of the EU Internal Serurity Agencies*, Paris: Centre d'Études sur les Conflits/Harmattan.
Blau, Peter M. (1964) *Exchange and Power in Social Life*. New York: J. Wiley.
Bobbio, Norberto (1981) 'La teoria dello stato e del potere', in Pietro Rossi, ed., *Max Weber e l'analisi del mondo*, Turin: Einaudi, 215–46.
—— (1996 [1969]) *Saggi sulla scienza politica in Italia*. 2nd edn. Rome and Bari: Editori Laterza.
Bourdieu, Pierre (1977) *Outline of a Theory of Practice*. Translated by Richard Nice. Cambridge: Cambridge University Press.

—— (1979) *La distinction. Critique sociale du jugement.* Paris: Les Éditions de Minuit.
—— (1980) *Le sens pratique.* Paris: Les Éditions de Minuit.
—— (1982) *Ce que parler veut dire. L'économie des échanges linguistiques.* Paris: Fayard.
—— (1984) *Homo academicus.* Paris: Les Éditions de Minuit.
—— (1989) *Noblesse d'état. Grandes écoles et esprit de corps.* Paris: Les Éditions de Minuit.
—— (1990) *In Other Words: Essays towards a Reflexive Sociology.* Translated by Matthew Adamson. Oxford: Polity Press.
—— (1994) *Raisons politiques. Sur la théorie de l'action.* Paris: Éditions du Seuil.
—— (2000a) *Propos sur le champ politique.* Lyon: Presses Universitaires de Lyon.
—— (2000b) *Les structures sociales de l'économie.* Paris: Les Éditions du Seuil.
—— (2001) *Language et pouvoir symbolique.* 2nd rev. and enlarged edn. Paris: Seuil.
Bourdieu, Pierre with Loïc J. D. Wacquant (1992) *Réponses. Pour une anthropologie réflexive.* Paris: Éditions du Seuil.
Brglez, Milan (2001) 'Reconsidering Wendt's Meta-Theory: Blending Scientific Realism with Social Constructivism', *Journal of International Relations and Development* 4(4): 339–62.
Brock, Lothar and Mathias Albert (1995) 'Entgrenzung der Staatenwelt. Zur Analyse weltgesellschaftlicher Entwicklungstendenzen', *Zeitschrift für Internationale Beziehungen* 2(2): 259–85.
Brooks, Stephen G. (1997) 'Dueling Realisms', *International Organization* 51(3): 445–77.
Brooks, Stephen G. and William C. Wohlforth (2000/01) 'Power, Globalization and the End of the Cold War: Reevaluating a Landmark Case for Ideas', *International Security* 25(3): 5–53.
Brown, Chris (1992) *International Relations Theory: New Normative Approaches.* New York: Harvester Wheatsheaf.
—— (1997) *Understanding International Relations.* Houndmills: Macmillan.
Bueno de Mesquita, Bruce (1985) 'Toward a Scientific Understanding of International Conflict: A Personal View', *International Studies Quarterly* 29(1): 121–36.
Bull, Hedley (1966) 'International Theory: The Case for a Classical Approach', *World Politics* 18(3): 361–77.
—— (1977) *The Anarchical Society: A Study of Order in World Politics.* London: Macmillan.
—— (1980) 'International Order and Foreign Policy: A Theoretical Sketch of Postwar International Politics by Frederick V. Kratochwil', *Third World Quarterly* 2(1): 134–7.
—— (1984) 'The Revolt against the West', in Hedley Bull and Adam Watson, eds, *The Expansion of International Society*, Oxford and New York: Clarendon Press, 217–28.
Bulmer, Martin (1979) 'Concepts in the Analysis of Qualitative Data', *Sociological Review* 27(4): 651–77.
Burton, John W. (1985) 'World Society and Human Needs', in Margot Light and A. J. R. Groom, eds, *International Relations: A Handbook of Current Theory*, London: Frances Pinter, 46–59.
—— (1986) *Global Conflict: The Domestic Sources of International Crisis.* 2nd edn. Brighton: Harvester Press.
Butler, Judith (1999) 'Performativity's Social Magic', in Richard Shusterman, ed., *Bourdieu: A Critical Reader*, Oxford: Blackwell, 113–28.
Buzan, Barry (1991) *People, States and Fear: An Agenda for International Security Studies in the Post-Cold War Era.* 2nd edn. New York: Harvester Wheatsheaf.
—— (2004a) *From International to World Society? English School Theory and the Social Structure of Globalisation.* Cambridge: Cambridge University Press.

—— (2004b) *The United States and Great Powers: World Politics in the Twenty-First Century*. Cambridge: Polity Press.
Buzan, Barry, Charles Jones and Richard Little (1993) *The Logic of Anarchy: Neorealism to Structural Realism*. New York: Columbia University Press.
Buzan, Barry, Ole Wæver and Jaap de Wilde (1998) *Security: A New Framework for Analysis*. Boulder, CO: Lynne Rienner.
Calleo, David P. (1982) *The Imperious Economy*. Cambridge, MA: Harvard University Press.
—— (1987) *Beyond American Hegemony: The Future of the Western Alliance*. New York: Basic Books.
Calleo, David and Susan Strange (1984) 'Money and World Politics', in Susan Strange, ed., *Paths to International Political Economy*, London: George Allen & Unwin, 91–125.
Campbell, David (1992) *Writing Security: United States Foreign Policy and the Politics of Identity*. Minneapolis, MN: University of Minnesota Press.
—— (1993) *Power without Principles: Sovereignty, Ethics and the Narratives of the Gulf War*. Boulder, CO: Lynne Rienner.
Campbell, David and Michael Dillon, eds (1993) *The Political Subject of Violence*. Manchester: Manchester University Press.
Camus, Albert (1942) *Le mythe de Sisyphe. Essai sur l'absurde*. Paris: Gallimard.
Caporaso, James A. (1978a) 'Introduction to the Special Issue of *International Organization* on Dependence and Dependency in the Global System', *International Organization* 32(1): 1–12.
—— (1978b) 'Dependence, Dependency and Power in the Global System: A Structural and Behavioural Analysis', *International Organization* 32(1): 13–43.
Caporaso, James A. and Stephen Haggard (1989) 'Power in the International Political Economy', in Richard J. Stoll and Michael D. Ward, eds, *Power in World Politics*, Boulder, CO: Lynne Rienner, 99–120.
Carlsnaes, Walter (1992) 'The Agency–Structure Problem in Foreign Policy Analysis', *International Studies Quarterly* 36(3): 245–70.
Carr, Edward Heller (1946) *The Twenty Years' Crisis: An Introduction to the Study of International Relations*. 2nd edn. London: Macmillan.
—— (1961) *What Is History?* 2nd edn. (1987) ed. by R. W. Davies. London: Penguin.
—— (2000 [1980]) 'An Autobiography', in Michael Cox, ed., *E. H. Carr: A Critical Appraisal*, Houndmills: Palgrave Macmillan, xiii–xxii.
Cederman, Lars-Erik and Christopher Daase (2003) 'Endogenizing Corporate Identities: The Next Step in Constructivist IR Theory', *European Journal of International Relations* 9(1): 5–35.
Checkel, Jeffrey T. (1997) *Ideas and International Political Change: Soviet/Russian Behaviour and the End of the Cold War*. New Haven and London: Yale University Press.
—— (1998) 'The Constructivist Turn in International Relations Theory', *World Politics* 50(2): 324–48.
—— (2001) 'Why Comply? Social Learning and European Identity Change', *International Organization* 55(3): 553–88.
—— (2007) 'Constructivism and EU Politics', in Knud-Erik Jørgensen, Mark Pollack and Ben Rosamond, eds, *Handbook of European Union Politics*, London: Sage, 57–76.
Choucri, Nazli (1980) 'International Political Economy: A Theoretical Perspective', in Ole R. Holsti, Randolph M. Siverson and Alexander L. George, eds, *Change in the International System*, Boulder, CO: Westview Press, 103–29.

Christensen, Cheryl (1977) 'Structural Power and National Security', in Klaus Knorr and Frank N. Trager, eds, *Economic Issues and National Security*, Kansas: Regents Press for the National Security Education Program, 127–59.

Claude, Inis L., Jr. (1956) *Swords into Plowshares: The Problems and Progress of International Organization*. New York: Random House.

—— (1962) *Power and International Relations*. New York: Random House.

—— (1989) 'The Balance of Power Revisited', *Review of International Studies* 15(2): 77–85.

Clegg, Stewart R. (1989) *Frameworks of Power*. London: Sage.

Coleman, James S. (1990) *Foundations of Social Theory*. Cambridge, MA: Belknap Press of Harvard University Press.

Collier, David and Steven Levitsky (1997) 'Democracy with Adjectives: Conceptual Innovation in Comparative Research', *World Politics* 49(3): 430–51.

Collier, David and James Mahon (1993) 'Conceptual "Stretching" Revisited: Adapting Categories in Comparative Research', *American Political Science Review* 87(4): 845–55.

Colombo, Alessandro (1999) 'L'Europa e la società internazionale. Gli aspetti culturali e istituzionali della convivenza internazionale di Raymond Aron, Martin Wight e Carl Schmitt', *Quaderni di Scienza Politica* 6(2): 251–301.

Connolly, William E. (1974) *The Terms of Political Discourse*. 2nd edn. Oxford: Martin Robertson.

Copeland, Dale C. (2000) 'The Constructivist Challenge to Structural Realism: A Review Essay', *International Security* 25(2): 187–212.

Cox, Andrew, Paul Furlong and Edward Page (1985) *Power in Capitalist Society: Theory, Explanations and Cases*. Brighton: Harvester Press/Wheatsheaf Books.

Cox, Michael (2000a) 'Introduction: E. H. Carr – a Critical Appraisal', in Michael Cox, ed., *E. H. Carr: A Critical Appraisal*, Houndmills: Palgrave Macmillan, 1–18.

——, ed. (2000b) *E. H. Carr: A Critical Appraisal*. Houndmills: Palgrave Macmillan.

Cox, Robert W. (1983) 'Gramsci, Hegemony and International Relations: An Essay in Method', *Millennium: Journal of International Studies* 12(2): 162–75.

—— (1986 [1981]) 'Social Forces, States and World Orders: Beyond International Relations Theory (+Postscript 1985)', in Robert O. Keohane, ed., *Neorealism and Its Critiques*, New York: Columbia University Press, 204–54.

—— (1987) *Production, Power and World Order. Social Forces in the Making of History*. New York: Columbia University Press.

Cronin, Bruce (1999) *Community under Anarchy: Transnational Identity and the Evolution of Cooperation*. New York: Columbia University Press.

Czempiel, Ernst-Otto (1981) *Internationale Politik. Ein Konfliktmodell*. Paderborn: Schöningh.

—— (1989) 'Internationalizing Politics: Some Answer to the Question of Who Does What to Whom', in Ernst-Otto Czempiel and James Rosenau, eds, *Global Changes and Theoretical Challenges: Approaches to World Politics for the 1990s*, Lexington, MA: Lexington Books, 117–34.

—— (1996a) 'Kants Theorem. Oder: warum sind die Demokratien (noch immer) nicht friedlich?' *Zeitschrift für Internationale Beziehungen* 3(1): 79–101.

—— (1996b) 'Theorie und Strategie. Überlegungen nach Hajo Schmidts Kommentar', *Zeitschrift für Internationale Beziehungen* 3(1): 117–22.

—— (2002) *Weltpolitik im Umbruch. Die Pax Americana, der Terrorismus und die Zukunft der internationalen Beziehungen*. Munich: Beck Verlag.

Daase, Christopher (1999) *Kleine Kriege – Große Wirkung. Wie unkonventionelle Kriegsführung die internationale Politik verändert*. Baden-Baden: Nomos Verlagsgesellschaft.

Dahl, Robert A. (1957) 'The Concept of Power', *Behavioural Science* 2(3): 201–15.
―― (1958) 'A Critique of the Ruling Elite Model', *American Political Science Review* 52: 463–69.
―― (1961) *Who Governs? Democracy and Power in an American City*. New Haven: Yale University Press.
―― (1968) 'Power', in David L. Sills, ed., *International Encyclopedia of the Social Sciences*, Vol. 12, New York: Free Press, 405–15.
―― (1976) *Modern Political Analysis*. 3rd edn. Upper Saddle River, NJ: Prentice Hall.
Debnam, Geoffrey (1984) *The Analysis of Power: A Realist Approach*. London: Macmillan.
Dessler, David (1989) 'What Is at Stake in the Agent–Structure Debate?' *International Organization* 43: 441–73.
Deudney, Daniel H. (2000) 'Regrounding Realism: Anarchy, Security and Changing Material Contexts', *Security Studies* 10(1): 1–42.
Deutsch, Karl W. (1966) *The Nerves of Government: Models of Political Communication and Control*. 2nd rev. edn. New York: The Free Press.
―― (1968) *The Analysis of International Relations*. Englewood Cliffs, NJ: Prentice Hall.
Deutsch, Karl W., Sidney A. Burrell, Robert A. Kann, Maurice Lee, Jr., Martin Lichterman, Raymond E. Lindgren, Francis L. Lowenheim and Richard W. Van Wagnen (1957) *Political Community in the North Atlantic Area: International Organization in the Light of Historical Experience*. Princeton: Princeton University Press.
Dezalay, Yves and Bryant G. Barth (2002) *The Internationalization of Palace Wars: Lawyers, Economists and the Contest to Transform Latin American States*. Chicago: The University of Chicago Press.
Donnelly, Jack (2000) *Realism and International Relations*. Cambridge: Cambridge University Press.
Doty, Roxanne Lynn (2000) 'Desire All the Way Down', *Review of International Studies* 26: 137–9.
Dowding, Keith (1991) *Rational Choice and Political Power*. Aldershot: Edward Elgar.
―― (1996) *Power*. Minneapolis: University of Minnesota Press.
Dreyfus, Hubert L. and Paul Rabinow (1983) *Michel Foucault: Beyond Structuralism and Hermeneutics*. 2nd edn. Chicago: The University of Chicago Press.
Drulák, Petr (2001) 'The Problem of Structural Change in Alexander Wendt's *Social Theory of International Politics*', *Journal of International Relations and Development* 4(4): 363–79.
―― (2006) 'Reflectivity and Structural Change', in Stefano Guzzini and Anna Leander, eds, *Constructivism and International Relations: Alexander Wendt and His Critics*, London, New York: Routledge, 140–59.
DuBois, Marc (1991) 'The Governance of the Third World: A Foucauldian Perspective on Power Relations in Development', *Alternatives* 16(1): 1–30.
Dunne, Tim (2000) 'Theories as Weapons: E. H. Carr and International Relations', in Michael Cox, ed., *E. H. Carr: A Critical Appraisal*, Houndmills: Palgrave Macmillan, 217–33.
Dunne, Timothy (1995) 'The Social Construction of International Society', *European Journal of International Relations* 1(3): 367–89.
Edelstein, David M. and Ronald R. Krebs (2005) 'Washington's Troubling Obsession with Public Diplomacy', *Survival* 47(1): 89–104.
Elman, Colin (1996) 'Horses for Courses: Why Not Neo-Realist Theories of Foreign Policy?' *Security Studies* 6(1): 7–53.
Elman, Colin and Miriam Fendius Elman (2002) 'How Not to Be Lakatos Intolerant: Appraising Progress in IR Research', *International Studies Quarterly* 46(2): 231–62.

Elster, Jon (1989) *Nuts and Bolts for the Social Sciences*. Cambridge: Cambridge University Press.
Evans, Graham and Jeffrey Newnham, eds (1990) *The Dictionary of World Politics: A Reference Guide to Concepts, Ideas and Institutions*. New York: Harvester Wheatsheaf.
Faber, Karl-Georg, Karl-Heinz Ilting and Christian Meier (1982) 'Macht, Gewalt', in Otto Brunner, Werner Conze and Reinhart Koselleck, eds, *Geschichtliche Grundbegriffe. Historisches Lexikon zur politisch–sozialen Sprache in Deutschland. Band 3*, Stuttgart: Klett–Cotta, 817–935.
Farr, James (1989) 'Understanding Conceptual Change Politically', in Terence Ball, James Farr and Russell L. Hanson, eds, *Political Innovation and Conceptual Change*, Cambridge: Cambridge University Press, 24–49.
Feaver, Peter D., Gunther Hellmann, Randall L. Schweller, Jeffrey W. Taliaferro, William C. Wohlforth, Jeffrey W. Legro and Andrew Moravcsik (2000) 'Correspondence. Brother, Can You Spare a Paradigm? (or Was Anybody Ever a Realist?)', *International Security* 25(1): 165–93.
Fierke, Karin (1998) *Changing Games, Changing Strategies: Critical Investigations in Security*. Manchester: Manchester University Press.
Fontaine, André (1965) *Histoire de la guerre froide. Tome I: De la révolution d'octobre à la guerre de Corée, 1917–1950*. Paris: Fayard.
Forsberg, Tuomas (1999) 'Power, Interest and Trust: Explaining Gorbachev's Choices at the End of the Cold War', *Review of International Studies* 25(4): 603–21.
Forum, on Alexander Wendt (2000) *Review of International Studies* 26(1): 123–80.
Foucault, Michel (1975) *Surveiller et punir. Naissance de la prison*. Paris: Gallimard.
—— (1977) 'Corso del 14 gennaio 1976', in *Microfisica del potere. Interventi politici*, Turin: Einaudi, 179–94.
Frei, Daniel (1969) 'Vom Mass der Macht. Überlegungen zum Grundproblem der internationalen Beziehungen', *Schweizer Monatshefte* 49(7): 642–54.
—— (1985) *Feindbilder und Abrüstung: Die gegenseitige Einschätzung der UdSSR und der USA*. Munich: Beck.
Friedman, Milton (1953) 'The Methodology of Positive Economics', in his *Essays in Positive Economics*, Chicago: Chicago University Press, 3–43.
Friedrich, Carl J. (1963) *Man and Government*. New York: McGraw Hill.
Frisch, Max (1954) *Stiller*. Frankfurt am Main: Suhrkamp.
Galbraith, John Kenneth (1978 [1967]) *The New Industrial State*. 3rd edn. Boston: Houghton Mifflin.
Galtung, Johan (1971) 'A Structural Theory of Imperialism', *Journal of Peace Research* 8(1): 81–117.
Garst, Daniel (1989) 'Thucydides and Neorealism', *International Studies Quarterly* 33(1): 3–27.
Gaventa, John (1980) *Power and Powerlessness: Quiescence and Rebellion in an Appalachian Valley*. Oxford: Clarendon Press.
Geller, Daniel S. and J. David Singer (1998) *Nations at War: A Scientific Study of International Conflict*. Cambridge: Cambridge University Press.
Germain, Randall (2000) 'E. H. Carr and the Historical Mode of Thought', in Michael Cox, ed., *E. H. Carr: A Critical Appraisal*, Houndmills: Palgrave Macmillan, 322–36.
Giddens, Anthony (1979) *Central Problems in Social Theory: Action, Structure, and Contradiction in Social Analysis*. London: Macmillan.
—— (1984) *The Constitution of Society: Outline of a Theory of Structuration*. Berkeley: The University of California Press.

Gill, Stephen and David Law (1988) *The Global Political Economy*. Brighton: Harvester Wheatsheaf.
―― (1989) 'Global Hegemony and the Structural Power of Capital', *International Studies Quarterly* 33(4): 475–99.
Gilpin, Robert (1968a) 'European Disunion and the Technology Gap', *The Public Interest* 10: 43–54.
―― (1968b) *France in the Age of the Scientific State*. Princeton: Princeton University Press.
―― (1968c) 'Of Course the Gap's Not Really Technological', *The Public Interest* 12: 124–9.
―― (1971) 'The Politics of Transnational International Relations', in Robert O. Keohane and Joseph S. Nye, Jr., eds, *Transnational Relations and World Politics*, Cambridge, MA: Harvard University Press, 48–69.
―― (1975a) 'Three Models of the Future', *International Organization* 29(1): 37–60.
―― (1975b) *U.S. Power and the Multinational Corporation: The Political Economy of Foreign Direct Investment*. New York: Basic Books.
―― (1977) 'Economic Interdependence and National Security in Historical Perspective', in Klaus Knorr and Frank N. Trager, eds, *Economic Issues and National Security*, Kansas: Regents Press, 19–66.
―― (1981) *War and Change in World Politics*. New York: Cambridge University Press.
―― (1982) 'Trade, Investment, and Technology Policy', in Herbert Giersch, ed., *Emerging Technologies: Consequences for Economic Growth, Structural Change, and Employment*, Tübingen: J. C. B. Mohr.
―― (1986 [1984]) 'The Richness of the Realist Tradition', in Robert O. Keohane, ed., *Neorealism and Its Critics*, New York: Columbia University Press, 301–21.
―― (1987a) 'American Policy in the Post-Reagan Era', *Dædalus* 166(3): 33–67.
―― (1987b) *The Political Economy of International Relations*, with the assistance of Jean Gilpin. Princeton: Princeton University Press.
―― (1988a) 'Development and Underdevelopment: Conflicting Perspectives on the Third World', in Sidney Hook, William O'Neill and Roger O'Toole, eds, *Philosophy, History and Social Action: Essays in Honor of Lewis Feuer*, Dordrecht: Kluwer Academic Publishers.
―― (1988b) 'The Theory of Hegemonic War', *Journal of Interdisciplinary History* 18(4): 591–613.
―― (1990) 'The Global Political System', in J. D. B. Miller and John Vincent, eds, *Order and Violence: Hedley Bull and International Relations*, Oxford: Clarendon Press, 112–39.
―― (1991) 'The Transformation of the International Political Economy', *Jean Monnet Chair Papers*. Florence: European Policy Unit at the European University Institute.
―― (2000) *The Challenge of Global Capitalism: The World Economy in the 21st Century*, with the assistance of Jean Gilpin. Princeton, NJ: Princeton University Press.
Glaser, Charles L. (2003) 'The Necessary and Natural Evolution of Structural Realism', in John A. Vasquez and Colin Elman, eds, *Realism and the Balance of Power: A New Debate*, Upper Saddle River, NJ: Prentice Hall, 266–79.
Goldstein, Judith and Robert O. Keohane (1993) 'Ideas and Foreign Policy: An Analytical Framework', in Judith Goldstein and Robert O. Keohane, eds, *Ideas and Foreign Policy: Beliefs, Institutions, and Political Change*, Ithaca, NY: Cornell University Press, 3–30.
Gramsci, Antonio (1981) *Noterelle sulla politica del Machiavelli. Quaderno 13*. Turin: Einaudi.

Grande, Edgar and Thomas Risse, eds (2000) *Globalisierung und die Handlungsfähigkeit des Nationalstaates*. Special Issue of *Zeitschrift für Internationale Beziehungen* 7(2).

Gray, John (1983) 'Political Power, Social Theory and Essential Contestability', in David Miller and Larry Siedentop, eds, *The Nature of Political Theory*, Oxford: Clarendon Press, 75–101.

Graz, Jean-Christophe (2003) 'How Powerful are Transnational Elite Clubs? The Social Myth of the World Economic Forum', *New Political Economy* 8(3): 321–40.

Grieco, Joseph M. (1988) 'Anarchy and the Limits of Cooperation: A Realist Critique of the Newest Liberal Institutionalism', *International Organization* 42(3): 485–507.

—— (1997) 'Realist International Theory and the Study of World Politics', in Michael W. Doyle and G. John Ikenberry, eds, *New Thinking in International Relations Theory*, Boulder, CO: Westview Press, 163–201.

Griffiths, Martin (1992) *Realism, Idealism and International Politics: A Reinterpretation*. London and New York: Routledge.

Grosser, Alfred (1972) *L'explication politique. Une introduction à l'analyse comparative*. Paris: Armand Colin.

Gutting, Gary (1980) 'Introduction', in Gary Gutting, ed., *Paradigms and Revolutions: Appraisals and Applications of Thomas Kuhn's Philosophy of Science*, Notre Dame: University of Notre Dame Press, 1–21.

Guzzini, Stefano (1987) 'T. S. Kuhn and International Relations: International Political Economy and the Inter-Paradigm Debate'. MSc(Econ) thesis, London School of Economics and Political Science.

—— (1992) 'The Continuing Story of a Death Foretold: Realism in International Relations and International Political Economy', *EUI Working Papers* 92/20. Florence: European University Institute.

—— (1993) 'Structural Power: The Limits of Neorealist Power Analysis', *International Organization* 47(3): 443–78.

—— (1994) 'Power Analysis as a Critique of Power Politics: Understanding Power and Governance in the Second Gulf War'. PhD dissertation, European University Institute.

—— (1997) 'Maintenir les dilemmes de la modernité en suspens: analyse et éthique poststructuralistes en Relations Internationales', in Klaus-Gerd Giesen, ed., *L'éthique de l'espace politique mondiale: Métissages interdisciplinaires*, Brussels: Bruylant, 247–85.

—— (1998) *Realism in International Relations and International Political Economy: The Continuing Story of a Death Foretold*. London and New York: Routledge.

—— (2000a) 'A Reconstruction of Constructivism in International Relations', *European Journal of International Relations* 6(2): 147–82.

—— (2000b) 'Strange's Oscillating Realism: Opposing the Ideal – and the Apparent', in Thomas C. Lawton, James N. Rosenau and Amy C. Verdun, eds, *Strange Power: Shaping the Parameters of International Relations and International Political Economy*, Aldershot: Ashgate, 215–28.

—— (2000c) 'The Use and Misuse of Power Analysis in International Theory', in Ronen Palan, ed., *Global Political Economy: Contemporary Theories*, London and New York: Routledge, 53–66.

—— (2001a) 'Calling for a Less "Brandish" and Less "Grand" Reconvention', *Review of International Studies* 27(3): 495–501.

—— (2001b) 'The Different Worlds of Realism in International Relations', *Millennium: Journal of International Studies* 30(1): 111–21.

―――― (2001c) 'The Significance and Roles of Teaching Theory in International Relations', *Journal of International Relations and Development* 4(2): 98–117.

―――― (2002a) 'Foreign Policy without Diplomacy: The Bush Administration at a Crossroads', *International Relations* 16(2): 291–7.

―――― (2002b) *'Power' in International Relations: Concept Formation between Conceptual Analysis and Conceptual History*. Working Paper 9. Copenhagen: Copenhagen Peace Research Institute.

―――― (2004a) '"The Cold War Is What We Make of It": When Peace Research Meets Constructivism in International Relations', in Stefano Guzzini and Dietrich Jung, eds, *Contemporary Security Analysis and Copenhagen Peace Research*, London and New York: Routledge, 40–52.

―――― (2004b) 'Constructivism and International Relations: An Analysis of Niklas Luhmann's Conceptualisation of Power', in Mathias Albert and Lena Hilkermeier, eds, *Observing International Relations: Niklas Luhmann and World Politics*, London and New York: Routledge, 208–22.

―――― (2004c) 'The Enduring Dilemmas of Realism in International Relations', *European Journal of International Relations* 10(4): 533–68.

―――― (2005) 'The Concept of Power: A Constructivist Analysis', *Millennium: Journal of International Studies* 33(3): 495–522.

―――― (2006) 'From (Alleged) Unipolarity to the Decline of Multilateralism? A Power-Theoretical Critique', in Edward Newman, Ramesh Thakur and John Tirman, eds, *Multilateralism under Challenge? Power, International Order and Structural Change*, Tokyo: United Nations University Press, 119–38.

―――― (2007) *Re-Reading Weber, Or: The Three Fields for the Analysis of Power in International Relations*. DIIS Working Papers 2007/29. Copenhagen: Danish Institute for International Studies.

―――― (2009) *On the Measure of Power and the Power of Measure*. DIIS Working Papers 28/2009. Copenhagen: Danish Institute for International Studies.

Guzzini, Stefano and Anna Leander (2001) 'A Social Theory for International Relations: An Appraisal of Alexander Wendt's Disciplinary and Theoretical Synthesis', *Journal of International Relations and Development* 4(4): 316–38.

Guzzini, Stefano, Heikki Patomäki and R. B. J. Walker (1995) 'Possibilities and Limits of Republican World Politics: A Concluding Trialogue', in Heikki Patomäki, ed., *Peaceful Changes in World Politics*, Tampere: Tampere Peace Research Institute, 404–30.

Haas, Ernst B. (1953) 'The Balance of Power: Prescription, Concept or Propaganda?' *World Politics* 5(3): 442–77.

―――― (1964) *Beyond the Nation-State: Functionalism and International Organization*. Stanford: Stanford University Press.

Habermas, Jürgen (1985) *Der philosophische Diskurs der Moderne. Zwölf Vorlesungen*. Frankfurt am Main: Suhrkamp.

―――― (1985 [1981]) *Theorie des kommunikativen Handelns. Band 1: Handlungstrationalität und gesellschaftliche Rationalisierung*. 3rd rev. edn. Frankfurt am Main: Suhrkamp.

―――― (2004) *Wahrheit und Rechtfertigung. Philosophische Aufsätze*. 2nd edn. Frankfurt am Main: Suhrkamp.

Hacking, Ian (1999) *The Social Construction of What?* Cambridge, MA: Harvard University Press.

Hall, Peter A. (2003) 'Aligning Ontology and Methodology in Comparative Research', in James Mahoney and Dietrich Rueschmeyer, eds, *Comparative Historical Analysis in Social Sciences*, Cambridge: Cambridge University Press, 373–404.

Hall, Rodney Bruce (1997) 'Moral Authority as a Power Resource', *International Organization* 51(4): 591–622.
Halliday, Fred (2000) 'Reason and Romance: The Place of Revolution in the Works of E. H. Carr', in Michael Cox, ed., *E. H. Carr: A Critical Appraisal*, Houndmills: Palgrave Macmillan, 258–79.
Hasenclever, Andreas, Peter Mayer and Volker Rittberger (1997) *Theories of International Regimes*. Cambridge: Cambridge University Press.
Haslam, Jonathan (2000) 'E. H. Carr's Search for Meaning, 1892–1982', in Michael Cox, ed., *E. H. Carr: A Critical Appraisal*, Houndmills: Palgrave Macmillan, 21–35.
Haugaard, Mark (2010) 'Power: A "Family Resemblance" Concept', *European Journal of Cultural Studies* 13(4): 419–38.
Hellmann, Gunther (2000) 'Realism + Idealism – Positivism = Pragmatism: IR Theory, United Germany and Its Foreign Policy', paper presented at the 41st Annual Convention of the International Studies Association, Los Angeles, 14–17 March 2000.
Hempel, Carl G. (1965) *Aspects of Scientific Explanation and Other Essays in the Philosophy of Science*. London: The Free Press.
Herz, John H. (1950) 'Idealist Internationalism and the Security Dilemma', *World Politics* 2(2): 157–80.
Hirschman, Alfred (1991) *The Rhetoric of Reaction: Perversity, Futility, Jeopardy*. Cambridge, MA: Belknap Press of Harvard University Press.
Hoffmann, John (1988) *State, Power and Democracy: Contentious Concepts in Practical Political Theory*. Brighton: Weatsheaf Books; New York: St. Martin's Press.
Hoffmann, Stanley (1978) *Primacy or World Order: American Foreign Policy since the Cold War*. New York: McGraw Hill.
Hollis, Martin and Steve Smith (1990) *Explaining and Understanding International Relations*. Oxford: Clarendon Press.
——— (1991) 'Beware of Gurus: Structure and Action in International Relations', *Review of International Studies* 17(4): 393–410.
——— (1992) 'Structure and Action: Further Comment', *Review of International Studies* 18(2): 187–8.
Holsti, K. J. (1985) *The Dividing Discipline: Hegemony and Diversity in International Theory*. Boston: Allen & Unwin.
Honneth, Axel (1992) *Kampf um Anerkennung. Zur moralischen Grammatik sozialer Konflikte*. Frankfurt am Main: Suhrkamp.
Hopf, Ted (1998) 'The Promise of Constructivism in International Relations Theory', *International Security* 23(1): 171–200.
Hopf, Ted, Friedrich Kratochwil and Richard Ned Lebow (2001) 'Reflexivity: Method and Evidence', in *International Encyclopedia of the Social and Behavioral Sciences*, Oxford: Elsevier, 12884–8.
Huntington, Samuel P. (1993a) 'The Clash of Civilizations?' *Foreign Affairs* 72(3): 22–42.
——— (1993b) 'Why International Primacy Matters', in Sean M. Lynn-Jones and Stephen E. Miller, eds, *The Cold War and After: Prospects for Peace*, Cambridge, MA: The MIT Press, 307–22.
Huysmans, Jef (1998) 'Security! What Do You Mean? From Concept to Thick Signifier', *European Journal of International Relations* 4(2): 226–55.
——— (1999) 'Know Your Schmitt', *Review of International Studies* 25(2): 323–8.
——— (2004) 'A Foucaultian View on Spill-Over: Freedom and Security in the EU', *Journal of International Relations and Development* 7(3): 294–318.

Jackson, Patrick Thaddeus (2001) 'Constructing Thinking Space: Alexander Wendt and the Virtues of Engagement', *Cooperation and Conflict* 36(1): 109–20.
Jackson, Patrick Thaddeus and Daniel H. Nexon (1999) 'Relations before States: Substance, Process and the Study of World Politics', *European Journal of International Relations* 5(3): 291–332.
Jaeger, Hans-Martin (1996) 'Konstruktionsfehler des Konstruktivismus in den internationalen Beziehungen', *Zeitschrift für Internationale Beziehungen* 3(2): 313–40.
James, Patrick (2002) *International Relations and Scientific Progress: Structural Realism Reconsidered*. Columbus: The Ohio State University Press.
Jenkins, Keith (2000) 'An English Myth? Rethinking the Contemporary Value of E. H. Carr's *What Is History?*' in Michael Cox, ed., *E. H. Carr: A Critical Appraisal*, Houndmills: Palgrave Macmillan, 304–21.
Jepperson, Ronald L., Alexander Wendt and Peter J. Katzenstein (1996) 'Norms, Identity and Culture in National Security', in Peter J. Katzenstein, ed., *The Culture of National Security*, New York: Columbia University Press, 33–75.
Jervis, Robert (1976) *Perception and Misperception in International Politics*. Princeton: Princeton University Press.
—— (1993) 'International Primacy: Is the Game Worth the Candle?' in Sean M. Lynn-Jones and Stephen E. Miller, eds, *The Cold War and After: Prospects for Peace*, Cambridge, MA: The MIT Press, 291–306.
—— (2003) 'Realism, Neoliberalism, and Cooperation: Understanding the Debate', in Colin Elman and Miriam Fendius Elman, eds, *Progress in International Relations Theory: Appraising the Field*, Cambridge, MA: MIT Press, 277–309.
Jones, Charles (1998) *E. H. Carr and International Relations*. Cambridge: Cambridge University Press.
Joseph, Sarah (1988) *Political Theory and Power*. Leiden: E. J. Brill.
Jouvenel, Bertrand de (1972) *Du pouvoir. Histoire naturelle de sa croissance*. Paris: Hachette.
Jung, Dietrich (1998) 'Weltgesellschaft als theoretisches Konzept der Internationalen Beziehungen', *Zeitschrift für Internationale Beziehungen* 5(2): 241–71.
Jørgensen, Knud-Erik (2000) 'Continental IR Theory: The Best Kept Secret', *European Journal of International Relations* 6(1): 9–42.
Kagan, Robert (1998) 'The Benevolent Empire', *Foreign Policy* 111: 24–35.
Kahler, Miles (1998) 'Rationality in International Relations', *International Organization* 52(4): 919–41.
Kaplan, Morton A. (1957) *System and Process in International Politics*. New York: J. Wiley.
—— (1969 [1966]) 'Variants on Six Models of the International System', in James Rosenau, ed., *International Politics and Foreign Policy: A Reader in Research and Theory*, New York: Free Press, 291–303.
Katzenstein, Peter J. (1985) *Small States in World Markets: Industrial Policy in Europe*. Ithaca: Cornell University Press.
Katzenstein, Peter J., Robert O. Keohane and Stephen D. Krasner (1998) '*International Organization* and the Study of World Politics', *International Organization* 52(4): 645–85.
Keck, Otto (1995) 'Rationales kommunikatives Handeln in den internationalen Beziehungen: ist eine Verbindung von Rational Choice und Habermas' Theorie des kommunikativen Handelns möglich?' *Zeitschrift für Internationale Beziehungen* 2(1): 5–48.
—— (1997) 'Zur sozialen Konstruktion des Rational-Choice Ansatzes. Einige Klarstellungen zur Rationalismus–Konstruktivismus Debatte'. *Zeitschrift für Internationale Beziehungen* 4(1): 139–51.

Kelman, Herbert C. (1958) 'Compliance, Identification, and Internalization: Three Processes of Attitude Change', *Journal of Conflict Resolution* 2(1): 51–60.
────── (1978) 'Israelis and Palestinians: Psychological Prerequisites for Mutual Acceptance', *International Security* 3(1): 162–86.
Kennan, George F. (1958) *Russia, the Atom and the West: The BBC Reith Lectures 1957.* Oxford: Oxford University Press.
────── (1967) *Memoirs, 1925–1950.* Boston: Little, Brown.
────── (1985–6) 'Morality and Foreign Policy', *Foreign Affairs* 64(2): 205–18.
Keohane, Robert O. (1980) 'The Theory of Hegemonic Stability and Changes in International Economic Regimes, 1967–1977', in Ole R. Holsti, Randolph M. Siverson and Alexander L. George, eds, *Change in the International System*, Boulder, CO: Westview Press, 131–62.
────── (1984) *After Hegemony: Cooperation and Discord in the World Political Economy.* Princeton: Princeton University Press.
────── (1986) 'Theory of World Politics: Structural Realism and Beyond', in Robert O. Keohane, ed., *Neorealism and Its Critics*, New York: Columbia University Press, 158–203.
────── (1989) *International Institutions and State Power: Essays in International Relations Theory.* Boulder, CO: Westview Press.
────── (1989 [1988]) 'International Institutions: Two Approaches', in Robert O. Keohane, ed., *International Institutions and State Power: Essays in International Relations Theory*, Boulder, CO: Westview Press, 158–79.
Keohane, Robert O. and Joseph S. Nye, Jr. (1977) *Power and Interdependence: World Politics in Transition.* Boston: Little, Brown.
────── (1987) 'Power and Interdependence Revisited', *International Organization* 41(4): 725–53.
Kertzer, David I. (1988) *Ritual, Politics, and Power.* New Haven: Yale University Press.
Khong, Yuen Foong (1992) *Analogies at War: Korea, Munich, Dien Bien Phu, and the Vietnam Decisions of 1965.* Princeton: Princeton University Press.
Kindleberger, Charles P. (1976) 'Systems of International Economic Organization', in David P. Calleo, ed., *Money and the Coming World Order*, New York: New York University Press for the Lehrmann Institute, 15–39.
────── (1981) 'Dominance and Leadership in the International Economy: Exploitation, Public Goods and Free Riders', *International Studies Quarterly* 25(2): 242–53.
────── (1986) 'International Public Goods without International Government', *American Economic Review* 76(1): 1–12.
────── (1987 [1973]) *The World in Depression, 1929–1939.* 2nd enlarged edn. Berkeley: University of California Press.
King, Gary, Robert O. Keohane and Sidney Verba (1994) *Designing Social Inquiry: Scientific Inference in Qualitative Research.* Princeton: Princeton University Press.
Kissinger, Henry A. (1957) *A World Restored: The Politics of Conservatism in a Revolutionary Era.* London: Victor Gollancz.
────── (1969) *American Foreign Policy: Three Essays.* 3rd edn. New York: W. W. Norton.
────── (1994) *Diplomacy.* New York: Simon & Schuster.
Klein, Bradley S. (1988) 'Hegemony and Strategic Culture: American Power Projection and Alliance Defence Politics', *Review of International Studies* 14(2): 133–48.
Klotz, Audie (1995) *Norms in International Relations: The Struggle against Apartheid.* Ithaca: Cornell University Press.
Klotz, Audie and Cecilia Lynch (2007) *Strategies for Research in Constructivist International Relations.* Armonk, NY: M. E. Sharpe.

Klotz, Audie and Deepa Prakash, eds (2008) *Qualitative Methods in International Relations: A Pluralist Guide*. Houndmills: Palgrave Macmillan.

Knorr, Klaus (1973) *Power and Wealth: The Political Economy of International Power*. London: Macmillan.

Koselleck, Reinhart (1979) *Vergangene Zukunft. Zur Semantik geschichtlicher Zeiten*. Frankfurt am Main: Suhrkamp Verlag.

Koskenniemi, Martti (2000) 'Carl Schmitt, Hans Morgenthau, and the Image of Law in International Relations', in Michael Byers, ed., *The Role of Law in International Politics*, Oxford: Oxford University Press, 17–34.

Koslowski, Rey and Friedrich Kratochwil (1994) 'Understanding Change in International Politics: The Soviet Empire's Demise and the International System', *International Organization* 48(2): 215–47.

Kramer, Mark (1999) 'Ideology and the Cold War', *Review of International Studies* 25(4): 539–76.

——— (2001) 'Realism, Ideology, and the End of the Cold War', *Review of International Studies* 27(1): 119–30.

Krasner, Stephen D. (1982a) 'Regimes and the Limits of Realism: Regimes as Autonomous Variables', *International Organization* 36(2): 497–510.

——— (1982b) 'Structural Causes and Regime Consequences: Regimes as Intervening Variables', *International Organization* 36(2): 185–205.

——— (1985a) *Structural Conflict: The Third World against Global Liberalism*. Berkeley: University of California Press.

——— (1985b) 'Toward Understanding in International Relations', *International Studies Quarterly* 29(1): 137–44.

——— (2000) 'Wars, Hotel Fires, and Plane Crashes', *Review of International Studies* 26: 131–6.

Kratochwil, Friedrich (1971) 'Politik und Politische Wissenschaften. Ein Diskussionsbeitrag zum Begriff des Politischen', *Zeitschrift für Politik* 18(2): 113–23.

——— (1978) *International Order and Foreign Policy: A Theoretical Sketch of Post-War International Politics*. Boulder, CO: Westview Press.

——— (1981) 'Alternative Criteria for Evaluating Foreign Policy', *International Interactions* 8(1–2): 105–22.

——— (1984a) 'Errors Have Their Advantage', *International Organization* 38(2): 305–20.

——— (1984b) 'Thrasymmachos Revisited: On the Relevance of Norms and the Study of Law for International Relations', *Journal of International Affairs* 37(2): 343–56.

——— (1988) 'Regimes, Interpretation and the "Science" of Politics: A Reappraisal', *Millennium: Journal of International Studies* 17(2): 263–84.

——— (1989a) 'The Challenge of Security in a Changing World', *Journal of International Affairs* 42(2): 119–41.

——— (1989b) *Rules, Norms and Decisions: On the Conditions of Practical and Legal Reasoning in International Relations and Domestic Affairs*. Cambridge: Cambridge University Press.

——— (1993) 'The Embarrassment of Changes: Neo-Realism and the Science of Realpolitik without Politics', *Review of International Studies* 19(1): 63–80.

——— (1995) 'Why Sisyphus is Happy: Reflections on the "Third Debate" and on Theorizing as a Vocation', *The Sejong Review* 3(1): 3–35.

——— (1996) 'Is the Ship of Culture at Sea or Returning?' in Yosef Lapid and Friedrich Kratochwil, eds, *The Return of Identity and Culture in IR Theory*, Boulder, CO: Lynne Rienner, 201–22.

―――― (1998a) 'Politics, Norms and Peaceful Change', *Review of International Studies* 24(5) (Special Issue: The Eighty Years' Crisis 1919–1999): 193–218.

―――― (1998b) 'Vergeßt Kant! Reflexionen zur Debatte über Ethik und internationale Politik', in Christine Chwaszcza and Wolfgang Kersting, eds, *Politische Philosophie der internationalen Beziehungen*, Frankfurt am Main: Suhrkamp, 96–149.

―――― (2000a) 'Constructing a New Orthodoxy? Wendt's 'Social Theory of International Politics' and the Constructivist Challenge', *Millennium: Journal of International Studies* 29(1): 73–101.

―――― (2000b) 'Theory and Political Practice: Reflections on Theory Building in International Relations', in Paul Wapner and Lester Edwin J. Ruiz, eds, *Principled World Politics: The Challenge of Normative International Relations*, Lanham, MD: Rowman & Littlefield, 50–64.

―――― (2005) 'Religion and (Inter-)National Politics: On the Heuristics of Identities, Structures and Agents', *Alternatives* 30(2): 113–40.

―――― (2006) 'History, Action and Identity: Revisiting The "Second" Great Debate and Assessing the Importance for Social Theory', *European Journal of International Relations* 12(1): 5–29.

―――― (2007a) 'Evidence, Inference, and Truth as Problems of Theory Building in the Social Sciences', in Richard Ned Lebow and Mark Irving Lichbach, eds, *Theory and Evidence in Comparative Politics and International Relations*, New York: Palgrave Macmillan, 25–54.

―――― (2007b) 'Of Communities, Gangs, Historicity and the Problem of Santa Claus: Replies to My Critics', *Journal of International Relations and Development* 10(1): 57–78.

―――― (2007c) 'Of False Premises and Good Bets: A Plea for a Pragmatic Approach to Theory Building (the Tartu Lecture)', *Journal of International Relations and Development* 10(1): 1–15.

―――― (2008) 'Constructivism: What It Is (Not) and How It Matters', in Donatella della Porta and Michael Keating, eds, *Approaches and Methodologies in the Social Sciences*, Cambridge: Cambridge University Press, 80–98.

Kratochwil, Friedrich and Yosef Lapid, eds (1996) *The Return of Culture and Identity in IR Theory*. Boulder, CO: Lynne Rienner.

Kratochwil, Friedrich and John Gerard Ruggie (1986) 'International Organization: A State of the Art on an Art of the State', *International Organization* 40(4): 753–75.

Krause, Keith (1991) 'Military Statecraft: Power and Influence in Soviet and American Arms Transfer Relationships', *International Studies Quarterly* 35(3): 313–36.

Krauthammer, Charles (1991) 'The Unipolar Moment', *Foreign Affairs* 70(1): 23–33.

―――― (2002–3) 'The Unipolar Moment Revisited', *The National Interest* (70): 5–17.

Krippendorff, Ekkehart (1975) *Internationales System als Geschichte*. Frankfurt am Main: Campus.

―――― (1977) *Internationale Beziehungen als Wissenschaft. Einführung 2*. Frankfurt am Main: Campus Verlag.

―――― (1985) *Staat und Krieg. Die historische Logik politischer Unvernunft*. Frankfurt am Main: Suhrkamp.

Kuhn, Thomas (1970) 'Reflections on My Critics', in Imre Lakatos and Alan Musgrave, eds, *Criticism and the Growth of Knowledge*, Cambridge: Cambridge University Press, 231–78.

―――― (1970 [1962]) *The Structure of Scientific Revolutions*. 2nd edn. Chicago: University of Chicago Press.

Kupchan, Charles A. (2002) *The End of the American Era: U.S. Foreign Policy and the Geopolitics of the Twenty-First Century*. New York: Alfred A. Knopf.

Kymlicka, Will (1995) *Multicultural Citizenship: A Liberal Theory of Minority Rights*. Oxford: Clarendon Press.

Lakatos, Imre (1970) 'Falsification and the Methodology of Scientific Research Programmes', in Imre Lakatos and Alan Musgrave, eds, *Criticism and the Growth of Knowledge*, Cambridge: Cambridge University Press, 91–196.

Lakoff, George (1991) 'Metaphor and War: The Metaphor System Used to Justify War in the Gulf', *Peace Research* 23(2–3): 25–32.

Lall, Sanjaya (1975) 'Is "Dependence" a Useful Concept in Analysing Underdevelopment?' *World Development* 3(6): 79–810.

Lapid, Yosef (1989) 'The Third Debate: On the Prospects of International Theory in a Post-Positivist Era', *International Studies Quarterly* 33(3): 235–54.

Leander, Anna (2000a) 'A "Nebbish Presence": The Neglect of Sociological Institutionalism in International Political Economy', in Ronen Palan, ed., *Global Political Economy: Contemporary Theories*, London and New York: Routledge, 184–96.

——— (2000b) 'Strange Looks on Developing Countries: A Neglected Kaleidoscope of Questions', in Thomas C. Lawton, James N. Rosenau and Amy C. Verdun, eds, *Strange Power: Shaping the Parameters of International Relations and International Political Economy*, Aldershot: Ashgate, 343–65.

——— (2001a) 'Dependency Today: Finance, Firms, Mafias and the State', *Third World Quarterly* 22(1): 115–28.

——— (2001b) 'The Globalisation Debate: Dead-Ends and Tensions to Explore (Review Essay)', *Journal of International Relations and Development* 4(3): 274–85.

——— (2001c) 'Pierre Bourdieu on Economics', *Review of International Political Economy* 8(2): 344–53.

——— (2005a) 'The Market for Force and Public Security: The Destabilizing Consequences of Private Military Companies', *Journal of Peace Research* 42(5): 605–22.

——— (2005b) 'The Power to Construct International Security: On the Significance of Private Military Companies', *Millennium: Journal of International Studies* 33(3): 803–26.

——— (2006a) *Eroding State Authority? Private Military Companies and the Legitimate Use of Force*. Rome: Rubbettino/CeMiSS.

——— (2006b) 'Shifting Political Identities and Global Governance of the Justified Use of Force', in Markus Lederer and Philipp S. Müller, eds, *Criticizing Global Governance*, Houndmills: Palgrave Macmillan, 125–43.

——— (2010) 'The Paradoxical Impunity of Private Military Companies: Authority and the Limits to Legal Accountability', *Security Dialogue* 41(5): 467–90.

——— (2011a) '*Habitus* and Field', in Robert Denemark, ed., *International Studies Compendium Project*, Oxford: Wiley–Blackwell, 3255–70.

——— (2011b) 'Risk and the Fabrication of Apolitical, Unaccountable Military Markets: The Case of the CIA "Killing Program"', *Review of International Studies* 37(5): 1–16.

Lebow, Richard Ned (1999) 'The Rise and Fall of the Cold War', *Review of International Studies* 25(Special Issue): 21–39.

Lebow, Richard Ned and Mark Irving Lichbach, eds (2007) *Theory and Evidence in Comparative Politics and International Relations*. Houndmills: Palgrave Macmillan.

Lebow, Richard Ned and Thomas Risse-Kappen, eds (1995) *International Relations Theory and the End of the Cold War*. New York: Columbia University Press.

Lebow, Richard Ned and Janice Gross Stein (1994) *We All Lost the Cold War*. Princeton: Princeton University Press.

Legro, Jeffrey W. and Andrew Moravcsik (1999) 'Is Anybody Still a Realist?' *International Security* 24(2): 5–55.
Linklater, Andrew (2000) 'E. H. Carr, Nationalism and the Future of the Sovereign State', in Michael Cox, ed., *E. H. Carr: A Critical Appraisal*, Houndmills: Palgrave Macmillan, 234–57.
Little, Richard (1988) 'Belief Systems in the Social Sciences', in Richard Little and Steve Smith, eds, *Belief Systems and International Relations*, Oxford: Basil Blackwell, 37–56.
—— (1989) 'Deconstructing the Balance of Power: Two Traditions of Thought', *Review of International Studies* 15(2): 87–100.
—— (1991) 'International Relations and the Methodological Turn', *Political Studies* 39(3): 463–78.
Lucarelli, Sonia and Roberto Menotti (2002) 'No-Constructivists' Land: International Relations in Italy in the 1990s', *Journal of International Relations and Development* 5(2): 114–42.
Luhmann, Niklas (1975) *Macht*. Stuttgart: Ferdinand Enke Verlag.
—— (1988 [1975]) *Macht*. 2nd edn. Stuttgart: Ferdinand Enke Verlag.
—— (1990) *Die Wissenschaft der Gesellschaft*. Frankfurt am Main: Suhrkamp.
—— (1990 [1981]) *Political Theory in the Welfare State*. Berlin: de Gruyter.
—— (1997) *Die Gesellschaft der Gesellschaft*. 2 vols. Frankfurt am Main: Suhrkamp.
—— (2000) *Die Politik der Gesellschaft*. Frankfurt am Main: Suhrkamp.
Luke, Timothy W. (1991) 'The Discipline of Security Studies and the Codes of Containment: Learning from Kuwait', *Alternatives* 16: 315–44.
Lukes, Steven (1974) *Power: A Radical View*. London: Macmillan.
—— (1977) 'Power and Structure', in his *Essays in Social Theory*, New York: Columbia University Press, 3–29.
—— (1979) 'Power and Authority', in T. Bottomore and R. Nisbet, eds, *History of Sociological Analysis*, London: Heinemann, 633–76.
—— (2005) *Power: A Radical View*. 2nd edn. London: Palgrave.
Lynn-Jones, Sean M., ed. (1991) *The Cold War and After: Prospects for Peace*. Cambridge, MA: The MIT Press.
MccGwire, Michael (1991) *Perestroika and Soviet National Security*. Washington, DC: The Brookings Institution.
Mackinder, Halford John (1944 [1919]) *Democratic Ideals and Reality: A Study in the Politics of Reconstitution*. Harmondsworth: Penguin.
McSweeney, Bill (1999) *Security, Identity and Interests: A Sociology of International Relations*. Cambridge: Cambridge University Press.
Madsen, Mikael Rask (2006) 'Transnational Fields: Elements of a Reflexive Sociology of the Internationalisation of Law', *Retfærd* 3(114): 34–41.
Malone, David M. and Yuen Foong Khong, eds (2003) *Unilateralism and US Foreign Policy: International Perspectives*. Boulder, CO: Lynne Rienner.
Mann, Michael (1986) *The Sources of Social Power, Vol. I: A History of Power from the Beginning to AD 1760*. Cambridge: Cambridge University Press.
—— (2003) *Incoherent Empire*. London: Verso.
Mannheim, Karl (1936) *Ideology and Utopia*. New York: Harvest Books.
Martin, Roderick (1977) *The Sociology of Power*. London: Routledge & Kegan Paul.
Mastanduno, Michael (1997) 'Preserving the Unipolar Moment: Realist Theories and US Grand Strategy after the Cold War', *International Security* 21(4): 49–88.
Mearsheimer, John (1990) 'Back to the Future: Instability in Europe after the Cold War', *International Security* 15(1): 5–56.

—— (2001) *The Tragedy of Great Power Politics*. New York: W. W. Norton.
Mearsheimer, John J. and Stephen M. Walt (2003) 'An Unnecessary War', *Foreign Policy* 134: 50–9.
Merlingen, Michael (1999) 'Die Relativität von Wahrheit dargestellt am Beispiel der Wirtschafts- und Währungsunion', *Zeitschrift für Internationale Beziehungen* 6(1): 93–128.
Merrit, Richard L. and Dina A. Zinnes (1989) 'Alternative Indexes of National Power', in Richard J. Stoll and Michael D. Ward, eds, *Power in World Politics*, Boulder, CO: Lynne Rienner, 11–28.
Meyers, Reinhard (1994) 'Virtuelle Scheingefechte im ontologischen Cyberspace? Nachfragen zum Duktus und zum Gehalt einer Theoriedebatte', *Zeitschrift für Internationale Beziehungen* 1(1): 127–37.
Miller, Peter (1987) *Domination and Power*. London: Routledge & Kegan Paul.
Milliken, Jennifer (1999) 'The Study of Discourse in International Relations: A Critique of Research and Methods', *European Journal of International Relations* 5(2): 225–54.
Moravcsik, Andrew (1996) 'Federalism and Peace: A Structural Liberal Perspective', *Zeitschrift für Internationale Beziehungen* 3(1): 123–32.
Morgenthau, Hans J. (1933) *La notion du 'politique' et la théorie des différends internationaux*. Paris: Sirey.
—— (1935) 'Théorie des sanctions internationales', *Revue de Droit International et de Législation Comparée* 36(3–4): 474–503.
—— (1936) 'Positivisme mal compris et théorie réaliste du Droit International', in Silvio A. Zavala, ed., *Colección de estudios históricos, jurídicos, pedagógicos y literarios*, Madrid: C. Bermejo, 446–65.
—— (1946) *Scientific Man vs. Power Politics*. Chicago: The University of Chicago Press.
—— (1948) *Politics among Nations: The Struggle for Power and Peace*. New York: Knopf.
—— (1962 [1958]) *Politics in the Twentieth Century. Volume II: The Impasse of American Foreign Policy*. Chicago: The University of Chicago Press.
—— (1965) *Vietnam and the United States*. Washington, DC: Public Affairs Press.
—— (1970 [1964]) 'The Intellectual and Political Functions of Theory', in *Truth and Power: Essays of a Decade 1960–1970*, London: Pall Mall Press, 248–61.
—— (1970 [1967]) 'Common Sense and Theories', in *Truth and Power: Essays of a Decade 1960–1970*, London: Pall Mall Press, 241–8.
Morriss, Peter (1987) *Power: A Philosophical Analysis*. Manchester: Manchester University Press.
—— (2002 [1987]) *Power: A Philosophical Analysis*. 2nd edn. Manchester: Manchester University Press.
Mouritzen, Hans (1997) 'Kenneth Waltz: A Critical Rationalist between International Politics and Foreign Policy', in Iver B. Neumann and Ole Wæver, eds, *The Future of International Relations: Masters in the Making?* London and New York: Routledge, 66–89.
Müller, Harald (1994) 'Internationale Beziehungen als kommunikatives Handeln. Zur Kritik der utilitaristischen Handlungstheorien', *Zeitschrift für Internationale Beziehungen* 1(1): 15–44.
—— (1995) 'Spielen hilft nicht immer. Die Grenzen des Rational-Choice-Ansatzes und der Platz der Theorie kommunikativen Handelns in der Analyse internationaler Beziehungen', *Zeitschrift für Internationale Beziehungen* 2(2): 379–99.
Nagel, Jack H. (1975) *The Descriptive Analysis of Power*. New Haven: Yale University Press.

Neufeld, Mark (1993) 'Reflexivity and International Theory', *Millennium: Journal of International Studies* 22(1): 53–76.
Neumann, Iver B. (1995) *Russia and the Idea of Europe: A Study in Identity and International Relations*. London and New York: Routledge.
―――― (1999) *Uses of the Other: The 'East' in European Identity Formation*. Minneapolis: University of Minnesota Press.
―――― (2001) *Mening, Materialitet, Makt: En innføring i diskursanalyse*. Bergen: Fakbogforlaget.
Neumann, Iver B. and Ole Wæver, eds (1997) *The Future of International Relations: Masters in the Making?* London and New York: Routledge.
Nicklas, Hans and Klaus-Jürgen Gantzel (1975) 'Außenpolitische Freund-Feindbilder in Der Bundesrepublik 1949–1971', in Vorstand der DGFK, ed., *Forschung für den Frieden. Fünf Jahre Deutsche Gesellschaft für Friedens- und Konfliktforschung. Eine Zwischenbilanz*, Boppard am Rhein: Harald Boldt, 231–44.
Nye, Joseph S., Jr. (1988) 'Neorealism and Neoliberalism', *World Politics* 40(2): 235–51.
―――― (1990a) *Bound to Lead: The Changing Nature of American Power*. New York: Basic Books.
―――― (1990b) 'Soft Power', *Foreign Policy* (80): 153–71.
―――― (2004) *Soft Power: The Means to Success in World Politics*. New York: Public Affairs.
Onuf, Nicholas Greenwood (1989) *World of Our Making: Rules and Rule in Social Theory and International Relations*. Columbia, SC: University of South Carolina Press.
Oppenheim, Felix E. (1981) *Political Concepts: A Reconstruction*. Oxford: Basil Blackwell.
Palan, Ronen (2000) 'A World of Their Making: An Evaluation of the Constructivist Critique in International Relations', *Review of International Studies* 26(4): 575–98.
Palan, Ronen P. and Brook M. Blair (1993) 'On the Idealist Origins of the Realist Theory of International Relations', *Review of International Studies* 19(4): 385–99.
Patman, Robert (1999) 'Reagan, Gorbachev and the Emergence of "New Political Thinking"', *Review of International Studies* 25(4): 577–601.
Patomäki, Heikki (1991) 'Concepts of "Action", "Structure", and "Power" in "Critical Social Realism": A Positive and Reconstructive Critique', *Journal for the Theory of Social Behaviour* 21(2): 221–50.
―――― (1992) 'What Is It that Changed with the End of the Cold War? An Analysis of the Problem of Identifying and Explaining Change', in Pierre Allan and Kjell Goldmann, eds, *The End of the Cold War: Evaluating Theories of International Relations*, Dordrecht: Martinus Nijhoff, 179–225.
―――― (1996) 'How to Tell Better Stories about World Politics', *European Journal of International Relations* 2(1): 105–33.
―――― (2001a) 'The Challenge of Critical Theories: Peace Research at the Start of the New Century', *Journal of Peace Research* 38(6): 723–37.
―――― (2001b) *Democratising Globalization: The Leverage of the Tobin Tax*. London: Zed Books.
―――― (2002) *After International Relations: Critical Realism and the (Re)Construction of World Politics*. London and New York: Routledge.
―――― (2008) *The Political Economy of Global Security: War, Future Crises and Changes in Global Governance*. London and New York: Routledge.
Patomäki, Heikki and Ole Wæver (1995) 'Introducing Peaceful Changes', in Heikki Patomäki, ed., *Peaceful Changes in World Politics*, Tampere: Tampere Peace Research Institute, Research Report No. 71, 3–27.

Patomäki, Heikki and Colin Wight (2000) 'After Postpositivism? The Promises of Critical Realism', *International Studies Quarterly* 44(2): 213–37.

Petrova, Margarita H. (2003) 'The End of the Cold War: A Battle or Bridging Ground between Rationalist and Ideational Approaches to International Relations?' *European Journal of International Relations* 9(1): 115–63.

Pizzorno, Alessandro (1994 [1993]) *Le radici della politica assoluta e altri saggi*. Milan: Feltrinelli.

Polsby, Nelson W. (1980) *Community, Power and Political Theory*. Rev. edn. New Haven: Yale University Press.

Portinaro, Pier Paolo (1999) *Il realismo politico*. Rome and Bari: Editori Laterza.

Powell, Robert (1994) 'Anarchy in International Relations: The Neorealist–Neoliberal Debate', *International Organization* 48(2): 313–44.

Prozorov, Sergei V. (2004) 'Three Theses on "Governance" and the Political', *Journal of International Relations and Development* 7(3): 267–93.

Ragin, Charles C. (1987) *The Comparative Method: Moving beyond Qualitative and Quantitative Strategies*. Berkeley: University of California Press.

—— (2000) *Fuzzy-Set Social Science*. Chicago: The University of Chicago Press.

Rawls, John (1985) 'Justice as Fairness: Political Not Metaphysical', *Philosophy and Public Affairs* 14(3): 223–51.

—— (1987) 'The Idea of an Overlapping Consensus', *Oxford Journal of Legal Studies* 7(1): 1–25.

Reus-Smit, Christian (1997) 'The Constitutional Structure of International Society and the Nature of Fundamental Institutions', *International Organization* 51(4): 555–89.

—— (2004) *American Power and World Order*. Cambridge: Polity Press.

Rich, Paul (2000) 'E. H. Carr and the Quest for Moral Revolution in International Relations', in Michael Cox, ed., *E. H. Carr: A Critical Appraisal*, Houndmills: Palgrave Macmillan, 198–216.

Richter, Rudolf (1994) 'Methodology from the Viewpoint of the Economic Theorist – Thirty Years On', *Journal of International and Theoretical Economics* 150(4): 589–608.

Riker, William H. (1964) 'Some Ambiguities in the Notion of Power', *American Political Science Review* 58(2): 341–9.

Ringmar, Erik (1997) 'Alexander Wendt: A Social Scientist Struggling with History', in Iver B. Neumann and Ole Wæver, eds, *The Future of International Relations: Masters in the Making?*, London and New York: Routledge, 269–89.

Risse, Thomas (2000) '"Let's Argue!" Communicative Action in World Politics', *International Organization* 54(1): 1–39.

Risse-Kappen, Thomas (1994a) 'Ideas Do Not Float Freely: Transnational Coalitions, Domestic Structures, and the End of the Cold War', *International Organization* 48(2): 185–214.

—— (1994b) 'Wie weiter mit dem "Demokratischen Frieden"?' *Zeitschrift für Internationale Beziehungen* 1(2): 367–79.

—— (1995) 'Reden ist nicht billig. Zur Debatte um Kommunikation und Rationalität', *Zeitschrift für Internationale Beziehungen* 2(1): 171–84.

Rittberger, Volker and Hartwig Hummel (1990) 'Die Disziplin "Internationale Beziehungen" im deutschsprachigen Raum auf der Suche nach ihrer Identität: Entwicklung und Perspektiven', in Volker Rittberger, ed., *Theorien der internationalen Beziehungen. Bestandsaufnahme und Forschungsperspektiven*, Opladen: Westdeutscher Verlag, 17–47.

Rosenau, James (1980 [1976]) 'Capabilities and Control in an Interdependent World', in James Rosenau, ed., *The Study of Global Interdependence: Essays on the Transnationalisation of World Affairs*, London: Frances Pinter, 35–52.
Rueschemeyer, Dietrich (1991) 'Different Methods – Contradictory Results? Research on Development and Democracy', *International Journal of Comparative Sociology* 32(1–2): 9–38.
Ruggie, John Gerard (1982) 'International Regimes, Transactions, and Change: Embedded Liberalism in the Postwar Economic Order', *International Organization* 36(2): 379–415.
—— (1986 [1983]) 'Continuity and Transformation in the World Polity: Toward a Neorealist Synthesis', in Robert O. Keohane, ed., *Neorealism and Its Critics*, New York: Columbia University Press, 131–57.
—— (1991) 'Embedded Liberalism Revisited: Institutions and Progress in International Economic Relations', in Emanuel Adler and Beverly Crawford, eds, *Progress in Postwar International Relations*, New York: Cambridge University Press, 202–34.
—— (1992) 'Multilateralism: The Anatomy of an Institution', *International Organization* 46(3): 561–98.
—— (1993) 'Territoriality and Beyond: Problematizing Modernity in International Relations', *International Organization* 47(1): 139–74.
—— (1998) *Constructing the World Polity: Essays on International Institutionalization*. London and New York: Routledge.
—— (2005) 'American Exceptionalism, Exemptionalism and Global Governance', in Michael Ignatieff, ed., *American Exceptionalism and Human Rights*, Princeton: Princeton University Press, 304–38.
Runyan, Anne Sisson and V. Spike Peterson (1991) 'The Radical Future of Realism: Feminist Subversions of IR Theory', *Alternatives* 16(1): 67–106.
Rupert, Mark (1995) *Producing Hegemony: The Politics of Mass Production and American Global Power*. Cambridge: Cambridge University Press.
Russell, Bertrand (1960 [1938]) *Power*. London: Unwin Books.
Said, Edward (1979) *Orientalism*. New York: Vintage Books.
Sartori, Giovanni (1970) 'Concept Misformation in Comparative Politics', *American Political Science Review* 64(4): 1033–53.
Sárváry, Katalin (1998) 'István Bibó (1943–1944): On the Equilibrium and Peace of Europe', paper presented at the 3rd Pan-European conference of the SGIR–ISA, Vienna, 16–19 September.
—— (2001) 'Devaluing Diplomacy? A Critique of Alexander Wendt's Conception of Progress and Politics', *Journal of International Relations and Development* 4(4): 380–402.
—— (2006) 'No Place for Politics? Truth, Progress and the Neglected Role of Diplomacy in Wendt's Theory of History', in Stefano Guzzini and Anna Leander, eds, *Constructivism and International Relations: Alexander Wendt and His Critics*, London and New York: Routledge, 160–80.
—— (2008) 'Democracy and International Relations: The Theory of István Bibó (1911–1979)', *Journal of International Relations and Development* 11(4): 385–414.
Schimmelfennig, Frank (1997) 'Rhetorisches Handeln in der internationalen Politik', *Zeitschrift für Internationale Beziehungen* 4(2): 219–54.
—— (2001) 'The Community Trap: Liberal Norms, Rhetorical Action, and the Eastern Enlargement of the European Union', *International Organization* 55(1): 47–80.
Schlichte, Klaus (1998) 'La Françafrique – postkolonialer Habitus und Klientelismus in der Französischen Afrikapolitik', *Zeitschrift für Internationale Beziehungen* 5(2): 309–43.

Schmalz-Bruns, Rainer (1995) 'Die Theorie des kommunikativen Handelns – eine Flaschenpost? Anmerkungen zur jüngsten Theoriedebatte in den internationalen Beziehungen', *Zeitschrift für Internationale Beziehungen* 2(2): 347–70.

—— (1999) 'Deliberativer Supranationalismus. Demokratisches Regieren jenseits des Nationalstaats', *Zeitschrift für Internationale Beziehungen* 6(2): 185–244.

Schmidt, Brian C. (1998) *The Political Discourse of Anarchy: A Disciplinary History of International Relations*. Albany: State University of New York Press.

—— (2002) 'On the History and Historiography of International Relations', in Walter Carlsnaes, Thomas Risse and Beth A. Simmons, eds, *Handbook of International Relations*, London: Sage, 3–22.

Schmidt, Hajo (1996) 'Kant und die Theorie der internationalen Beziehungen. Vom Nutzen und den Problemen einer aktualisierten Kantlektüre – Ein Kommentar zu E.-O. Czempiel', *Zeitschrift für Internationale Beziehungen* 3(1): 103–16.

Schneider, Gerald (1994) 'Rational Choice und kommunikatives Handeln. Eine Replik auf Harald Müller', *Zeitschrift für Internationale Beziehungen* 1(2): 357–66.

Schutz, Alfred (1962) *The Problem of Social Reality: Collected Papers 1*. The Hague: Martinus Nijhoff.

—— (1962 [1953]) 'On the Methodology of the Social Sciences', in his *The Problem of Social Reality*, The Hague: Martinus Nijhoff, 3–47.

Schweller, Randall L. (1997) 'New Realist Research on Alliances: Refining, Not Refuting, Waltz's Balancing Position', *American Political Science Review* 91(4): 927–30.

—— (2003) 'The Progressiveness of Neoclassical Realism', in Colin Elman and Miriam Fendius Elman, eds, *Progress in International Relations Theory: Appraising the Field*, Cambridge, MA: MIT Press, 311–47.

Schweller, Randall L. and William C. Wohlforth (2000) 'Power Test: Evaluating Realism in Response to the End of the Cold War', *Security Studies* 9(3): 60–107.

Searle, John R. (1995) *The Construction of Social Reality*. New York: The Free Press.

Sellin, Volker (1978) 'Politik', in Otto Brunner, Werner Conze and Reinhart Koselleck, eds, *Geschichtliche Grundbegriffe. Historisches Lexikon zur Politisch–Sozialen Sprache in Deutschland. Band 4*, Stuttgart: Klett–Cotta, 789–874.

Senghaas, Dieter (1972) *Rüstung und Militarismus*. Frankfurt am Main: Suhrkamp.

—— (1987) *Konfliktformationen im internationalen System*. Frankfurt am Main: Suhrkamp.

—— (1992) *Friedensprojekt Europa*. Frankfurt am Main: Suhrkamp.

Simmel, Georg (1908) *Soziologie. Untersuchungen über die Formen der Vergesellschaftung*. Berlin: Duncker & Humblot.

Skinner, Quentin (1989) 'Language and Political Change', in Terence Ball, James Farr and Russell L. Hanson, eds, *Political Innovation and Conceptual Change*, Cambridge: Cambridge University Press, 6–23.

—— (2002) *Visions of Politics, Vol. I: Regarding Method*. Cambridge: Cambridge University Press.

Sklar, Richard L. (1983) 'On the Concept of Power in Political Economy', in Dalmas H. Nelson and Richard L. Sklar, eds, *Towards a Humanistic Science of Politics: Essays in Honor of F. Dunham Wortmuth*, Lanham, MD: University Press of America, 179–206.

Skocpol, Theda, ed. (1984) *Visions and Method in Historical Sociology*. Cambridge, MA: Cambridge University Press.

—— (1987 [1979]) *States and Social Revolutions: A Comparative Analysis of France, Russia, and China*. Cambridge, MA: Cambridge University Press.

Smith, Steve (1995) 'The Self-Images of a Discipline', in Ken Booth and Steve Smith, eds, *International Relations Theory Today*, Oxford: Polity Press, 1–37.

—— (2000) 'Wendt's World', *Review of International Studies* 26: 151–63.
Snidal, Duncan (1985) 'The Limits of Hegemonic Stability Theory', *International Organization* 39(4): 579–614.
Sparti, Davide (1992) *Se un leone potesse parlare. Indagine sul comprendere e lo spiegare*. Florence: Sansoni.
—— (1996) *Soggetti al tempo. Identità personale tra analisi filosofica e costruzione sociale*. Milan: Feltrinelli.
Spegele, Roger D. (1996) *Political Realism in International Theory*. Cambridge: Cambridge University Press.
Staniland, Martin (1985) *What Is Political Economy?* New Haven: Yale University Press.
Steinbruner, John D., Jr. (1974) *The Cybernetic Theory of Decision: New Dimensions of Political Analysis*. Princeton, NJ: Princeton University Press.
Stephanson, Anders (2000) 'The Lessons of *What Is History?*' in Michael Cox, ed., *E. H. Carr: A Critical Appraisal*, Houndmills: Palgrave, 283–303.
Sterling-Folker, Jennifer (1997) 'Realist Environment, Liberal Process, and Domestic-Level Variables', *International Studies Quarterly* 41(1): 1–25.
—— (2002) 'Realism and the Constructivist Challenge: Rejecting, Reconstructing, or Rereading', *International Studies Review* 4(1): 73–97.
Stopford, John and Susan Strange with John S. Henley (1991) *Rival States, Rival Firms: Competition for World Market Shares*. Cambridge: Cambridge University Press.
Strange, Susan (1971) *Sterling and British Policy*. London: Oxford University Press.
—— (1975) 'What Is Economic Power and Who Has It?' *International Journal* 30(2): 207–24.
—— (1976) 'International Monetary Relations', in Andrew Shonfield, ed., *International Economic Relations of the Western World, 1959–1971, Vol. 2*, Oxford: Oxford University Press.
—— (1982) '*Cave! Hic Dragones*: A Critique of Regime Analysis', *International Organization* 36(2): 479–96.
—— (1984) 'What about International Relations?' in Susan Strange, ed., *Paths to International Political Economy*, London: Frances Pinter, 183–98.
—— (1985) 'International Political Economy: The Story So Far and the Way Ahead', in W. Ladd Hollist and F. Lamond Tullis, eds, *The International Political Economy*, Boulder, CO: Westview Press, 13–25.
—— (1986) *Casino Capitalism*. London: Basil Blackwell.
—— (1987) 'The Persistent Myth of Lost Hegemony', *International Organization* 41(4): 551–74.
—— (1988) *States and Markets: An Introduction to International Political Economy*. New York: Basil Blackwell.
—— (1989) 'Toward a Theory of Transnational Empire', in Ernst-Otto Czempiel and James Rosenau, eds, *Global Changes and Theoretical Challenges: Approaches to World Politics for the 1990s*, Lexington, MA: D. C. Heath, 161–76.
—— (1990) 'The Name of the Game', in N. Rizopoulos, ed., *Sea-Changes: American Foreign Policy in a World Transformed*, New York: Council on Foreign Relations Press, 238–74.
—— (1996) *The Retreat of the State: The Diffusion of Power in the World Economy*. Cambridge: Cambridge University Press.
—— (1998) *Mad Money*. Manchester: Manchester University Press.
Suganami, Hidemi (1996) *On the Causes of War*. Oxford: Clarendon Press.

—— (2001) 'Alexander Wendt and the English School', *Journal of International Relations and Development* 4(4): 403–23.
Suskind, Ron (2004) 'Without a Doubt', *New York Times Magazine*, 17 October.
Taylor, Charles (1992) *Multiculturalism and the Politics of Recognition*. Princeton: Princeton University Press.
Taylor, Philip M. (1992) *War and the Media: Propaganda and Persuasion in the Gulf War.* Manchester: Manchester University Press.
Thies, Cameron (2002) 'Progress, History and Identity in International Relations Theory: The Case of the Idealist–Realist Debate', *European Journal of International Relations* 8(2): 147–85.
Tilly, Charles (1995) 'To Explain Political Processes', *American Journal of Sociology* 100(6): 1594–610.
Tucker, Robert W. (1952) 'Professor Morgenthau's Theory of "Realism"', *American Political Science Review* 46: 214–24.
—— (2001) 'The International Criminal Court Controversy', *World Policy Journal* 18(2): 71–81.
Tully, James (1988) 'The Pen Is a Mighty Sword: Quentin Skinner's Analysis of Politics', in James Tully, ed., *Meaning and Context: Quentin Skinner and His Critics*, Cambridge: Polity Press, 7–25.
Vasquez, John A. (1983) *The Power of Power Politics: A Critique*. London: Frances Pinter.
—— (1987) 'The Steps to War: Toward a Scientific Explanation of Correlates of War Findings', *World Politics* 40(1): 108–45.
—— (1997) 'The Realist Paradigm and Degenerative Versus Progressive Research Programs: An Appraisal of Neotraditional Research on Waltz's Balancing Proposition', *American Political Science Review* 91(4): 899–912.
—— (1998) *The Power of Power Politics: From Classical Realism to Neotraditionalism*. Cambridge: Cambridge University Press.
Vauchez, Antoine (2011) 'Interstitial Power in Fields of Limited Statehood: Introducing a "Weak Field" Approach to the Study of Transnational Settings', *International Political Sociology* 5(3): 340–5.
Vertzberger, Yaakov (1986) 'Foreign Policy-Makers as Practical Intuitive Historians: Applied History and Its Shortcomings', *International Studies Quarterly* 30(2): 223–47.
Wæver, Ole (1989a) *Beyond the "Beyond" of Critical International Theory*. COPRI Working Papers 1/1989. Copenhagen: Copenhagen Peace Research Institute.
—— (1989b) *Tradition and Transgression in International Relations: A Post–Ashleyan Position*. Working Paper 24/1989. Copenhagen: Copenhagen Peace Research Institute.
—— (1995) 'Securitization and Desecuritization', in Ronnie Lipschutz, ed., *On Security*, New York: Columbia University Press, 46–86.
—— (1996) 'The Rise and Fall of the Inter-Paradigm Debate', in Steve Smith, Ken Booth and Marysia Zalewski, eds, *International Theory: Positivism and Beyond*, Cambridge: Cambridge University Press, 149–84.
—— (1997a) 'Figures of International Thought: Introducing Persons Instead of Paradigms', in Iver B. Neumann and Ole Wæver, eds, *The Future of International Relations: Masters in the Making?*, London and New York: Routledge, 1–37.
—— (1997b) 'John G. Ruggie: Transformation and Institutionalization', in Iver B. Neumann and Ole Wæver, eds, *The Future of International Relations: Masters in the Making?* London and New York: Routledge, 170–204.
—— (1998) 'The Sociology of a Not So International Discipline: American and European Developments in International Relations', *International Organization* 52(4): 687–728.

Walker, R. B. J. (1980) *Political Theory and the Transformation of World Politics.* Occasional papers No. 8.
——— (1987) 'Realism, Change and International Political Theory', *International Studies Quarterly* 31(1): 65–86.
——— (1988–9) *Ethics, Modernity and the Theory of International Relations,* unpublished manuscript presented at the Centre for International Studies, Princeton University.
——— (1989) 'History and Structure in the Theory of International Relations', *Millennium: Journal of International Studies* 18(2): 163–83.
——— (1990) 'Security, Sovereignty, and the Challenge of World Politics', *Alternatives* 15(1): 3–27.
——— (1991) 'State Sovereignty and the Articulation of Political Space/Time', *Millennium: Journal of International Studies* 20(3): 445–61.
——— (1993a) *Inside/Outside: International Relations as Political Theory.* Cambridge: Cambridge University Press.
——— (1993b) 'Violence, Modernity, Silence: From Weber to International Relations', in David Campbell and Michael Dillon, eds, *The Political Subject of Violence,* Manchester: Manchester University Press, 137–60.
Wallace, William (1996) 'Truth and Power; Monks and Technocrats: Theory and Practice in International Relations', *Review of International Studies* 22: 301–21.
Walt, Stephen M. (1997) 'The Progressive Power of Realism', *American Political Science Review* 91(4): 931–5.
——— (1999) 'Rigor or Rigor Mortis? Rational Choice and Security Studies', *International Security* 23(4): 5–48.
——— (2002a) 'The Enduring Relevance of the Realist Tradition', in Ira Katznelson and Helen V. Milner, eds, *Political Science: State of the Discipline,* New York: Norton, 197–230.
——— (2002b) 'Keeping the World "Off Balance": Self-Restraint and U.S. Foreign Policy', in G. John Ikenberry, ed., *America Unrivaled: The Future of the Balance of Power,* Ithaca: Cornell University Press, 121–54.
Waltz, Kenneth N. (1969 [1967]) 'International Structure, National Force and the Balance of World Power', in James A. Rosenau, ed., *International Politics and Foreign Policy: A Reader in Research and Theory,* New York: The Free Press, 304–14.
——— (1979) *Theory of International Politics.* Reading, MA: Addison-Wesley.
——— (1986) 'A Response to My Critics', in Robert O. Keohane, ed., *Neorealism and Its Critics,* New York: Columbia University Press, 322–45.
——— (1990) 'Realist Thought and Neorealist Theory', *Journal of International Affairs* 44(1): 21–38.
——— (1997) 'Evaluating Theories', *American Political Science Review* 91(4): 913–17.
——— (2003) 'Thoughts about Assessing Theories', in Colin Elman and Miriam Fendius Elman, eds, *Progress in International Relations Theory: Appraising the Field,* Cambridge, MA: MIT Press, vii–xii.
Ward, Hugh (1987) 'Structural Power – A Contradiction in Terms?' *Political Studies* 35(4): 593–610.
Webb, Michael and Stephen D. Krasner (1989) 'Hegemonic Stability Theory: An Empirical Assessment', *Review of International Studies* 15(2): 56–76.
Weber, Max (1980 [1921–2]) *Wirtschaft und Gesellschaft. Grundriss der verstehenden Soziologie.* 5th rev. edn. Tübingen: J. C. B. Mohr (Paul Siebeck).
——— (1988 [1919]) 'Wissenschaft als Beruf', in *Gesammelte Aufsätze zur Wissenschaftslehre,* Tübingen: J. C. B. Mohr (Paul Siebeck), 582–613.

―― (1988 [1922]) *Gesammelte Aufsätze zur Wissenschaftslehre*, Tübingen: J. C. B. Mohr (Paul Siebeck).
Weldes, Jutta (1996) 'Constructing National Interests', *European Journal of International Relations* 2(3): 275–318.
―― (1999) *Constructing National Interests: The United States and the Cuban Missile Crisis*. Minneapolis: University of Minnesota Press.
Weller, Christoph (2000) *Die öffentliche Meinung in der Außenpolitik. Eine konstruktivistische Perspektive*. Wiesbaden: Westdeutscher Verlag.
―― (2001) 'Feindbilder. Ansätze und Probleme ihrer Erforschung', *InIIS–Arbeitspapier* Nr. 22, 2001. Bremen: Universität Bremen/Institut für Interkulturelle und Internationale Studien (InIIS).
Wendt, Alexander (1987) 'The Agent–Structure Problem in International Relations', *International Organization* 41(3): 335–70.
―― (1991) 'Bridging the Theory/Meta-theory Gap in International Relations', *Review of International Studies* 17(4): 383–92.
―― (1992a) 'Anarchy Is What States Make of It: The Social Construction of Power Politics', *International Organization* 46(2): 391–425.
―― (1992b) 'Levels of Analysis Vs. Agents and Structures: Part III', *Review of International Studies* 18(2): 181–5.
―― (1999) *Social Theory of International Politics*. Cambridge: Cambridge University Press.
―― (2000) 'On the Via Media: A Response to the Critics', *Review of International Studies* 26: 165–80.
―― (2003) 'Why a World State Is Inevitable: Teleology and the Logic of Anarchy', *European Journal of International Relations* 9(4): 491–542.
―― (2006) 'Social Theory as Cartesian Science: An Auto-Critique from a Quantum Perspective', in Stefano Guzzini and Anna Leander, eds, *Constructivism and International Relations: Alexander Wendt and His Critics*, London, New York: Routledge, 181–219.
Wendt, Alexander and Raymond Duvall (1989) 'Institutions and International Order', in Ernst-Otto Czempiel and James Rosenau, eds, *Global Changes and Theoretical Challenges: Approaches to World Politics for the 1990s*, Lexington, MA: Lexington Books, 51–74.
Wiberg, Håkan (1992) 'Peace Research and Eastern Europe', in Pierre Allan and Kjell Goldmann, eds, *The End of the Cold War: Evaluating Theories of International Relations*, Dordrecht: Martinus Nijhoff, 147–78.
―― (1993) 'Scandinavia', in Richard D. Burns, ed., *Encyclopedia of Arms Control and Disarmament, Vol. 1*, New York: Scribner, 209–26.
―― (2000) 'Security Communities: Emanuel Adler, Michael Barnett and Anomalous Northerners', *Cooperation and Conflict* 35(3): 289–98.
Wight, Colin (1996) 'Incommensurability and Cross-Paradigm Communication in International Relations Theory: "What's the Frequency Kenneth?"', *Millennium: Journal of International Studies* 25(2): 291–319.
―― (1999) 'They Shoot Dead Horses Don't They? Locating Agency in the Agent–Structure Problematique', *European Journal of International Relations* 5(1): 109–42.
―― (2007a) 'Inside the Epistemological Cave All Bets Are Off', *Journal of International Relations and Development* 10(1): 40–56.
―― (2007b) 'A Response to Friedrich Kratochwil: Why Shooting the Messenger Does Not Make the Bad News Go Away', *Journal of International Relations and Development* 10(3): 301–15.

Wight, Martin (1966) 'Why Is There No International Theory?' in Herbert Butterfield and Martin Wight, eds, *Diplomatic Investigations*, Cambridge: Cambridge University Press, 17–34.

Wilson, Peter (2000) 'Carr and His Early Critics: Responses to *The Twenty Years' Crisis, 1939–1946*', in Michael Cox, ed., *E. H. Carr: A Critical Appraisal*, Houndmills: Palgrave Macmillan, 165–97.

Wohlforth, William C. (1993) *The Elusive Balance: Power and Perceptions during the Cold War*. Ithaca, NY: Cornell University Press.

—— (1994/95) 'Realism and the End of the Cold War', *International Security* 19(3): 91–129.

—— (1998) 'Reality Check: Revising Theories of World Politics in Response to the End of the Cold War', *World Politics* 50(4): 650–80.

—— (1999) 'The Stability of a Unipolar World', *International Security* 24(1): 5–41.

—— (2000) 'Ideology and the Cold War', *Review of International Studies* 26(2): 327–31.

—— (2003) 'Measuring Power – and the Power of Theories', in John A. Vasquez and Colin Elman, eds, *Realism and the Balance of Power: A New Debate*, Upper Saddle River, NJ: Prentice Hall, 250–65.

Wolfers, Arnold (1962) *Discord and Collaboration: Essays on International Politics*. Baltimore: The Johns Hopkins University Press.

'World Politics' (2001) *The Economist*, 3–9 March.

Wrong, Dennis H. (1988 [1979]) *Power: Its Forms, Bases and Uses*. 2nd edn. Oxford: Basil Blackwell.

Zakaria, Fareed (1998) *From Wealth to Power: The Unusual Origins of America's World Role*. Princeton: Princeton University Press.

Zehfuß, Maja (1998) 'Sprachlosigkeit schränkt ein. Zur Bedeutung von Sprache in konstruktivistischen Theorien', *Zeitschrift für Internationale Beziehungen* 5(1): 109–37.

Zehfuss, Maja (2001a) 'Constructivism and Identity: A Dangerous Liaison', *European Journal of International Relations* 7(3): 315–48.

—— (2001b) 'Constructivisms in International Relations: Wendt, Onuf and Kratochwil', in Knud-Erik Jørgensen and Karin M. Fierke, eds, *Constructing International Relations: The Next Generation*, Armonk, NY: M. E. Sharpe, 54–75.

—— (2002) *Constructivism in International Relations: The Politics of Reality*. Cambridge: Cambridge University Press.

Zürn, Michael (1994) '*We Can Do Much Better!* Aber muß es gleich auf Amerikanisch sein? Zum Vergleich der Disziplin "Internationale Beziehungen" in den USA und in Deutschland', *Zeitschrift für Internationale Beziehungen* 1(1): 91–114.

—— (1997) '"Positives Regieren" jenseits des Nationalstaates. Zur Implementation internationaler Umweltregime', *Zeitschrift für Internationale Beziehungen* 4(1): 41–68.

INDEX

Note: Page numbers in **bold** type represent **figures**.

academic communities in Europe 298
actors 31; capabilities 23; cost-efficient strategy 182; meaning for 201–2; motives 279; power as actor-based concept 45; self-consciously aware 196; social 100; value systems 65, 115, *see also* agents
Adler, E. 245, 271, 275
agency (human) 37
agent concept 8, 210; Bourdieu 91
agent power 7; concept 22, 30; and impersonal governance 40–2
agent–structure: approach 261; tension 40
agents 26, 29; behaviour 25; economic capital 95; empowerment 35; identity 41; identity formation 266; privilege specific 42; properties 260, *see also* actors
America *see* United States of America (USA)
American dilemma (Cold War) 151
American Service Members' Protection Act (2001) 150
analysis: bargaining level 15
analytical conceptual analysis 220–6
anarchy 112, 120, 222, 249; logic of 238–9; as social construct (Wendt) 244, 252
applied studies 286, 303
Aron, R. 3, 49, 116–17, 138–9, 164, 193
Art, R. 118, 119

Ashley, R. 34, 35, 103, 104, 120; dissident power analysis 36; political power of hegemony 36; power links 213–14; rituals of power 214; social theory of IR 265; and Wendt, A. 16
Austin, J.L. 98
authority: and legitimacy 10
autopoiesis 84

Bachrach, P.: and Baratz, M.S. 4–5, 21, 23, 32, 103, 229
balance of power 118, 157, 239; Morgenthau 238–9; nineteenth-century 160; as symbol of realism 139–40
Baldwin, D. 3, 4, 16, 20, 86, 96; causal link between power and control 53–4; coercive power 23; framework 22, 28; fungibility of power 51, 118, 119, 157, 211; multidimensional context 25–6; Peloponnesian War (economic sanctions) 55; relational power analysis 23–4, **26**; single international power structure 118; state understanding 101; unintended influence of power 31; unrealized power paradox 69
Banks, M. 19; hoover-effect of realism 121
Baratz, M.S.: and Bachrach, P. 4–5, 21, 23, 32, 103, 229
Barnes, B. 201, 276

Barnett, M. 245
Beck, U. 194; reflexive modernity 191, 192
Becker, G. 126
Behnke, A. 264
benefit fallacy of power 58, 211, 212
Berki, R.N. 129
Bernstein, R. 85
bias (ritualized mobilization) 97–8
Bielefeld School 233
Bobbio, N. 129, 185
Bound to Lead (Nye) 181
Bourdieu, P. 7, 11; act of social magic 102, 103; agent concept 91; *doxa* 35; *habitus* 202; *sens pratique* (action and practices) 207, **208**; stratification theory 206
Bourdieu's field theory 59, 90–1, 205–10, 265; analysis of power in IR 101–2; language and authority 97–8; measure of power and power of measure 102–3; non-reactive anticipation 97; politics, state, power 99–101; power as disposition (capacity) 101; power as relational capital 95–6; social stratification and elites 99; symbolic violence 96–7
Bretton Woods 63–4, 152, 169, 181, 182, 230–1
British Foreign Office 178
British ideology (harmony of interests) 167
Brown, C. 124, 288
Bull, H. 59, 118, 119, 130, 250; great powers 82
Bulmer, M. 223
Bush, G.H.W. 147; First Gulf War 209
Bush, G.W.: administration 146–51; foreign policy shortcomings 147–8; 'who is not for us . . .' 149
Buzan, B. 74–5; and Wæver, O. 71, 229–30

Camus, A. 284–5
capital: analysis of 95; economic and cultural 99; economic, social and cultural 206; power of 33; symbolic capital 96
capitalism 165
Caporaso, J. 32, 56; and Krasner, S. 21, 43–4; structural power 57
Carr, E.H. 129, 133, 137, 142, 144; double heritage of realism 185; harmony of interests critique 143–4; rich contextualization of work 141, see also *E.H. Carr: A Critical Appraisal* (Cox); *Twenty Years' Crisis, The* (Carr)

Cartesian anxiety 281
Casino Capitalism (Strange) 183
causal efficacy 8
causal power 80; and educated guesses 53–5
causal theorising 256
causality 5, 221, 279; chain 28–9
Checkel, J. 197, 209–10
choice-theoretical power concept 15, 20, 21
Christensen, C. 56
Clash of Civilization thesis (Huntington) 220, 292
class: struggle 100; system 167
Claude, I. 139, 239
coercive power (Baldwin) 23–4, 54
Cold War (1947–91) 82–3, 102, 147; American dilemma 151; diplomacy 133; end 195–7, 242, 243, 290, 291, 302; end and reflexive modernity 192–7; is what we make of it 237–46; origins 290; political practices (Kratochwil) 276; Second (1980s) 196; self-fulfilling prophecy 237–8; shared background knowledge 277; Soviet retrenchment 291; Soviet Union forced to give in 291; Soviet Union, non-military factors 231, 291; and strength of democracy 149
collective memory 207
common knowledge 259
communication: power as medium 224–5; reflexive process 296
community power literature 80
conceptual analysis: aims and limits 17–19; as conceptual history and genealogy 232–5; as means 221–3; reflexivity loops in IR 230–2
conceptual history 280
Connolly, W. 92, 212, 228–9
conservative dilemma in IR 134; critique of science as defence of realism 125–7; Kissinger on Metternich 123; meta-theoretical and post-positivist arguments 125; micro–macro link 121–2; no pragmatist way out of realist dilemma 127–8; realist scope conditions 121, 122
constructivism 5, 77, 127, 219–20; and cognitive psychology 209–10; common-sense action 191; in IR 189–216; linking of levels of action and observation 210–15; meaning of power 226; as meta-theory subsuming all others 248; phenomenal world, external to thought 200; reconstruction 190; and reflexivity on process 242–6

conversion failures 3, 51, 68–9, 148
Copenhagen School of security studies 245
Correlates of War research project 242–3, 288
corruption 85
counterfactual reasoning 18
Cox, M. 136–7
Cox, R. 33, 176

Dahl, R. 3, 4, 9, 80, 94; relational power 114, *see also Who Governs?* (Dahl)
data speaking to us 287, 288
Davos 104
Definitionshoheit 6–7
democracy: different meanings 222
dependency concept 57
détente 240
deterrence practices: and 'autism' 241
Deutsch, K.W. 240, 241
diplomacy 277
diplomatic culture 124
diplomatic staff: classical education 294; State Department recruitment 296; UK training 287
diplomats: need to agree first on what counts 70, 102, 119
dispositional conceptualization of power (Morriss) **30**
Dividing Discipline (Holsti) 140
domains and levels (power) 9–10, **10**
dominance (Perroux) 31
Donnelly, J. 130, 136, 140; defining realism 137–8, *see also Realism and International Relations* (Donnelly)
Doty, R.L. 254, 256
double hermeneutics 201–3, 210
Dowding, K. 41, 58, 203–4, 212, 229
doxa (Bourdieu) 35, 206
doxic acceptance 97
doxic subordination 97
Dunne, T. 144
Durkheim, D.É. 9
Duvall, R.: and Wendt, A. 18

eclecticism 190
economic adjustment programmes 169; beggar-thy-neighbour policies 173
economic theory 49; micro- 156; and modelling behaviour 117; neo-classical 156
economics: link to medicine (Richter) 289
Economy and Society (Weber) 223, 255
economy (world): governments control 184; Keynesian control 184

egoism 204
E.H. Carr: A Critical Appraisal (Cox) 136–7; Bolshevik Revolution 142; British Empire 142; Carr's internal contradictions 141–4; historical positivism 142; *Life and Times* 141; overall impressions of Carr 141–2; Russian section 141
elites: and social stratification 99
elitism 142
embedded liberalism 235
English School of International Relations 67, 196, 262, 263, 265, 266
epistemological constructivism 197, 198–201; gestalt-switch 199
equilibrium 276–7
European integration 240
European Journal of International Relations 298
European Monetary System (EMS): 1992 crisis 27–8, 56–7

facts (necessary theory-dependence) 289, 290
Feindbilder (enemy-images) 240, 241–2
Foreign Direct Investment (FDI) 161; new 173
foreign policy: containment and deterrence 238; goals (classical) 49; USA 73
Fortress America illusion 148, 150–1
Foucauldian genealogical power conceptualization 34
Foucault, M. 11, 40, 42, 95, 101, 131; discourse concept 259–60
France: US multinational corporations 154
Frankfurt critical theory 271
Frankfurt School 194
free-rider 58, 64, 211
Frei, D. 71, 83, 103, 229, 231
Friedman, M. 126, 199, 281
Frisch, M. 219
fungibility 4, 5, 49, 116; Baldwin 51, 118, 119, 157, 211; Keohane 117; of money 24, 66; of power (low) 24–5, 50, 88, 231

Galtung, J. 243
game-theoretical approach 16
Germany: academic IR community 296–7; Historical School 234; *Ostpolitik* 2, 13, 245; public lawyers, political realism 88; reunification 292; Saarland 2

Giddens, A. 203, 258; structuration theory 205
Gill, S.: and Law, D. 32–3, 59
Gilpin, R. 152–3, 154, 161–3, 165–6, 179; attempt to dynamism realism 171; individual or group permanence 157–8; meta-theoretical critique 17; moral pessimism and human nature 156; neo-mercantilism 155; ontological ambiguities and methodological individualism 155–8; power–money analogy 156–7; research programme 153, 155; social formations 164, 174, *see also War and Change in World Politics* (Gilpin)
globalization debate 292
Gorbachev, M. 118; New Thinking 196, 291
governance 40, 44, 99; international 103; poststructuralist view 41; and structural power 55
governments: control over world economy 184
Gramsci, A. 9, 33, 59
Gramscian analysis 40
Gramscian School 57–8
Gray, J. 225
Great Depression 291–2
great powers 153
Grieco, J.M. 134
Griffiths, M. 130
Grosser, A. 293
Gulf War (1990–1) 207–9; international media 209; Saddam Hussein as modern Hitler 35, 209; self-censorship 209; weapons of mass-destruction 209
Guzzini, S.: coping strategies 2; PhD thesis on power 1

Haas, E. 239
Haas, P. 245
Habermas, J. 194, 256
habitus 206
Hague Invasion Act, The (2002) 150
Halliday, F. 143
harmony of interests 176; British ideology 167
Hassner, P. 28
Hegemonic Stability Theory (HST) 63, 72, 75, 168; causal propositions 64
hegemony 9, 33, 59, 165, 167; political power of (Ashley) 36; two-sided 167
Hellmann, G. 127
hermeneutical skill 296
Herrschaft (authority/rule) 34, 96–7

Hirschman, A. 129, 143, 176
history: conceptual 280; cyclical theory 113, 250; lessons 291; structure as conceived product 206
Hoffmann, S. 151
Hollis, M.: and Smith, S. 16
Holsti, K.J. 113, 140
homo economicus 16
human agency 37
human nature 157–8; characteristics 261
human practice 283
human understanding: and social reality 279
humanist ethics 283–5
Huntington, S.: Clash of Civilization thesis 220
Huysmans, J. 229–30

ideational phenomena 279
identity dilemma in IR 110, 111–21; amity and enmity 120; macro-assumption of anarchy 112, 120; micro-assumption of self-interest 112; power indeterminacy and micro-macro link 114–20; realism as indistinguishable science 120–1; which realism 111–14
Imagined Communities (Anderson) 195
impersonal governance: and agent power 40–2
impersonal power 34
indirect institutional power 181
industrial capitalism 167
industrial society 194
inflation: global 168
influence through resources (reductionist understanding) 67
Inter-Paradigm Debate: teaching theory in (IR) 300–1
interactionist rational-choice approaches 19, 31
international business civilization 266
international liberal order 63; and decline of *Pax Americana* 168–71
international monetary relations 168
international order: after (1989) 277–8
international political economy (IPE) 17, 154, 159–61; definition and ideologies 161–3; dialogue between Lenin and Kautsky 166–8; neo-mercantilist limits 171–4; power–materialist discipline 176; resources and outcomes link 51–5
international politics: mutual role-taking 277–8; practice and practices 276; symbolic communication and problem of order 273–8

international relations (IR): Bourdieu and analysis of power 101–2; classical American framing 290; communicability (shared experience) 132–3; concept of power 62; conservative dilemma 110; constructivism in 189–216; dilemmas, accepting (limits and opportunities) 130–3; economic mode of explanation 16; four great debates 300; journals (leading) of field 296; lessons of dilemma 128–33; physical violence and power (Luhmann's link) 87–9; power as killer argument 3, 5; realism as twofold negation 128–30, 131, 132; reconceptualization of power 235; research inspired by constructivism and peace research 244–6; substitution of power 82–3; tenets of constructivism in 197–215; theoretical debate 189; Western European conference life 298, *see also* conservative dilemma in IR; identity dilemma in IR; realism; teaching theory in IR
international relations theory: sociological turn 77
international system: ruling indicator 48; unipolarity 232
international system of rule (nonformalistic understanding) 43
interparadigm debate 18
interpretive practice: and reflexivity 278–80
intersubjective power 214–15
intersubjectivity *vs* individualism 203–5
Italy: teaching theory in IR 297

jeopardy thesis 176
Jouvenel, B. de 234
judgement: and science 280–3

Kant, I. 198, 294; categories and possibility of knowledge 225–6
Kantian cultures 263
Kautsky, K.J. 168
Kelman, H. 239–40
Kennan, G.F. 149
Keohane, R. 50, 117, 192, 290; causal role of power 52; hegemony 168; and Nye, J., Jr 16, 20–1, 50, 52, 54, 250; rational actor approach 52, **53**
Kertzer, D. 34
Keynesian revolution 165
Kissinger, H.A. 2, 82, 110, 120, 151, 194–5; 'absolute security' 149; 'Metternich and Conservative Dilemma' 123; State Department recruitment 296; study of international order 276
Knorr, K. 31
knowledge: limited and prone to change 294; social construction 201, 213
Korb, L. 150
Krasner, S. 22–3, 25, 28, 125, 190, 254; and Caporaso, J. 21, 43–4; metapower 26, 27, 32, 43, 56
Kratochwil, F. 284; forms of constructivism 270; humanist ethics 283–5; international politics 273–8; interpretive practice and reflexivity 278–80; intersubjective ontology clash 270; political practices 276; problem-driven research 269; qualitative methods 270; and Ruggie, J.G. 268; sanctions 278; science and judgement 280–3; scientific proofs 281–2; scrabble analogy 281; strategy to deny contradictions 269–70
Kuhn, T. 18, 85, 199, 201, 220, 281; paradigms 200, 207, 223, 253; production of knowledge (his understanding) 199

Lakatosian falsificationism 127, 199
language: and authority (Bourdieu's field theory) 97–8; -based constructivists 261; and intersubjectivity 205; making thinking possible 260; no private language (Wittgenstein) 205; rules 275
Lauxerois, J. 1
Law, D.: and Gill, S. 32–3, 59
leadership 52
legal positivism 249
legitimacy 67
Legro, J.: and Moravcsik, A. 110, 121, 122, 133–4
Lenin, V.I. 168, 183
Levitt, T. 152
liberal anti-totalitarian ideal 284
liberalism 161, 170, 173; and political economy 163
looping effect 71, 78, 191, 219, 244
Lucarelli, S.: and Menotti, R. 297
luck 229
Luhmann's systems theory 282; autopoiesis of political system 83–6; causal, relational and multidimensional power 79–80; code of generalized symbols 81; conceptualization of media of communication 84–5; constructivism

and power 89–91; functional differentiation 91; *hierarchies* 82; *history* 82; inner logic of code 85; negative sanctions 86–7, 88–9; physical violence and power in IR 87–9; positive sanctions 86, 87, 89; power as medium of communication 79–83; power and political system 83–91; power, socially constructed through communication 81, 224–5; social construction of reality 81; social relevance or power 83–4; substitution of power 82–3; synchronic element 79; system-theoretical and communicative twist 80–2
Lukes, S. 9, 37, 71, 97, 222, 227–8
lump-of-power fallacy 5, 48–51, 117

Machtausübung (realization of power) 81
Machtkunst (art/craft of power/governing) 233–4
Machtüberlegenheit (power superiority) 86
Machtunterlegenheit (power inferiority) 86
Mad Money (Strange) 183, 185
Mainstream International Relations 197
Mann, M. 168
Mannheim, K. 176
market theory: Waltzian 16
Marshall Plan (1948–52) 149
Marxism 156, 165
materialist theory of action 113
meaning: social constructed 205
Mearsheimer, J. 4, 115, 116, 292
media of communication 78, 91
Menotti, R.: and Lucarelli, S. 297
mercantilism: benign 170
meta-power (Krasner) 23, 26, 27, 32, 43, 56
meta-theoretical dependency 223–6
meta-theoretical enlargement 262
meta-theory: pragmatist turn 272
Metternich, K. von 110
military field: vision and division 103
military security 74
Mille, P. 225
money: attribution of value (Searle) 201; fungibility 24, 66
Monroe Doctrine 147
Moravcsik, A.: and Legro, J. 110, 121, 122, 133–4
Morgenthau, H.J. 47, 115, 116, 120, 249, 295; Aristocracy International 194; balance of power 238–9; human nature 157; nationalistic universalism 158; realism in IR 123–4; sanctions 278

Morriss, P. 37, 58, 65, 227; categories of ability 30–1; dispositional conceptualization of power **30**; non-epistemic power 31, 181; passive power 38, 39
motives 225; and will 224–5
Müller, H. 245
multilateralism 61–76; perception and missing measure of power 69–70; performative and reflexive aspects of power 71–2
multinational corporations (MNCs) 162–3, 183
mutual connection 10
mutually assured destruction (MAD) 88, 147

national interest: defining 119
National Missile Defence (NMD) of USA 147, 148
National Security 245; US strategy 148
neo-institutionalism 262
neo-institutionalist analysis 51
neo-mercantilism (dynamizing) 163–8
neo-mercantilist (limits in IPE) 171–4
neo–neo synthesis 262
neo-realism 15, 16, 251; conceptual critique of power 17–22; indeterminacy 138
non-causal power and prediction 52–3
non-decision making 32, 56, 72
non-epistemic power (Morriss) 31
non-intentional effects 212
non-intentional power (Strange) 28, 31
Nye, J., Jr 56, 74, 181; and Keohane, R. 16, 20–1, 50, 52, 54, 250; multidimensional character of power 67–8; soft power 68

oil 153
oil shock 152
Oppenheim, F. 221, 223–4, 225
Orientalism (Said) 195
Ostpolitik 2, 13, 245
overload fallacy of power analysis 8, 37–9, 94

Parsonian systems theory 87
Parsons, T. 80, 87
passive power: Morriss 38, 39
Patomäki, H. 238, 271
Pax Americana 154, 160, 165, 183; decline and international liberal order 168–71
Pax Britannica 160

peace research 237; Correlates of War research project 242–3, 288; *Feindbilder* (enemy-images) 240, 241–2; normative tradition 243; as study of process pathologies 239–40
peace research-cum constructivism: paradoxical success 242–4
Peloponnesian War (431–404 BC): economic sanctions (Baldwin) 55
performative conceptual analysis 218, 226–32; effect of power 227–30
Perrou, F. 31
petroleum 153
philosophical idealism 253
physical violence 89; symbiotic mechanism 87
Pizzorno, A. 85
pluralism 85
political agency 71
political analysis: classical 9
political discourse: what power does 92
political economy: globalization 173; and liberalism 163; and power materialism 177–9
political hierarchy 100
political order 99
political realism 111; double heritage 176; tensions 143
political scientists: retrospective insight 293
political system: autopoiesis of 83–6
political theory: power debate 21
politics: art of possible 103, 181, 198, 212; depoliticization 103, 229; global 1; negative sanctions 86–7; world politics 104
Politics Among Nations (Morgenthau) 124
Polsby, N. 58, 211, 229
Popper, K. 284
positivism 127, 198, 255
post-modernity 194
post-positivism 255
post-structuralism (metatheoretical outlook) 36
post-structuralists 131
Potsdam 23–4
Powell, C. 149
Power: A Philosophical Analysis (Morriss) 227
power analysis: domains of 8–11; four-tier dispositional 94; presumed double link 60; single measure 3–4
power: arguments 3; and constructivism 5–7; materialism and political economy 177–9; materialist approaches 61; and money analogy 3–4; in neorealism 17–22; resources 22
power explanations: classical circularity 95–6
Power and Interdependence (Keohane and Nye) 52, 56; paradigm 262
power phenomena: contemporary IR and IPE 42–4; dyadic conceptualization **41**
power-as-benefit fallacy 37–8
public goods 64, 168; international 27

Ragin, C. 256
rational choice 19, 31, 58, 203–4; theories (agency assumptions) 39
rationalism: thick 260
Rawlsian liberal political philosophy 170
realism 250–1; anti-apparent 129, 143–4; as anti-idealism 129, 182; balance of power as symbol 139–40; critique of science as defence 125–7; different worlds of in IR 136–45; as indistinguishable science 120–1; Inter-Paradigm Debate 120; in IR 109–35; as mainly negative approach 143; oscillating (Strange) 175–85; and power 2–5; utilitarian 157; world as it is 110–11
Realism and International Relations (Donnelly) 136, 140, 145; defining realism 137–8, 141; on human nature 138
realist theory of action 114
realist writings (diversity) 111
realpolitik 78, 110, 124, 129, 131, 132, 244, 272
reflexive modernity 192–7
reflexivity 77, 248, 280; and interpretive practice 278–80
regime: analysis 52; theory 45, 180, 268–9
relational concepts of power 4–5, 22–6
relational phenomenon 5
relational power behaviour 23; sentry and unarmed intruder 4–5
Reus-Smit, C. 68, 69
Rhetoric of Reaction, The (Hirschman) 176
Richter, R. 289
Riker, W. 28–9
Ringmar, E. 263
rites and power 34–5
Rival States and Rival Firms (Stopford and Strange) 178
Roosevelt administration 183
Rosecrance, W.S. 156
routine actions 42
Ruggie, J. G. 260; and Kratochwil, F. 268

rule-like inference-guidance devices 277
rump materialism 253–6
Russia: government 5; military might 118; New Thinking 291; nineteenth-century intellectuals 143; Soviet legitimacy crisis (1980s) 291
Russian 6
Rust, M. 151

Saarbrücken 2; University 2
Saarland 2
sanctions 88–9; politics and power 86–7
Scharpf, F. 74
Schmidt, B. 130
science and judgement 280–3
scientific method courses 255
scientific proofs 281–2
scientific realism 248
Searle, J.R. 98; background abilities 201; money and attribution of value 201, 219
second face of power (Bachrach and Baratz) 21, 32
securitization 71–2, 75; de-securitization 89
security 229–30; meaning and action 245; Microsoft theory 74; utility function 156–7; and world order 62
self-awareness (theoretical) 294
self-fulfilling prophecies 220, 239, 244; Cold War 237–8
self-interest 112
self-reflexivity 303
Sellin, V. 233, 234
Senghaas, D. 241
shared beliefs 219, 261
shared meanings and understanding 275
shared rules of game 276
Simmel, G. 85
Singer, D.J. 288
Skinner, Q. 233
social actors 100
social event (right meaning) 202, 254
social formations (Gilpin) 164, 174
social psychology 240
social reality: construction of 201; dimension of political power 213; and human understanding 279
social sciences: political implications 215; Weberian tradition 131
social theories of action 93
Social Theory of International Politics (Wendt) 247, 265, 271; synthesis **257**
social-science concepts 228
societal norms 25, 26

socioeconomic dynamics 165–6
sociological approach: classical (holistic) 261
sociological constructivism 197
sociology of international power 104
sociopolitical order 11
soft power 69; apparent decline in US power 180–4; idealist streak in 180–2; Nye 68; US 102, 211, 231
Soviet legitimacy crisis (1980s) 291
speech act theory 98
Spegele, R.D. 134
Stalin, J. 23–4
state: as collective actor 158; dynamics 163–5; failed states 6; inter-state system 263; interests and behaviour 63; intervention in international markets 292; role given to 265; social structure 170; theory 154, 163, 171, 172
state-system (cultural theory) 261–4
Stephanson, A. 142
Stiller (Frisch) 219
Strange, S. 26–7, 28; non-intentional power 28, 31; relational and structural power 56; structural power 42, 68, 72, 177, 230–1; unintended effects 29
Strange's oscillating realism 175–85; political economy and power materialism 177–9; retreat or reform of realism 184–5; two poles of 175–7
structural coupling 84, 85
structural power 15–46; beyond neorealism 21–2; as dispositional concept 26–31; and governance 55; impersonal power 31–6; indirect institutional power 22, 56; and international rule 7–8; as non-intentional power 56–7; overload fallacies 37–9; related concepts and meanings **21**; relational concept (power as) 22–6; as systematic bias 57–60; unintended effects 181
structural reductionism 38–9
superpower relations 241
supervenience 259
Suskind, R. 75
suspicion (political theories) 176

teaching theory in IR: academic communities in Europe 298; applied studies 286, 303; classical types of courses 302–3; conflation between theory and academia 302; constitutive function of theories 299; criticism of empiricism 289; data speaking to us

287, 288; diplomatic staff and classical education 294; educational argument 287, 292–6; four great debates 300; Germany's academic IR community 296–7; hermeneutical skill 296; history of thought 300; Inter-Paradigm Debate 300–1; Italy 297; language and culture of other countries 295; logical argument 288–92; meta-theory/theory-content in courses 299–300, 301–2; political/academic argument 296–9; practical note 299–302; significant role of teaching 302; top–down manner of teaching 301; training to be aware of others' assumptions 292
technology gap 152–3, 169
theory (constitutive functions) 294
theory courses 286; conflation between theory and academia 302
Theory of International Politics (Waltz) 113, 125–7, 154, 178, 198, 250–1
Third World 23, 44, 169, 172, 195
Thucydides 154, 156
Tobin Tax 271
trading gains and losses 231
traffic light (social science analysis) 201–2
transnational corporations (TNCs) 183
transnational empire 27
Truman, H.S. 23–4
truth: belief that something is true 288; classical correspondence theory 281; nature of 123; value of an explanation 283
Twenty Years' Crisis, The (Carr) 144, 176; anti-ideal position 177

unilateralism: power of 73–5; as strategy to redefine power 70–1
unintended consequences 72
unintended influence 57
unipolarity: influence and legitimacy 66–9; international system 232; power as aggregate resource analysis 64–5; unilateralism and hegemonic stability 63–4; US foreign policy 62
United States of America (USA): debt to other countries 169; democracy (nature of) 8, 9; empire and own reality 75; fear of religious-nationalist attacks 147; foreign policy 62, 70, 73, 124, 146–51; foreign policy post-World War II 295; foreign policy remilitarization 148, 149; foreign policy and unipolarity 62; Fortress America illusion 148, 150–1; GNP 183; hegemonic decline 26–7;

justifying exemptionalism 72–3; military self-reliance 148; Monroe Doctrine 147; multilateralization of military 150–1; National Missile Defence (NMD) 147, 148; National Security strategy 148; non-territorial empire 180, 182–4; perceived arrogance of power 150; perceived decline 230–1; preponderance in world affairs 63, 66, 75; primacy 69, 151; soft power 102, 180–4, 211, 231; take it or leave it diplomacy 147, 149; ungovernance 182–4; unilateralism 71, 73, 74, 146; as world policeman 148
unrealized power paradox 51, 69
USSR: military might 118; New Thinking 291; Soviet legitimacy crisis (1980s) 291
utility maximization 49, 115

value-dependence 227–8
value-maximization 204
Vasquez, J. 109–10, 112, 125
Vermeidungsalternative (avoidance/alternative) 81
Vietnam War (1955–75): conversion failure 3, 51, 68–9; paradox of unrealized power 117; US decline in power following 180–1; US disengagement 82
violence: domestication 250; symbolic 96–7; as ultimate power 88; 'your money or your life' 23–4, 54
voluntarism 197

Wæver, O. 245; and Buzan, B. 71, 229–30
Walker, R.B.J. 131, 195
Wallace, W. 287
Walt, S. 128
Waltz, K.N. 4, 16, 20, 43, 48–9, 151; actors security maximization 115; analogy between power and money 50, 117; empiricist trait 199; narrow understanding or IR 252; neorealism 36; power differentials (stability) 64; realist scope conditions 122; structural realism 258, *see also Theory of International Politics* (Waltz)
war: against terrorism 146, 149; utilitarian theory 160
War and Change in World Politics (Gilpin) 154
Ward, H. 39
Weber, M. 10–11, 34, 96–7, 100, 193, 223; clash of Gods 273–4; social action

4, 114–15; status group approach 207; understanding of power 65, 79–80, 86
welfare state 153, 165
Weller, C. 241
Wendt, A. 132, 247, 259; anarchy 244; and Ashley, R. 16; and Duvall, R. 18
Wendt's constructivism 247–67; cultural theory of state-system 261–4; disciplinary orthodoxy and theoretical heterodoxy 264–6; dualist ontology 256–61; heterodox social theory of IR 252–64; individualism and multiple readability 259; micro- and macro-level combination 258; orthodoxy in disciplinary identity or IR 249–52; rump materialism 253–6; synthesising apparently contradictory positions 253; understanding of international politics 265–6
What is History? (Carr) 142
Who governs? (Dahl) 8, 48
Wight, C. 282, 283
will and motives 224–5
Wohlforth, W.C. 67, 69, 120
Wolfers, A. 52, 116, 120, 239, 262
World Wars: I (1914–18) 160, 239; II (1939–45) 239
Wrong, D. 37

Zeitschrift für Internationale Beziehungen 298
Zürn, M. 298

Taylor & Francis
eBooks
FOR LIBRARIES

ORDER YOUR FREE 30 DAY INSTITUTIONAL TRIAL TODAY!

Over 23,000 eBook titles in the Humanities, Social Sciences, STM and Law from some of the world's leading imprints.

Choose from a range of subject packages or create your own!

Benefits for you
- Free MARC records
- COUNTER-compliant usage statistics
- Flexible purchase and pricing options

Benefits for your user
- Off-site, anytime access via Athens or referring URL
- Print or copy pages or chapters
- Full content search
- Bookmark, highlight and annotate text
- Access to thousands of pages of quality research at the click of a button

For more information, pricing enquiries or to order a free trial, contact your local online sales team.

UK and Rest of World: online.sales@tandf.co.uk
US, Canada and Latin America:
e-reference@taylorandfrancis.com

www.ebooksubscriptions.com

A flexible and dynamic resource for teaching, learning and research.